Skip·Beat!

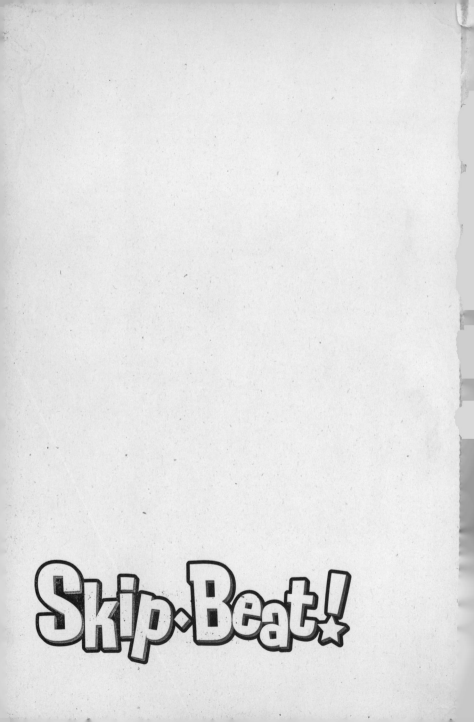

Shojo Beat

Skip·Beat!

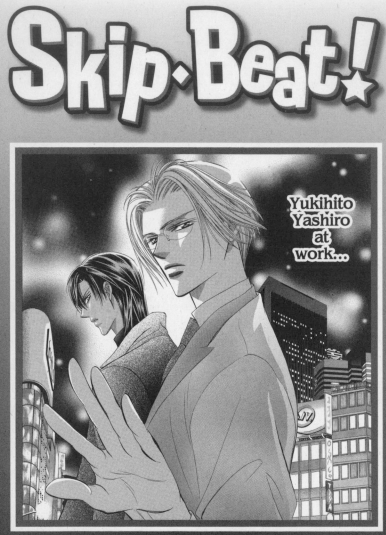

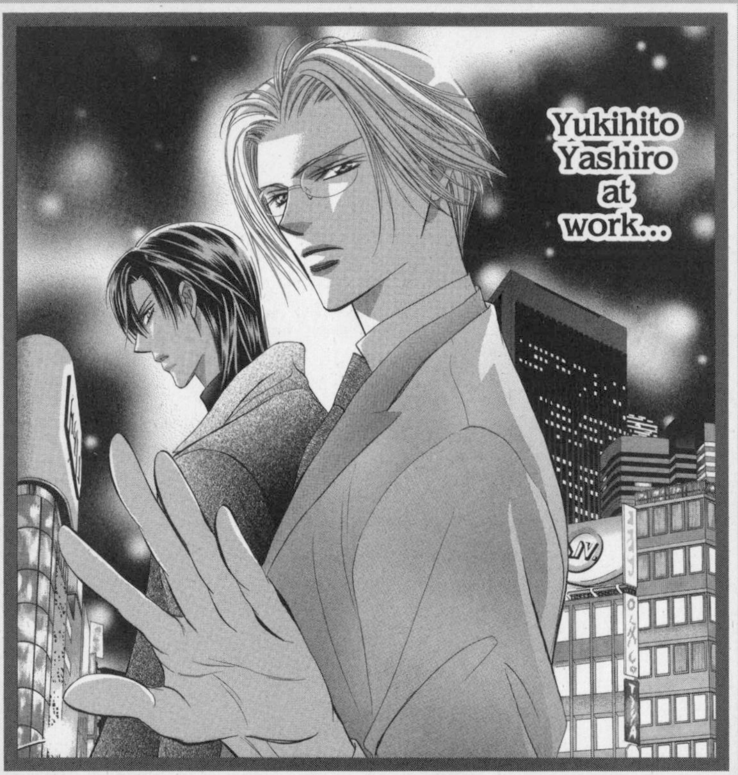
Yukihito Yashiro at work...

20

Story & Art by Yoshiki Nakamura

Skip·Beat!

Volume 20

CONTENTS

Act 115 Lucky Number 24 ----- 5

Act 116 Lucky Number 24 ----- 35

Act 117 Lucky Number 24 ----- 65

Act 118 Lucky Number 24 ----- 95

Act 119 Lucky Number 24 ----- 125

Act 120 Lucky Number 25 ----- 155

End Notes ----- 185

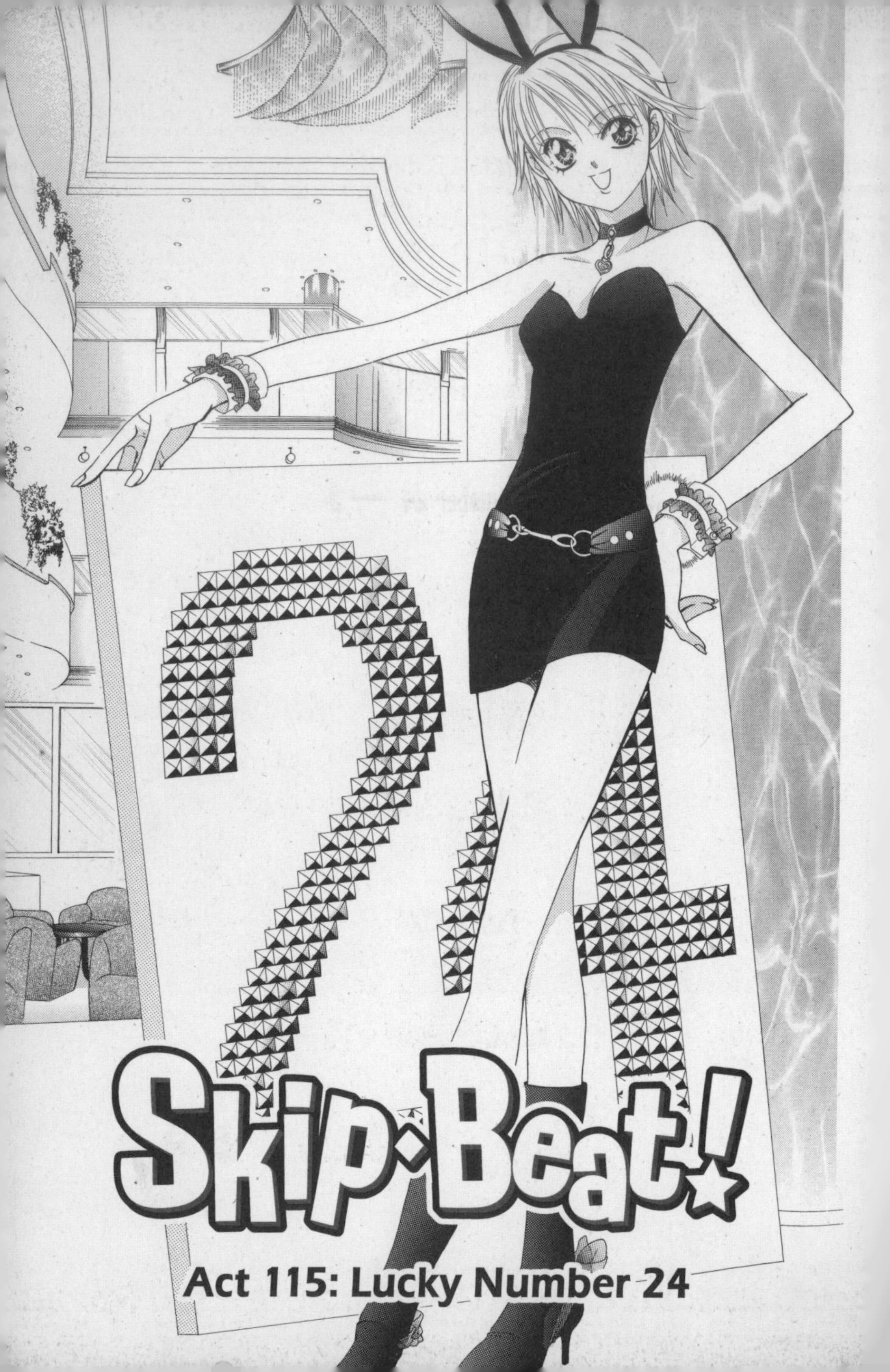
Skip·Beat!
Act 115: Lucky Number 24

"Aaaah, I'm bored. I wish something interesting would happen."

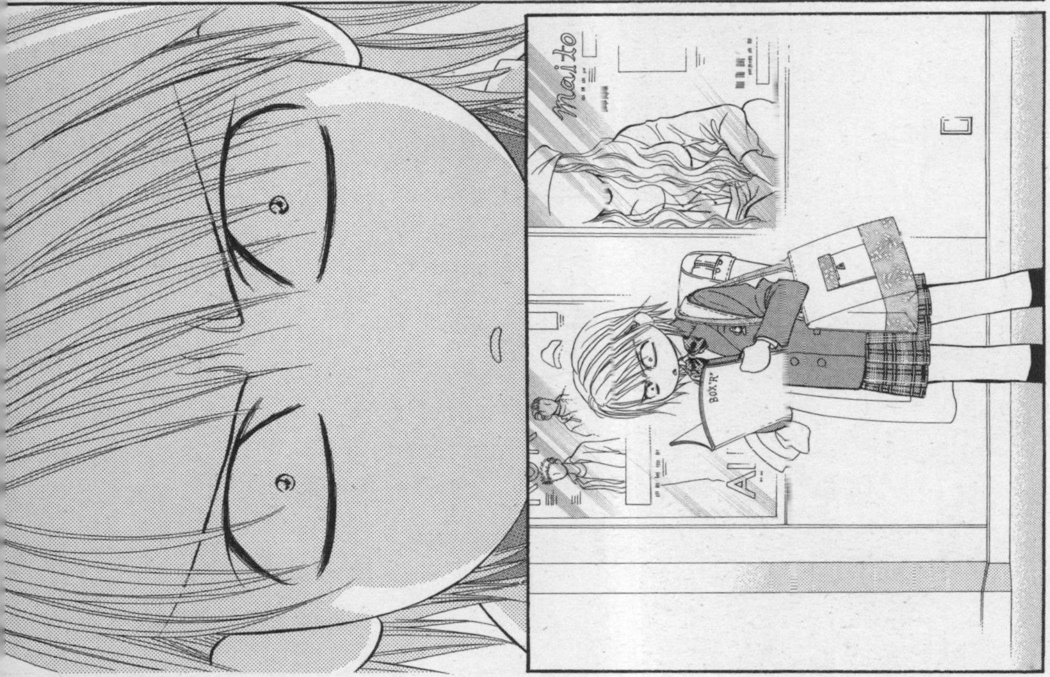
maito
BOX"R"

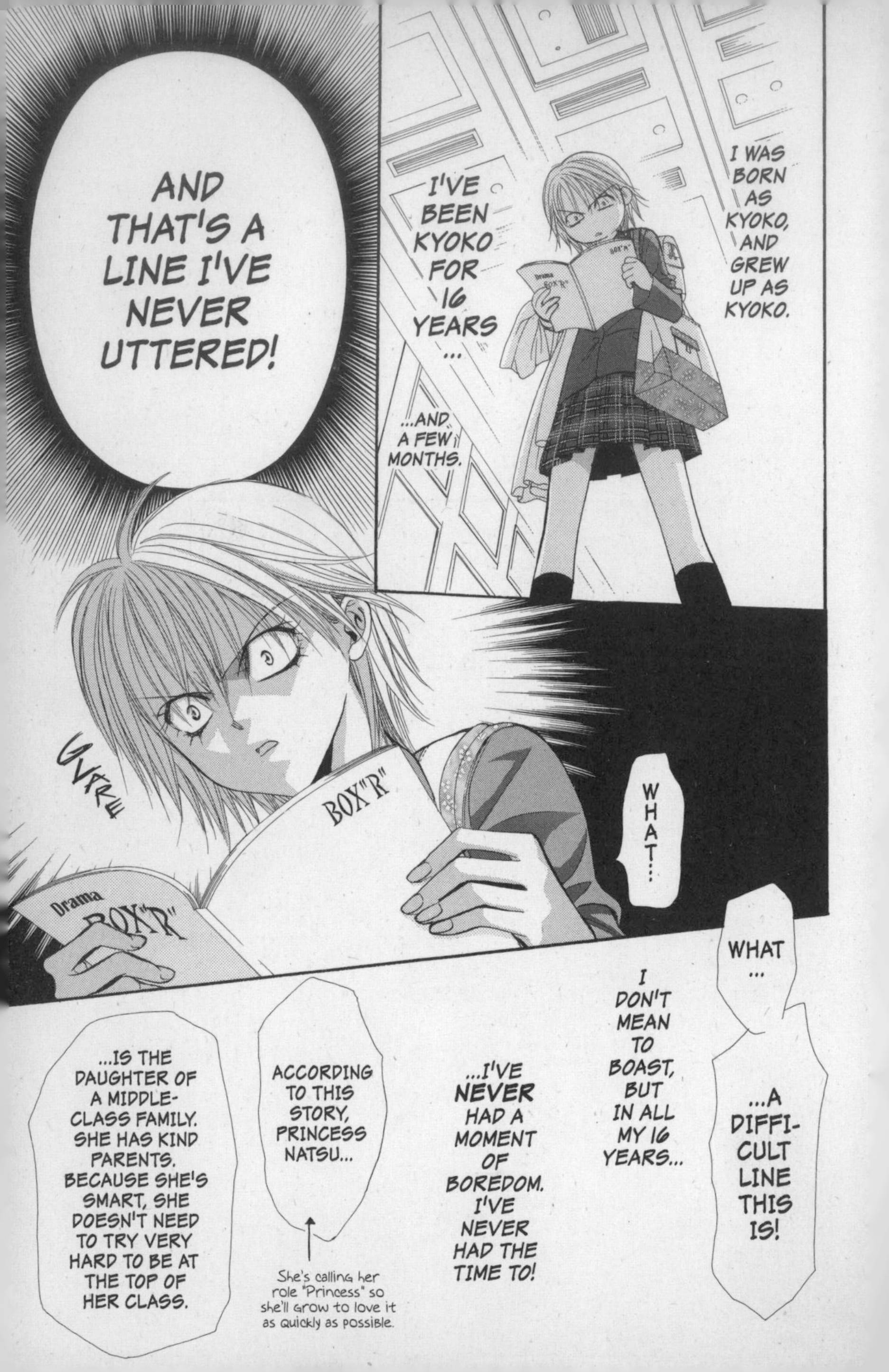
I WAS BORN AS KYOKO, AND GREW UP AS KYOKO.
I'VE BEEN KYOKO FOR 16 YEARS...
...AND A FEW MONTHS.
AND THAT'S A LINE I'VE NEVER UTTERED!
WHAT...
WHAT... ...A DIFFICULT LINE THIS IS!
I DON'T MEAN TO BOAST, BUT IN ALL MY 16 YEARS...
...I'VE NEVER HAD A MOMENT OF BOREDOM. I'VE NEVER HAD THE TIME TO!
ACCORDING TO THIS STORY, PRINCESS NATSU...
She's calling her role "Princess" so she'll grow to love it as quickly as possible.
...IS THE DAUGHTER OF A MIDDLE-CLASS FAMILY. SHE HAS KIND PARENTS. BECAUSE SHE'S SMART, SHE DOESN'T NEED TO TRY VERY HARD TO BE AT THE TOP OF HER CLASS.

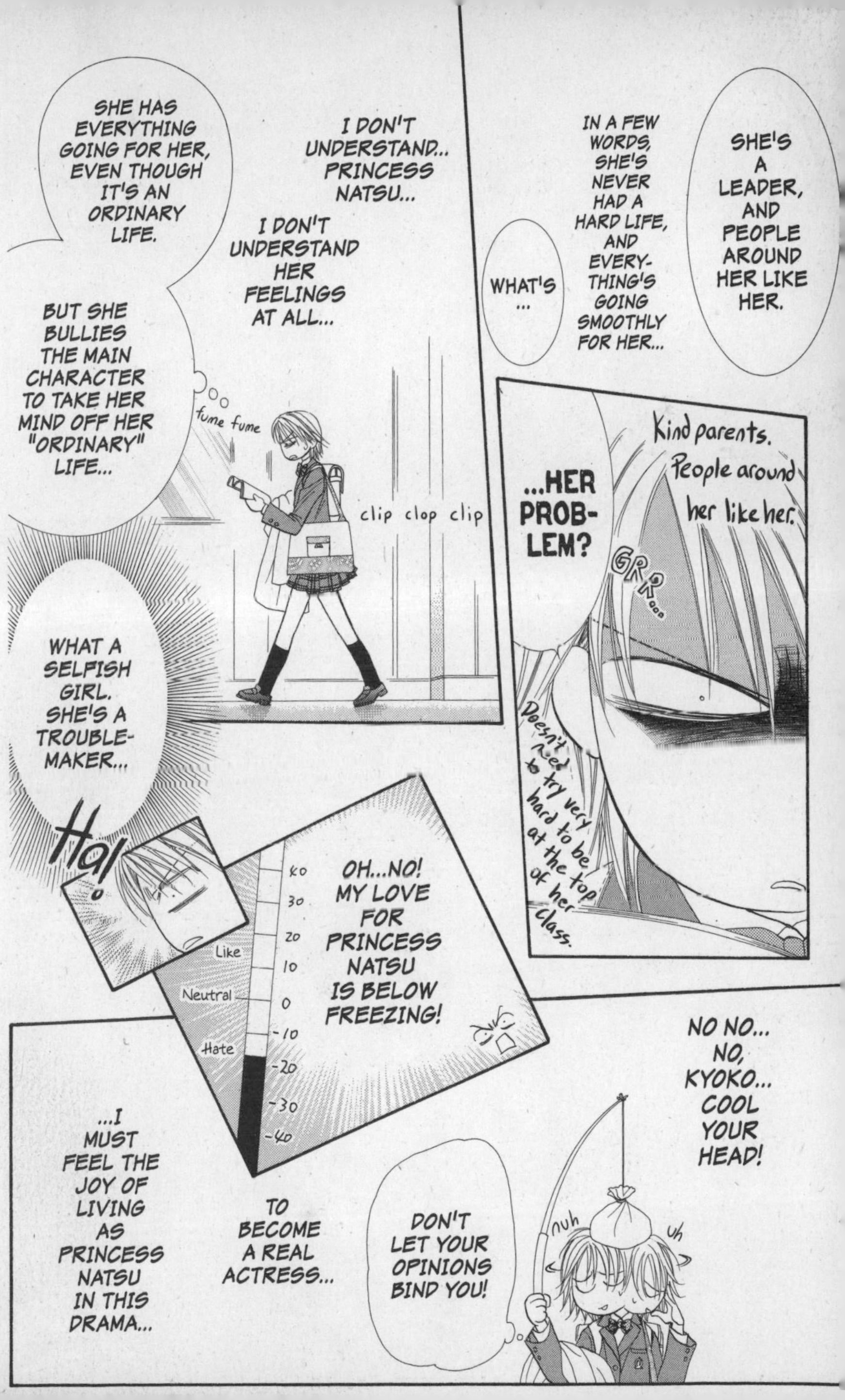
SHE'S A LEADER, AND PEOPLE AROUND HER LIKE HER.
IN A FEW WORDS, SHE'S NEVER HAD A HARD LIFE, AND EVERY-THING'S GOING SMOOTHLY FOR HER...
WHAT'S ...
...HER PROB-LEM?
Kind parents. People around her like her.
GRRR...
Doesn't need to try very hard to be at the top of her class.
I DON'T UNDERSTAND... PRINCESS NATSU...
I DON'T UNDERSTAND HER FEELINGS AT ALL...
SHE HAS EVERYTHING GOING FOR HER, EVEN THOUGH IT'S AN ORDINARY LIFE.
BUT SHE BULLIES THE MAIN CHARACTER TO TAKE HER MIND OFF HER "ORDINARY" LIFE...
fume fume
clip clop clip
WHAT A SELFISH GIRL. SHE'S A TROUBLE-MAKER...
Ha!
40
30
20
10
0
-10
-20
-30
-40
Like
Neutral
Hate
OH...NO! MY LOVE FOR PRINCESS NATSU IS BELOW FREEZING!
NO NO... NO, KYOKO... COOL YOUR HEAD!
nuh
uh
DON'T LET YOUR OPINIONS BIND YOU!
TO BECOME A REAL ACTRESS...
...I MUST FEEL THE JOY OF LIVING AS PRINCESS NATSU IN THIS DRAMA...

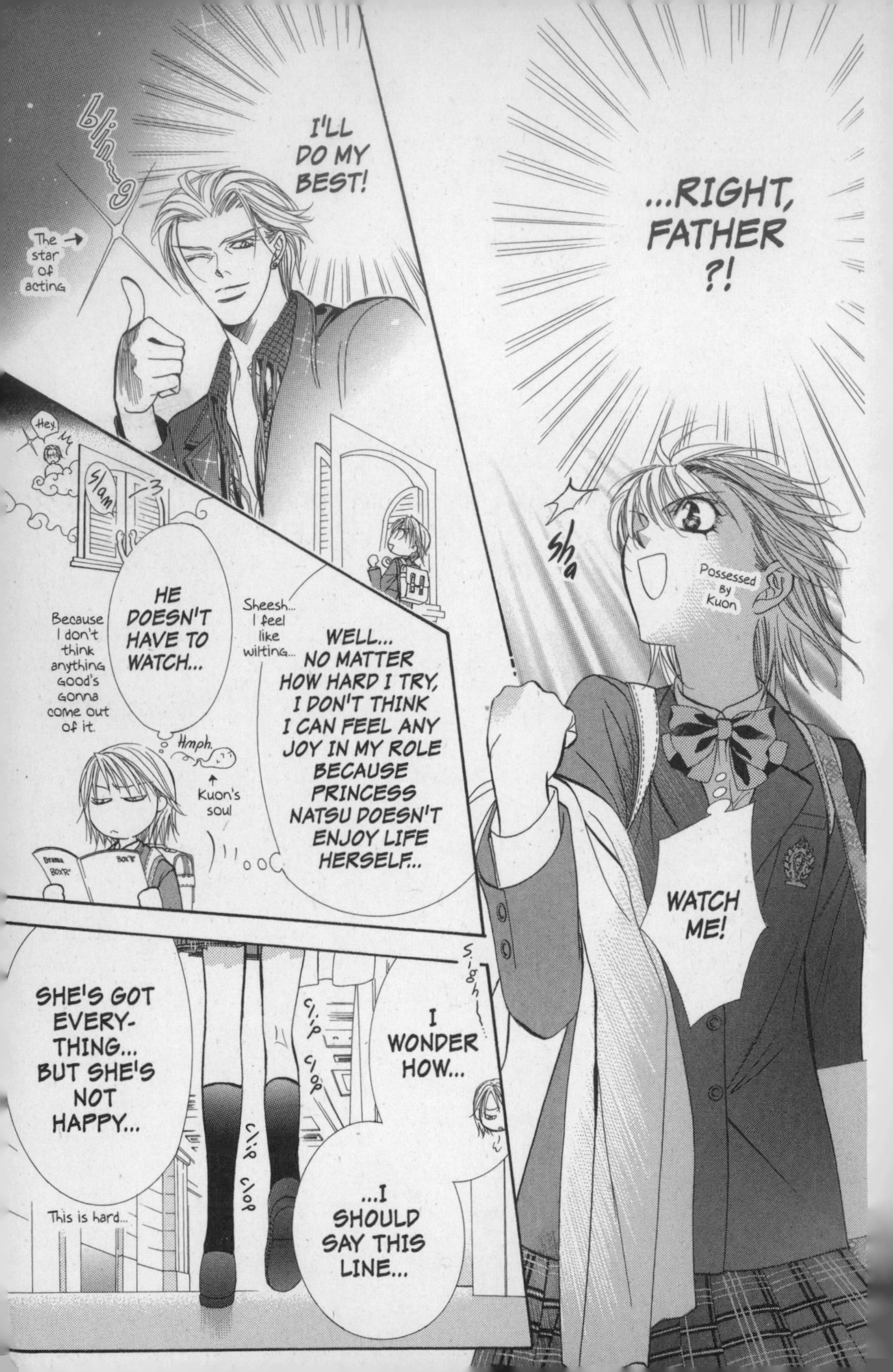
...RIGHT, FATHER?!
sha
Possessed By Kuon
WATCH ME!
blin~g
The star of acting
I'LL DO MY BEST!
Hey.
slam
Sheesh... I feel like wilting...
WELL... NO MATTER HOW HARD I TRY, I DON'T THINK I CAN FEEL ANY JOY IN MY ROLE BECAUSE PRINCESS NATSU DOESN'T ENJOY LIFE HERSELF...
HE DOESN'T HAVE TO WATCH...
Because I don't think anything good's gonna come out of it.
Hmph.
Kuon's soul
Sigh
I WONDER HOW...
clip clop
...I SHOULD SAY THIS LINE...
clip clop
SHE'S GOT EVERY-THING... BUT SHE'S NOT HAPPY...
This is hard...

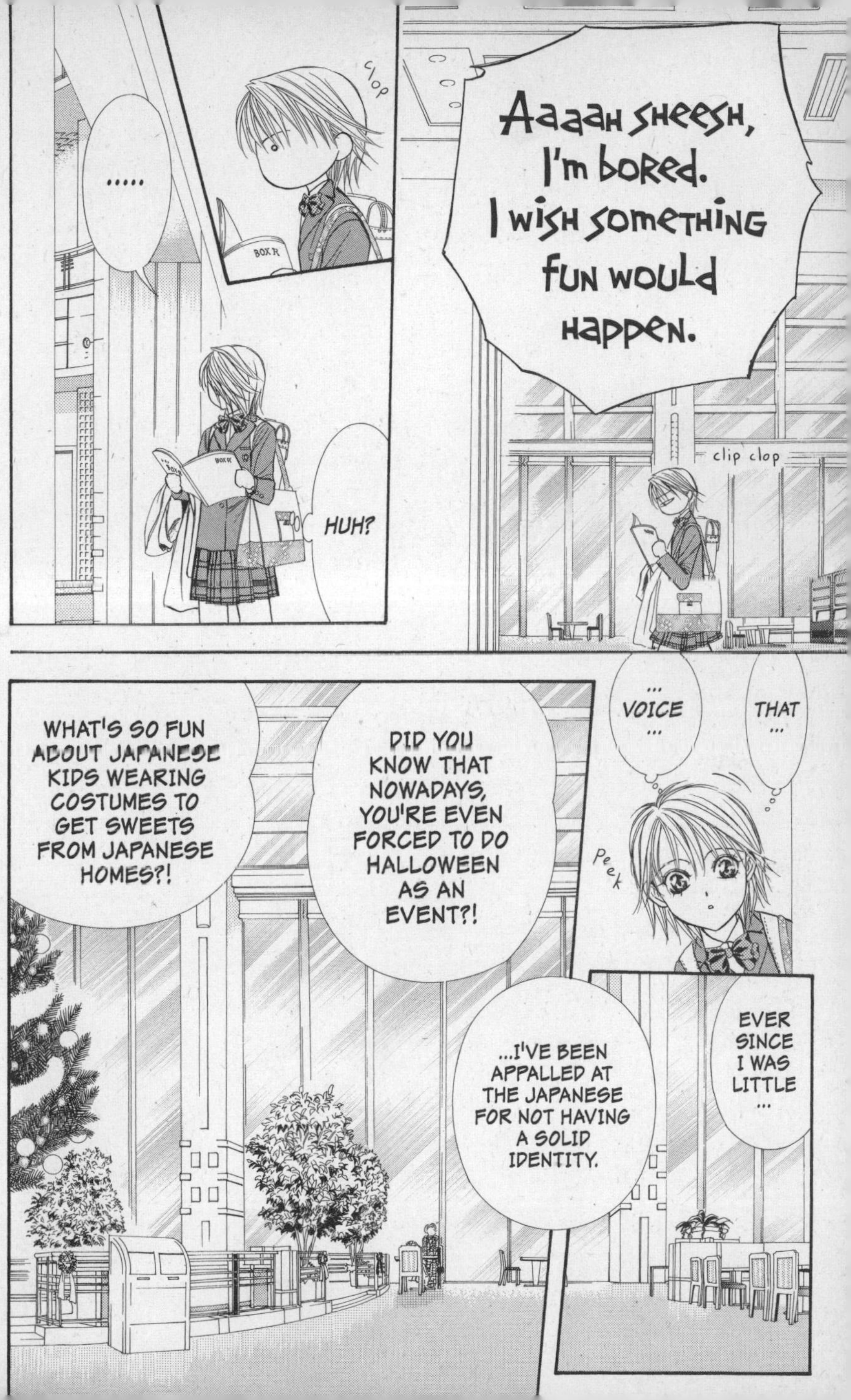
Aaaah sheesh, I'm bored. I wish something fun would happen.
clip clop
clop
.....
HUH?
THAT ...
... VOICE ...
Peek
EVER SINCE I WAS LITTLE ...
...I'VE BEEN APPALLED AT THE JAPANESE FOR NOT HAVING A SOLID IDENTITY.
DID YOU KNOW THAT NOWADAYS, YOU'RE EVEN FORCED TO DO HALLOWEEN AS AN EVENT?!
WHAT'S SO FUN ABOUT JAPANESE KIDS WEARING COSTUMES TO GET SWEETS FROM JAPANESE HOMES?!

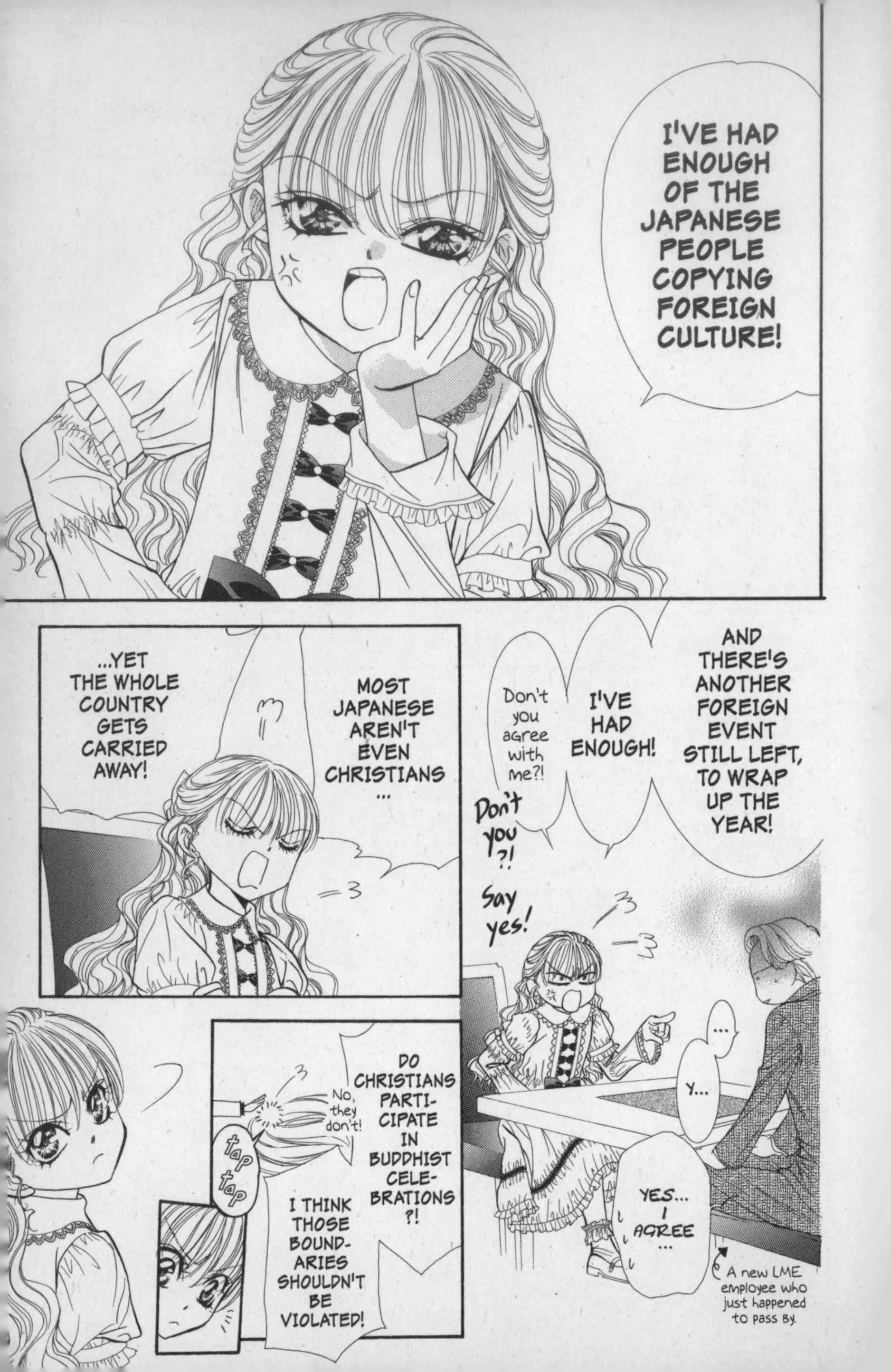
I'VE HAD ENOUGH OF THE JAPANESE PEOPLE COPYING FOREIGN CULTURE!
AND THERE'S ANOTHER FOREIGN EVENT STILL LEFT, TO WRAP UP THE YEAR!
I'VE HAD ENOUGH!
Don't you agree with me?!
Don't you ?!
Say yes!
...
Y...
YES... I AGREE ...
A new LME employee who just happened to pass by.
MOST JAPANESE AREN'T EVEN CHRISTIANS ...
...YET THE WHOLE COUNTRY GETS CARRIED AWAY!
DO CHRISTIANS PARTICI-PATE IN BUDDHIST CELE-BRATIONS ?!
No, they don't!
I THINK THOSE BOUND-ARIES SHOULDN'T BE VIOLATED!
tap tap

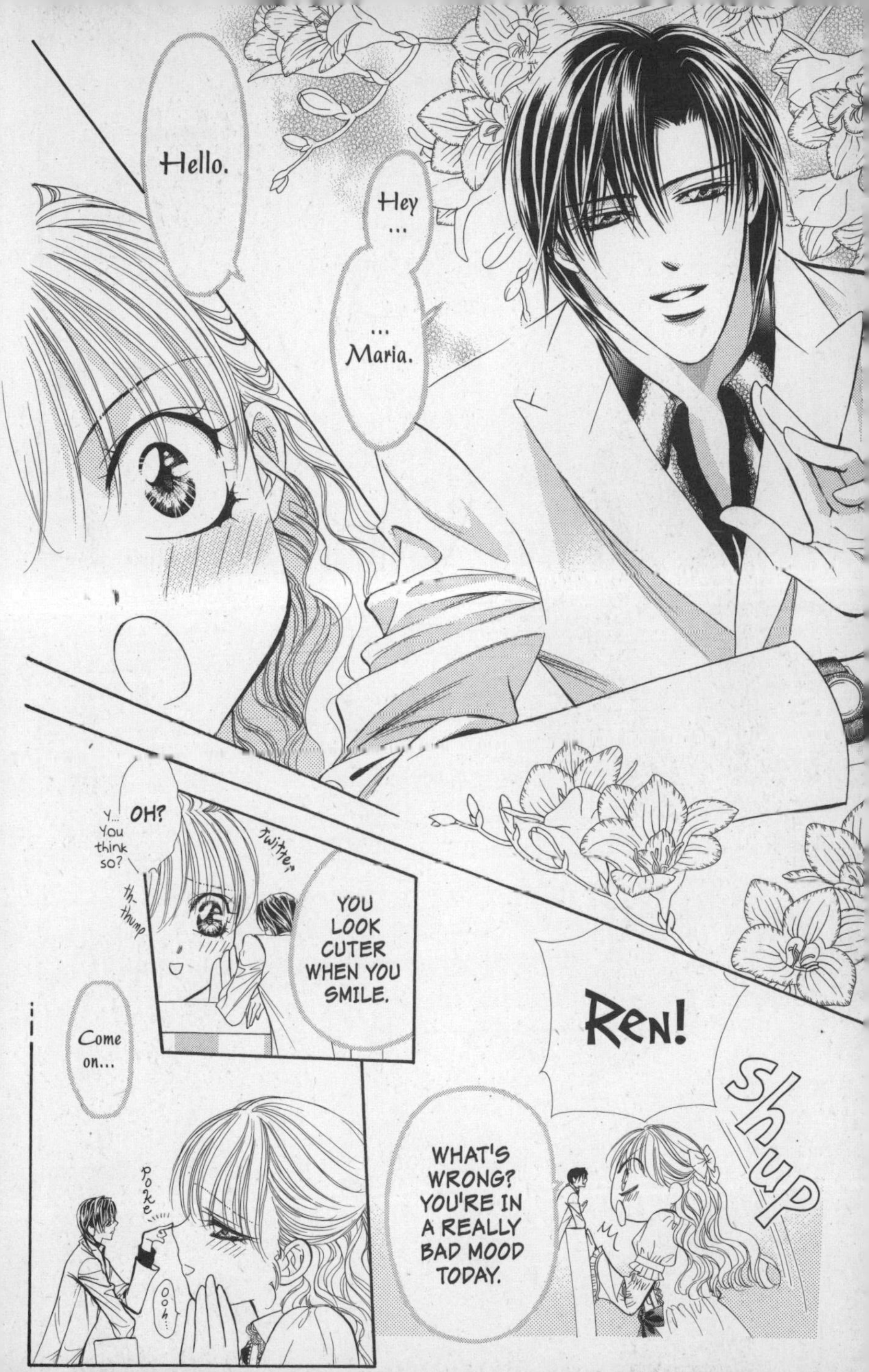
Hey
...
...
Maria.
Hello.
Ren!
Shup
WHAT'S WRONG? YOU'RE IN A REALLY BAD MOOD TODAY.
YOU LOOK CUTER WHEN YOU SMILE.
twitter
OH?
Y... You think so?
th-thump
Come on...
poke
ooh...

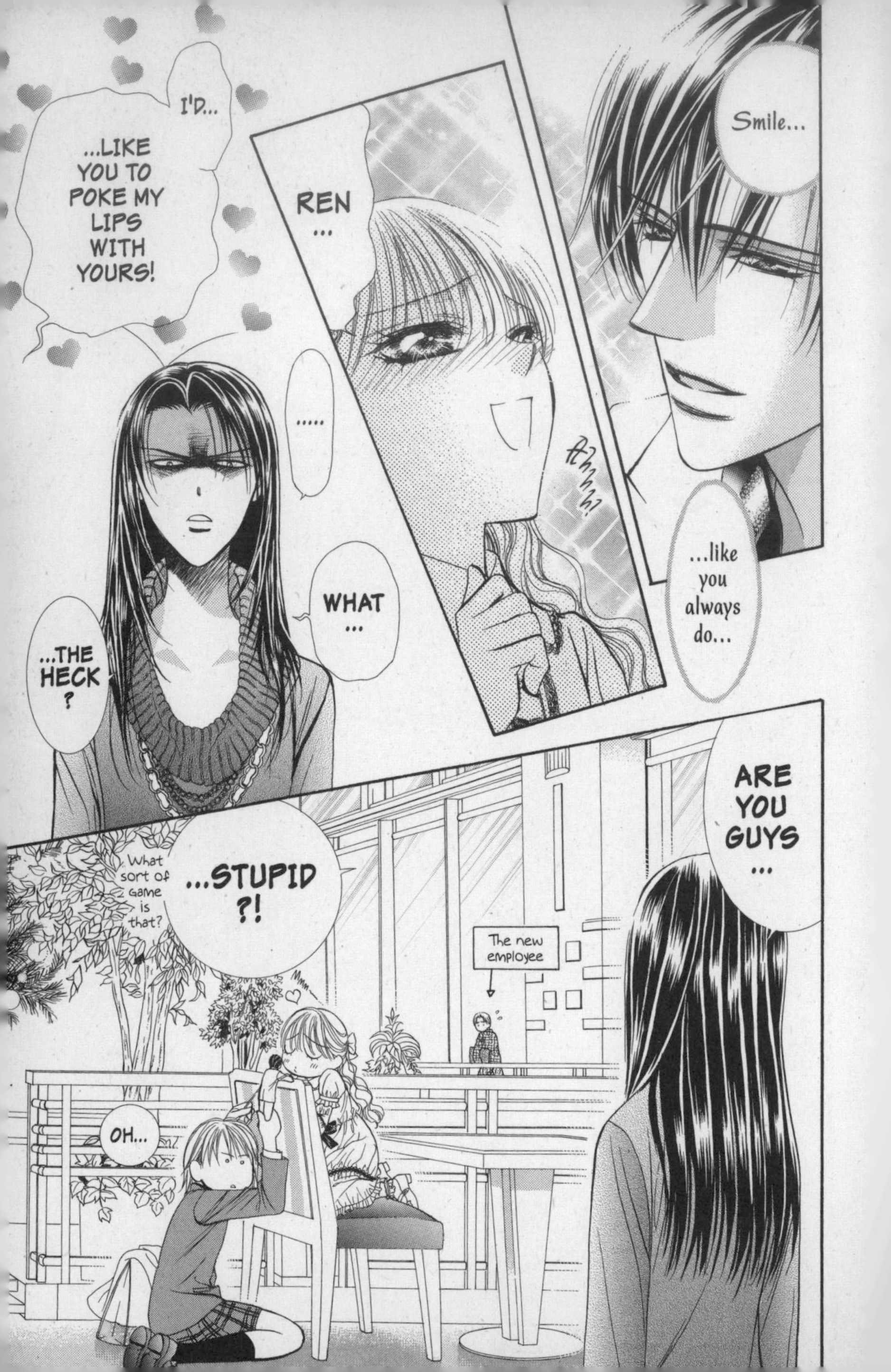
Smile...
...like you always do...
REN...
I'D...
...LIKE YOU TO POKE MY LIPS WITH YOURS!
.....
WHAT...
...THE HECK?
ARE YOU GUYS...
...STUPID?!
What sort of game is that?
The new employee
Mmm ♡
OH...

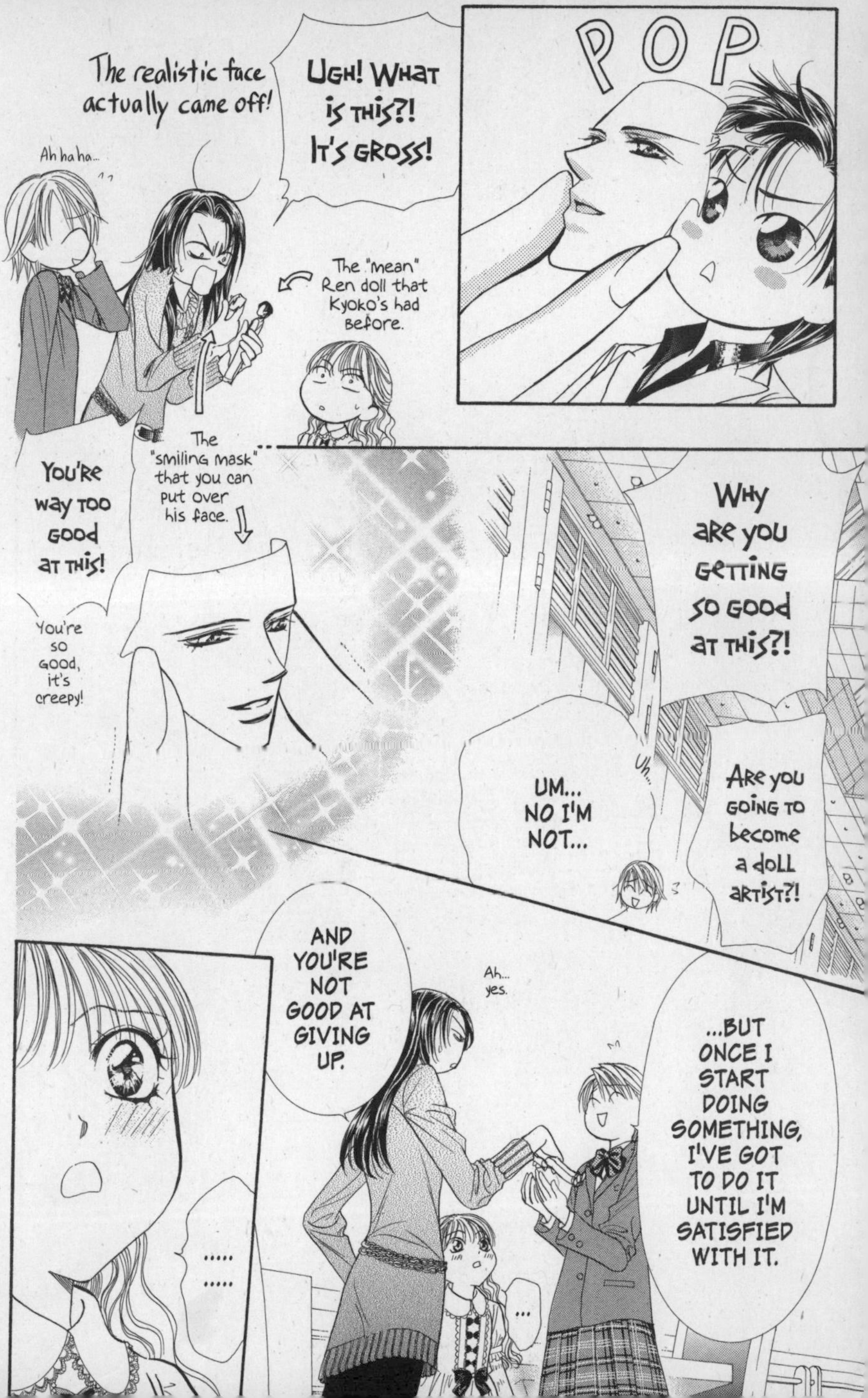
POP
UGH! WHAT IS THIS?! IT'S GROSS!
The realistic face actually came off!
Ah ha ha...
The "mean" Ren doll that Kyoko's had before.
WHY ARE YOU GETTING SO GOOD AT THIS?!
ARE YOU GOING TO BECOME A DOLL ARTIST?!
Uh...
UM... NO I'M NOT...
The "smiling mask" that you can put over his face.
YOU'RE WAY TOO GOOD AT THIS!
You're so good, it's creepy!
...BUT ONCE I START DOING SOMETHING, I'VE GOT TO DO IT UNTIL I'M SATISFIED WITH IT.
Ah... yes.
AND YOU'RE NOT GOOD AT GIVING UP.
...
.....
.....

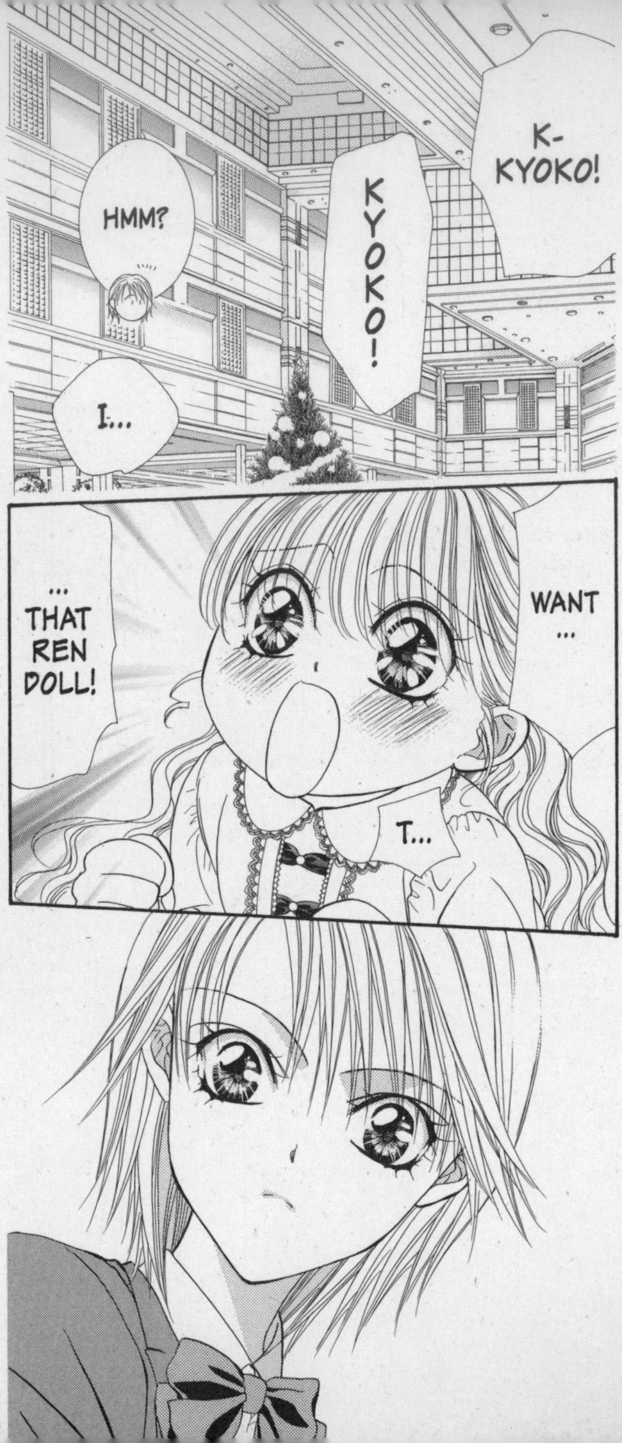
K-KYOKO!
KYOKO!
HMM?
I...
WANT ...
T...
... THAT REN DOLL!
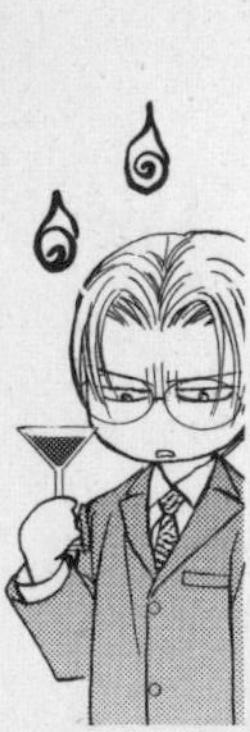

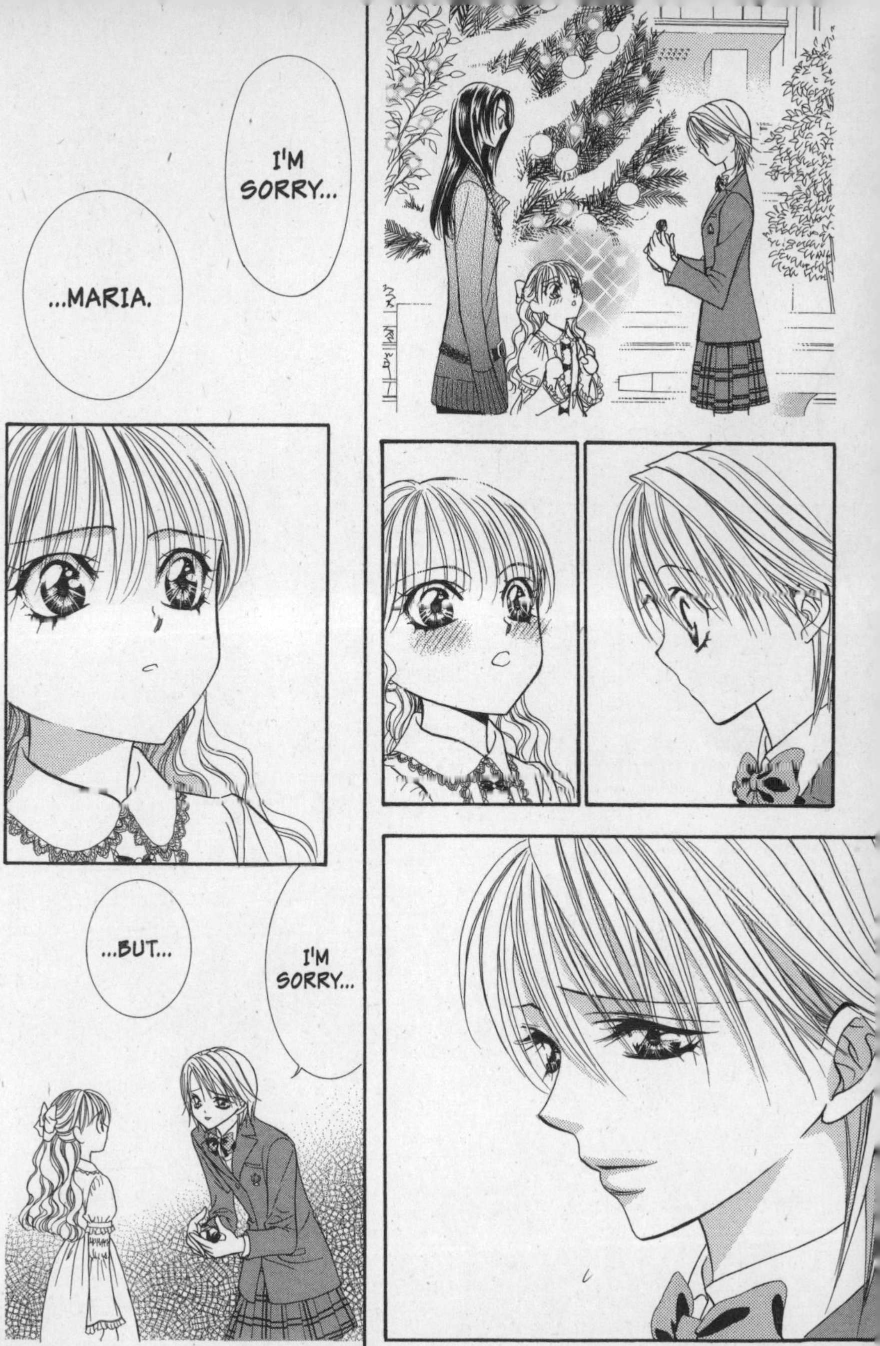
I'M SORRY...
...MARIA.
I'M SORRY...
...BUT...

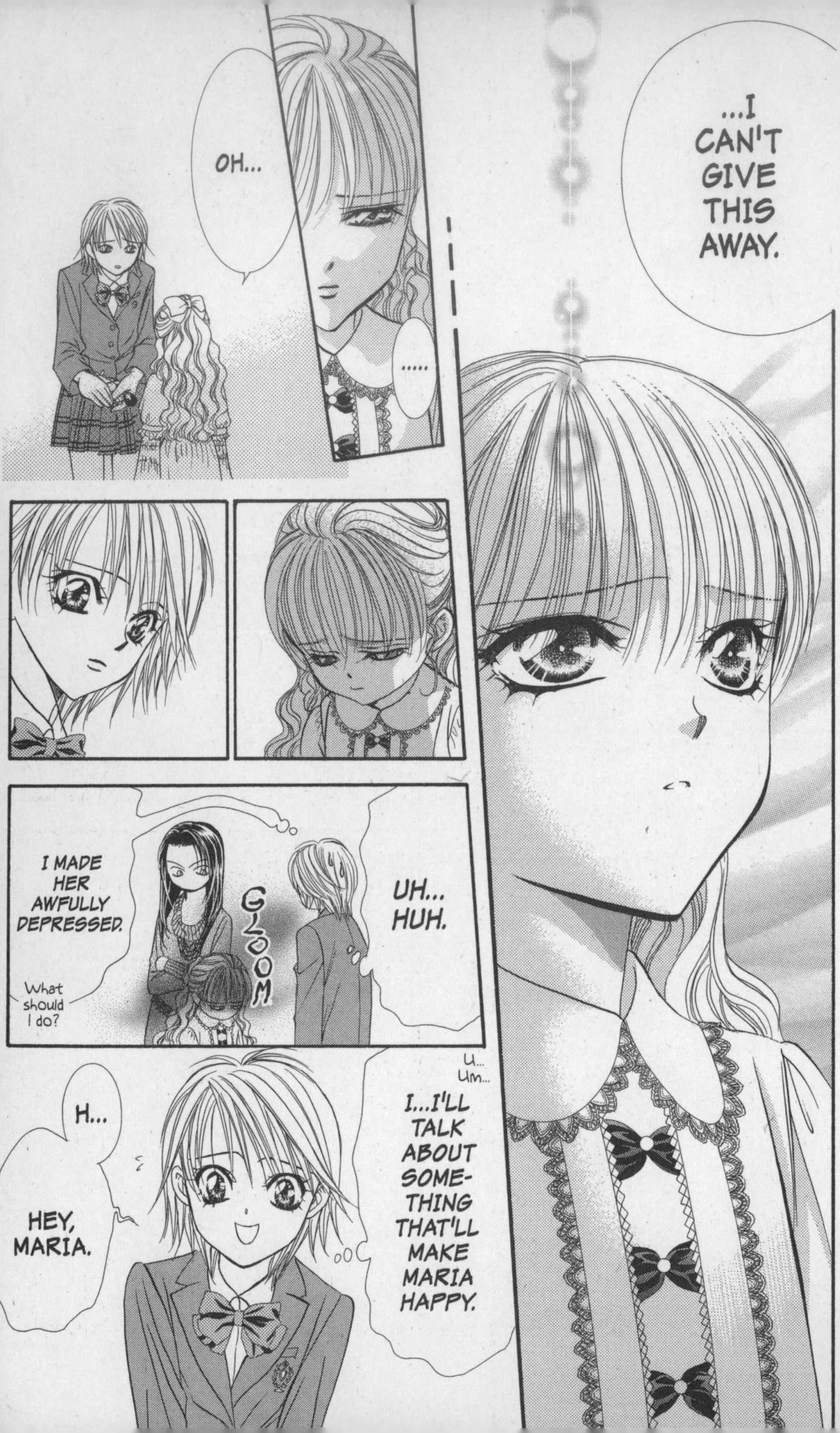
...I CAN'T GIVE THIS AWAY.
.....
OH...
UH... HUH.
GLOOM
I MADE HER AWFULLY DEPRESSED.
What should I do?
U... Um...
I...I'LL TALK ABOUT SOMETHING THAT'LL MAKE MARIA HAPPY.
H...
HEY, MARIA.

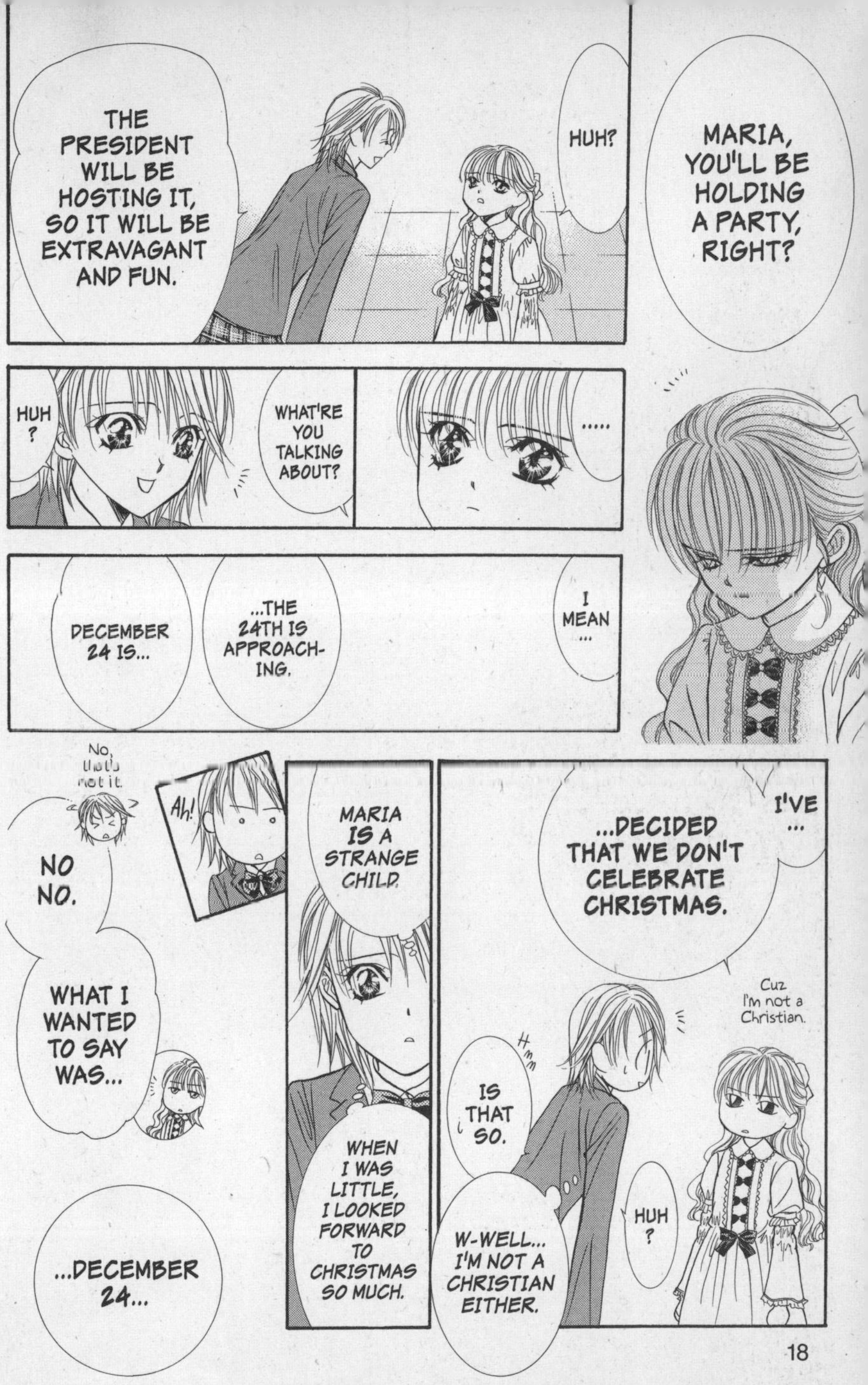
MARIA, YOU'LL BE HOLDING A PARTY, RIGHT?
HUH?
THE PRESIDENT WILL BE HOSTING IT, SO IT WILL BE EXTRAVAGANT AND FUN.
.....
HUH ?
WHAT'RE YOU TALKING ABOUT?
I MEAN ...
...THE 24TH IS APPROACH-ING.
DECEMBER 24 IS...
I'VE ...
...DECIDED THAT WE DON'T CELEBRATE CHRISTMAS.
Cuz I'm not a Christian.
Hmm
IS THAT SO.
HUH ?
W-WELL... I'M NOT A CHRISTIAN EITHER.
MARIA IS A STRANGE CHILD.
WHEN I WAS LITTLE, I LOOKED FORWARD TO CHRISTMAS SO MUCH.
Ah!
No, that's not it.
NO NO.
WHAT I WANTED TO SAY WAS...
...DECEMBER 24...

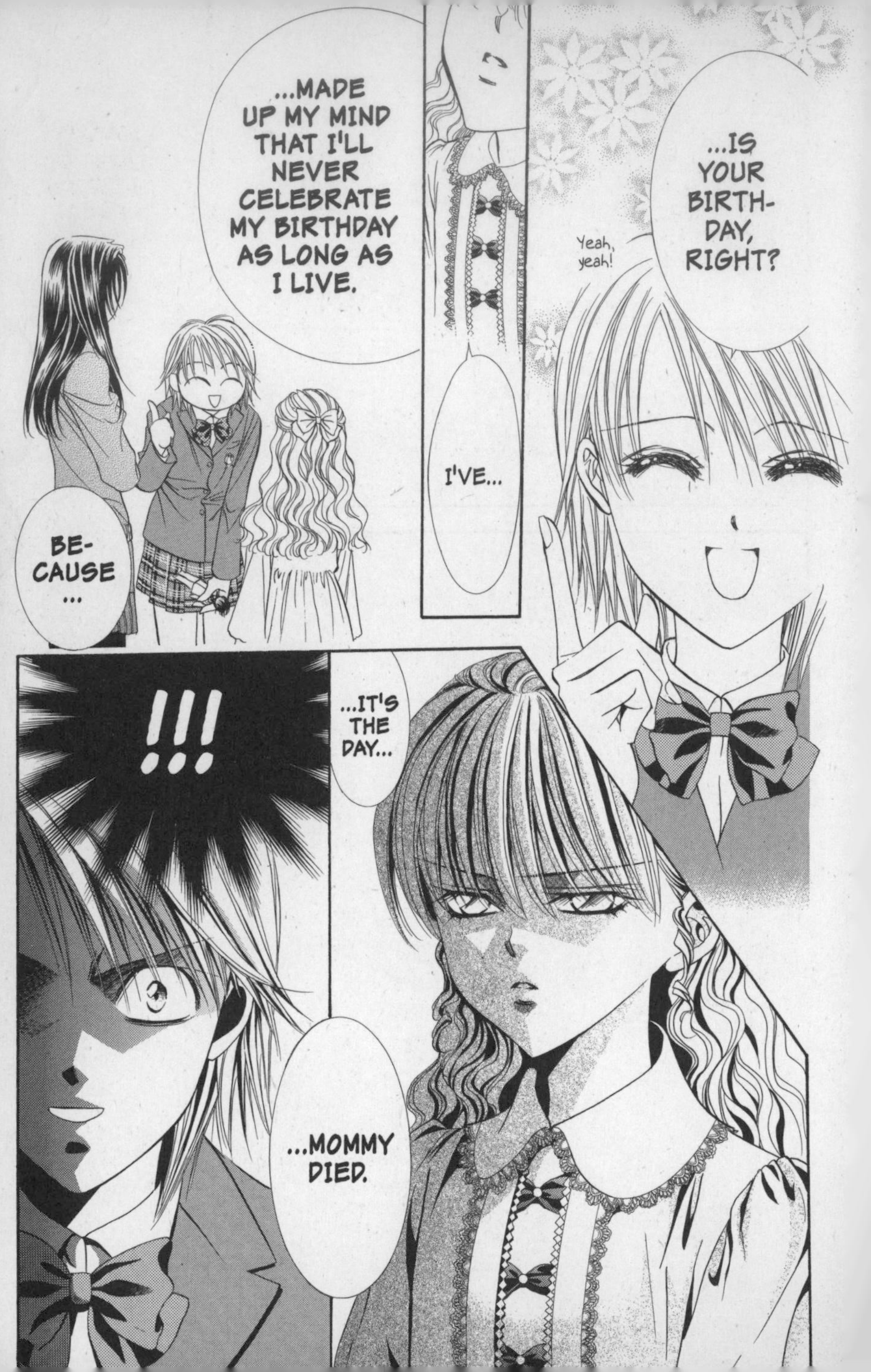
...IS YOUR BIRTH-DAY, RIGHT?
Yeah, yeah!
I'VE...
...MADE UP MY MIND THAT I'LL NEVER CELEBRATE MY BIRTHDAY AS LONG AS I LIVE.
BE-CAUSE ...
...IT'S THE DAY...
...MOMMY DIED.
!!!

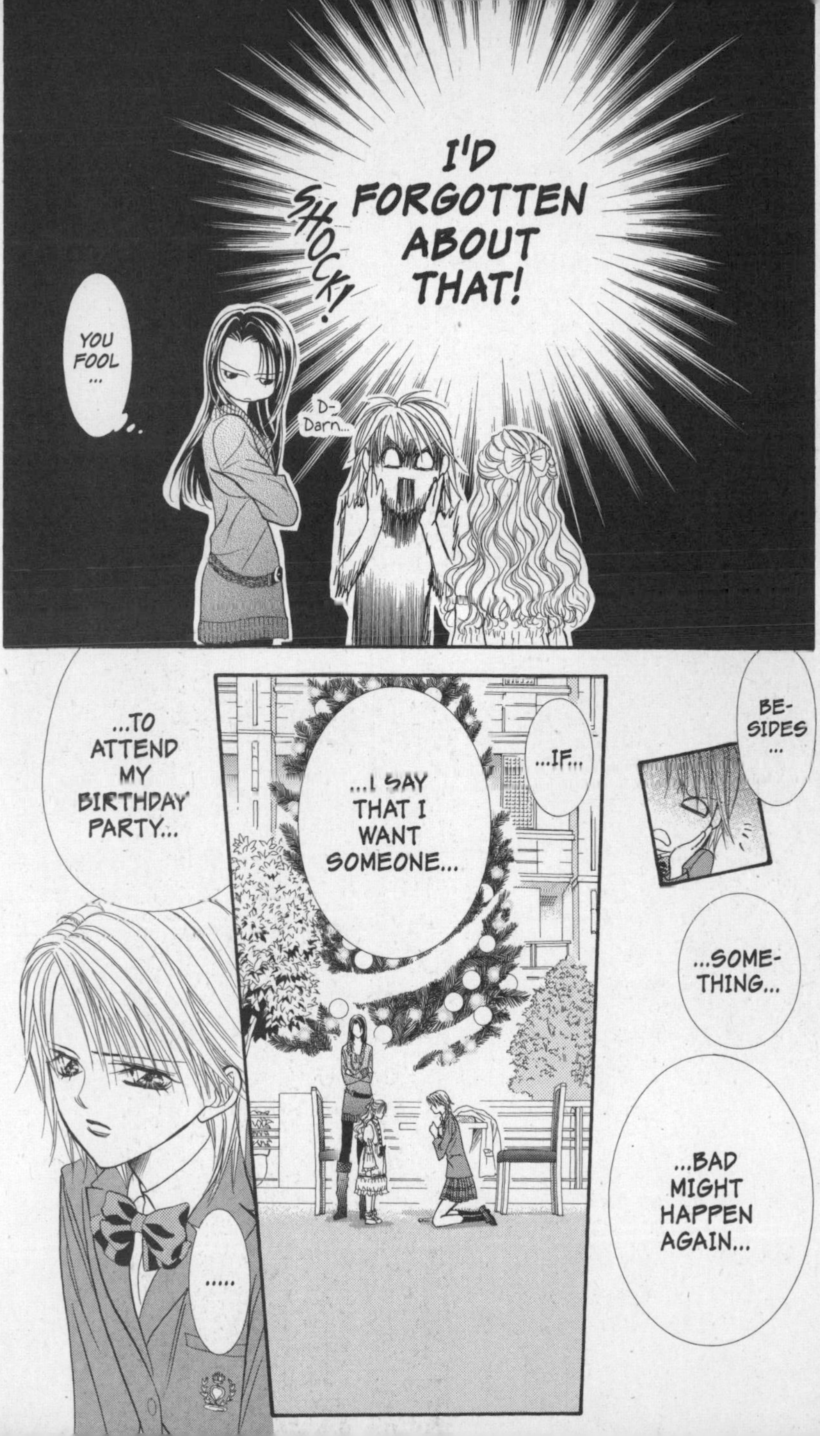
I'D FORGOTTEN ABOUT THAT!
SHOCK!
D-Darn...
YOU FOOL...
BE-SIDES...
...IF...
...I SAY THAT I WANT SOMEONE...
...TO ATTEND MY BIRTHDAY PARTY...
...SOME-THING...
...BAD MIGHT HAPPEN AGAIN...
.....

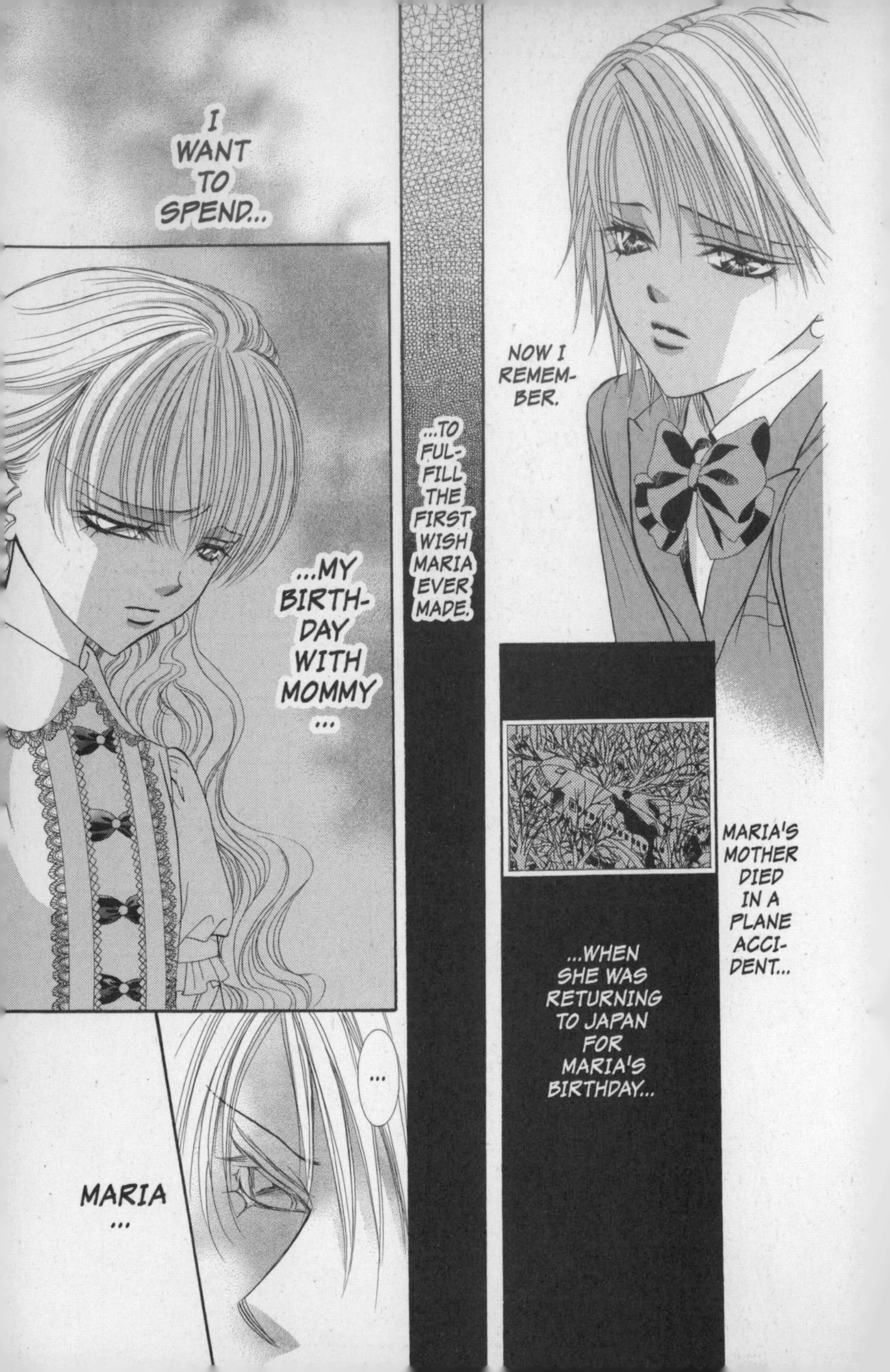
NOW I REMEMBER.
MARIA'S MOTHER DIED IN A PLANE ACCIDENT...
...WHEN SHE WAS RETURNING TO JAPAN FOR MARIA'S BIRTHDAY...
...TO FULFILL THE FIRST WISH MARIA EVER MADE.
I WANT TO SPEND...
...MY BIRTHDAY WITH MOMMY...
...
MARIA...

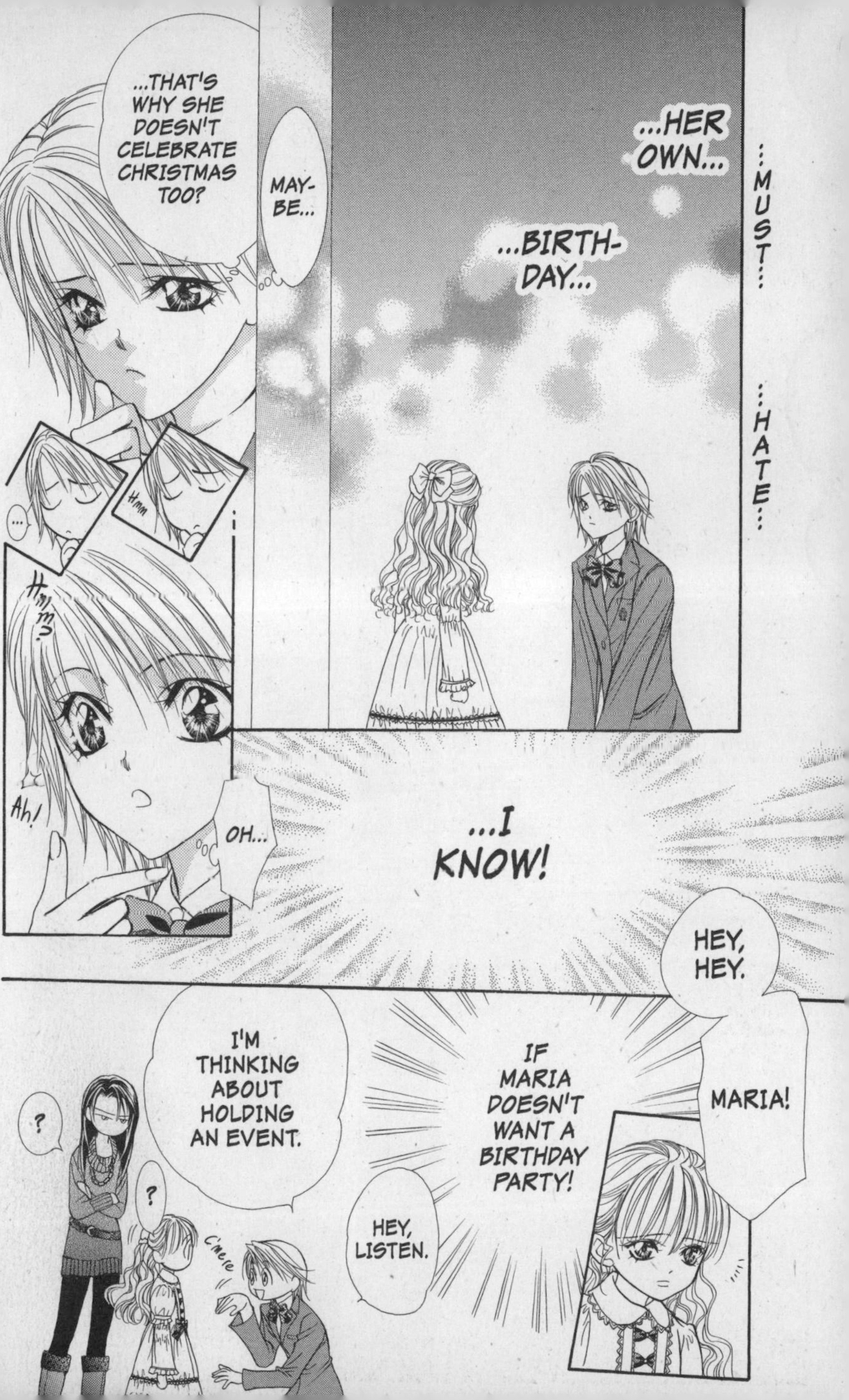
...MUST...
...HATE...
...HER OWN...
...BIRTH-DAY...
...THAT'S WHY SHE DOESN'T CELEBRATE CHRISTMAS TOO?
MAY-BE...
Hmm
...
Hmm?
Ah!
OH...
...I KNOW!
HEY, HEY.
MARIA!
IF MARIA DOESN'T WANT A BIRTHDAY PARTY!
HEY, LISTEN.
I'M THINKING ABOUT HOLDING AN EVENT.
C'mere
?
?

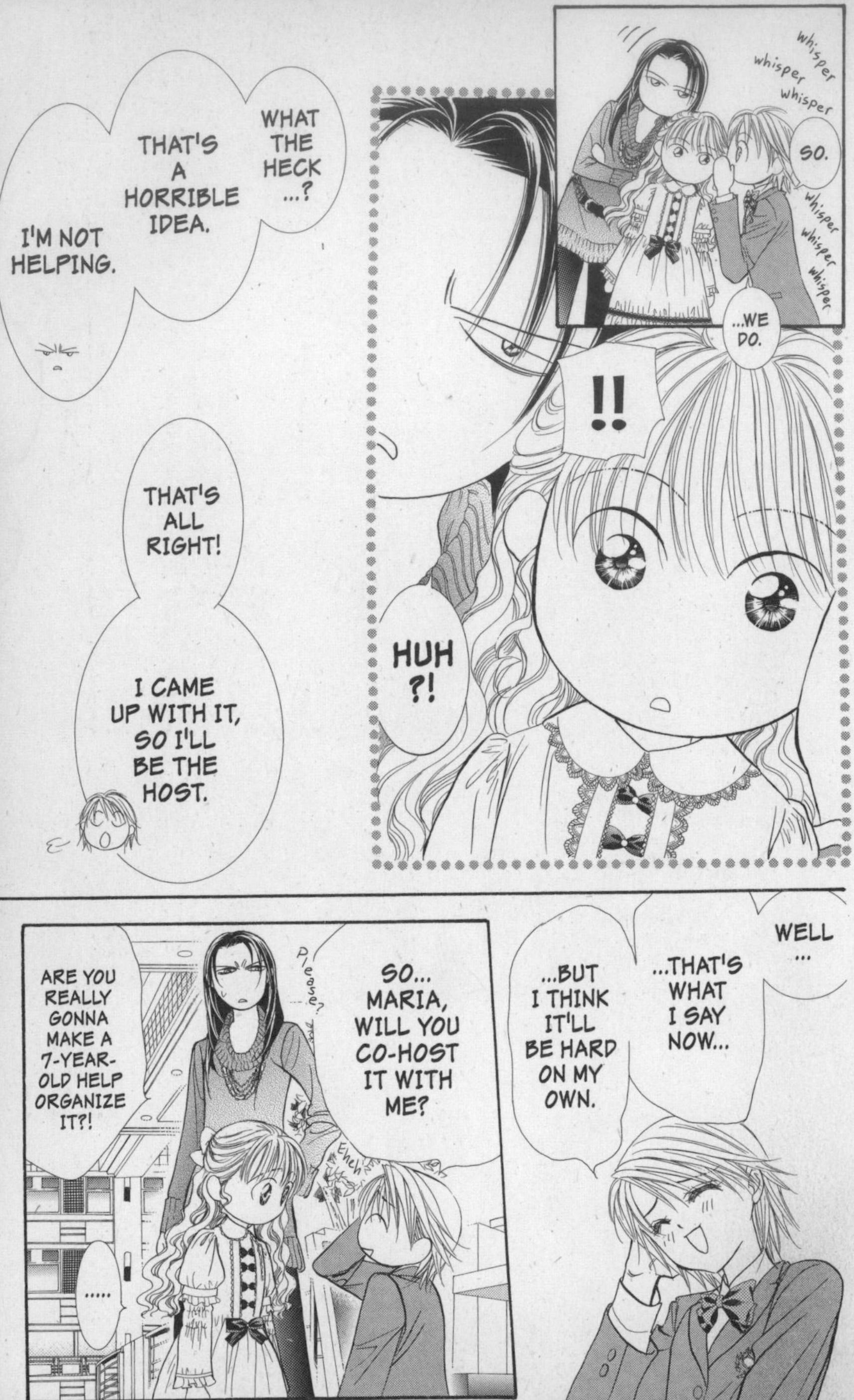
whisper whisper whisper
SO.
whisper whisper whisper
...WE DO.
!!
HUH?!
WHAT THE HECK ...?
THAT'S A HORRIBLE IDEA.
I'M NOT HELPING.
THAT'S ALL RIGHT!
I CAME UP WITH IT, SO I'LL BE THE HOST.
WELL ...
...THAT'S WHAT I SAY NOW...
...BUT I THINK IT'LL BE HARD ON MY OWN.
SO... MARIA, WILL YOU CO-HOST IT WITH ME?
Please?
Eheh
ARE YOU REALLY GONNA MAKE A 7-YEAR-OLD HELP ORGANIZE IT?!
.....

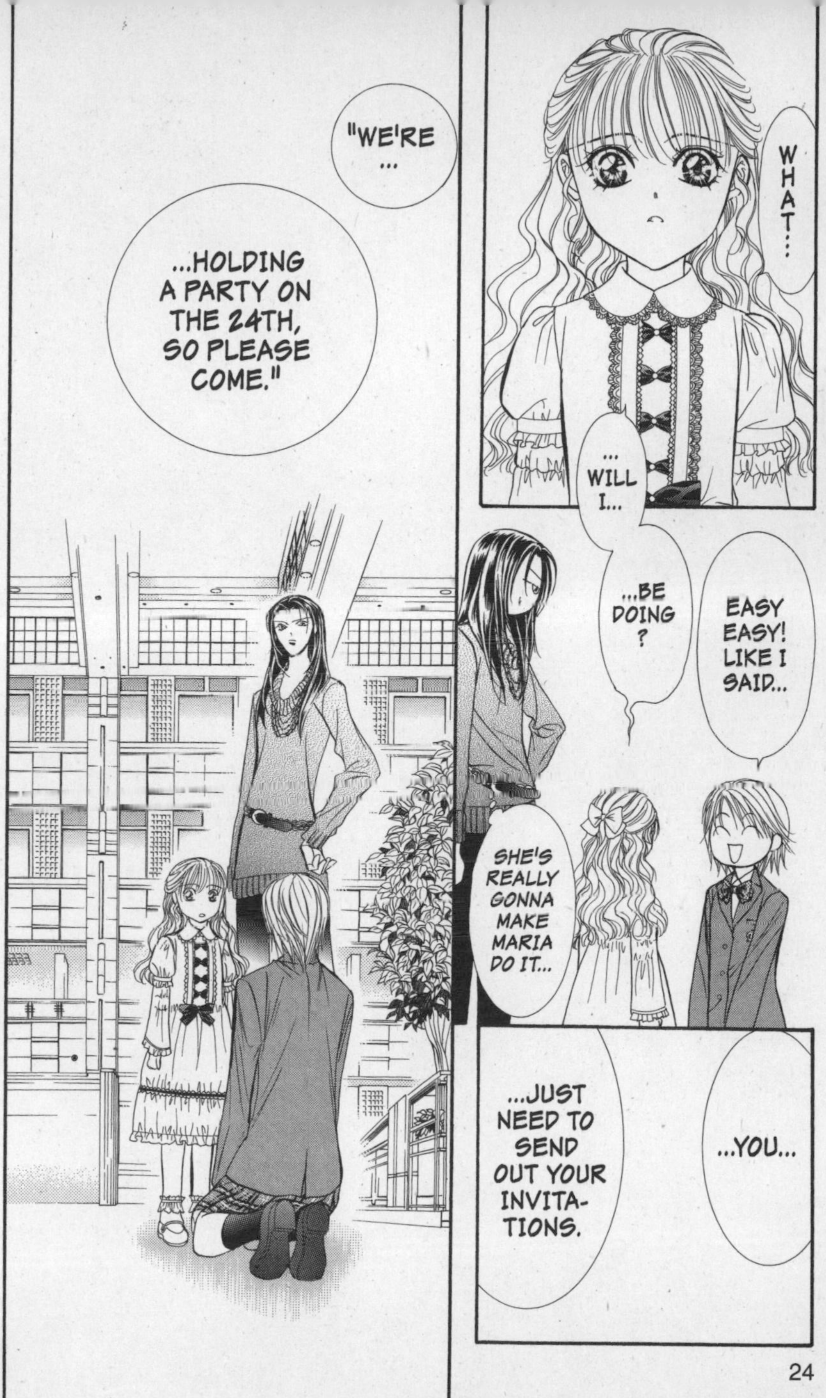
WHAT...
...WILL I...
...BE DOING?
EASY EASY! LIKE I SAID...
SHE'S REALLY GONNA MAKE MARIA DO IT...
...YOU...
...JUST NEED TO SEND OUT YOUR INVITATIONS.
"WE'RE ...
...HOLDING A PARTY ON THE 24TH, SO PLEASE COME."

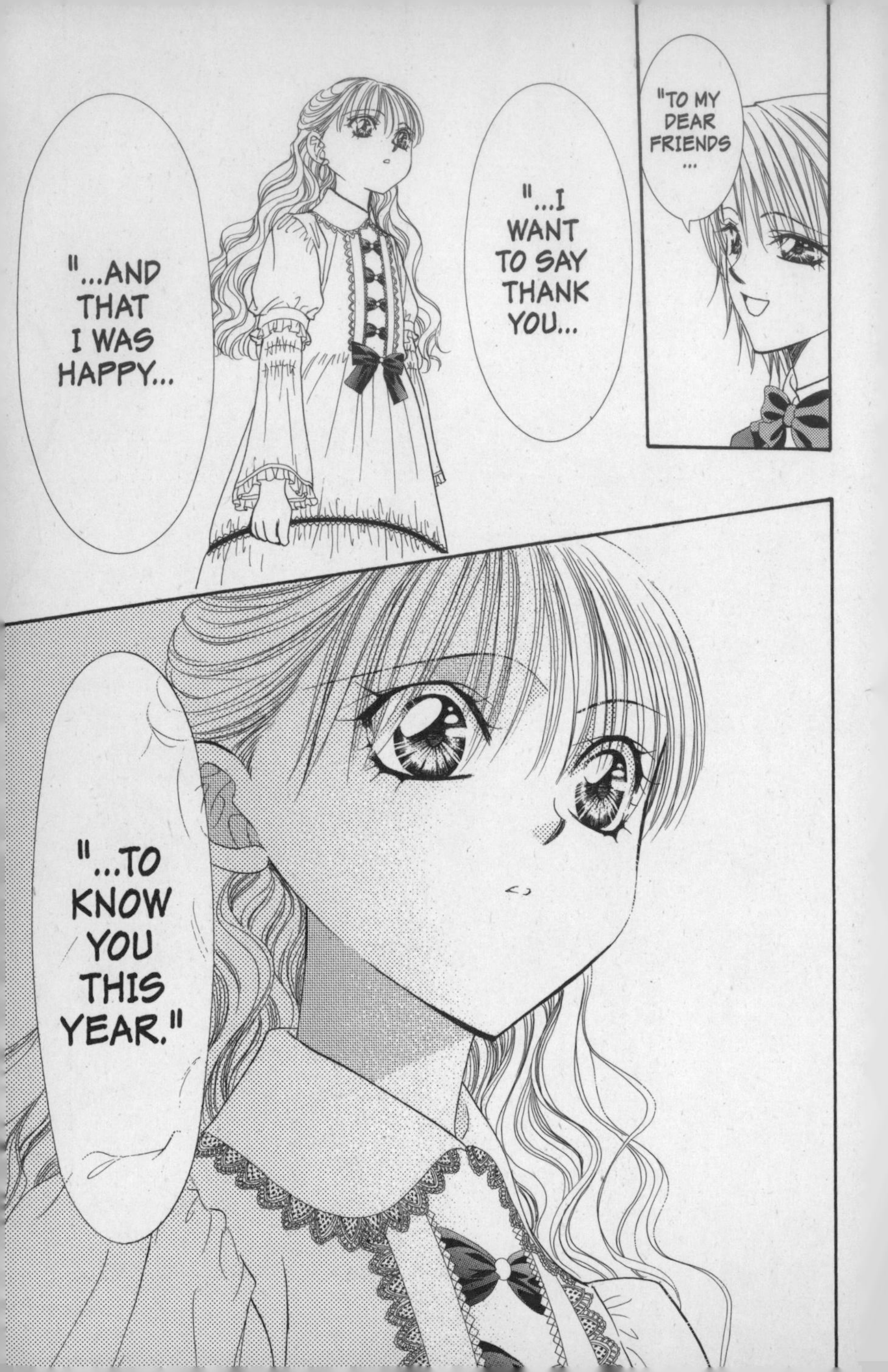
"TO MY DEAR FRIENDS ...
"...I WANT TO SAY THANK YOU...
"...AND THAT I WAS HAPPY...
"...TO KNOW YOU THIS YEAR."

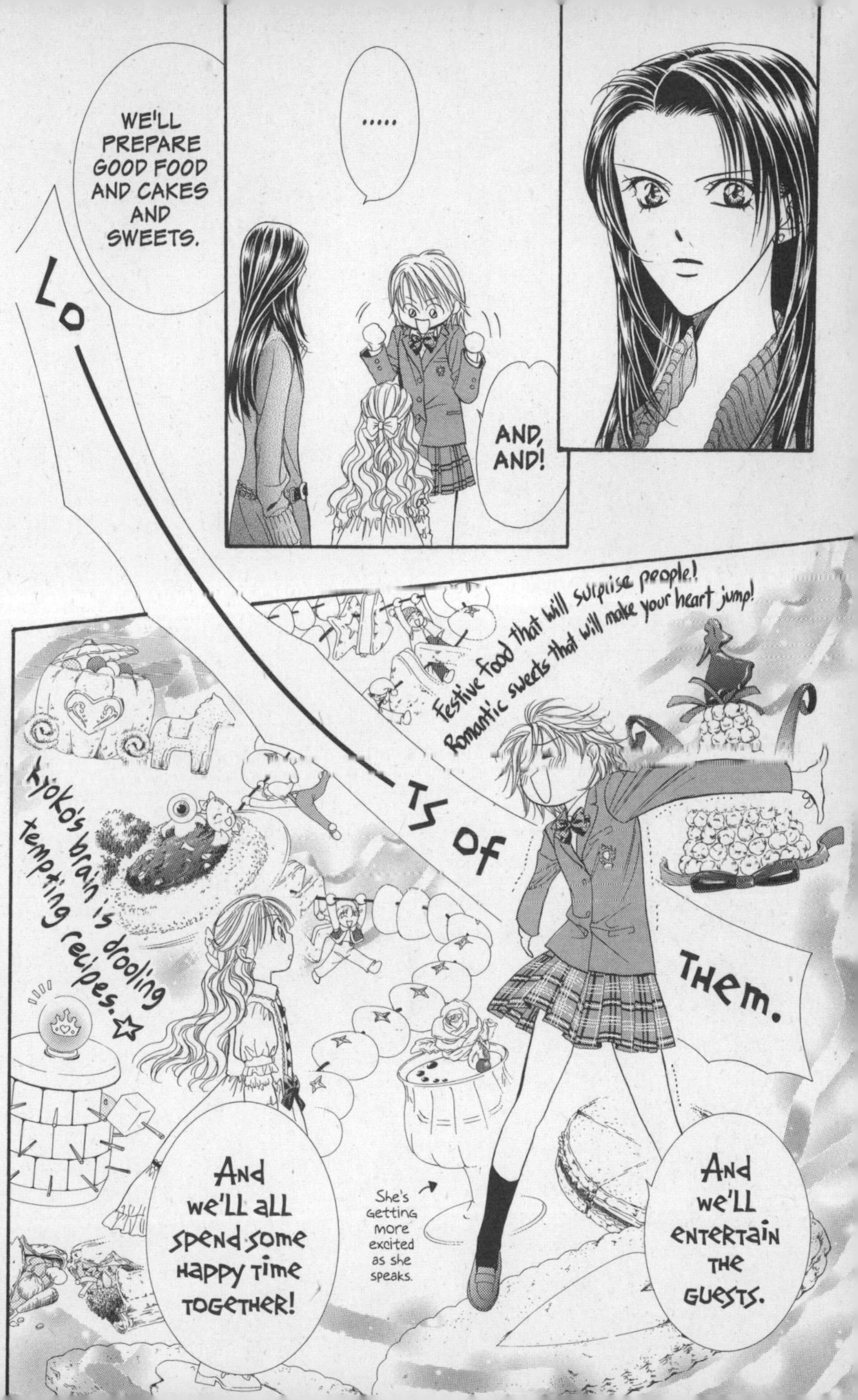
.....
AND, AND!
WE'LL PREPARE GOOD FOOD AND CAKES AND SWEETS.
LO—TS OF THEM.
Festive food that will surprise people!
Romantic sweets that will make your heart jump!
And we'll entertain the guests.
She's getting more excited as she speaks.
And we'll all spend some happy time together!
Kyoko's brain is drooling tempting recipes.☆

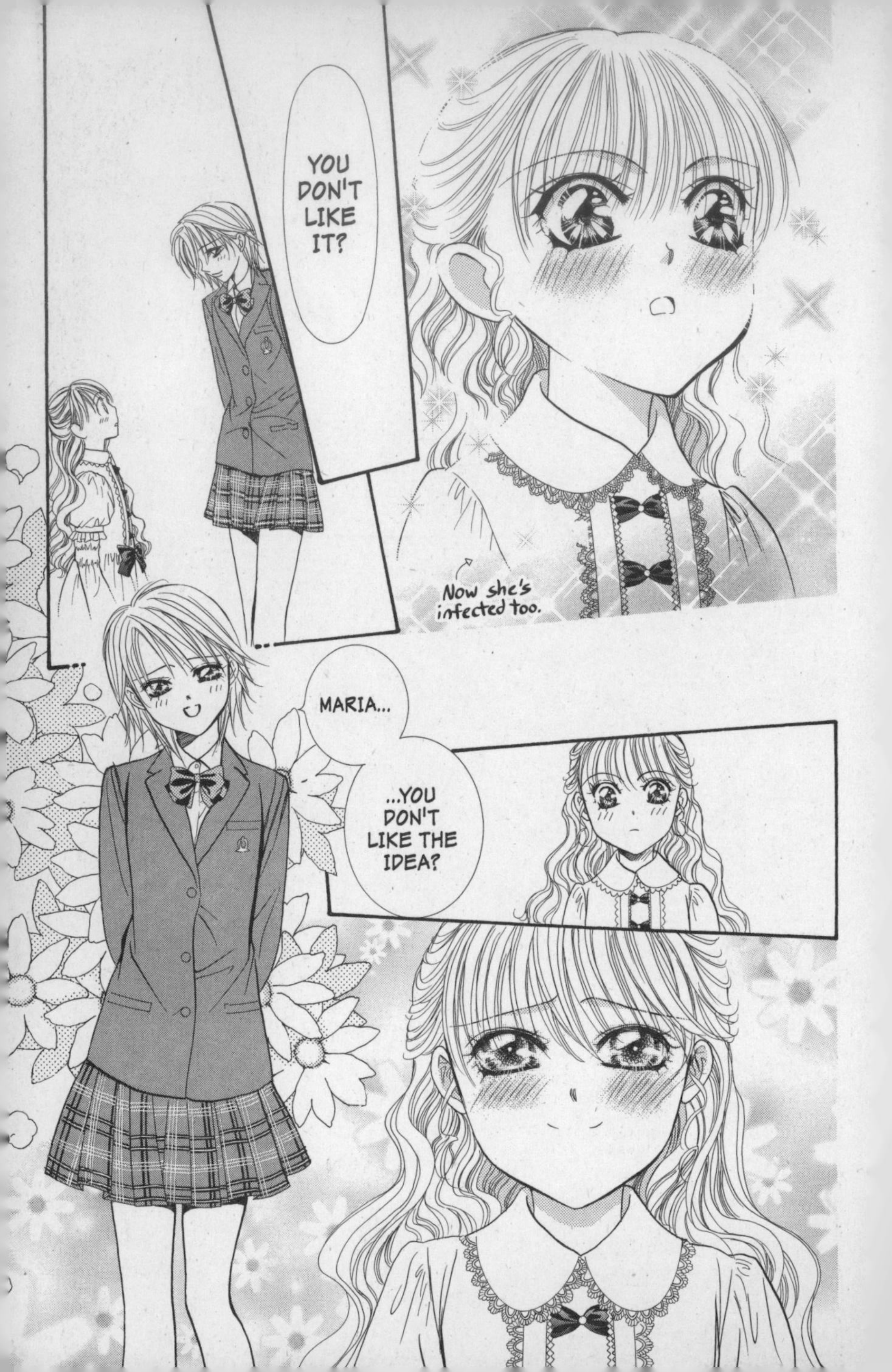
Now she's infected too.
YOU DON'T LIKE IT?
MARIA...
...YOU DON'T LIKE THE IDEA?

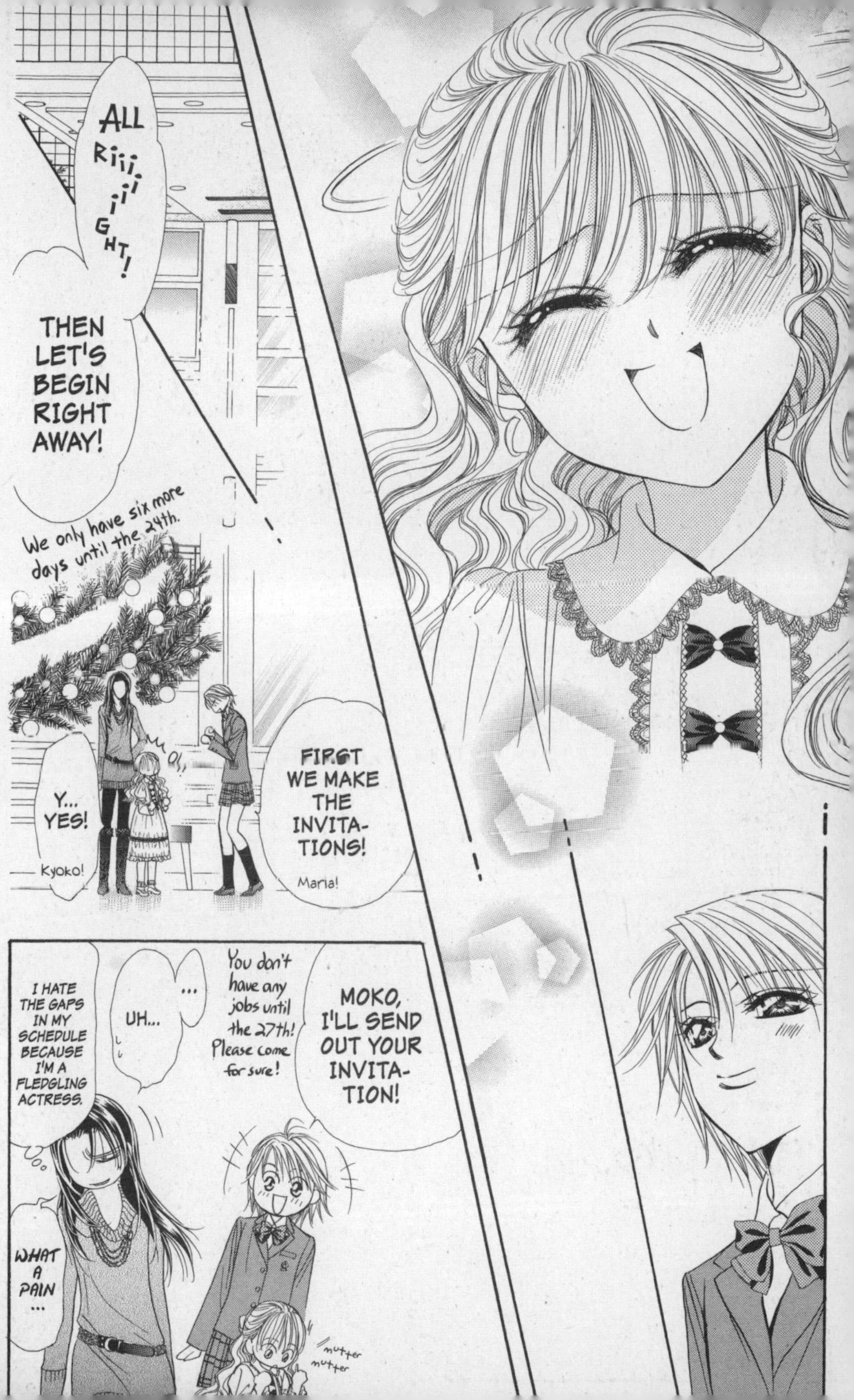

ALL RIiiiiIGHT!
THEN LET'S BEGIN RIGHT AWAY!
We only have six more days until the 24th.
FIRST WE MAKE THE INVITATIONS!
Maria!
Y... YES!
—— Kyoko!
MOKO, I'LL SEND OUT YOUR INVITATION!
You don't have any jobs until the 27th! Please come for sure!
...
UH...
I HATE THE GAPS IN MY SCHEDULE BECAUSE I'M A FLEDGLING ACTRESS.
WHAT A PAIN ...
mutter mutter

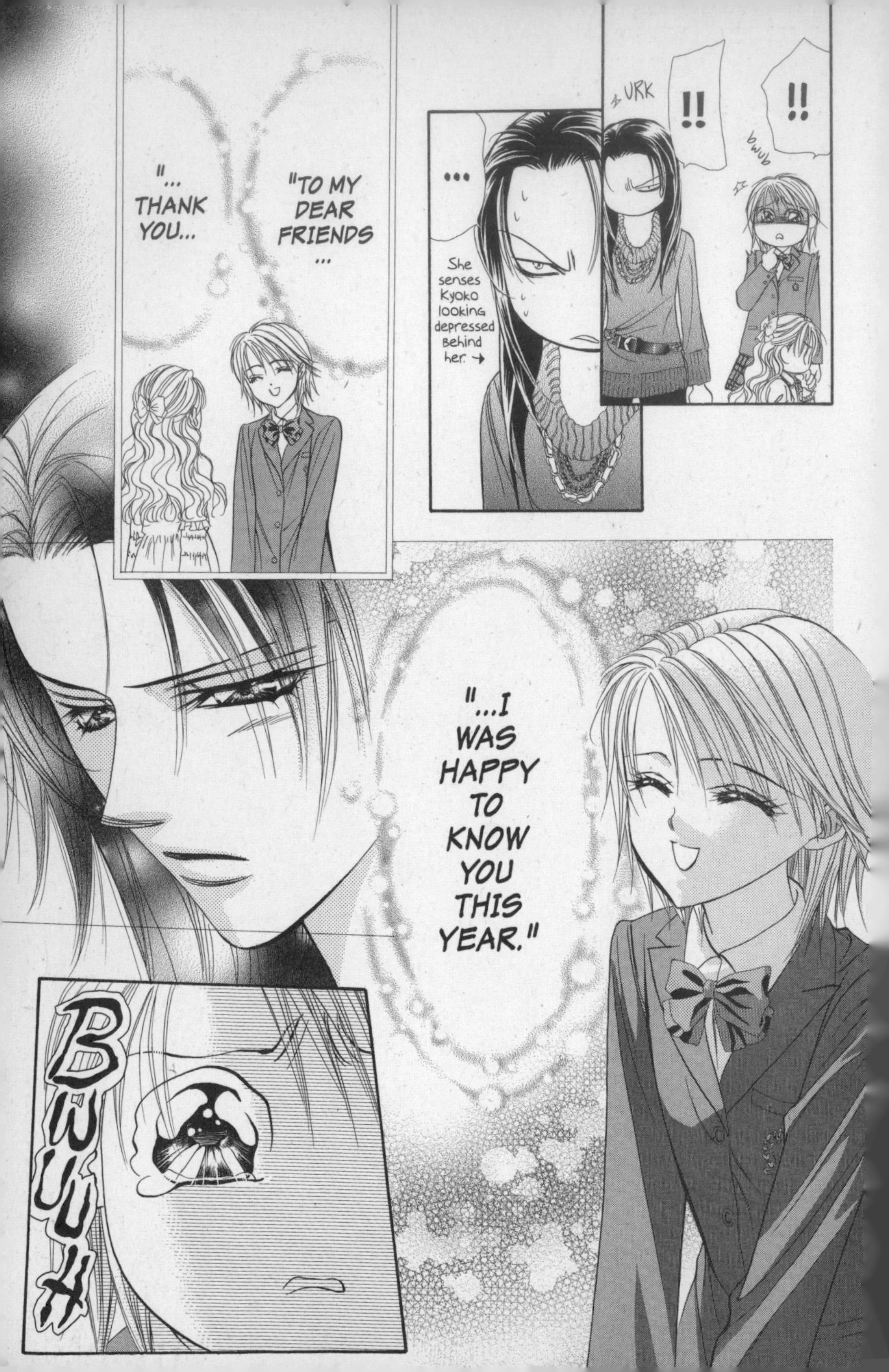
!!
bwub
!!
URK
...
She senses Kyoko looking depressed behind her. →
"TO MY DEAR FRIENDS ...
"... THANK YOU...
"...I WAS HAPPY TO KNOW YOU THIS YEAR."
BWUH

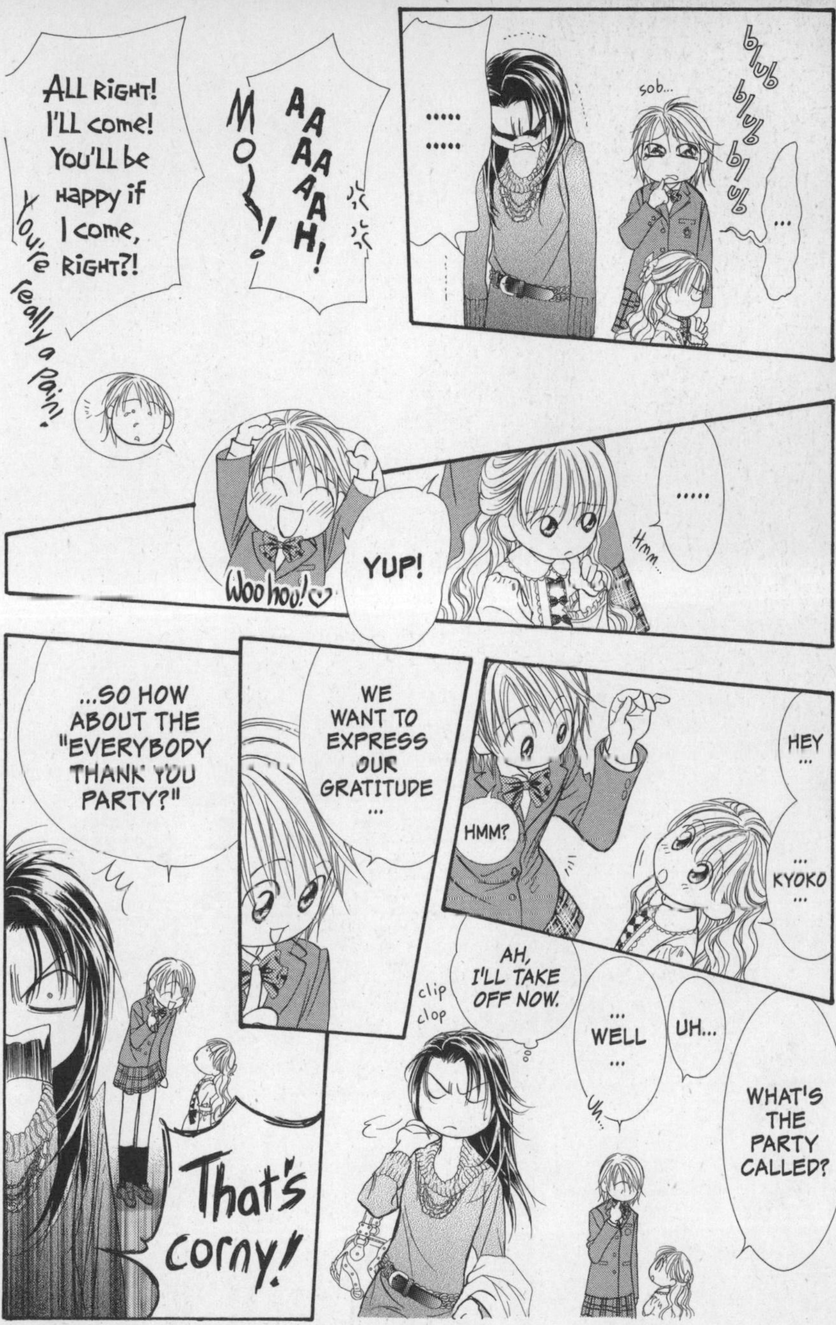

......
......
sob...
blub blub blub
...
AAAAAAH!
MO~!
ALL RIGHT! I'LL come! You'LL be happy if I come, RIGHT?!
You're really a pain!
.....
Hmm...
YUP!
Woohoo!♡
HEY... ...KYOKO...
HMM?
WHAT'S THE PARTY CALLED?
UH...
...WELL...
Uh...
AH, I'LL TAKE OFF NOW.
clip clop
WE WANT TO EXPRESS OUR GRATITUDE...
...SO HOW ABOUT THE "EVERYBODY THANK YOU PARTY?"
That's corny!

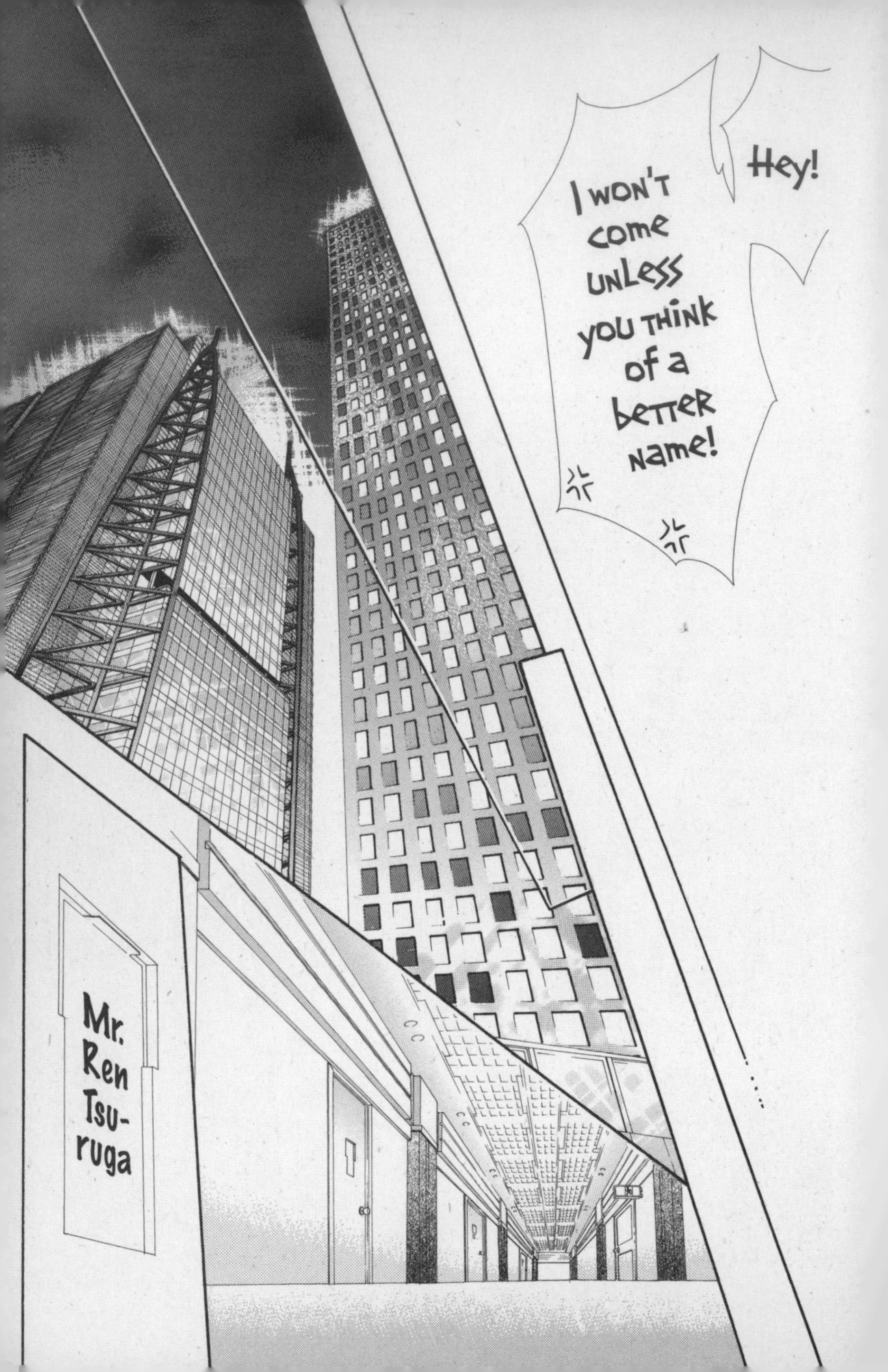
Hey! I won't come unless you think of a better name!
...
Mr. Ren Tsuruga

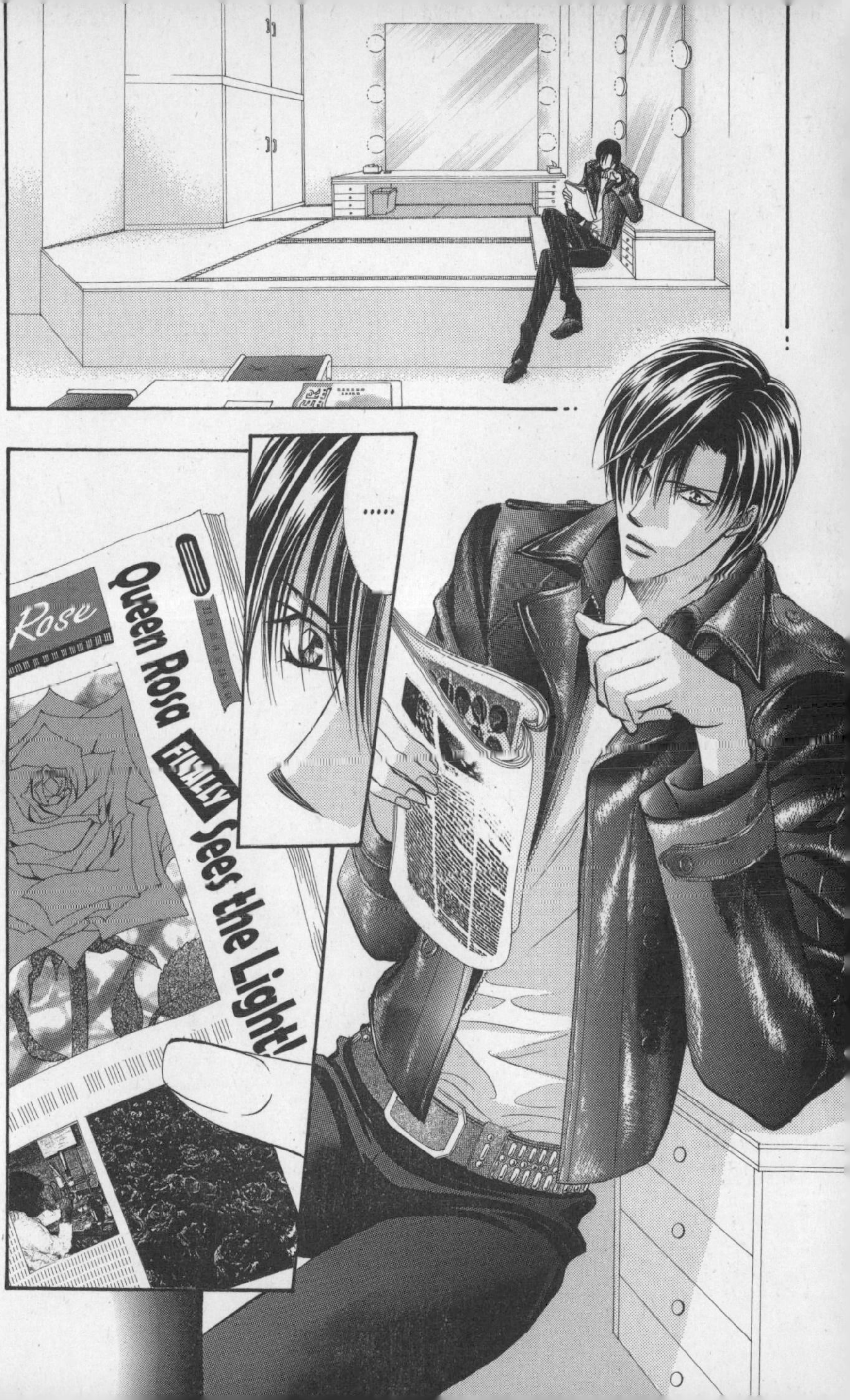
......
Rose
Queen Rosa FINALLY Sees the Light!

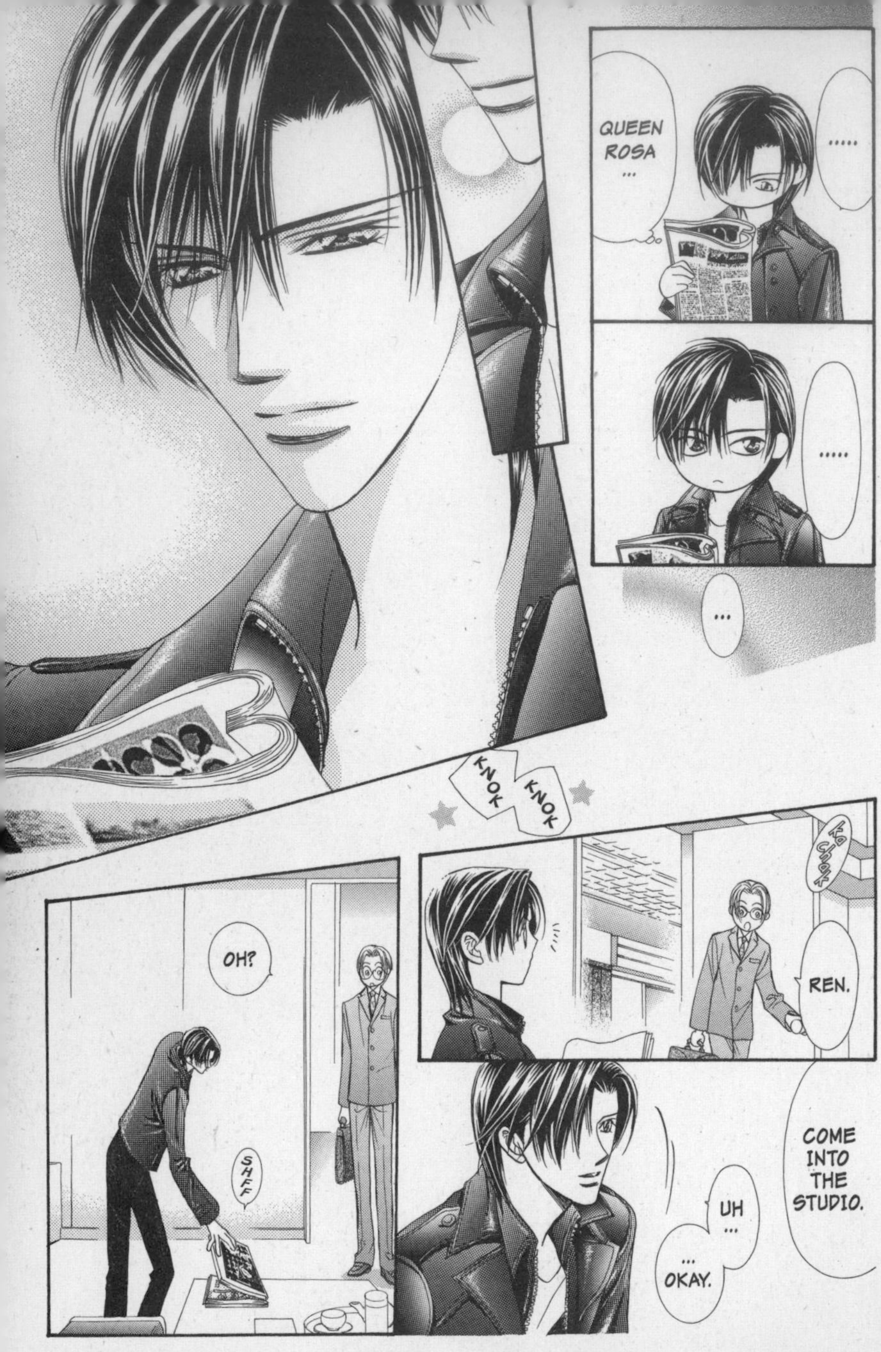
.....
QUEEN ROSA ...
.....
...
KNOK KNOK
KA CHAK
REN.
COME INTO THE STUDIO.
UH ...
... OKAY.
OH?
SHFF

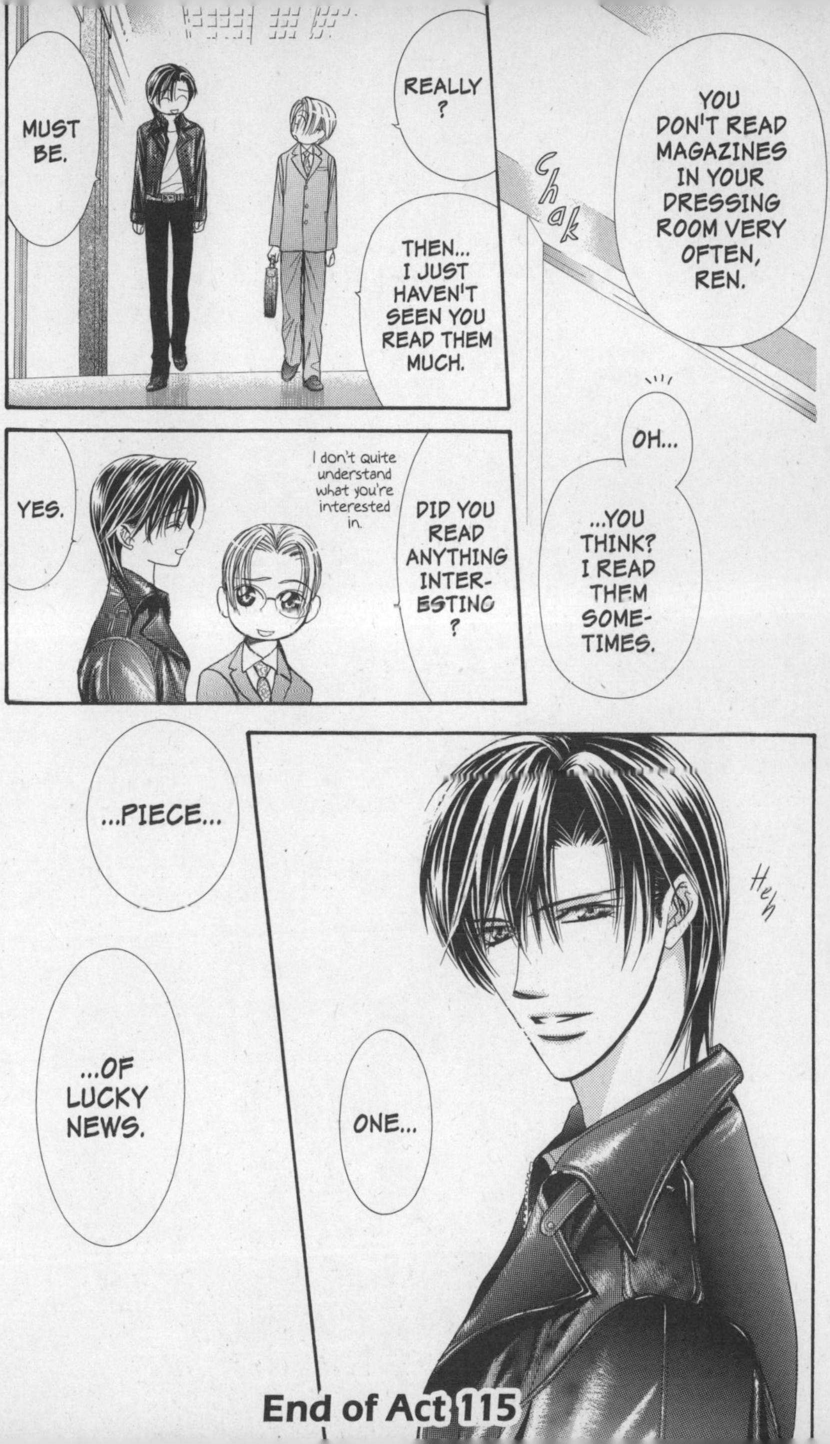
Chak
YOU DON'T READ MAGAZINES IN YOUR DRESSING ROOM VERY OFTEN, REN.
OH...
...YOU THINK? I READ THEM SOMETIMES.
REALLY?
THEN... I JUST HAVEN'T SEEN YOU READ THEM MUCH.
MUST BE.
DID YOU READ ANYTHING INTER-ESTING?
I don't quite understand what you're interested in.
YES.
Heh
ONE...
...PIECE...
...OF LUCKY NEWS.
End of Act 115

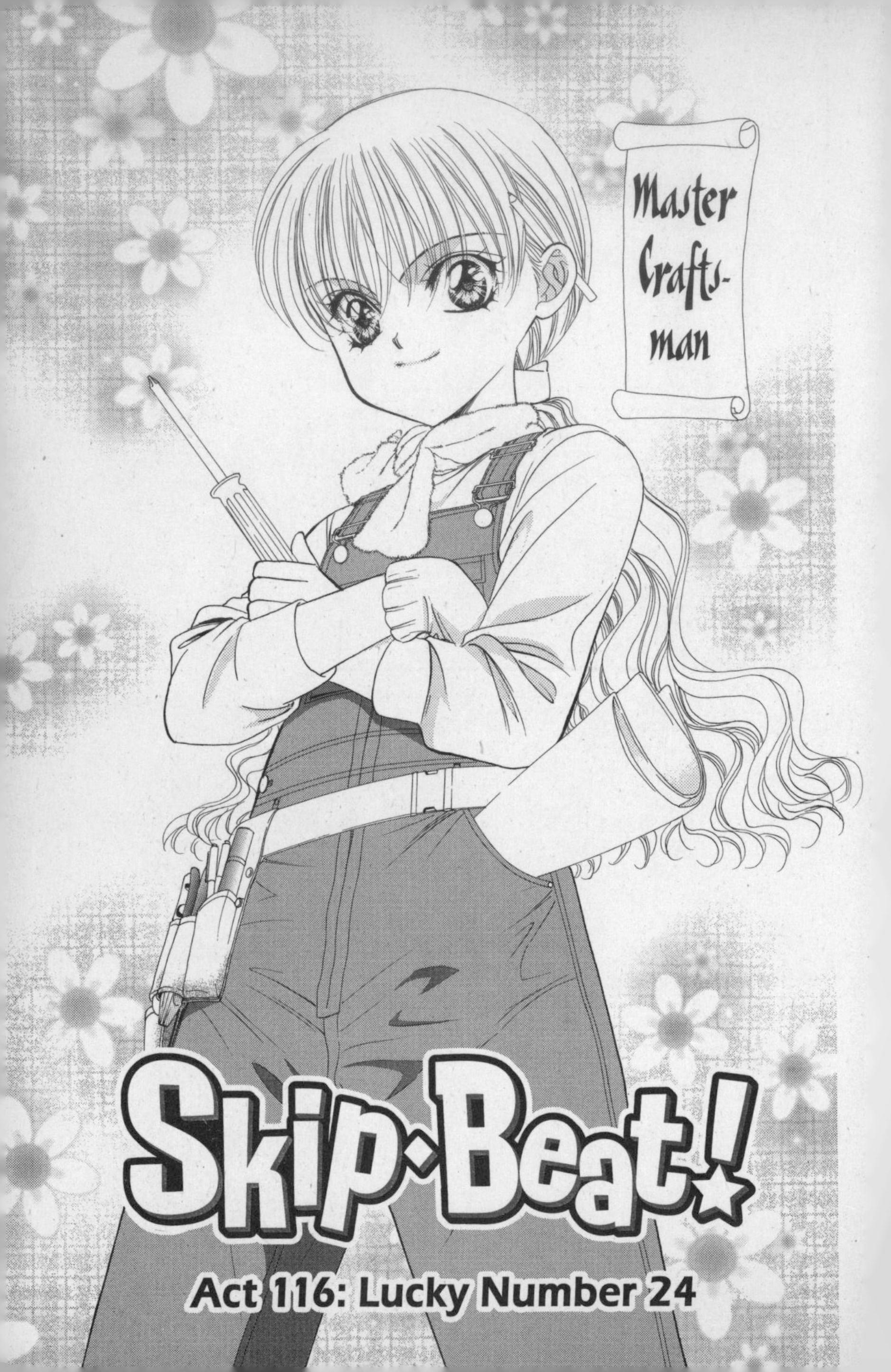
Master Crafts-man
Skip·Beat!
Act 116: Lucky Number 24

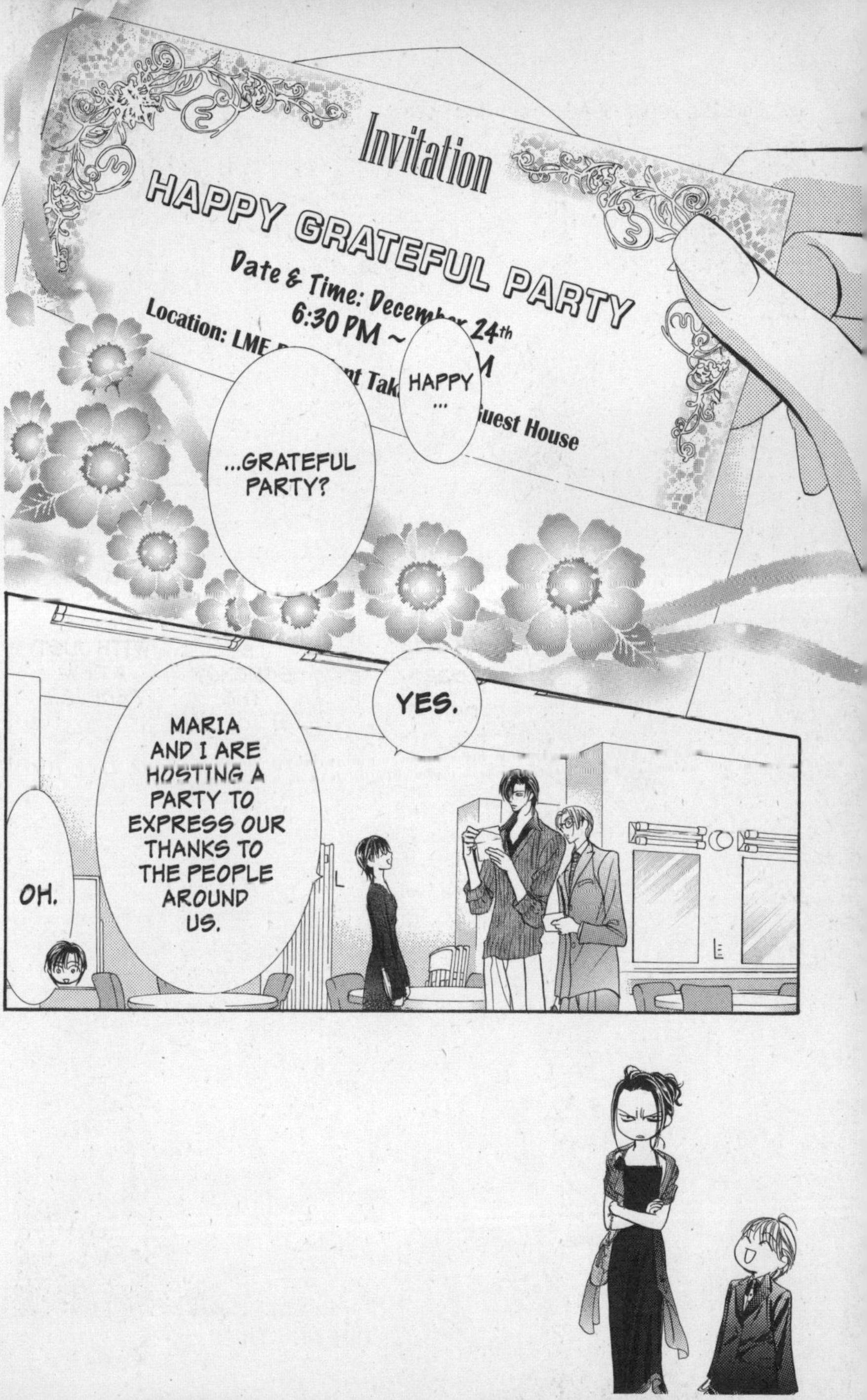
Invitation
HAPPY GRATEFUL PARTY
Date & Time: Decem 24th
6:30 PM ~ M
Location: LME nt Tak uest House
HAPPY ...
...GRATEFUL PARTY?
YES.
MARIA AND I ARE HOSTING A PARTY TO EXPRESS OUR THANKS TO THE PEOPLE AROUND US.
OH.

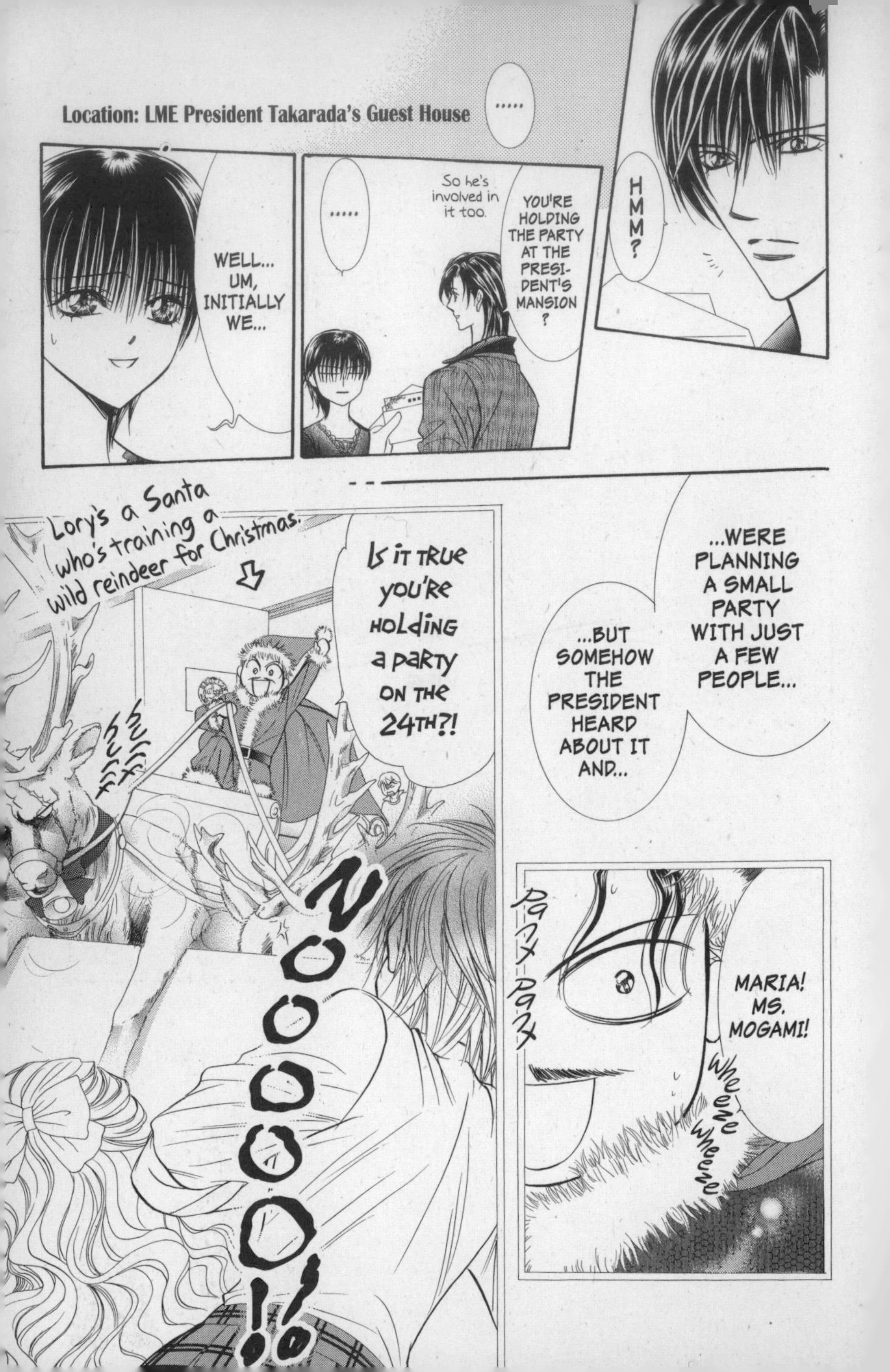

Location: LME President Takarada's Guest House
......
HMM?
YOU'RE HOLDING THE PARTY AT THE PRESIDENT'S MANSION?
So he's involved in it too.
......
WELL... UM, INITIALLY WE...
...WERE PLANNING A SMALL PARTY WITH JUST A FEW PEOPLE...
...BUT SOMEHOW THE PRESIDENT HEARD ABOUT IT AND...
MARIA! MS. MOGAMI!
Pant Pant
wheeze wheeze
Is it true you're holding a party on the 24th?!
Lory's a Santa who's training a wild reindeer for Christmas.
huff huff
NOOOOO!!

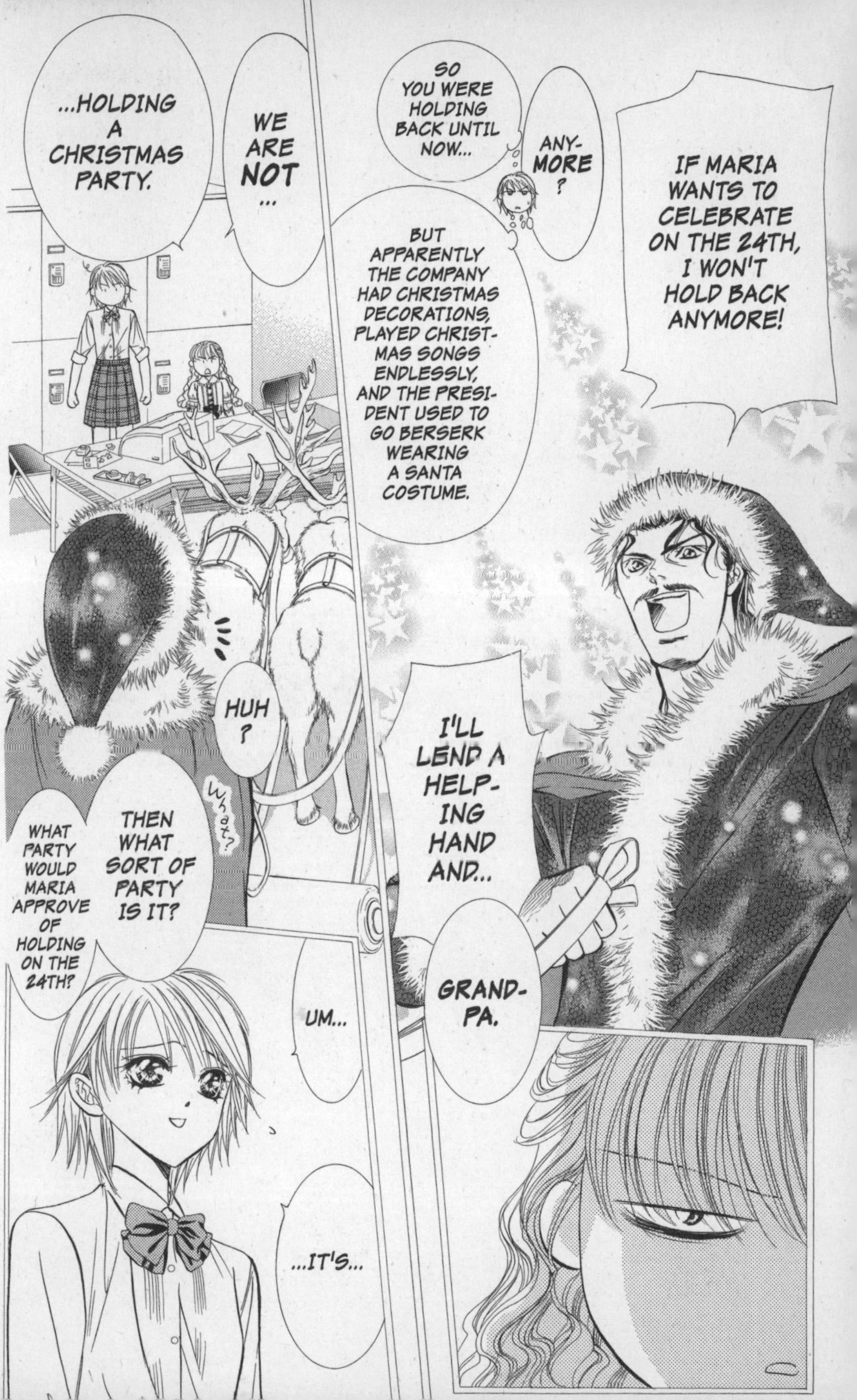
IF MARIA WANTS TO CELEBRATE ON THE 24TH, I WON'T HOLD BACK ANYMORE!
ANY-MORE?
SO YOU WERE HOLDING BACK UNTIL NOW...
BUT APPARENTLY THE COMPANY HAD CHRISTMAS DECORATIONS, PLAYED CHRIST-MAS SONGS ENDLESSLY, AND THE PRESI-DENT USED TO GO BERSERK WEARING A SANTA COSTUME.
I'LL LEND A HELPING HAND AND...
GRAND-PA.
WE ARE NOT...
...HOLDING A CHRISTMAS PARTY.
HUH?
What?
THEN WHAT SORT OF PARTY IS IT?
WHAT PARTY WOULD MARIA APPROVE OF HOLDING ON THE 24TH?
UM...
...IT'S...

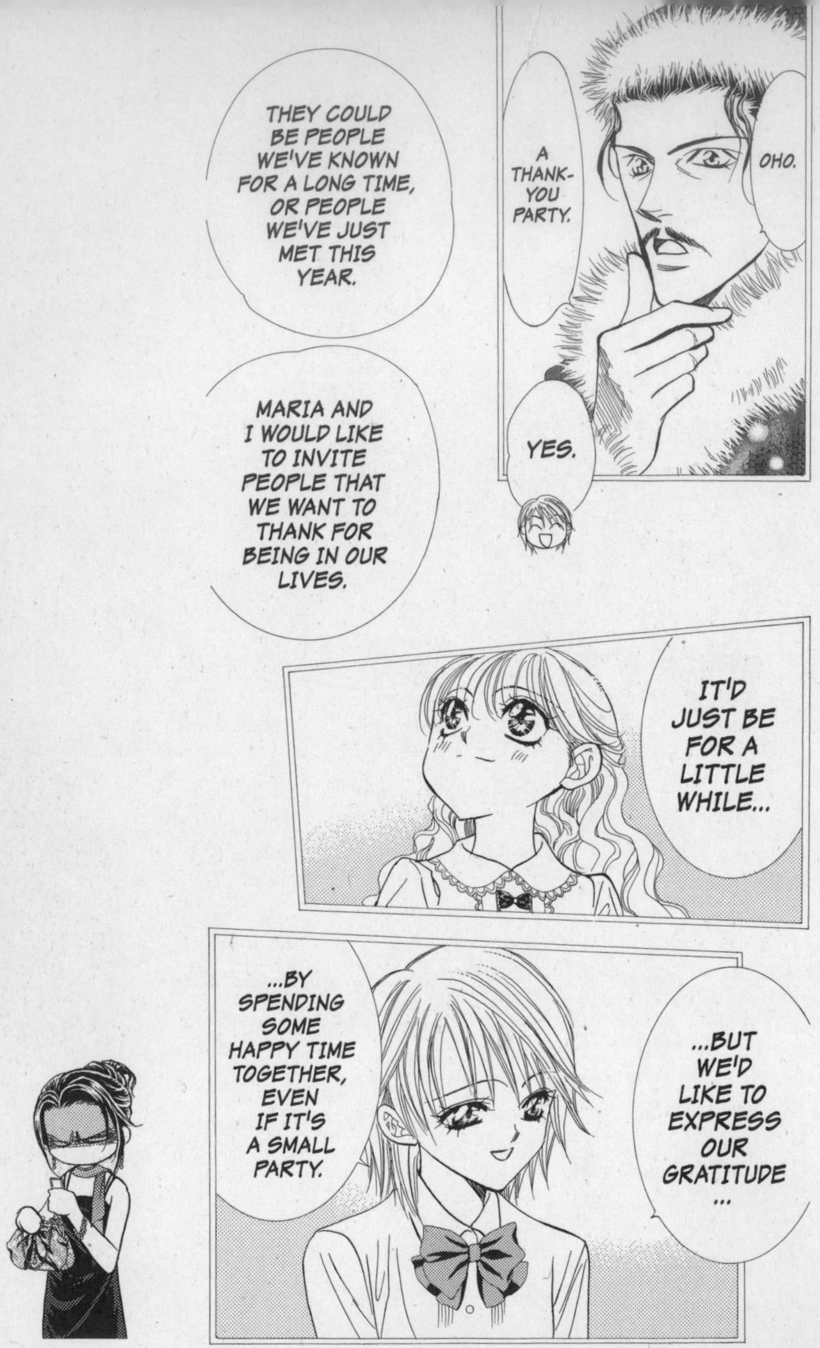
OHO.
A THANK-YOU PARTY.
YES.
THEY COULD BE PEOPLE WE'VE KNOWN FOR A LONG TIME, OR PEOPLE WE'VE JUST MET THIS YEAR.
MARIA AND I WOULD LIKE TO INVITE PEOPLE THAT WE WANT TO THANK FOR BEING IN OUR LIVES.
IT'D JUST BE FOR A LITTLE WHILE...
...BUT WE'D LIKE TO EXPRESS OUR GRATITUDE...
...BY SPENDING SOME HAPPY TIME TOGETHER, EVEN IF IT'S A SMALL PARTY.

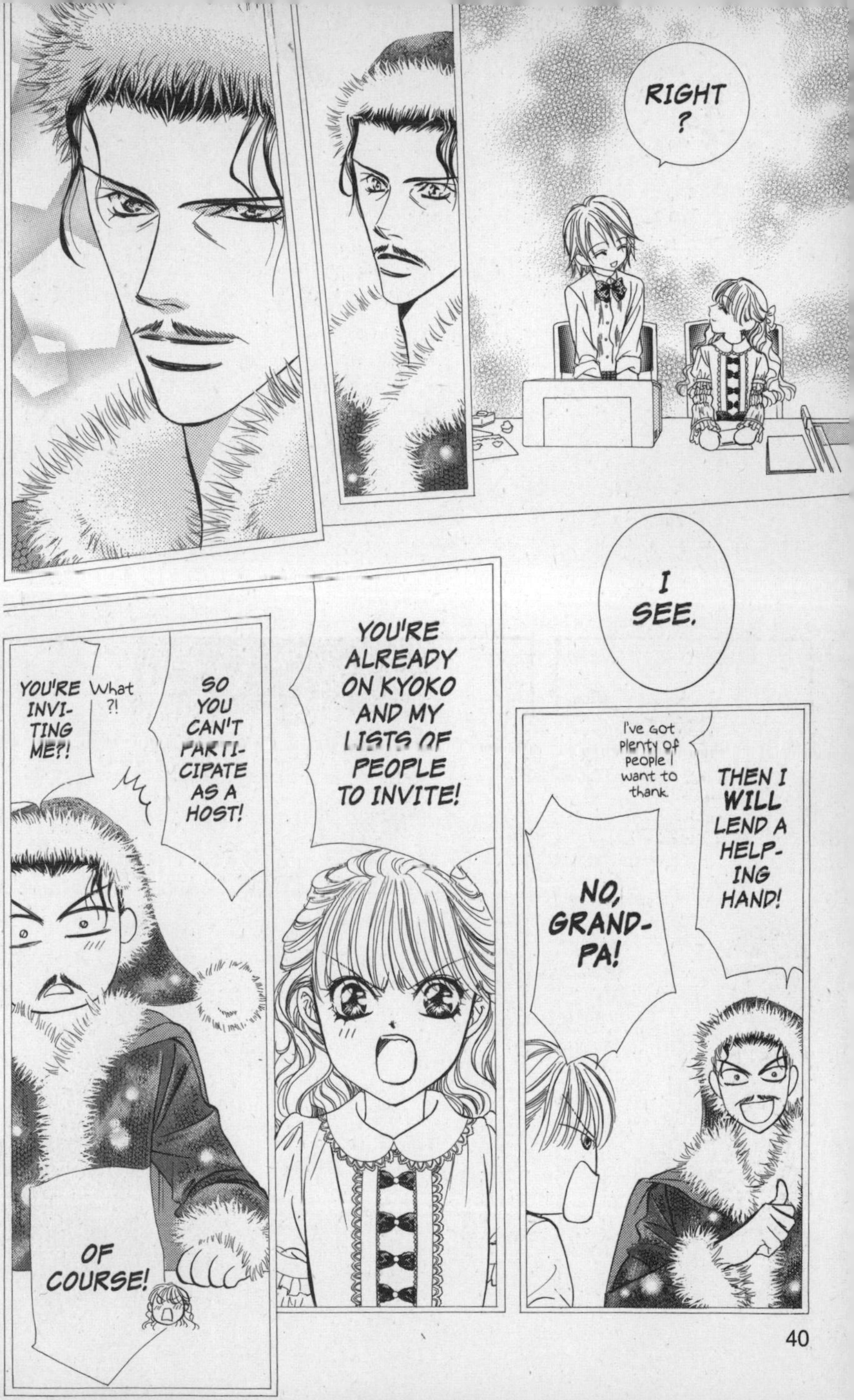
RIGHT ?
I SEE.
THEN I WILL LEND A HELPING HAND!
I've got plenty of people I want to thank.
NO, GRANDPA!
YOU'RE ALREADY ON KYOKO AND MY LISTS OF PEOPLE TO INVITE!
SO YOU CAN'T PARTICIPATE AS A HOST!
What ?!
YOU'RE INVITING ME?!
OF COURSE!

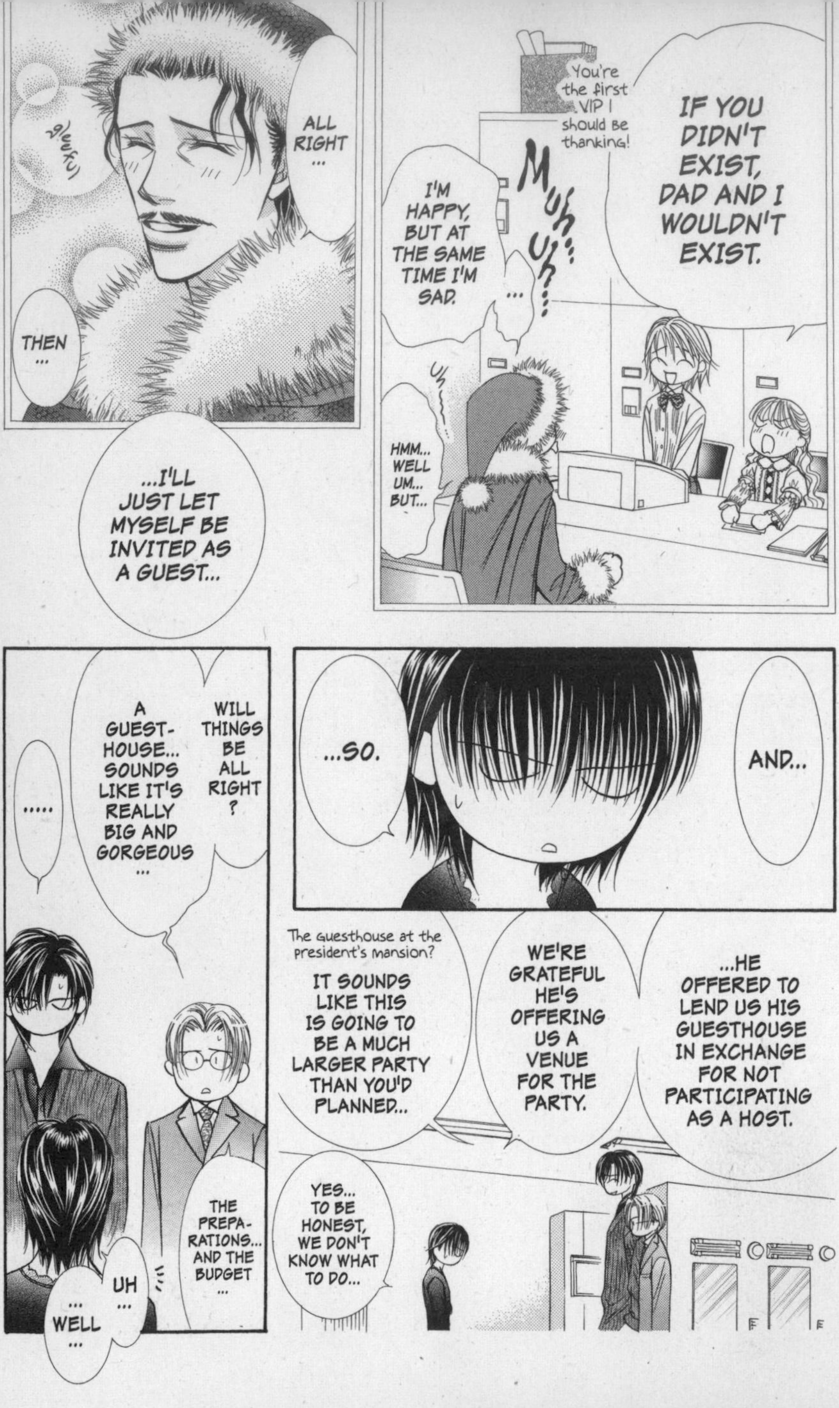
IF YOU DIDN'T EXIST, DAD AND I WOULDN'T EXIST.
You're the first VIP I should be thanking!
Muh uh...
I'M HAPPY, BUT AT THE SAME TIME I'M SAD.
...
Uh-
HMM... WELL UM... BUT...
ALL RIGHT ...
THEN ...
...I'LL JUST LET MYSELF BE INVITED AS A GUEST...
AND...
...SO.
...HE OFFERED TO LEND US HIS GUESTHOUSE IN EXCHANGE FOR NOT PARTICIPATING AS A HOST.
WE'RE GRATEFUL HE'S OFFERING US A VENUE FOR THE PARTY.
The guesthouse at the president's mansion?
IT SOUNDS LIKE THIS IS GOING TO BE A MUCH LARGER PARTY THAN YOU'D PLANNED...
YES... TO BE HONEST, WE DON'T KNOW WHAT TO DO...
WILL THINGS BE ALL RIGHT?
A GUEST-HOUSE... SOUNDS LIKE IT'S REALLY BIG AND GORGEOUS ...
.....
THE PREPA-RATIONS... AND THE BUDGET ...
UH ...
... WELL ...

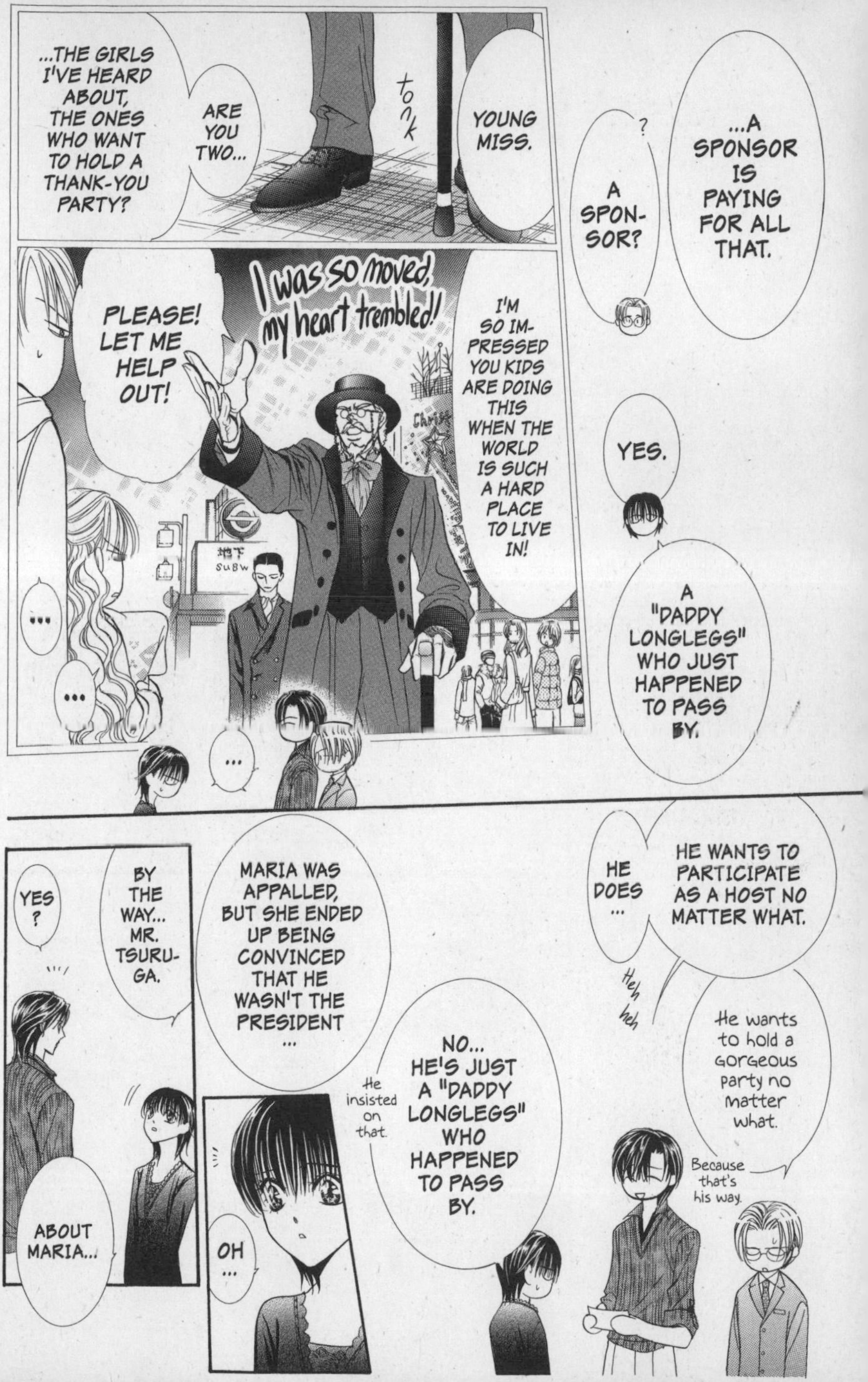
...A SPONSOR IS PAYING FOR ALL THAT.
?
A SPONSOR?
YES.
A "DADDY LONGLEGS" WHO JUST HAPPENED TO PASS BY.
YOUNG MISS.
tonk
ARE YOU TWO...
...THE GIRLS I'VE HEARD ABOUT, THE ONES WHO WANT TO HOLD A THANK-YOU PARTY?
I'M SO IMPRESSED YOU KIDS ARE DOING THIS WHEN THE WORLD IS SUCH A HARD PLACE TO LIVE IN!
I was so moved, my heart trembled!
PLEASE! LET ME HELP OUT!
...
...
...
HE WANTS TO PARTICIPATE AS A HOST NO MATTER WHAT.
HE DOES...
Heh heh
He wants to hold a gorgeous party no matter what.
Because that's his way.
MARIA WAS APPALLED, BUT SHE ENDED UP BEING CONVINCED THAT HE WASN'T THE PRESIDENT...
NO... HE'S JUST A "DADDY LONGLEGS" WHO HAPPENED TO PASS BY.
He insisted on that.
OH...
BY THE WAY... MR. TSURUGA.
YES?
ABOUT MARIA...

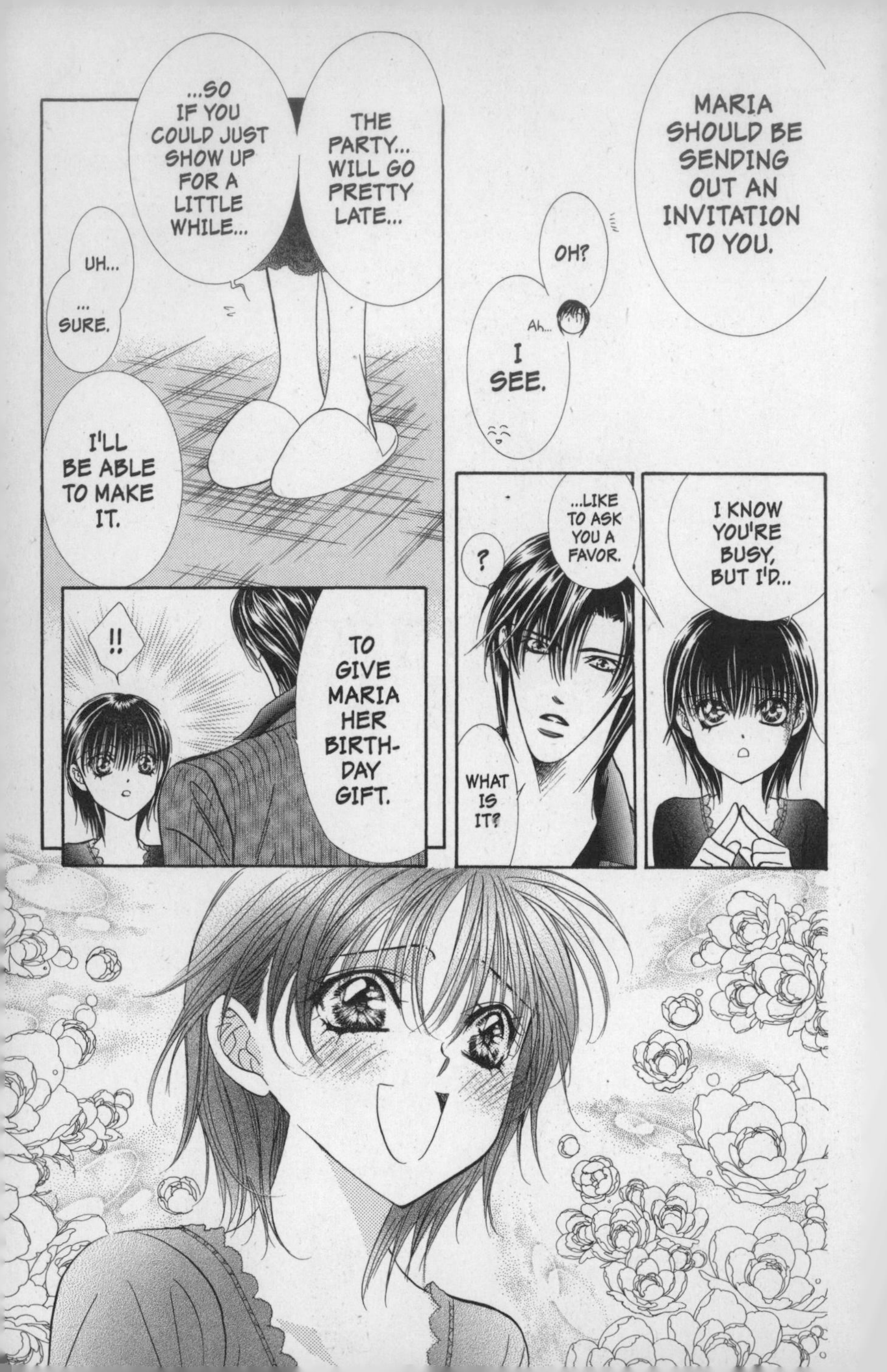
MARIA SHOULD BE SENDING OUT AN INVITATION TO YOU.
OH?
Ah... I SEE.
THE PARTY... WILL GO PRETTY LATE...
...SO IF YOU COULD JUST SHOW UP FOR A LITTLE WHILE...
UH... ...SURE.
I'LL BE ABLE TO MAKE IT.
I KNOW YOU'RE BUSY, BUT I'D...
...LIKE TO ASK YOU A FAVOR.
?
WHAT IS IT?
!!
TO GIVE MARIA HER BIRTHDAY GIFT.

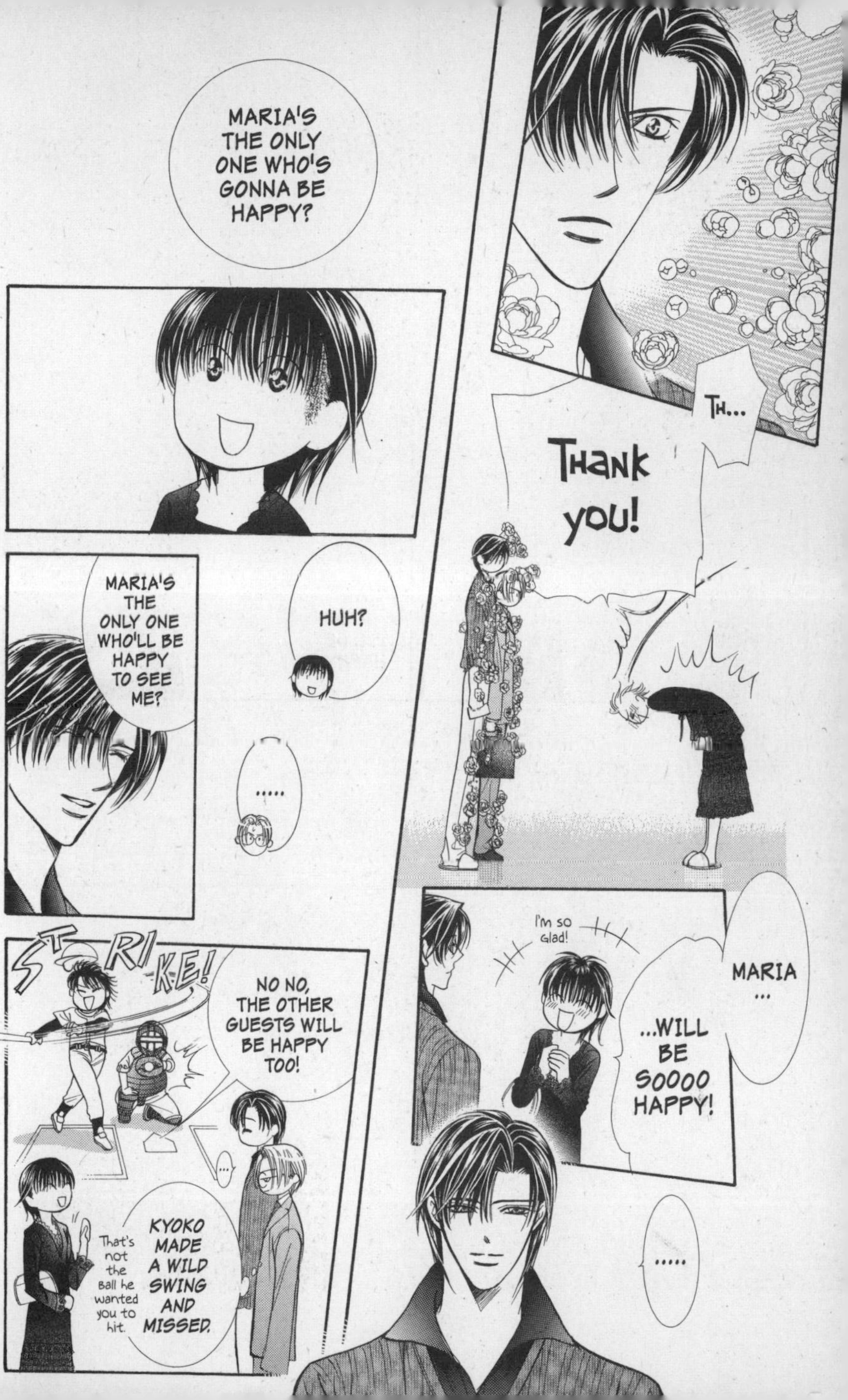
TH...
THANK you!
MARIA ...
...WILL BE SOOOO HAPPY!
I'm so Glad!
.....
MARIA'S THE ONLY ONE WHO'S GONNA BE HAPPY?
HUH?
MARIA'S THE ONLY ONE WHO'LL BE HAPPY TO SEE ME?
.....
STRIKE!
NO NO, THE OTHER GUESTS WILL BE HAPPY TOO!
...
KYOKO MADE A WILD SWING AND MISSED.
That's not the Ball he wanted you to hit.

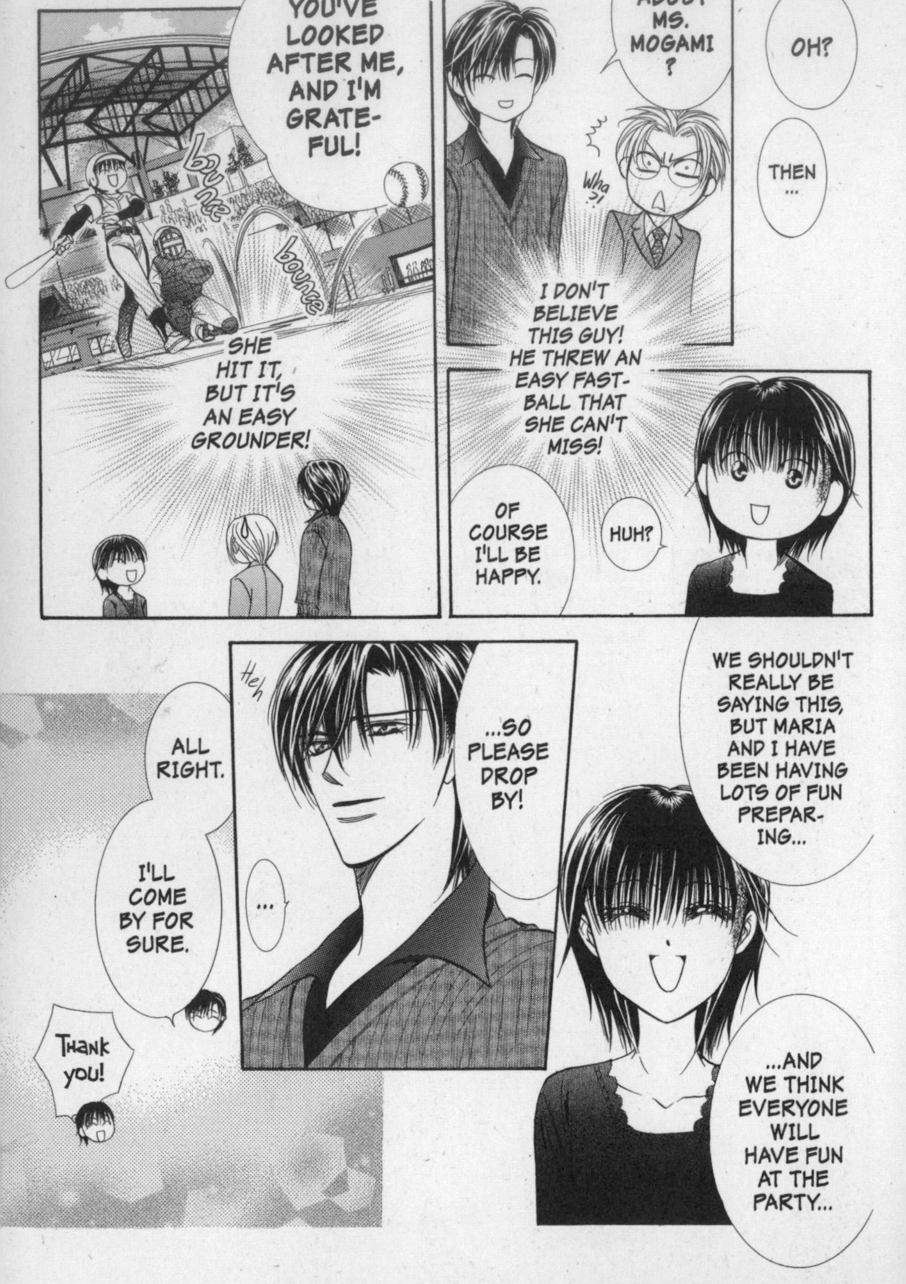
OH?
THEN...
...WHAT ABOUT MS. MOGAMI?
Wha?!
I DON'T BELIEVE THIS GUY! HE THREW AN EASY FAST-BALL THAT SHE CAN'T MISS!
HUH?
OF COURSE I'LL BE HAPPY.
YOU'VE LOOKED AFTER ME, AND I'M GRATE-FUL!
bounce
bounce
SHE HIT IT, BUT IT'S AN EASY GROUNDER!
WE SHOULDN'T REALLY BE SAYING THIS, BUT MARIA AND I HAVE BEEN HAVING LOTS OF FUN PREPAR-ING...
...AND WE THINK EVERYONE WILL HAVE FUN AT THE PARTY...
...SO PLEASE DROP BY!
Heh
...
ALL RIGHT.
I'LL COME BY FOR SURE.
Thank you!

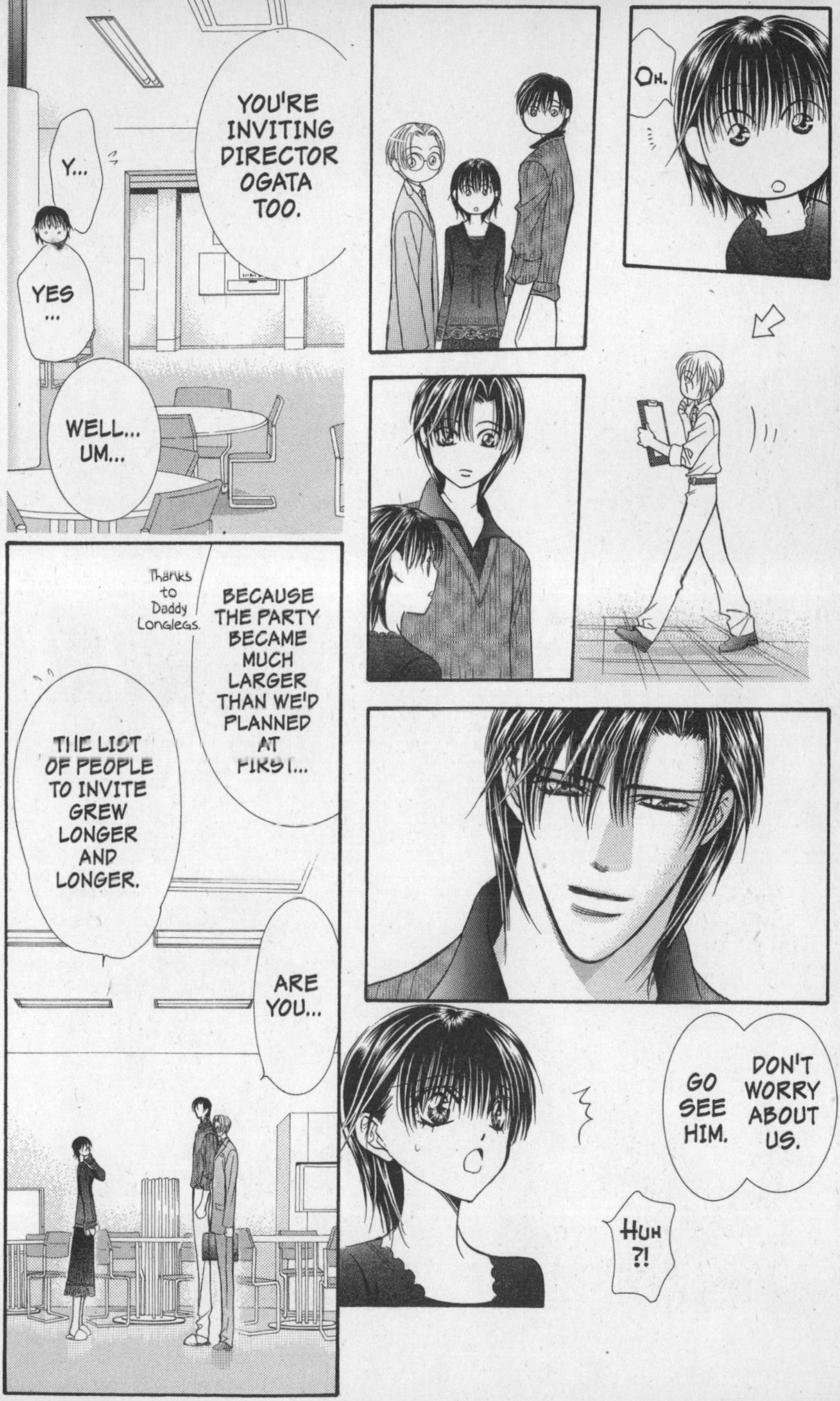
OH.
YOU'RE INVITING DIRECTOR OGATA TOO.
Y...
YES ...
WELL... UM...
BECAUSE THE PARTY BECAME MUCH LARGER THAN WE'D PLANNED AT FIRST...
Thanks to Daddy Longlegs.
THE LIST OF PEOPLE TO INVITE GREW LONGER AND LONGER.
ARE YOU...
DON'T WORRY ABOUT US.
GO SEE HIM.
HUH ?!

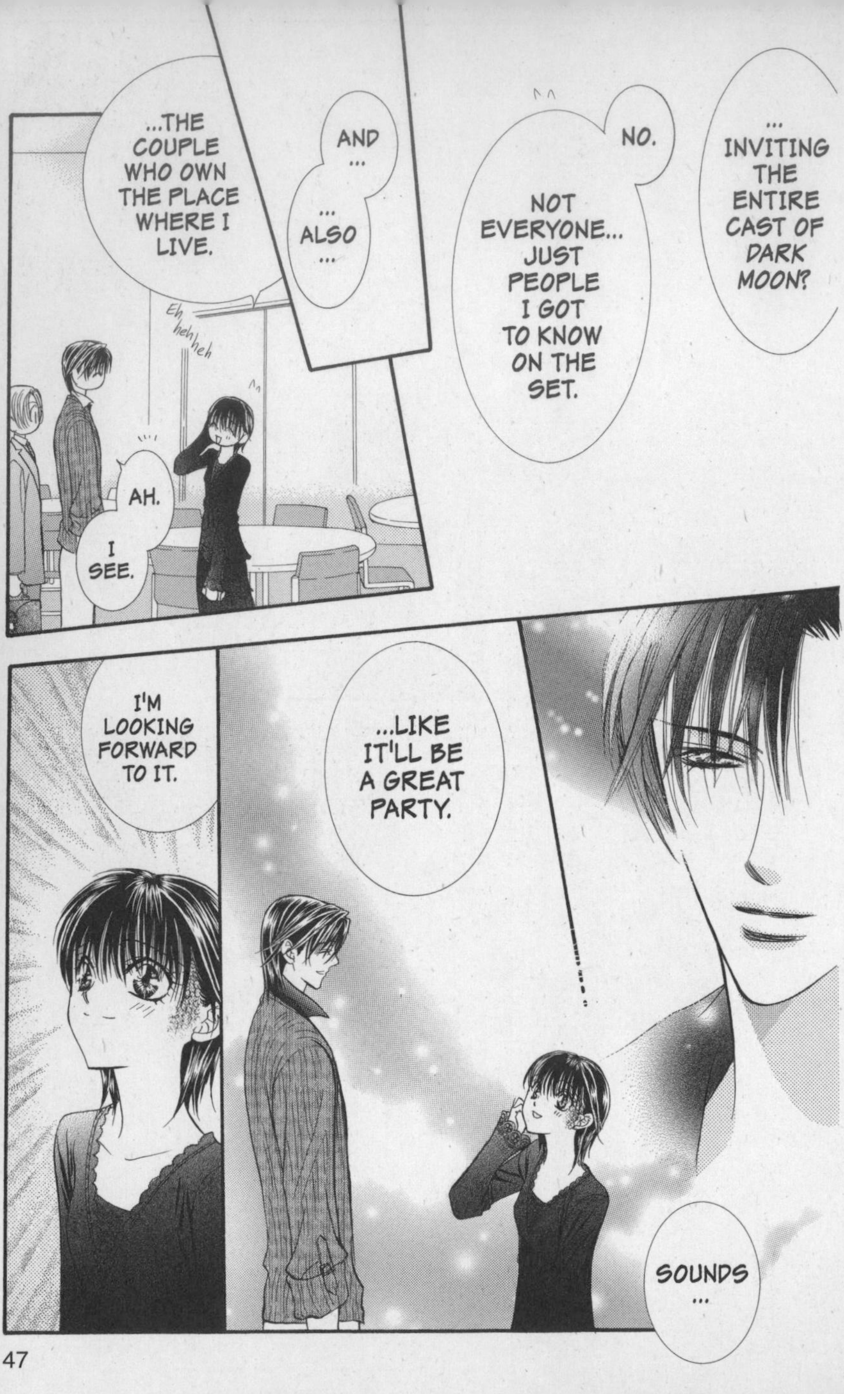
...INVITING THE ENTIRE CAST OF DARK MOON?
NO.
NOT EVERYONE... JUST PEOPLE I GOT TO KNOW ON THE SET.
AND ...
... ALSO ...
...THE COUPLE WHO OWN THE PLACE WHERE I LIVE.
Eh heh heh
AH.
I SEE.
SOUNDS ...
...LIKE IT'LL BE A GREAT PARTY.
I'M LOOKING FORWARD TO IT.

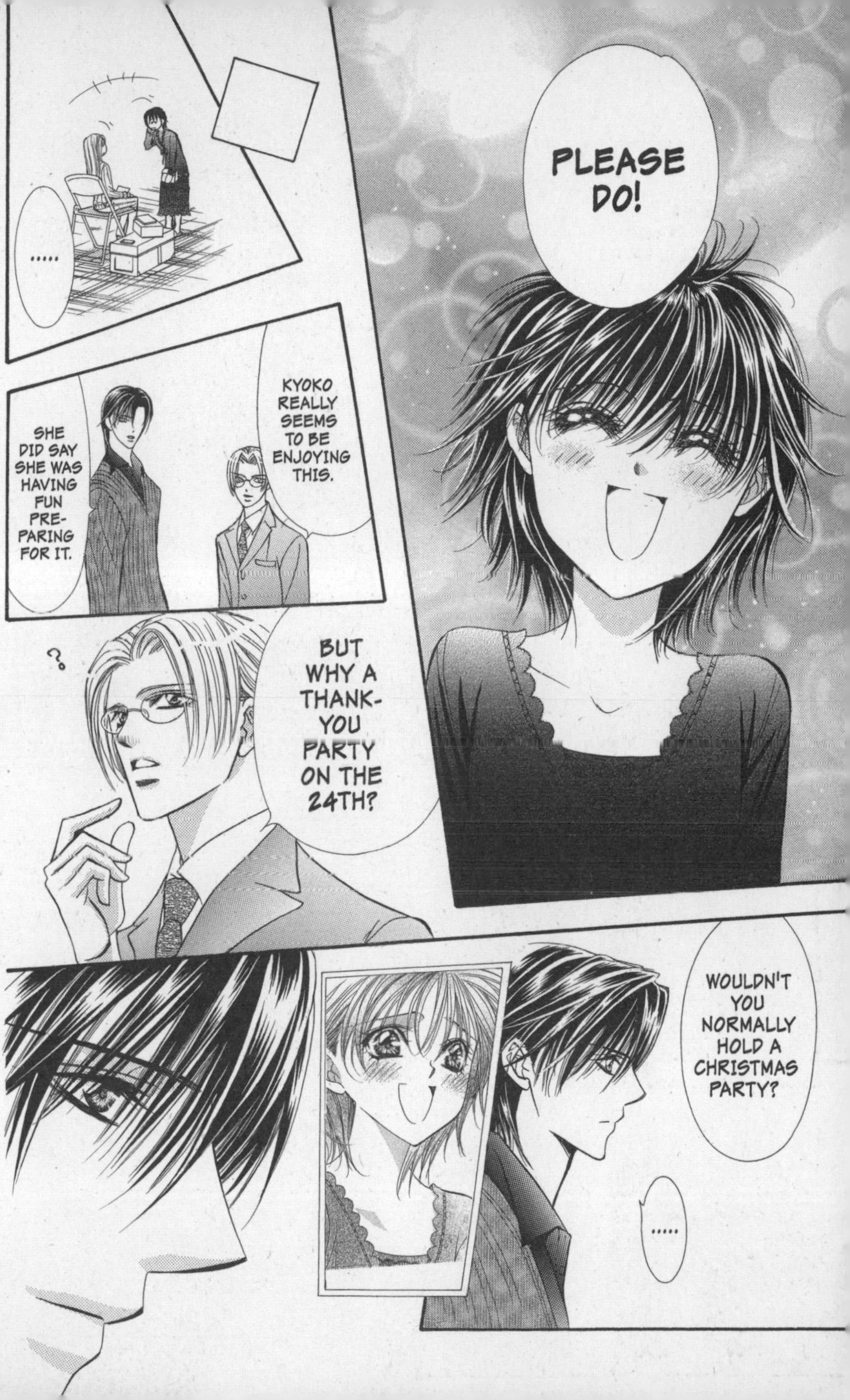
PLEASE DO!
.....
KYOKO REALLY SEEMS TO BE ENJOYING THIS.
SHE DID SAY SHE WAS HAVING FUN PRE-PARING FOR IT.
?
BUT WHY A THANK-YOU PARTY ON THE 24TH?
WOULDN'T YOU NORMALLY HOLD A CHRISTMAS PARTY?
.....

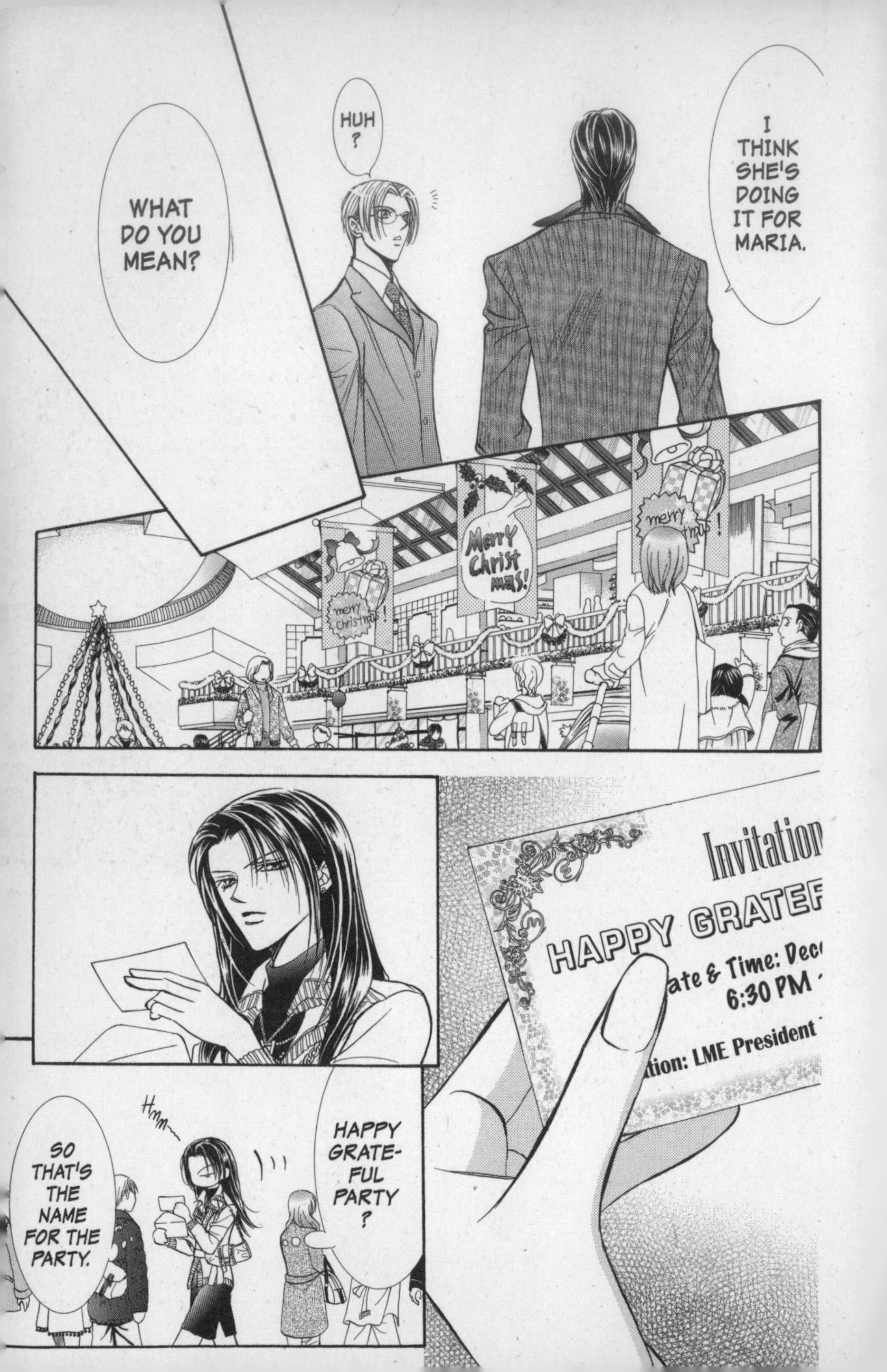
I THINK SHE'S DOING IT FOR MARIA.
HUH?
WHAT DO YOU MEAN?
Merry Christmas!
merry christmas!
merry christmas!
Invitation
6:30 PM
LME President
HAPPY GRATE-FUL PARTY?
Hmm~
SO THAT'S THE NAME FOR THE PARTY.

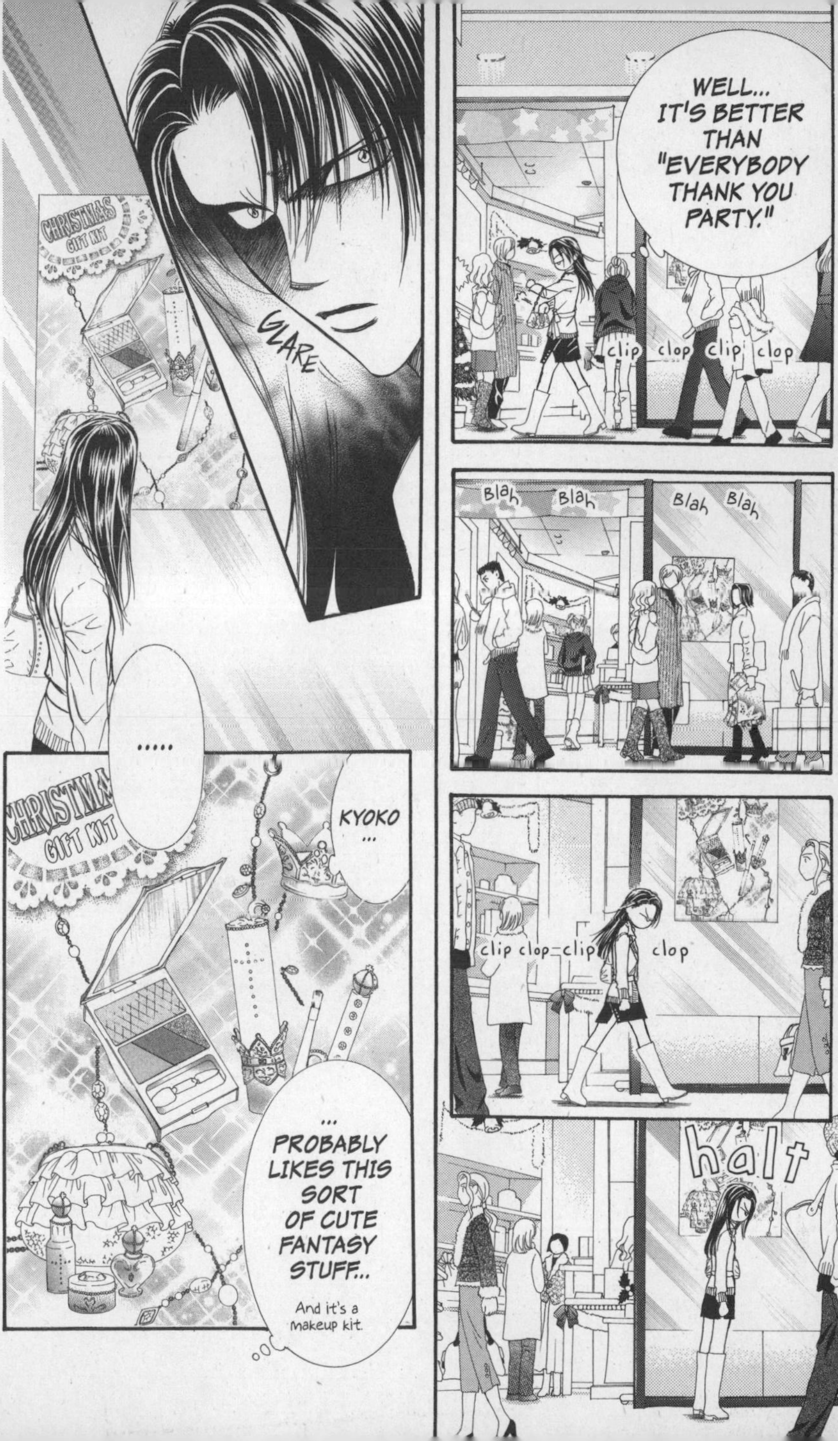
WELL... IT'S BETTER THAN "EVERYBODY THANK YOU PARTY."
clip clop clip clop
Blah Blah Blah Blah
clip clop clip clop
halt
CHRISTMAS GIFT KIT
GLARE
.....
CHRISTMAS GIFT KIT
KYOKO ...
... PROBABLY LIKES THIS SORT OF CUTE FANTASY STUFF...
And it's a makeup kit.

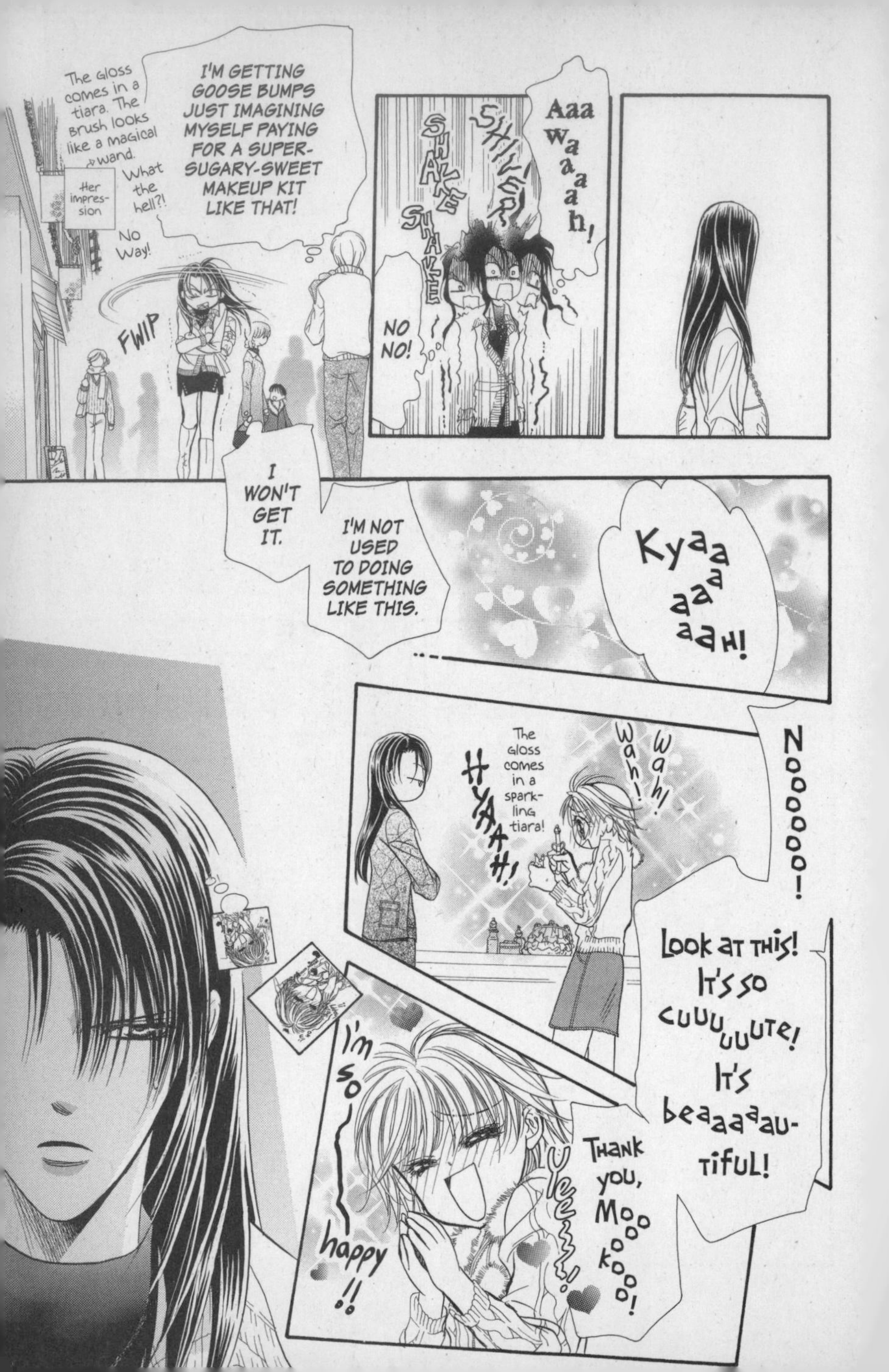
Aaa waaaah!
SHIVER!
SHAKE SHAKE
NO NO!
I'M GETTING GOOSE BUMPS JUST IMAGINING MYSELF PAYING FOR A SUPER-SUGARY-SWEET MAKEUP KIT LIKE THAT!
The gloss comes in a tiara. The brush looks like a magical wand.
What the hell?!
Her impression
No Way!
FWIP
I WON'T GET IT.
Kyaaaaaaah!
...
I'M NOT USED TO DOING SOMETHING LIKE THIS.
Nooooooo!
Wah! Wah!
The gloss comes in a sparkling tiara!
HYAAAH!
Look at this! It's so cuuuuuute! It's beaaaaau-tiful!
Thank you, Mooooooko!
Yeeees!
I'm so happy!!

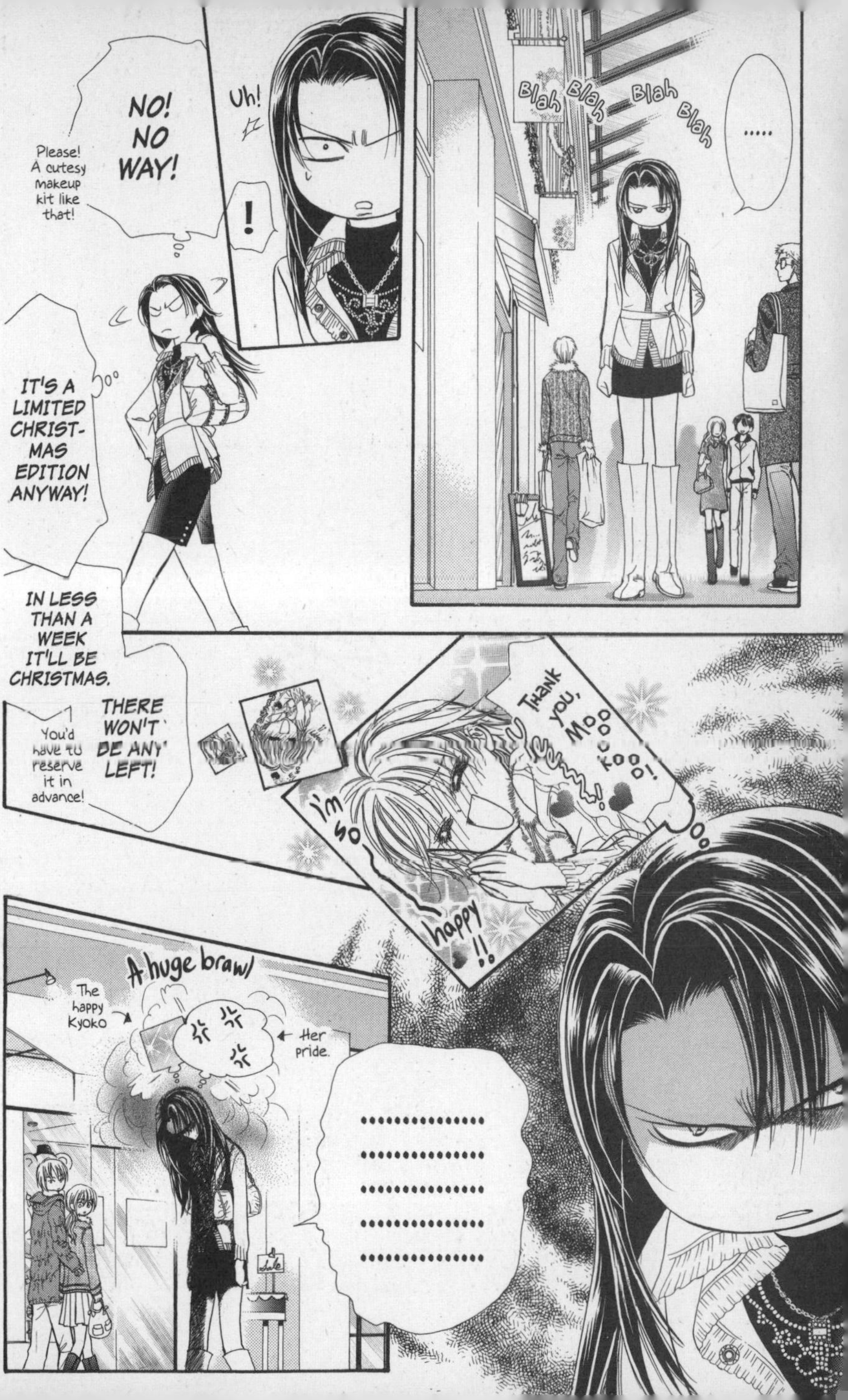
Blah Blah Blah Blah
.....
Uh!
!
NO! NO WAY!
Please! A cutesy makeup kit like that!
IT'S A LIMITED CHRISTMAS EDITION ANYWAY!
IN LESS THAN A WEEK IT'LL BE CHRISTMAS.
THERE WON'T BE ANY LEFT!
You'd have to reserve it in advance!
Thank you, Moooookooo!
I'm so~ happy!!
....
A huge brawl
The happy Kyoko
Her pride.

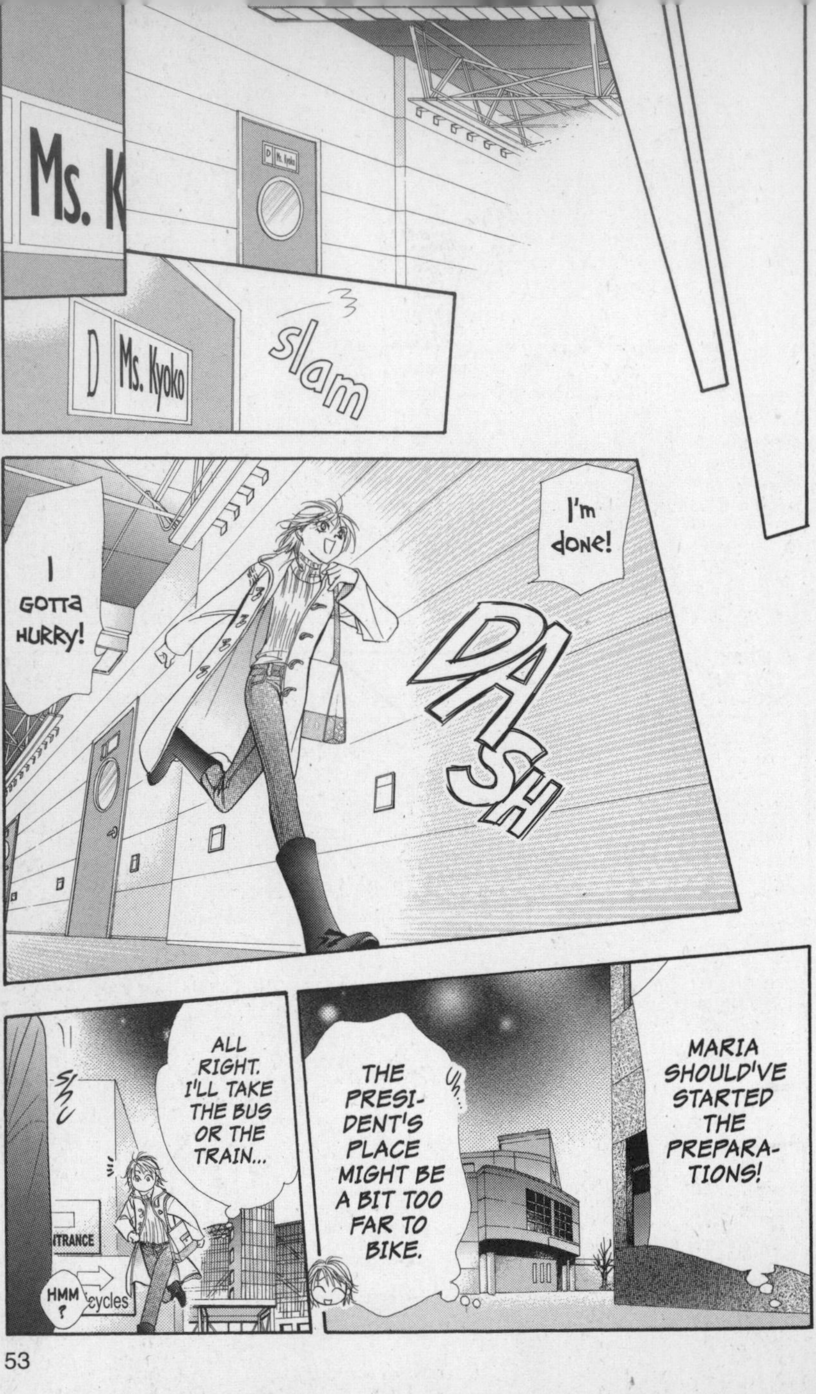
Ms. K
D Ms. Kyoko
D Ms. Kyoko
slam
I'm done!
DASH
I GOTTA HURRY!
MARIA SHOULD'VE STARTED THE PREPARATIONS!
Uh...
THE PRESIDENT'S PLACE MIGHT BE A BIT TOO FAR TO BIKE.
ALL RIGHT. I'LL TAKE THE BUS OR THE TRAIN...
HMM?

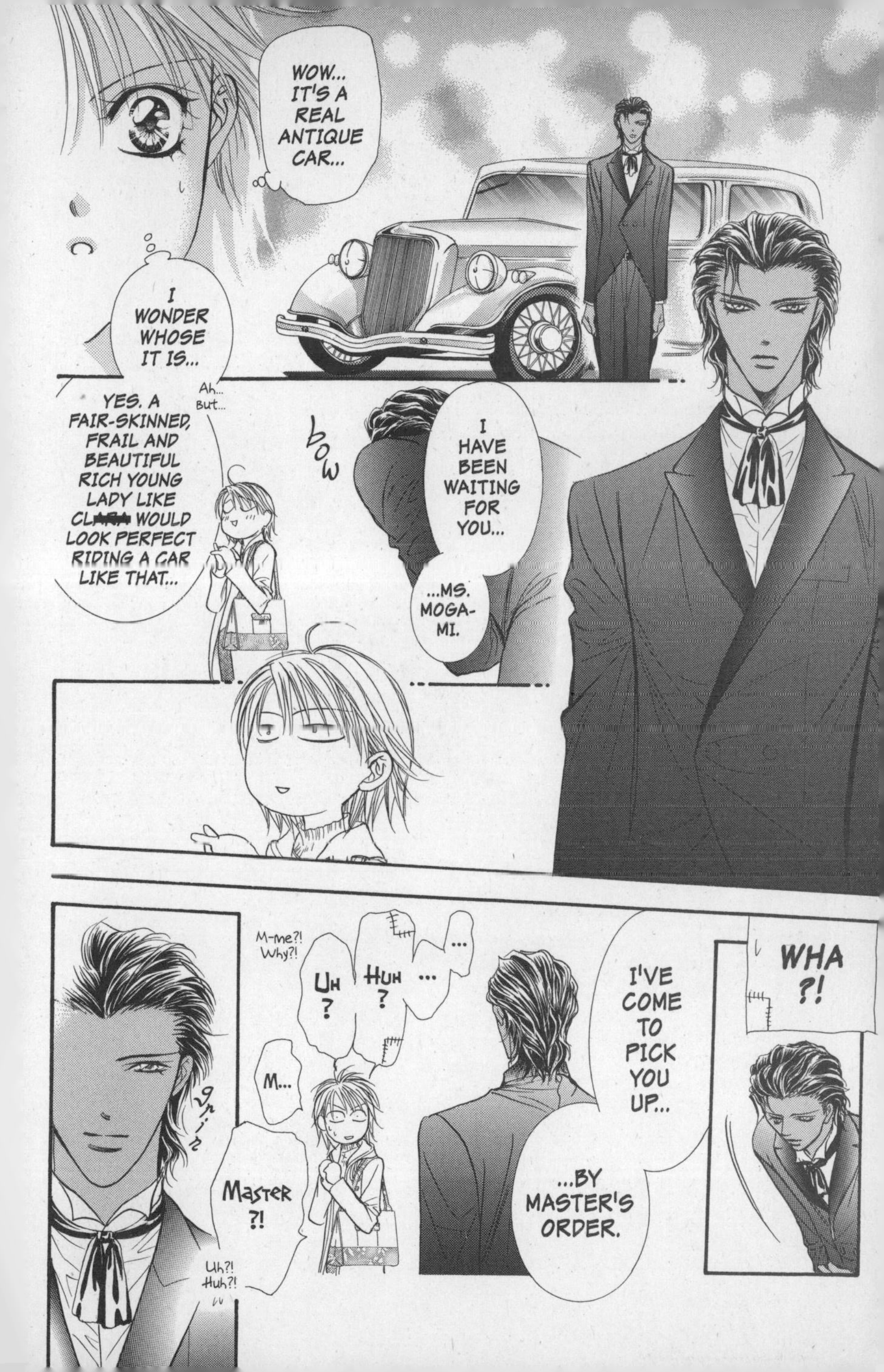
WOW... IT'S A REAL ANTIQUE CAR...
I WONDER WHOSE IT IS...
YES. A FAIR-SKINNED, FRAIL AND BEAUTIFUL RICH YOUNG LADY LIKE CL[redacted] WOULD LOOK PERFECT RIDING A CAR LIKE THAT...
Ah... But...
bow
I HAVE BEEN WAITING FOR YOU...
...MS. MOGA-MI.
WHA ?!
I'VE COME TO PICK YOU UP...
...BY MASTER'S ORDER.
M-me?! Why?!
...
HUH ?
...
UH ?
M...
Master ?!
Uh?! Huh?!
grin

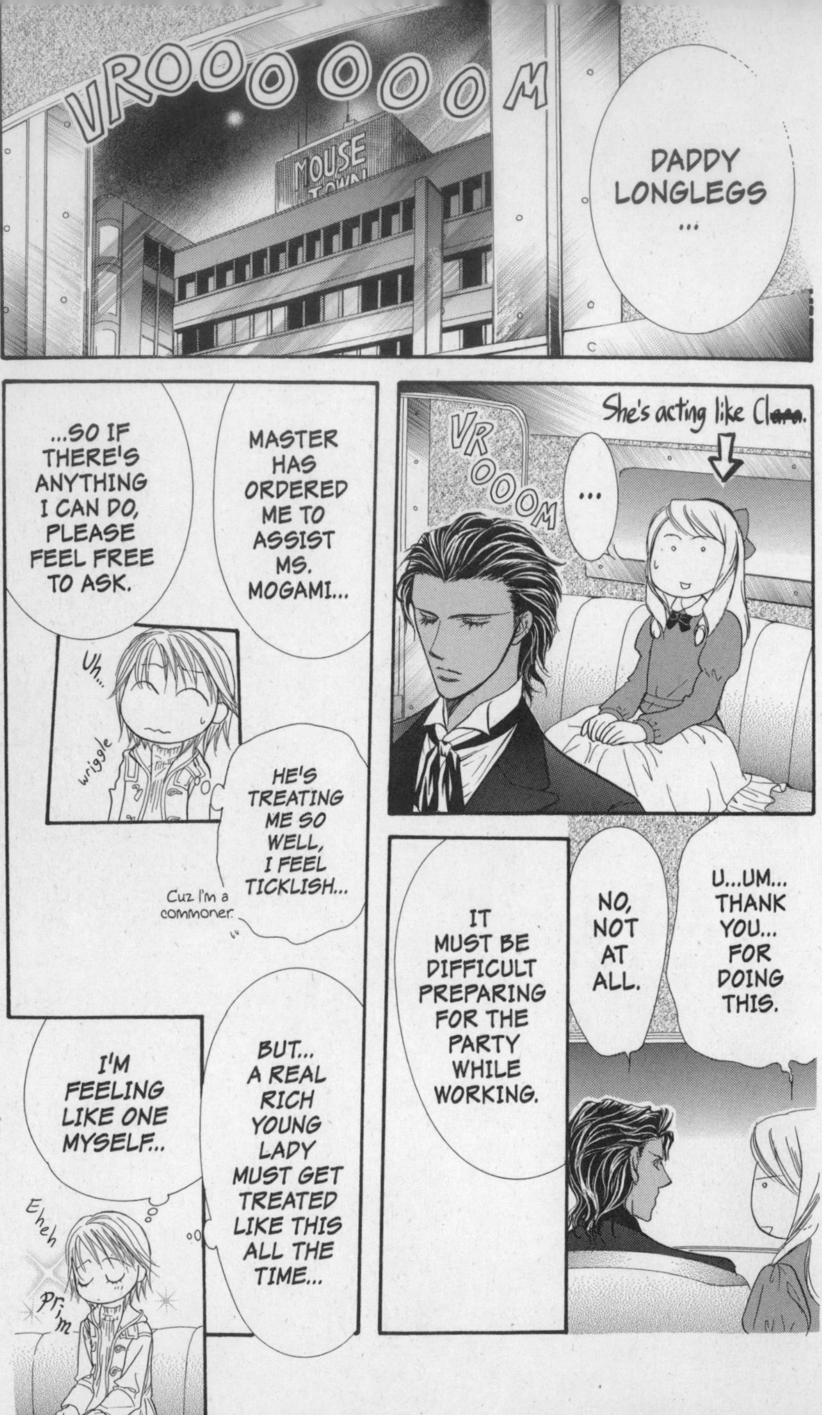
DADDY LONGLEGS ...
VROOOOOOOM
MOUSE TOWN
She's acting like Clara.
VROOOM
...
MASTER HAS ORDERED ME TO ASSIST MS. MOGAMI...
...SO IF THERE'S ANYTHING I CAN DO, PLEASE FEEL FREE TO ASK.
Uh...
wriggle
HE'S TREATING ME SO WELL, I FEEL TICKLISH...
Cuz I'm a commoner.
U...UM... THANK YOU... FOR DOING THIS.
NO, NOT AT ALL.
IT MUST BE DIFFICULT PREPARING FOR THE PARTY WHILE WORKING.
BUT... A REAL RICH YOUNG LADY MUST GET TREATED LIKE THIS ALL THE TIME...
I'M FEELING LIKE ONE MYSELF...
Eheh
Prim

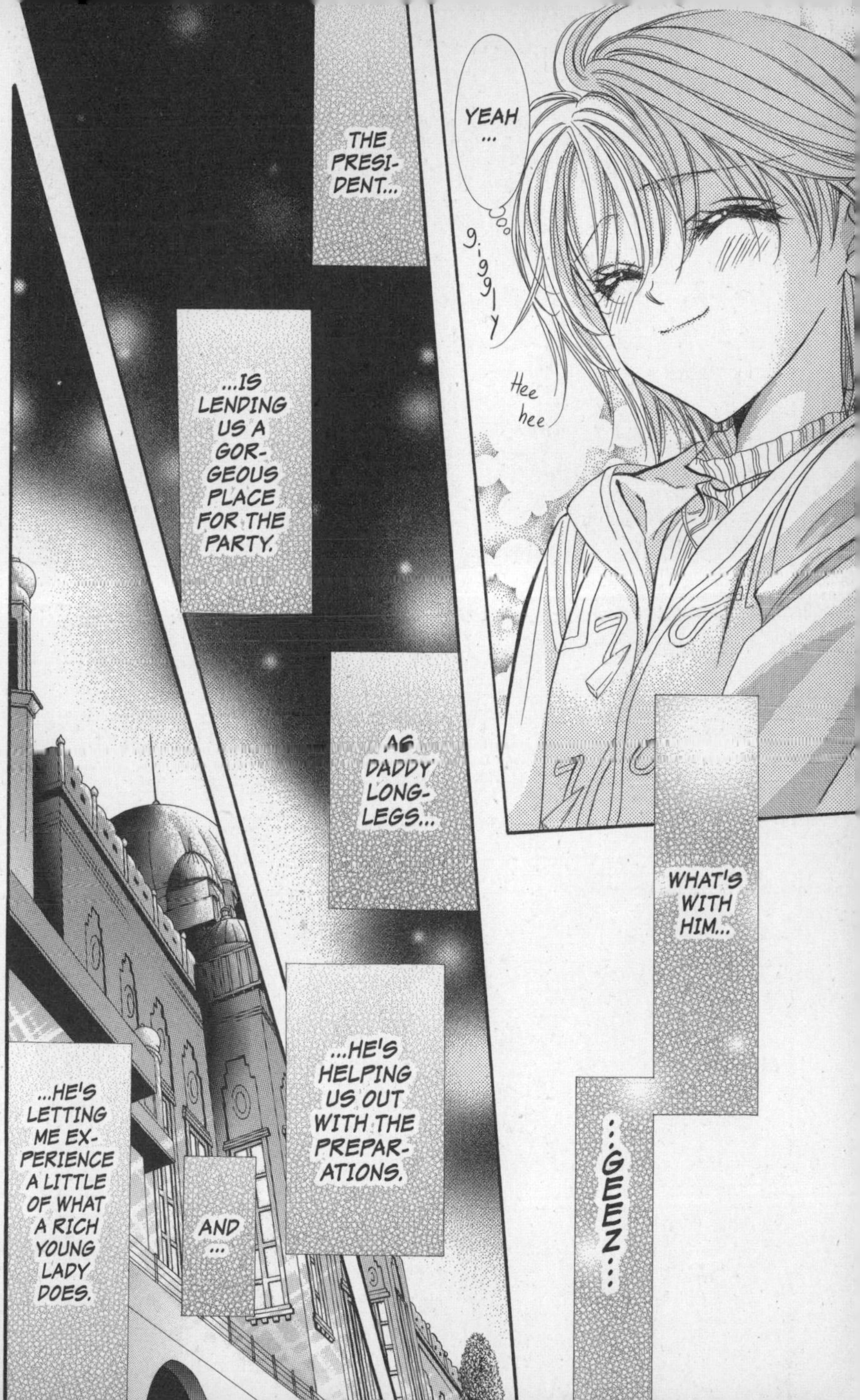
YEAH ...
giggly
Hee hee
WHAT'S WITH HIM...
...GEEZ...
THE PRESIDENT...
...IS LENDING US A GORGEOUS PLACE FOR THE PARTY.
AS DADDY LONG-LEGS...
...HE'S HELPING US OUT WITH THE PREPARATIONS.
AND ...
...HE'S LETTING ME EXPERIENCE A LITTLE OF WHAT A RICH YOUNG LADY DOES.

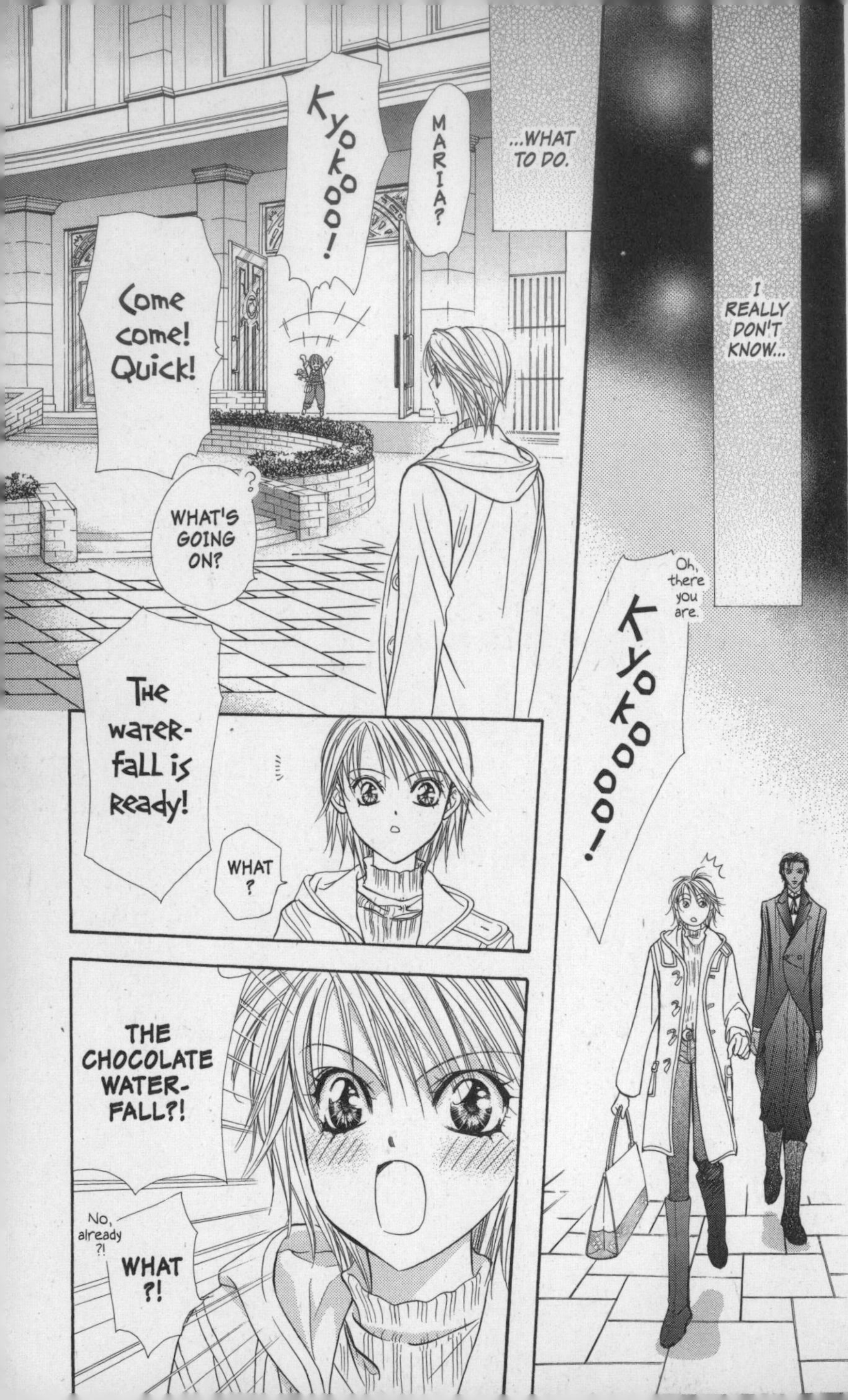
I REALLY DON'T KNOW...
...WHAT TO DO.
KYOKOOOO!
Oh, there you are.
KYOKOO!
MARIA?
Come come! Quick!
WHAT'S GOING ON?
The water-fall is ready!
WHAT?
THE CHOCOLATE WATER-FALL?!
WHAT?!
No, already?!

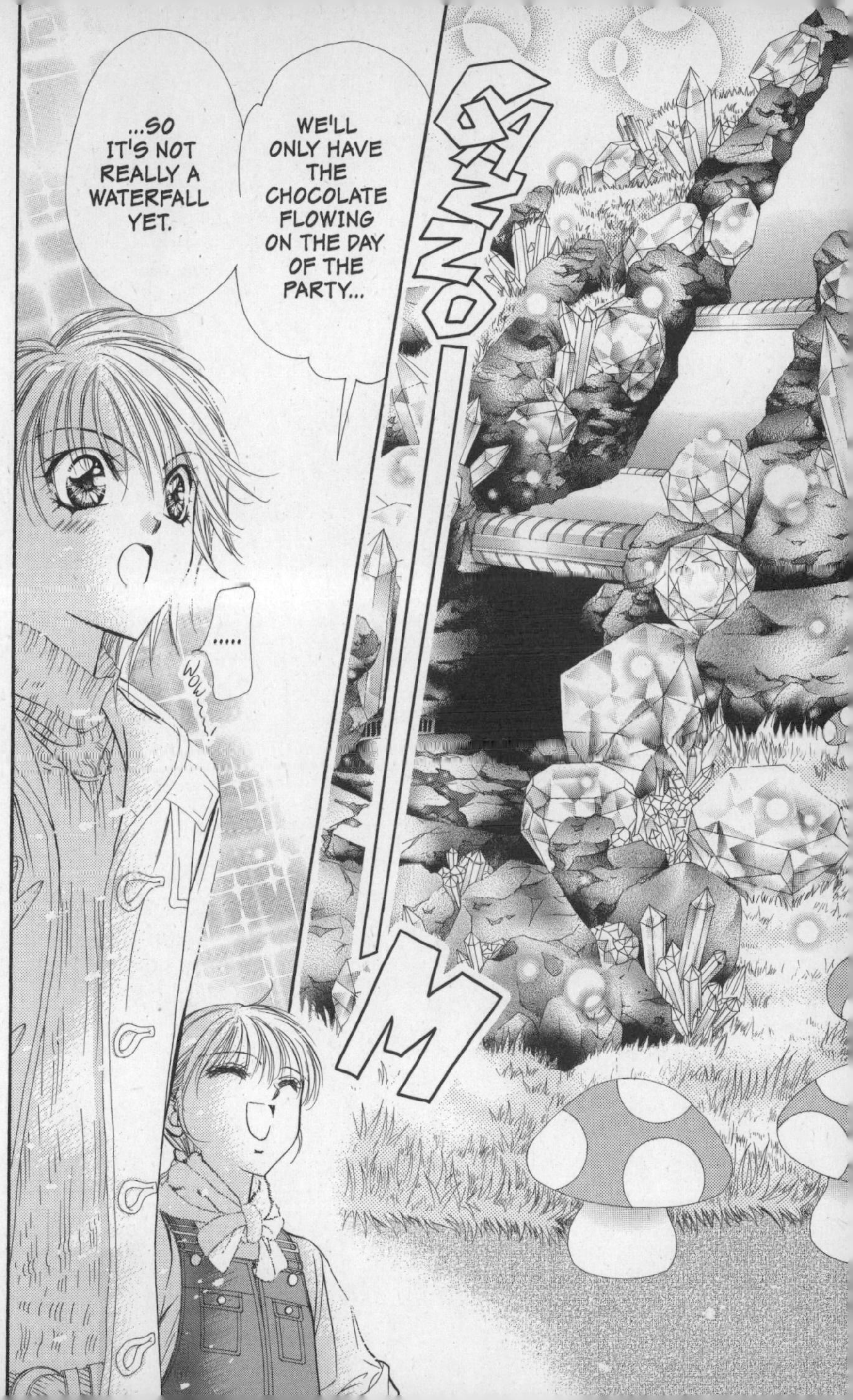
WE'LL ONLY HAVE THE CHOCOLATE FLOWING ON THE DAY OF THE PARTY...
...SO IT'S NOT REALLY A WATERFALL YET.
.....
WOW...

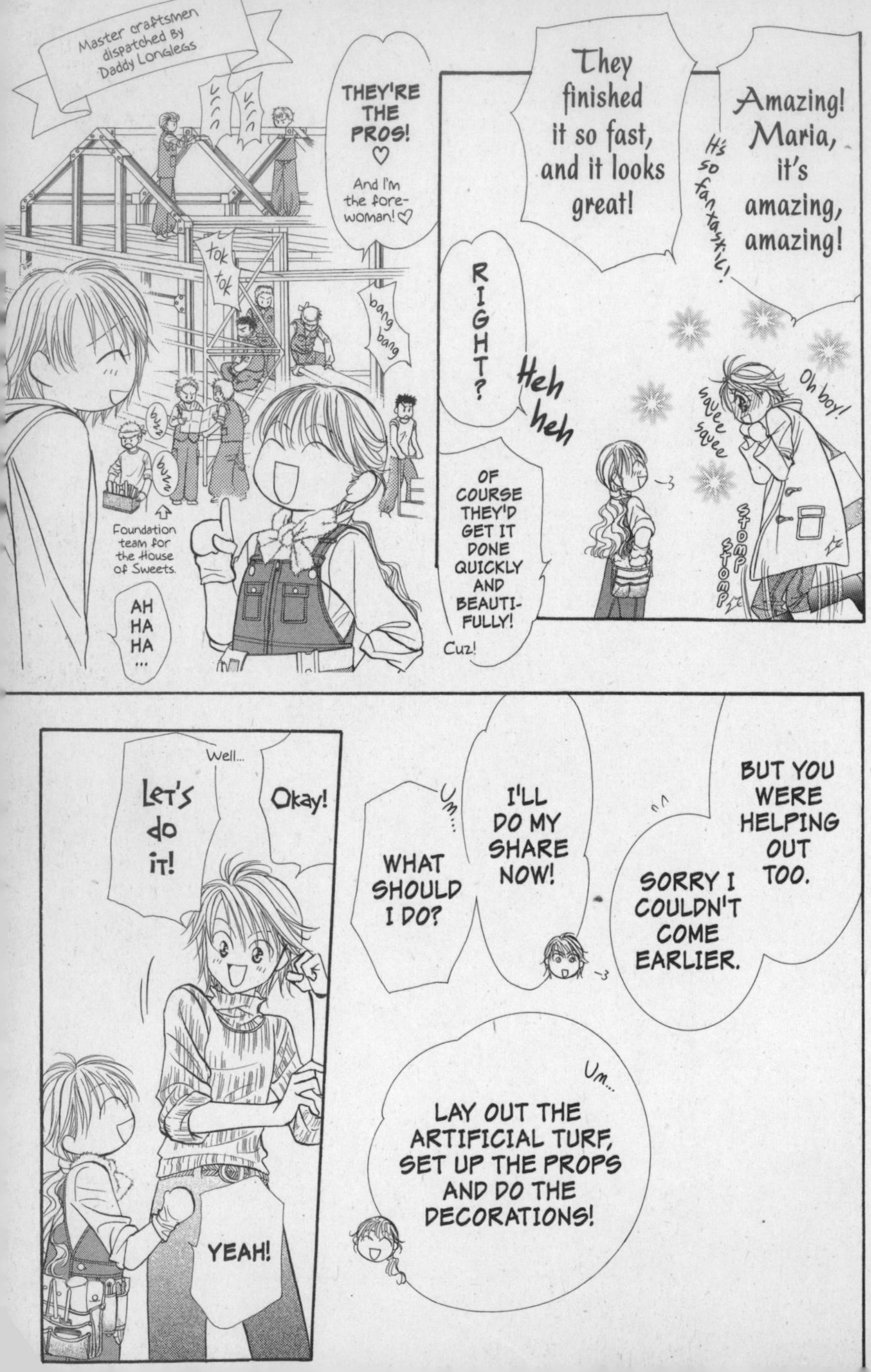
Amazing! Maria, it's amazing, amazing!
It's so fantastic!
They finished it so fast, and it looks great!
Oh boy!
squee squee
STOMP STOMP STOMP
RIGHT?
Heh heh
OF COURSE THEY'D GET IT DONE QUICKLY AND BEAUTIFULLY!
Cuz!
Master craftsmen dispatched by Daddy Longlegs
THEY'RE THE PROS! ♡
And I'm the fore-woman! ♡
tok tok
bang bang
buzz
buzz
Foundation team for the House of Sweets.
AH HA HA ...
BUT YOU WERE HELPING OUT TOO.
SORRY I COULDN'T COME EARLIER.
I'LL DO MY SHARE NOW!
Um...
WHAT SHOULD I DO?
Um...
LAY OUT THE ARTIFICIAL TURF, SET UP THE PROPS AND DO THE DECORATIONS!
Well...
Okay!
Let's do it!
YEAH!

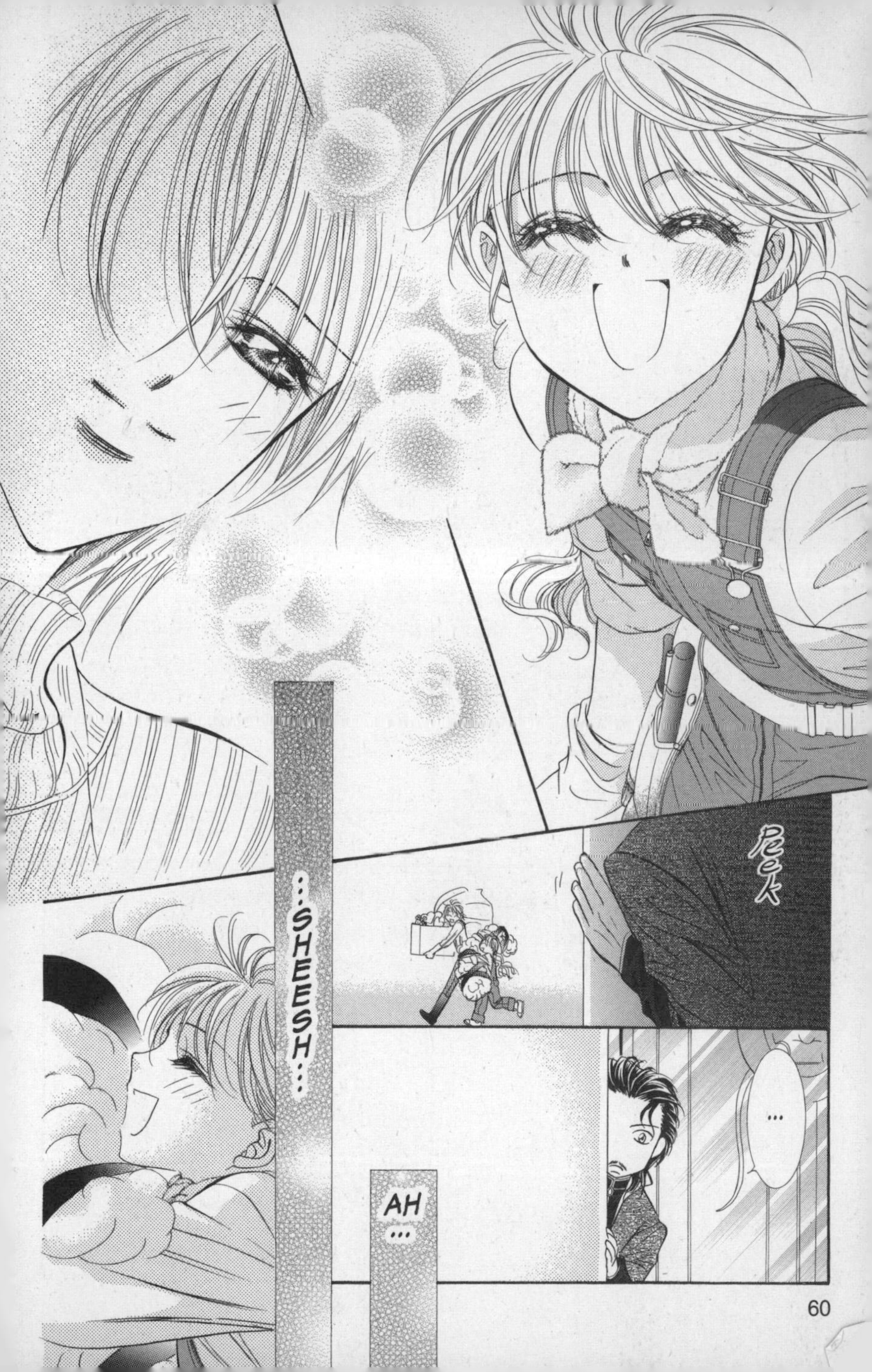
PECK
...SHEESH...
...
AH ...

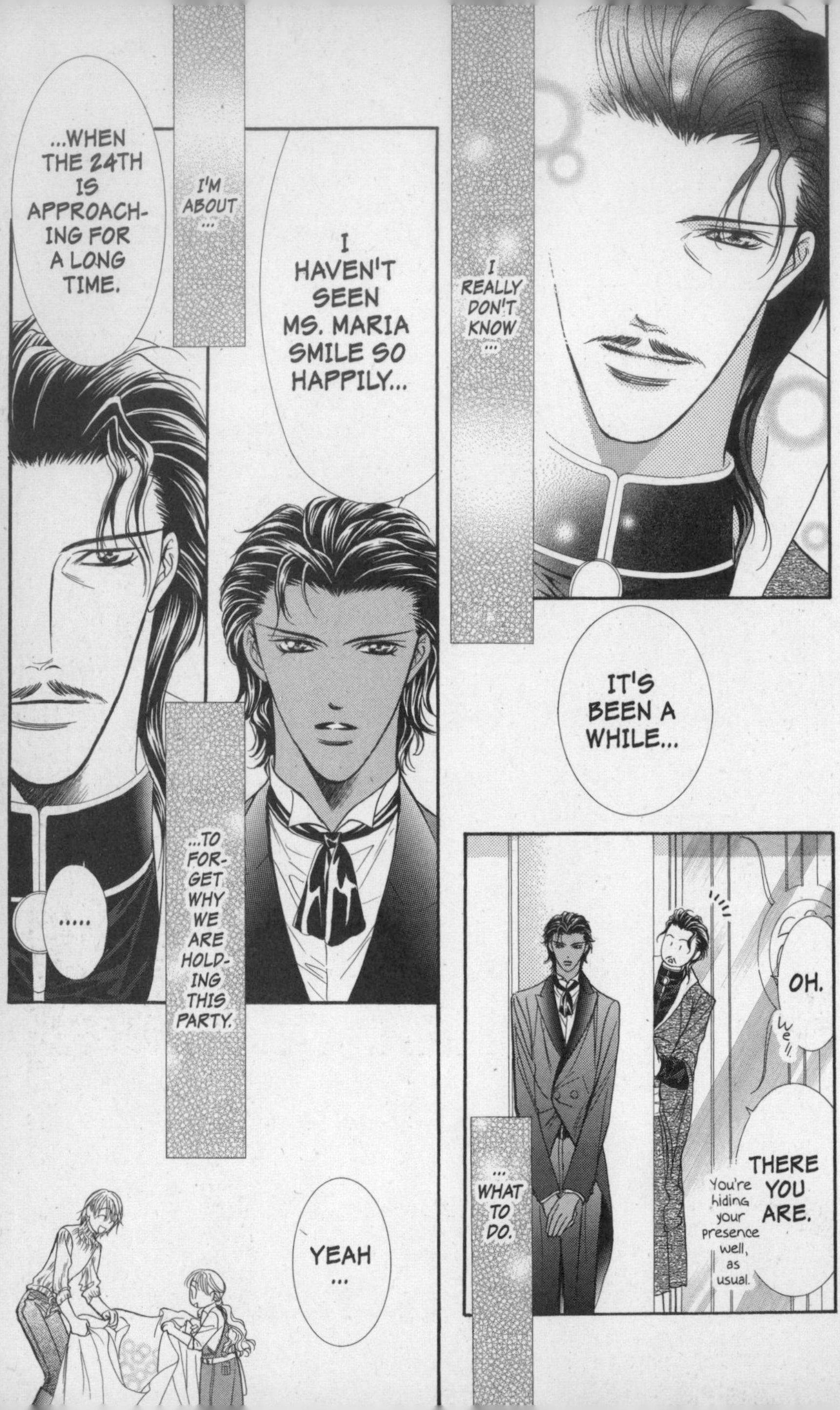
I REALLY DON'T KNOW ...
IT'S BEEN A WHILE...
OH.
Well.
THERE YOU ARE.
You're hiding your presence well, as usual.
... WHAT TO DO.
I HAVEN'T SEEN MS. MARIA SMILE SO HAPPILY...
...WHEN THE 24TH IS APPROACHING FOR A LONG TIME.
I'M ABOUT ...
.....
...TO FORGET WHY WE ARE HOLDING THIS PARTY.
YEAH ...

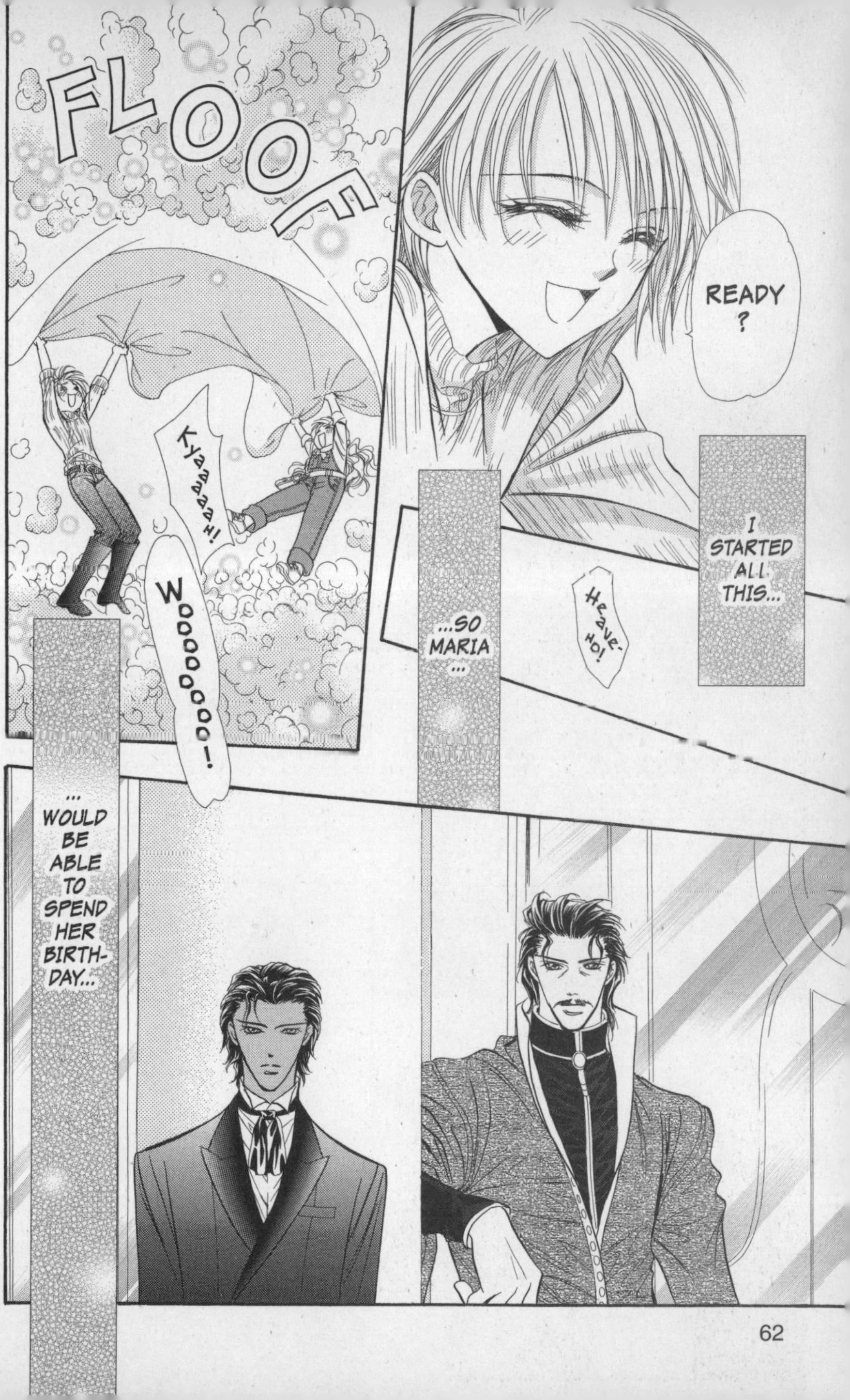
READY?
I STARTED ALL THIS...
Heave-ho!
...SO MARIA...
FLOOF
Kyaaaaaah!
WOOOOOOOOO!
...WOULD BE ABLE TO SPEND HER BIRTHDAY...

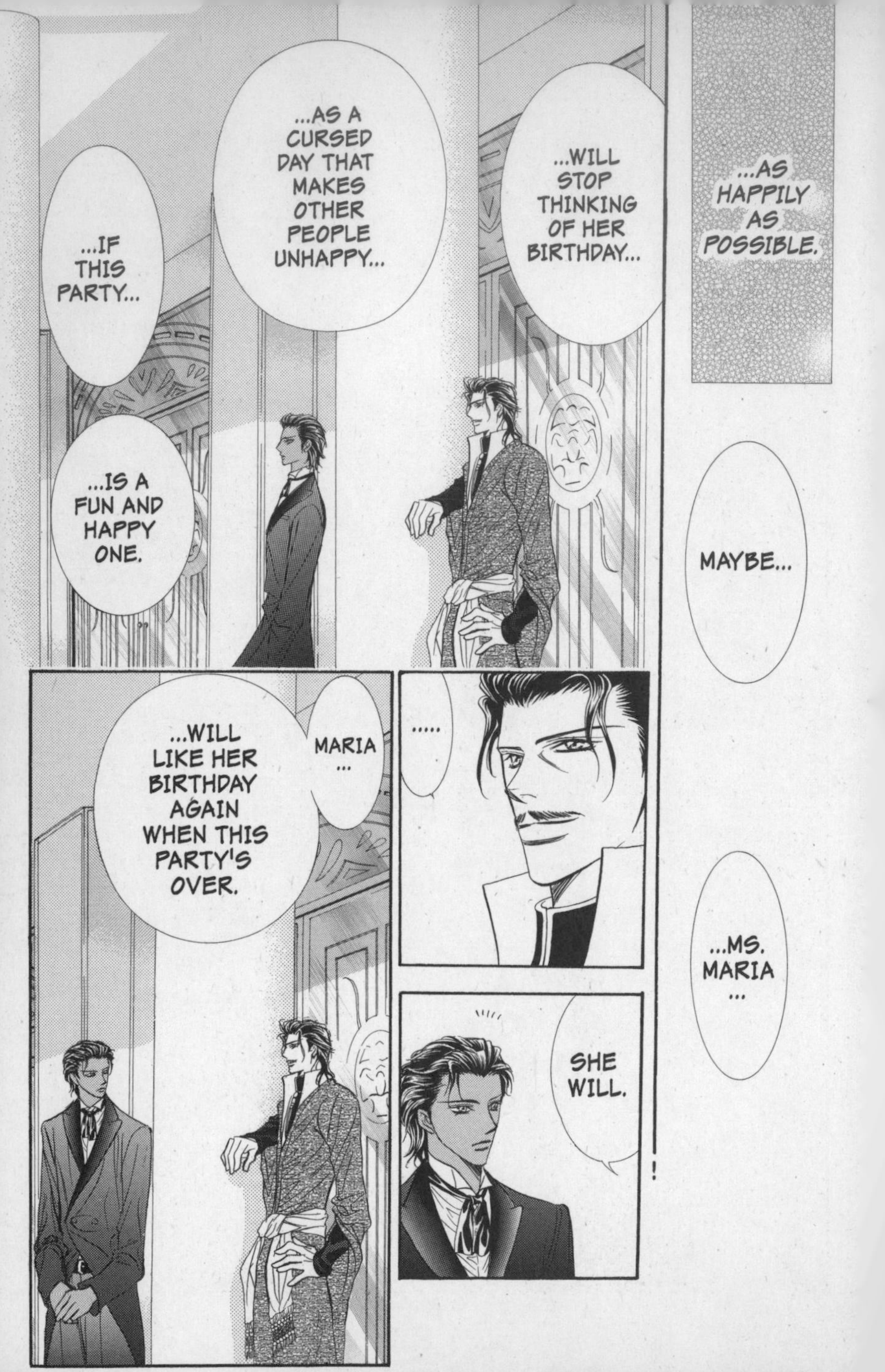
...AS HAPPILY AS POSSIBLE.
MAYBE...
...MS. MARIA ...
...WILL STOP THINKING OF HER BIRTHDAY...
...AS A CURSED DAY THAT MAKES OTHER PEOPLE UNHAPPY...
...IF THIS PARTY...
...IS A FUN AND HAPPY ONE.
.....
SHE WILL.
MARIA ...
...WILL LIKE HER BIRTHDAY AGAIN WHEN THIS PARTY'S OVER.

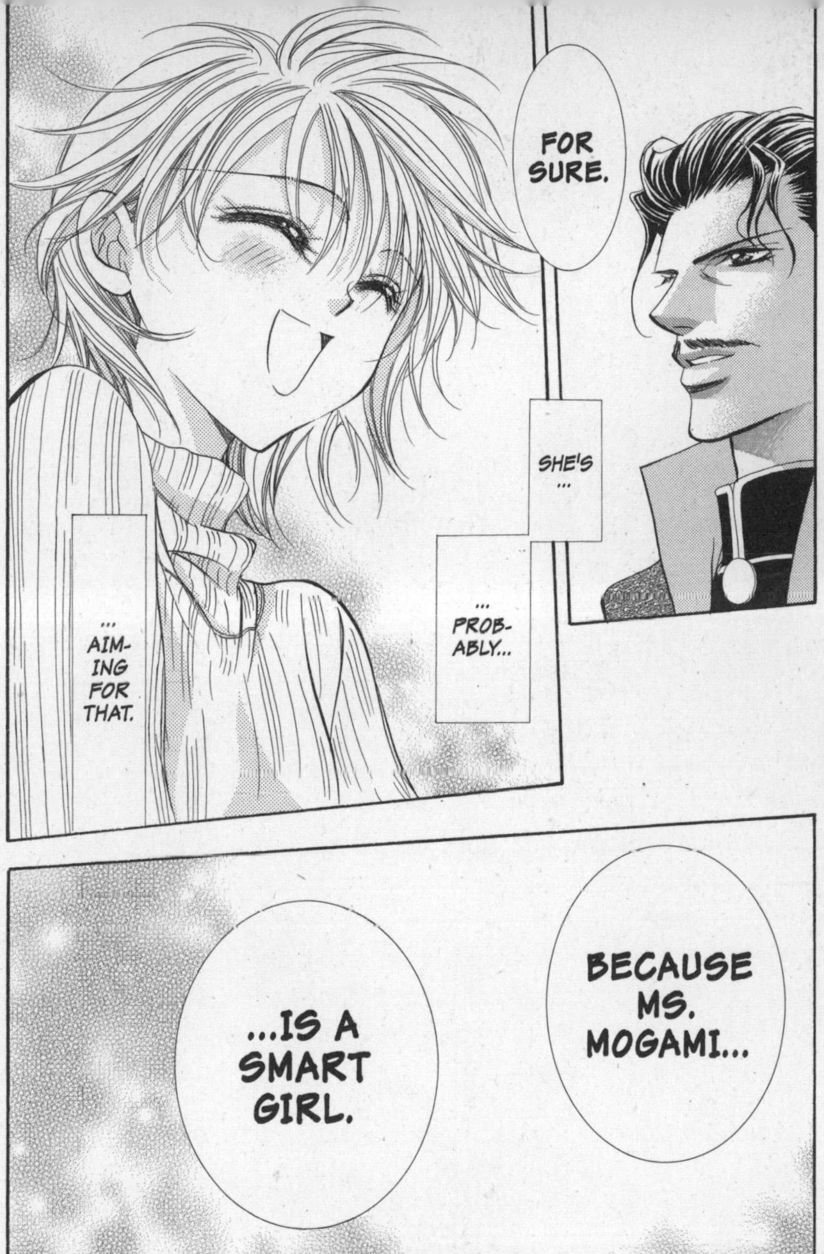
FOR SURE.
SHE'S ...
... PROBABLY...
... AIMING FOR THAT.
BECAUSE MS. MOGAMI...
...IS A SMART GIRL.

End of Act 116

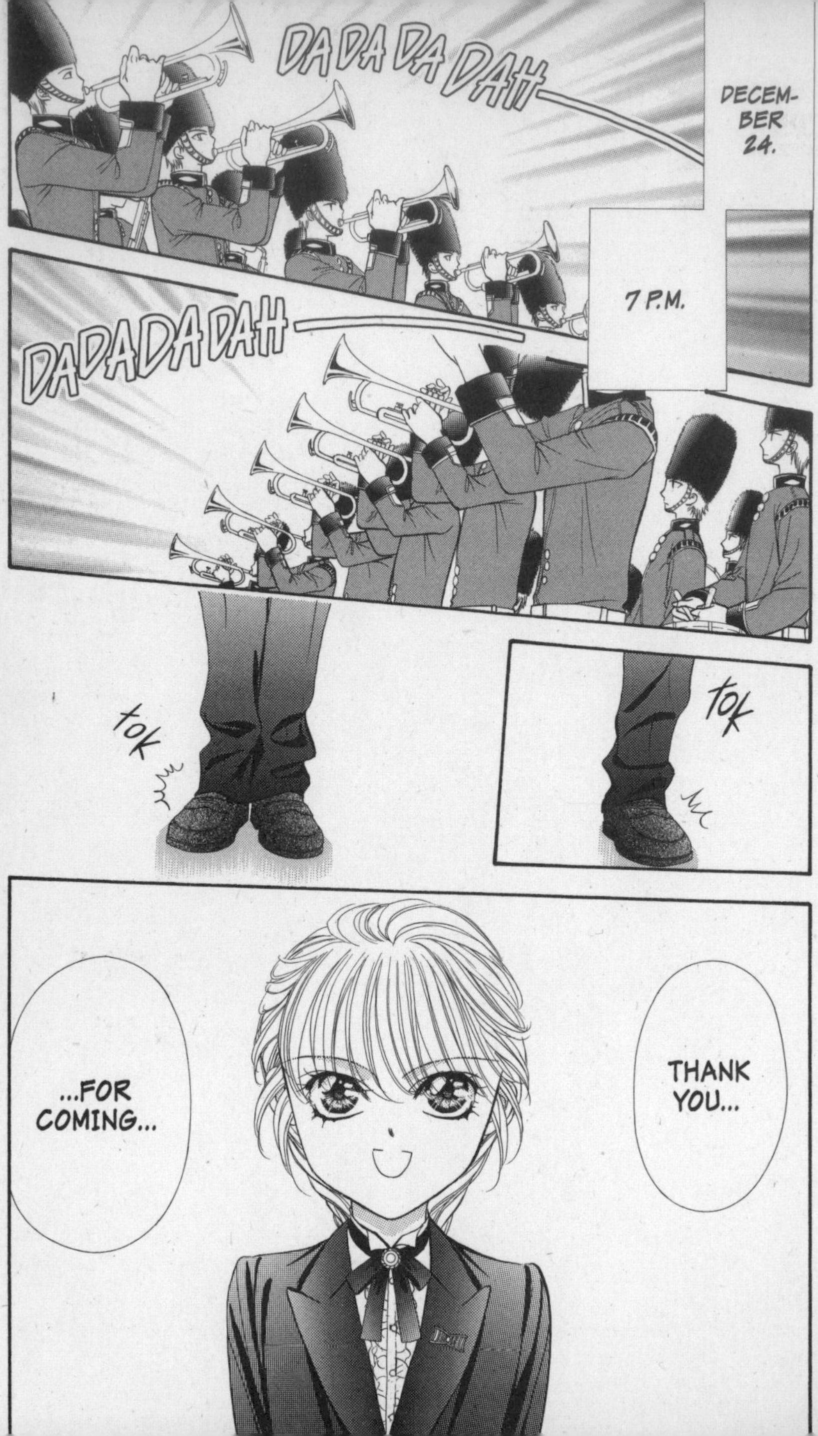
DECEMBER 24.
DA DA DA DAH
7 P.M.
DADADADAH
TOK
TOK
THANK YOU...
...FOR COMING...

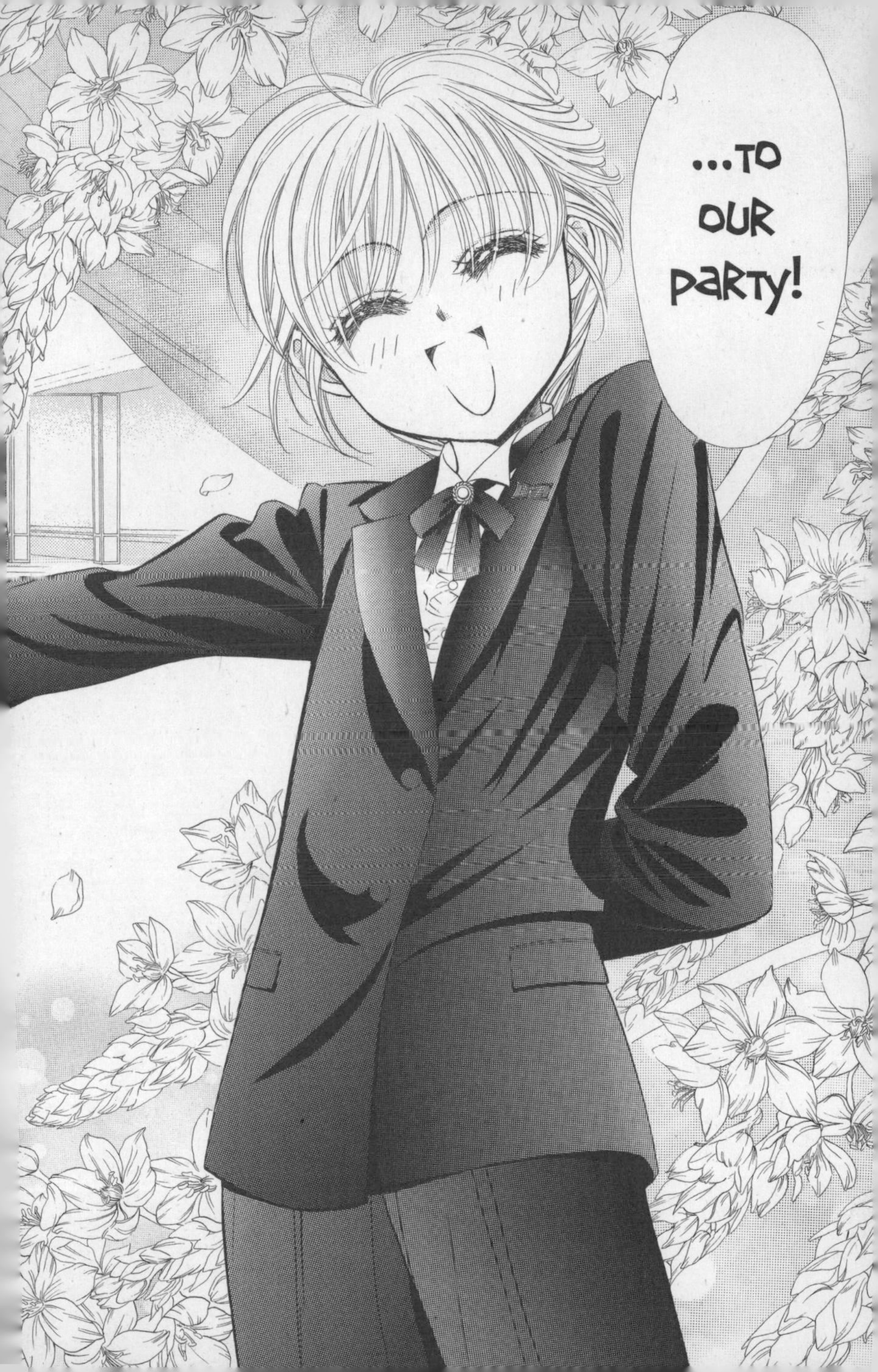
...TO OUR PARTY!

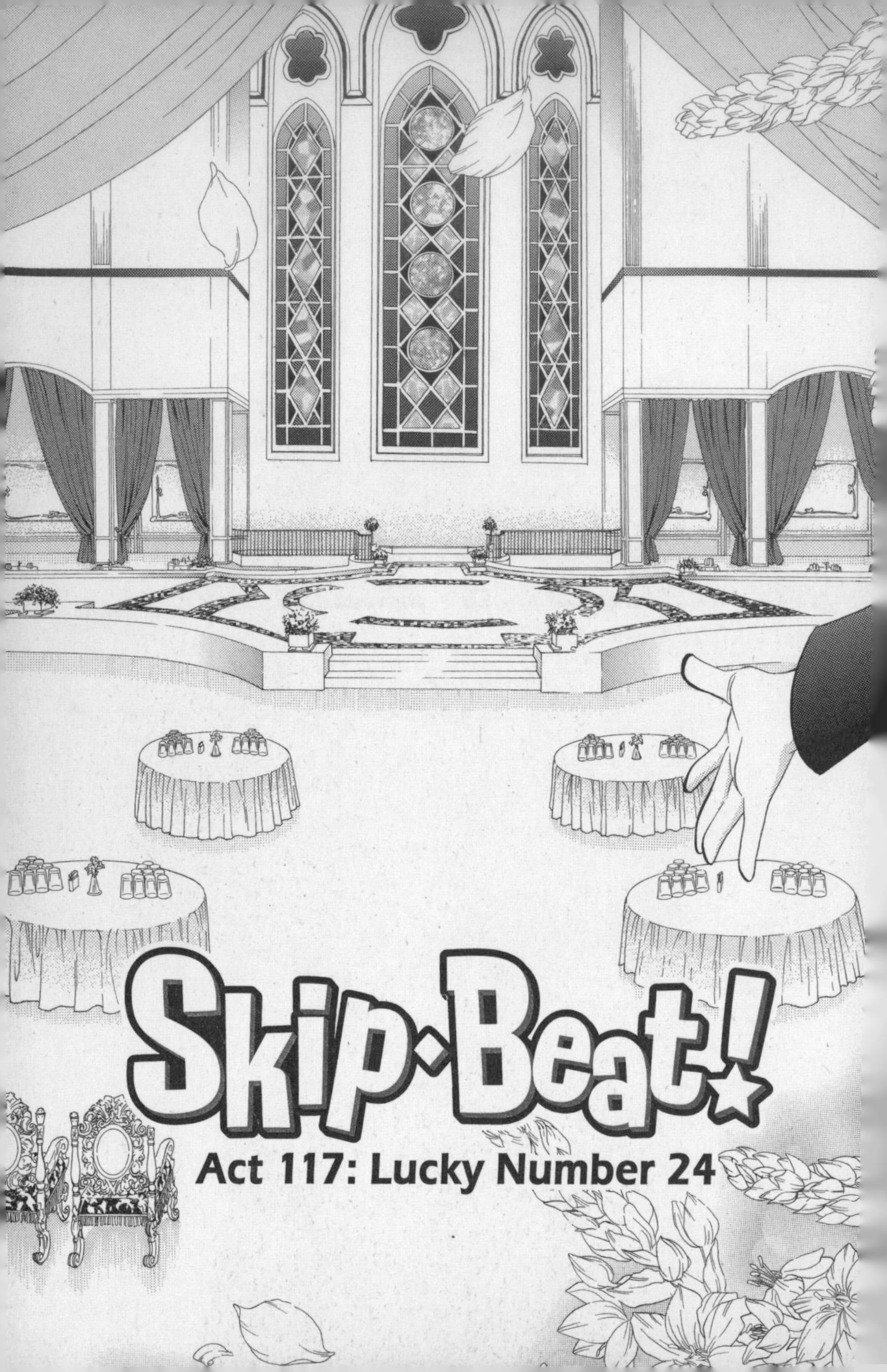
Skip·Beat!
Act 117: Lucky Number 24

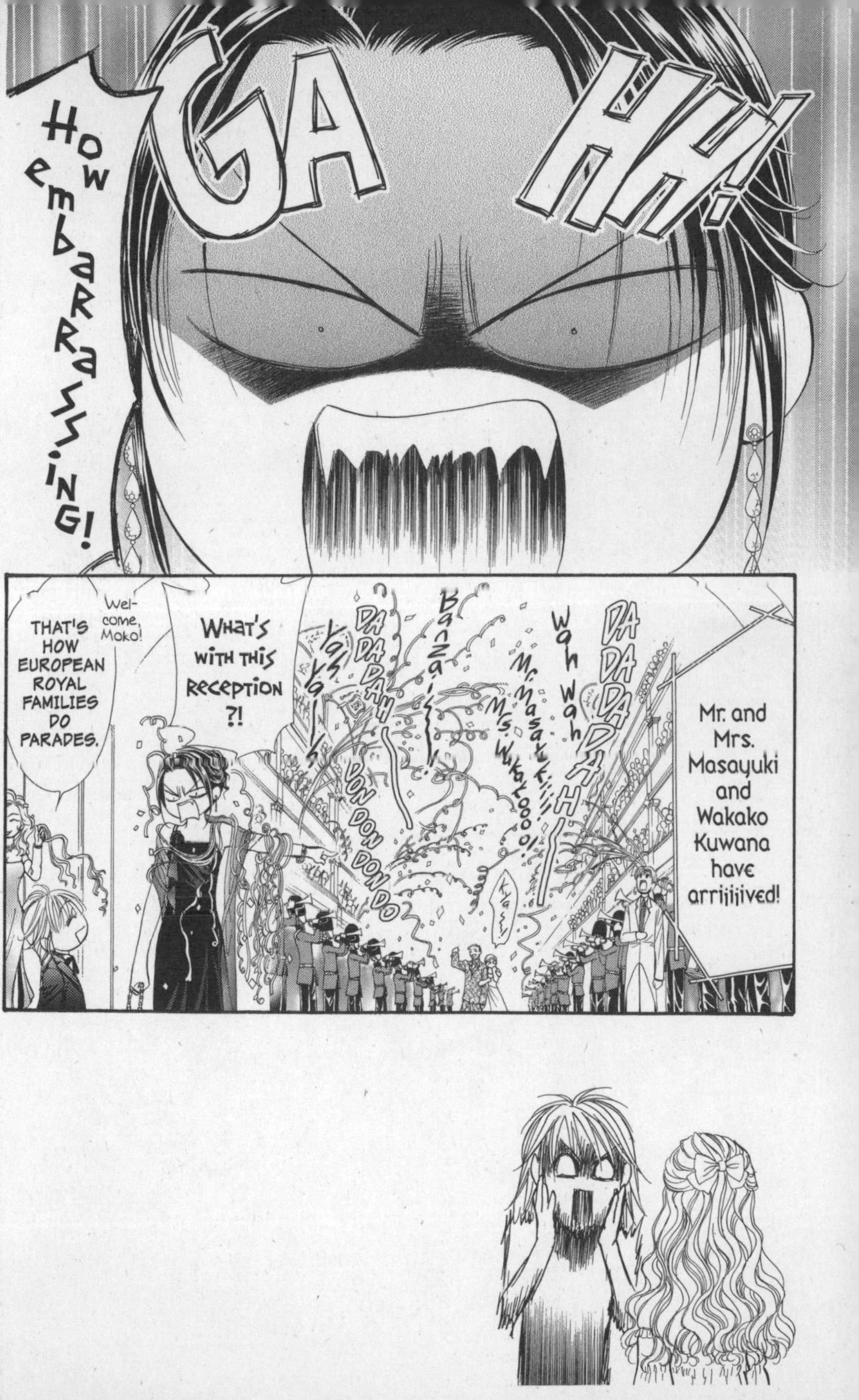
GAHH!
How embarrassing!
Mr. and Mrs. Masayuki and Wakako Kuwana have arriiiiived!
DA DA DA DA DAH
Wah wah
Mr. Masayuki!
Mrs. Wakakooo!
Banzai!
DA DA DAH
Yah yah
DON DON DON DO
What's with this reception?!
Wel-come, Moko!
THAT'S HOW EUROPEAN ROYAL FAMILIES DO PARADES.

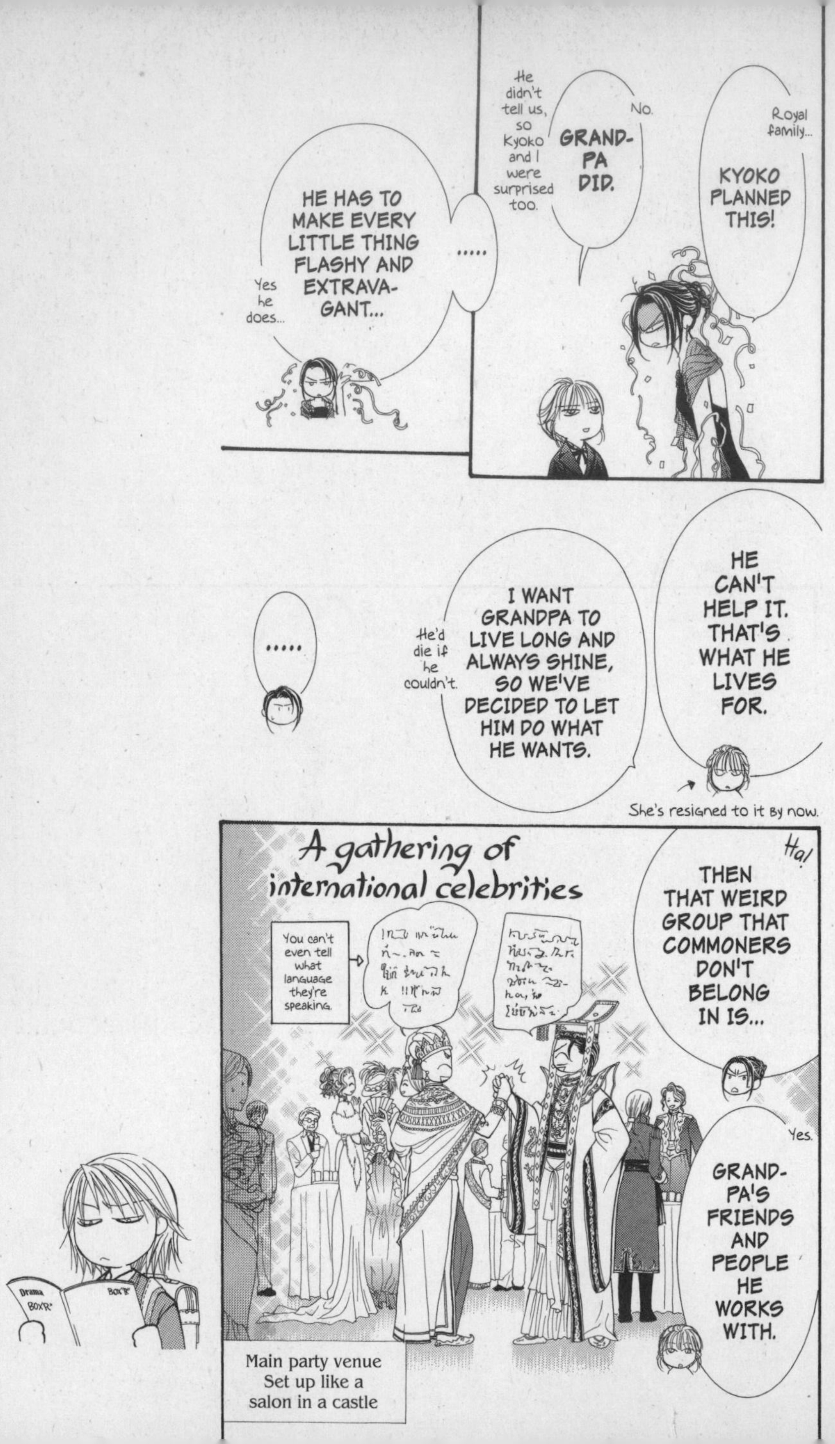
Royal family...
KYOKO PLANNED THIS!
No.
GRANDPA DID.
He didn't tell us, so Kyoko and I were surprised too.
.....
HE HAS TO MAKE EVERY LITTLE THING FLASHY AND EXTRAVAGANT...
Yes he does...
HE CAN'T HELP IT. THAT'S WHAT HE LIVES FOR.
I WANT GRANDPA TO LIVE LONG AND ALWAYS SHINE, SO WE'VE DECIDED TO LET HIM DO WHAT HE WANTS.
He'd die if he couldn't.
She's resigned to it by now.
......
Ha!
THEN THAT WEIRD GROUP THAT COMMONERS DON'T BELONG IN IS...
Yes.
GRANDPA'S FRIENDS AND PEOPLE HE WORKS WITH.
A gathering of international celebrities
You can't even tell what language they're speaking.
Main party venue Set up like a salon in a castle
Drama BOX"R"

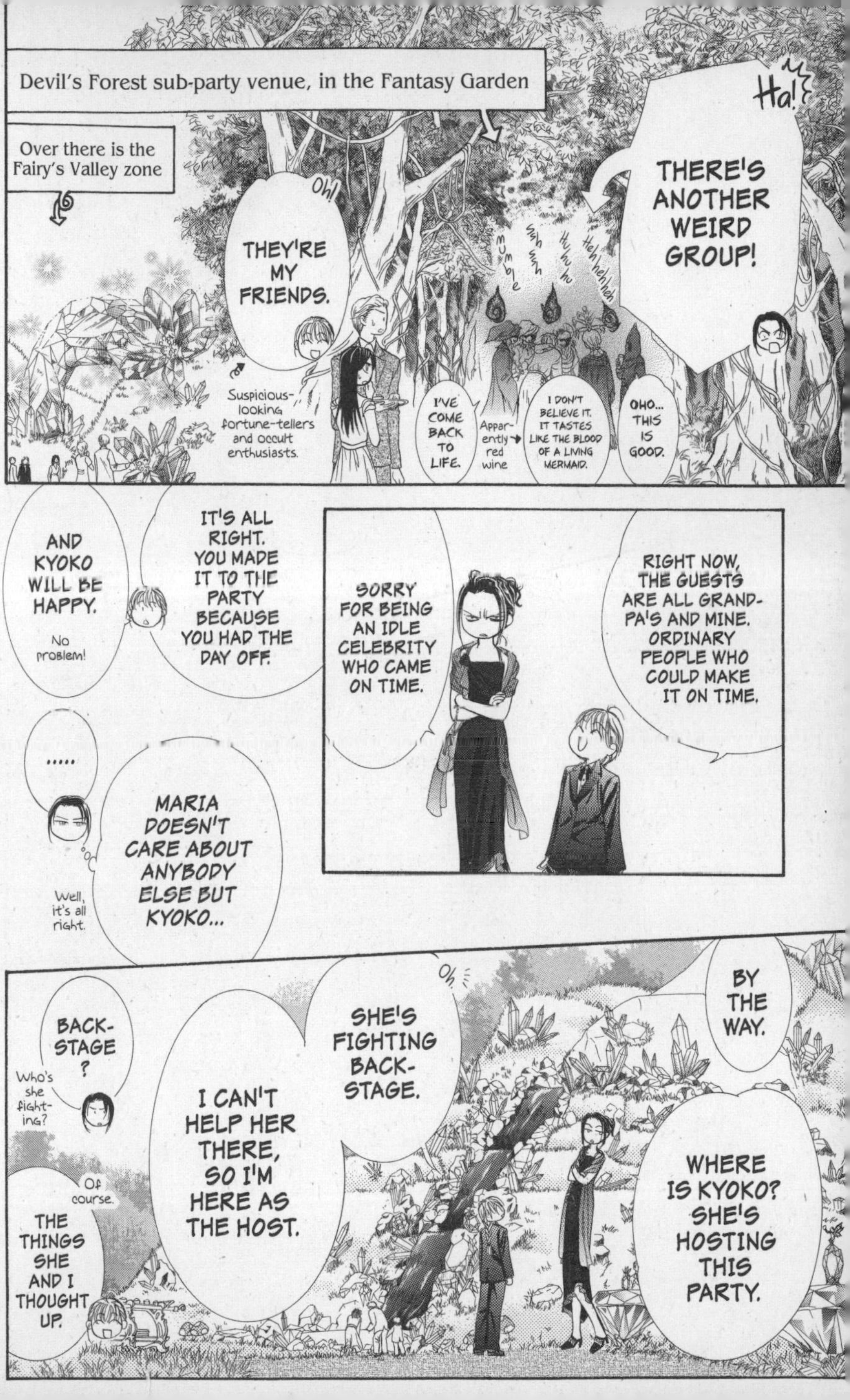
Devil's Forest sub-party venue, in the Fantasy Garden
Ha!
THERE'S ANOTHER WEIRD GROUP!
Heh hehheh
Hu hu hu
Ssh ssh
Mumble
Oh!
THEY'RE MY FRIENDS.
Over there is the Fairy's Valley zone
OHO... THIS IS GOOD.
I DON'T BELIEVE IT. IT TASTES LIKE THE BLOOD OF A LIVING MERMAID.
Apparently red wine
I'VE COME BACK TO LIFE.
Suspicious-looking fortune-tellers and occult enthusiasts.
RIGHT NOW, THE GUESTS ARE ALL GRAND-PA'S AND MINE. ORDINARY PEOPLE WHO COULD MAKE IT ON TIME.
SORRY FOR BEING AN IDLE CELEBRITY WHO CAME ON TIME.
IT'S ALL RIGHT. YOU MADE IT TO THE PARTY BECAUSE YOU HAD THE DAY OFF.
AND KYOKO WILL BE HAPPY.
No problem!
......
MARIA DOESN'T CARE ABOUT ANYBODY ELSE BUT KYOKO...
Well, it's all right.
BY THE WAY.
WHERE IS KYOKO? SHE'S HOSTING THIS PARTY.
Oh.
SHE'S FIGHTING BACK-STAGE.
I CAN'T HELP HER THERE, SO I'M HERE AS THE HOST.
BACK-STAGE?
Who's she fight-ing?
Of course.
THE THINGS SHE AND I THOUGHT UP.

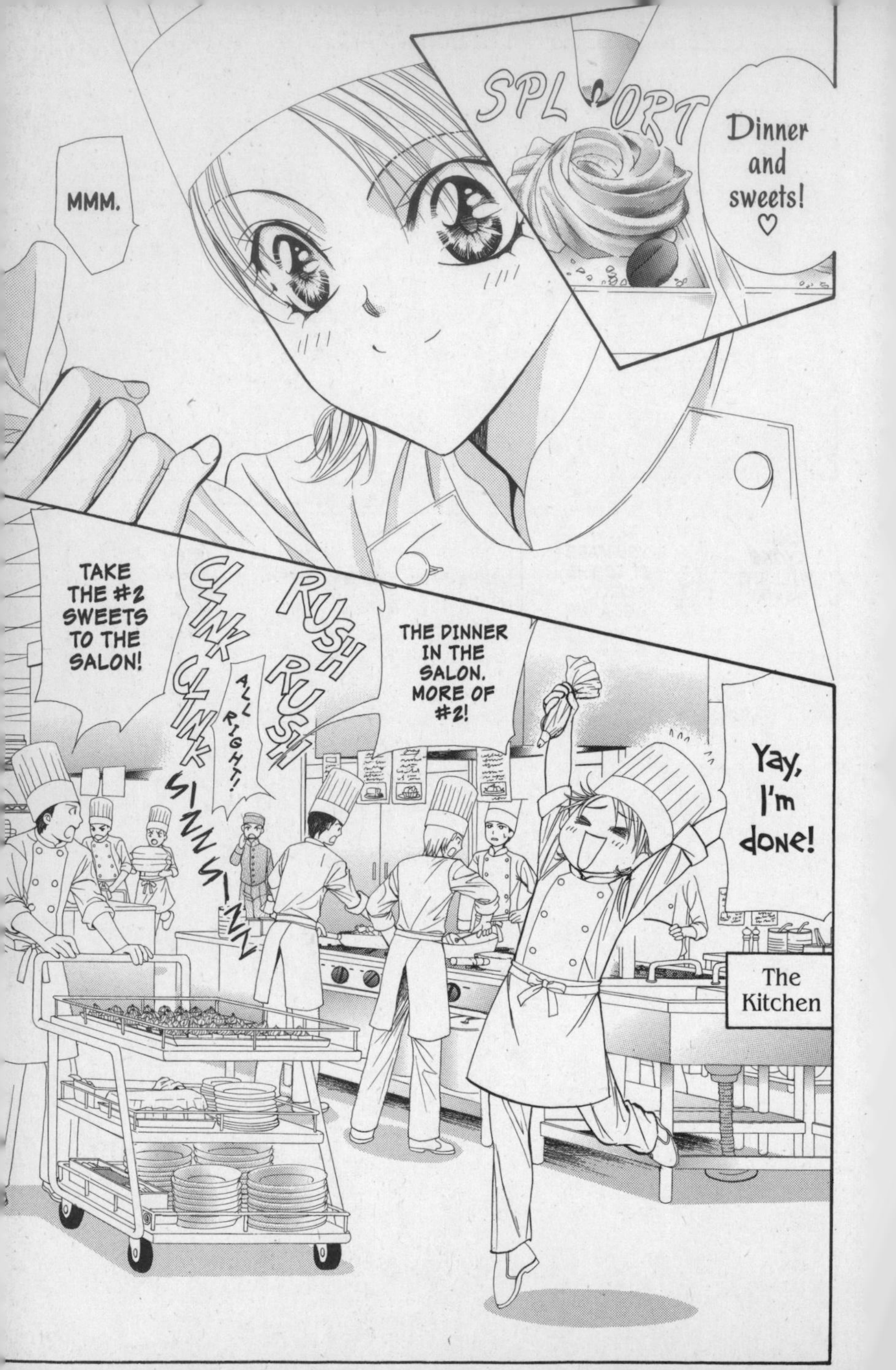
SPLORT
Dinner and sweets! ♡
MMM.
Yay, I'm done!
The Kitchen
THE DINNER IN THE SALON. MORE OF #2!
RUSH RUSH
ALL RIGHT!
CLINK CLINK
SIZZ SIZZ
TAKE THE #2 SWEETS TO THE SALON!

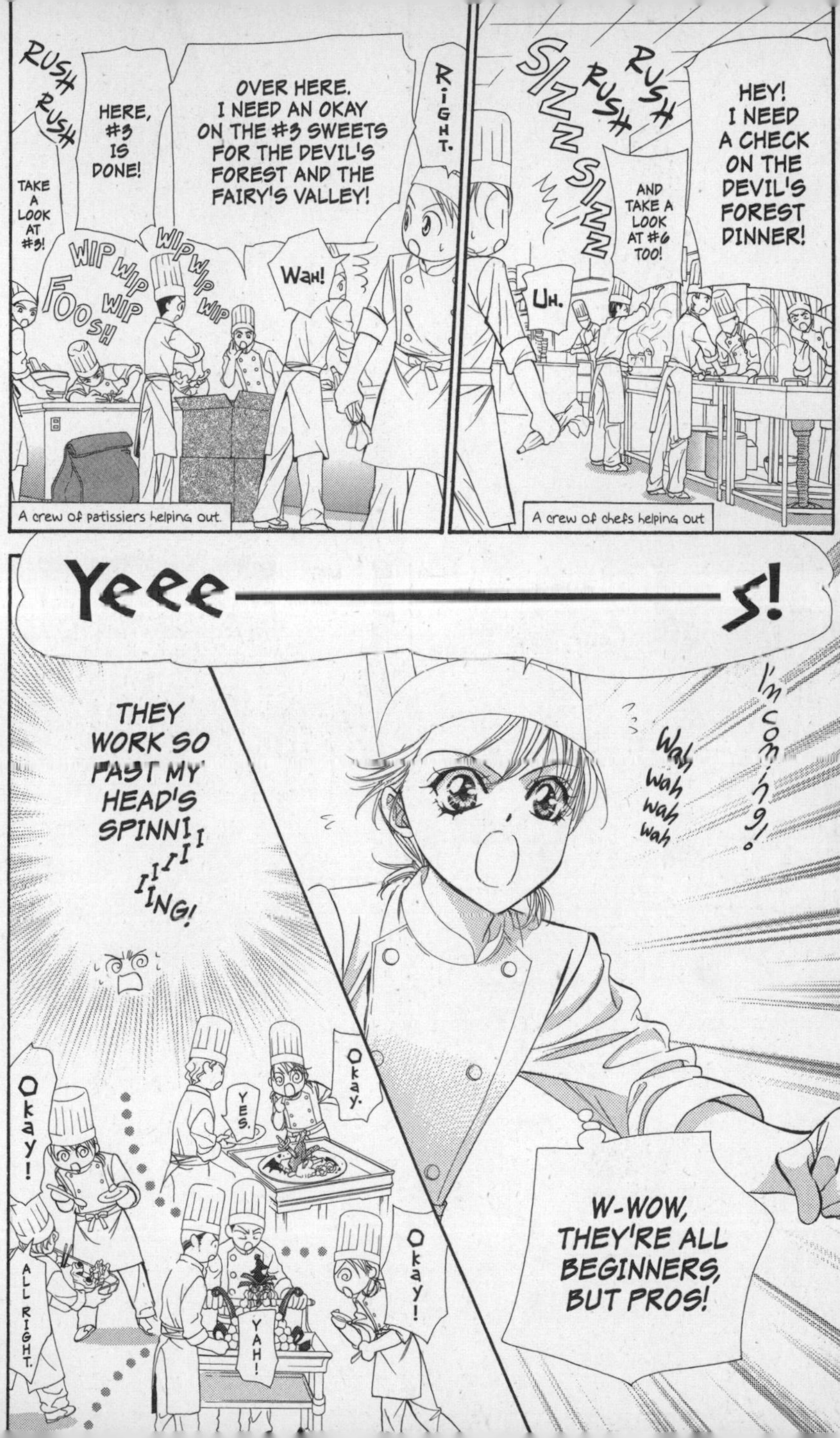
RUSH RUSH
SIZZ SIZZ
HEY! I NEED A CHECK ON THE DEVIL'S FOREST DINNER!
AND TAKE A LOOK AT #6 TOO!
UH.
A crew of chefs helping out
RIGHT.
OVER HERE. I NEED AN OKAY ON THE #3 SWEETS FOR THE DEVIL'S FOREST AND THE FAIRY'S VALLEY!
Wah!
HERE, #3 IS DONE!
RUSH RUSH
TAKE A LOOK AT #3!
WIP WIP WIP WIP WIP
FOOSH
A crew of patissiers helping out.
Yeee——s!
I'm coming!
Wah wah wah wah
W-WOW, THEY'RE ALL BEGINNERS, BUT PROS!
THEY WORK SO FAST MY HEAD'S SPINNIIIIIING!
Okay.
YES.
Okay!
Okay!
YAH!
ALL RIGHT.

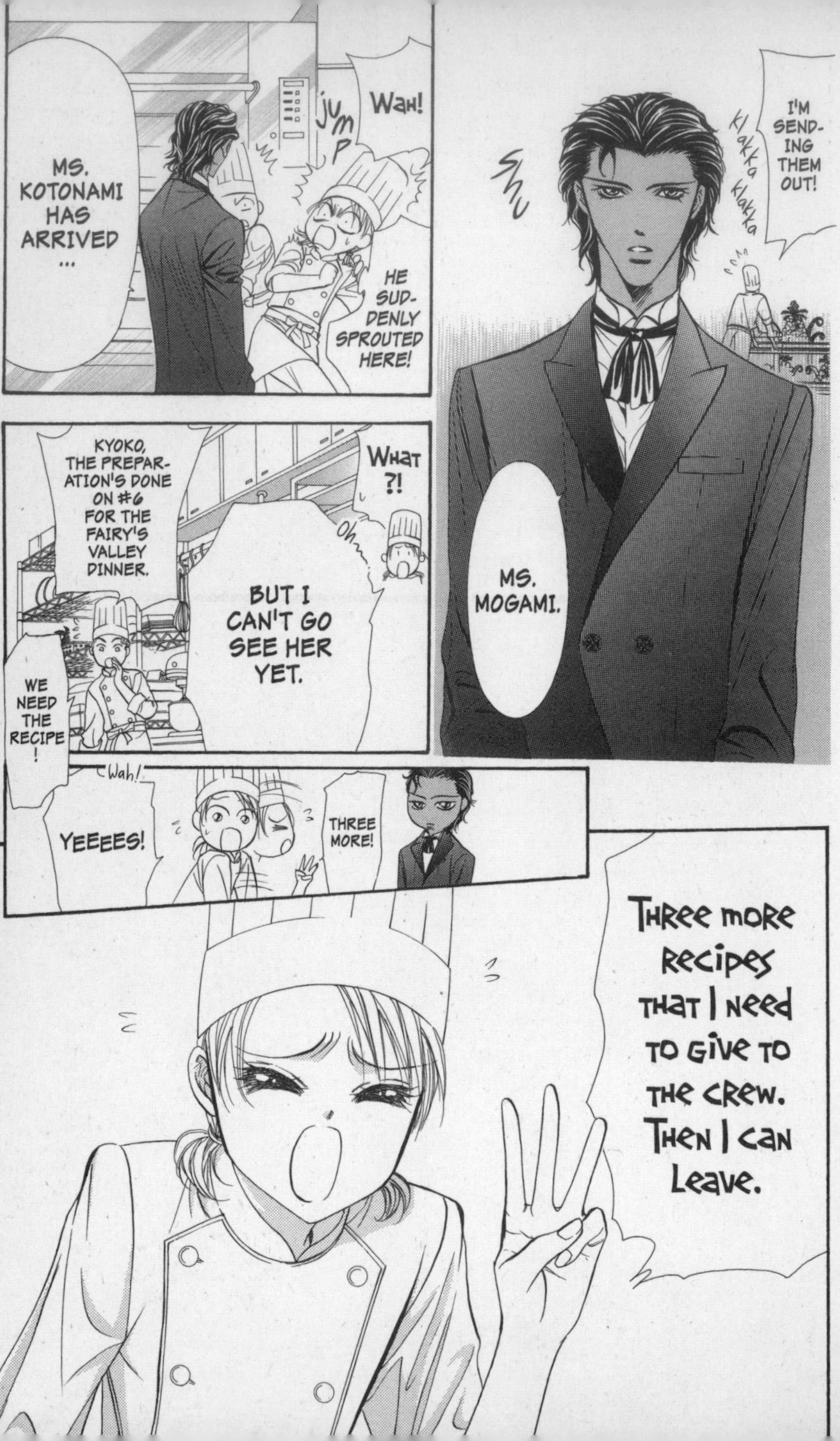
I'M SENDING THEM OUT!
klakka klakka
shu
MS. MOGAMI.
WAH!
jump
MS. KOTONAMI HAS ARRIVED ...
HE SUDDENLY SPROUTED HERE!
WHAT ?!
KYOKO, THE PREPARATION'S DONE ON #6 FOR THE FAIRY'S VALLEY DINNER.
Oh...
BUT I CAN'T GO SEE HER YET.
WE NEED THE RECIPE!
THREE MORE!
YEEEES!
Wah!
Three more recipes that I need to give to the crew. Then I can leave.

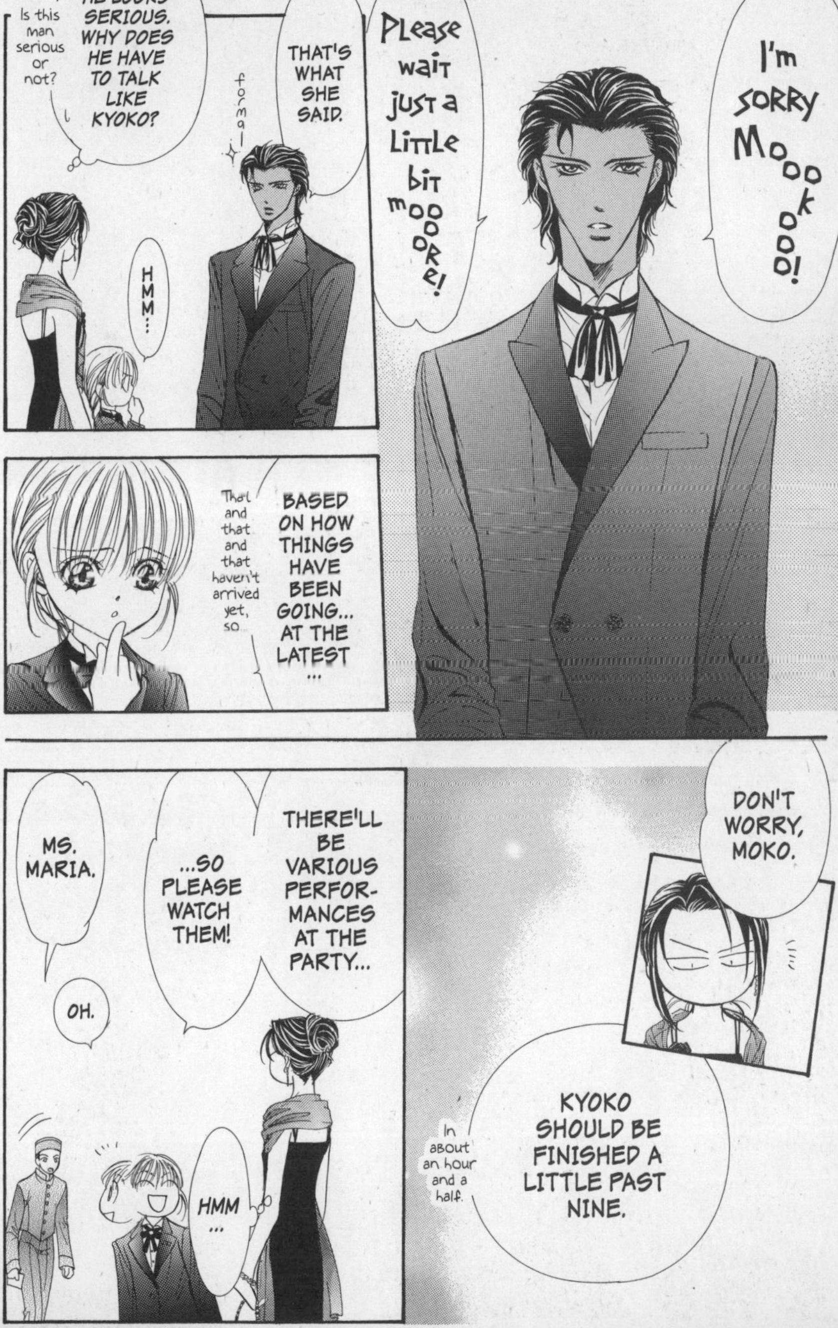
I'm SORRY MOOOKOOO!
Please wait just a little bit mooooore!
THAT'S WHAT SHE SAID.
formal
HE LOOKS SERIOUS. WHY DOES HE HAVE TO TALK LIKE KYOKO?
Is this man serious or not?
HMM...
BASED ON HOW THINGS HAVE BEEN GOING... AT THE LATEST...
That and that and that haven't arrived yet, so...
DON'T WORRY, MOKO.
KYOKO SHOULD BE FINISHED A LITTLE PAST NINE.
In about an hour and a half.
THERE'LL BE VARIOUS PERFORMANCES AT THE PARTY...
...SO PLEASE WATCH THEM!
MS. MARIA.
OH.
HMM...

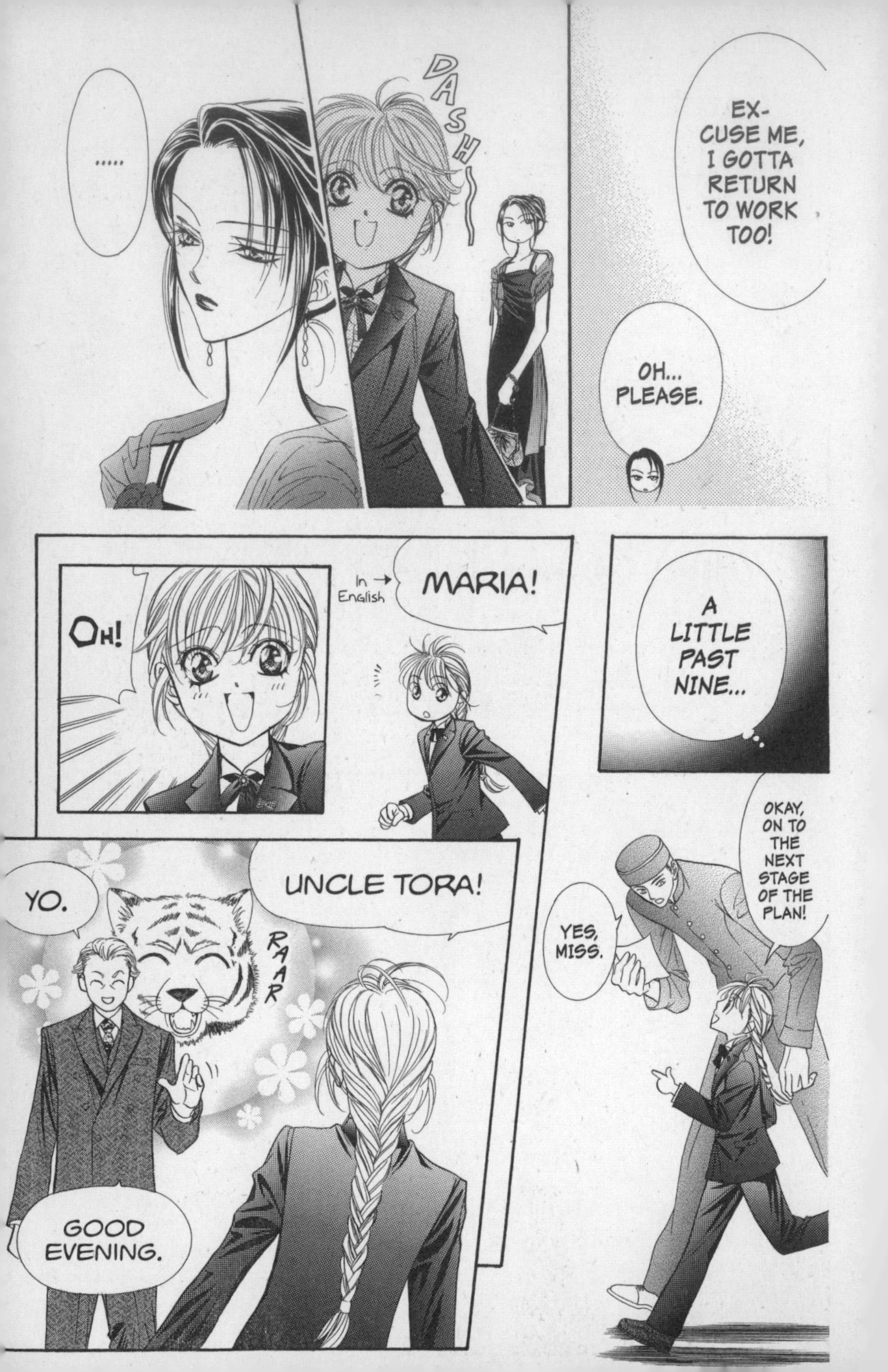

EX-CUSE ME, I GOTTA RETURN TO WORK TOO!
OH... PLEASE.
DASH
.....
A LITTLE PAST NINE...
In English
MARIA!
OH!
OKAY, ON TO THE NEXT STAGE OF THE PLAN!
YES, MISS.
UNCLE TORA!
YO.
RAAR
GOOD EVENING.

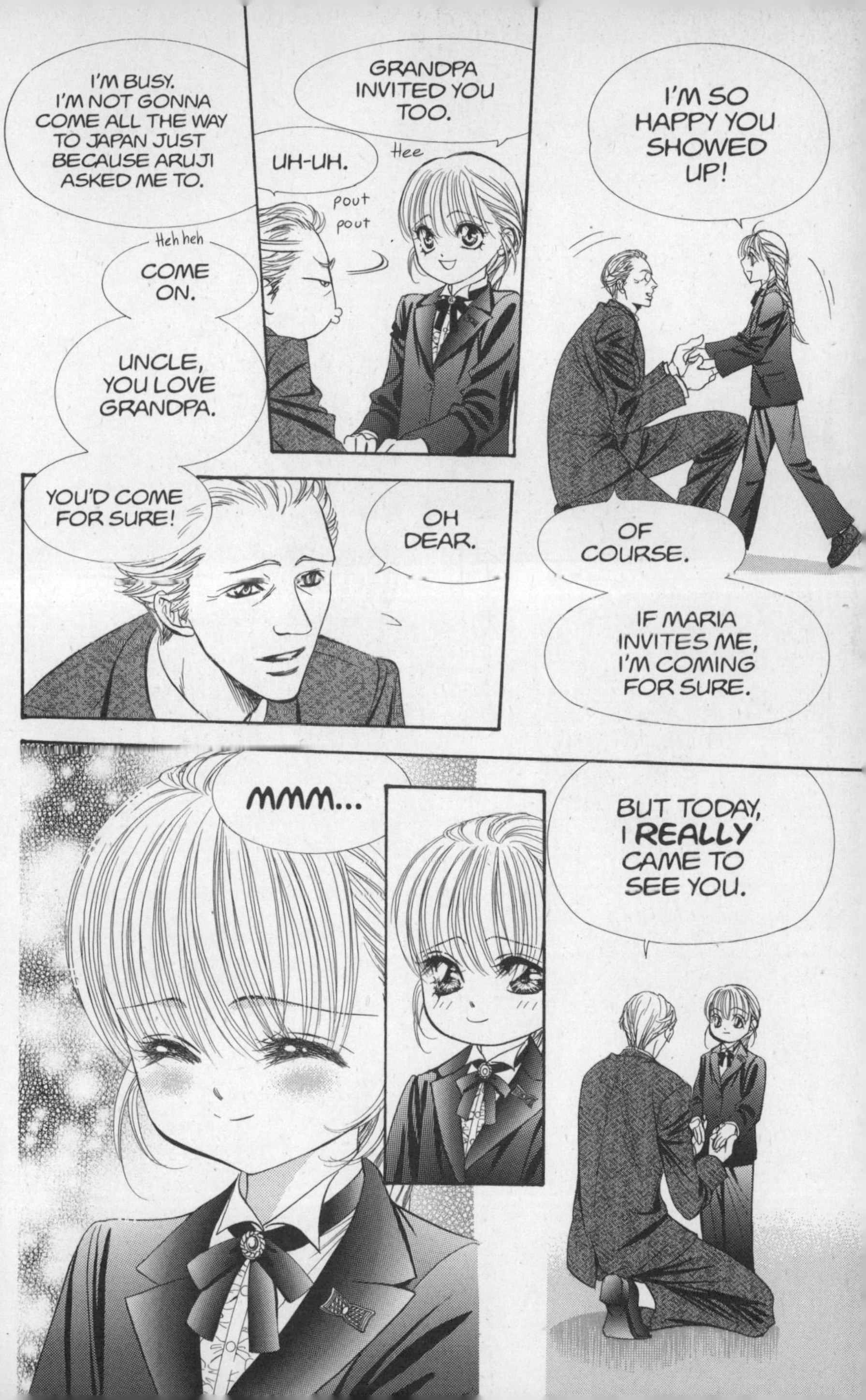
I'M SO HAPPY YOU SHOWED UP!
OF COURSE.
IF MARIA INVITES ME, I'M COMING FOR SURE.
GRANDPA INVITED YOU TOO.
Hee
UH-UH.
pout pout
I'M BUSY. I'M NOT GONNA COME ALL THE WAY TO JAPAN JUST BECAUSE ARUJI ASKED ME TO.
Heh heh
COME ON.
UNCLE, YOU LOVE GRANDPA.
YOU'D COME FOR SURE!
OH DEAR.
BUT TODAY, I REALLY CAME TO SEE YOU.
MMM...

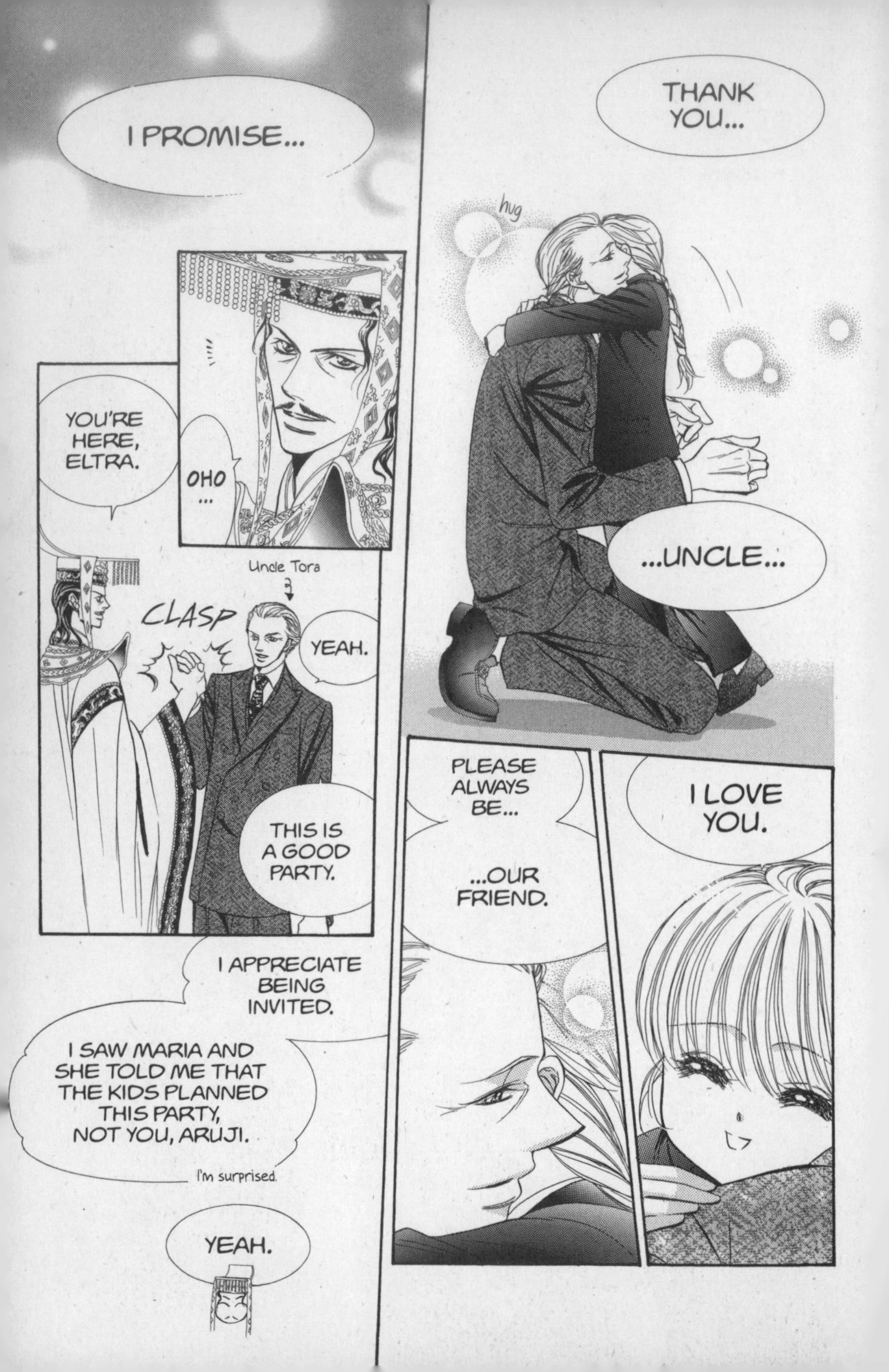
THANK YOU...
hug
...UNCLE...
I LOVE YOU.
PLEASE ALWAYS BE...
...OUR FRIEND.
I PROMISE...
OHO ...
YOU'RE HERE, ELTRA.
Uncle Tora
CLASP
YEAH.
THIS IS A GOOD PARTY.
I APPRECIATE BEING INVITED.
I SAW MARIA AND SHE TOLD ME THAT THE KIDS PLANNED THIS PARTY, NOT YOU, ARUJI.
I'm surprised.
YEAH.

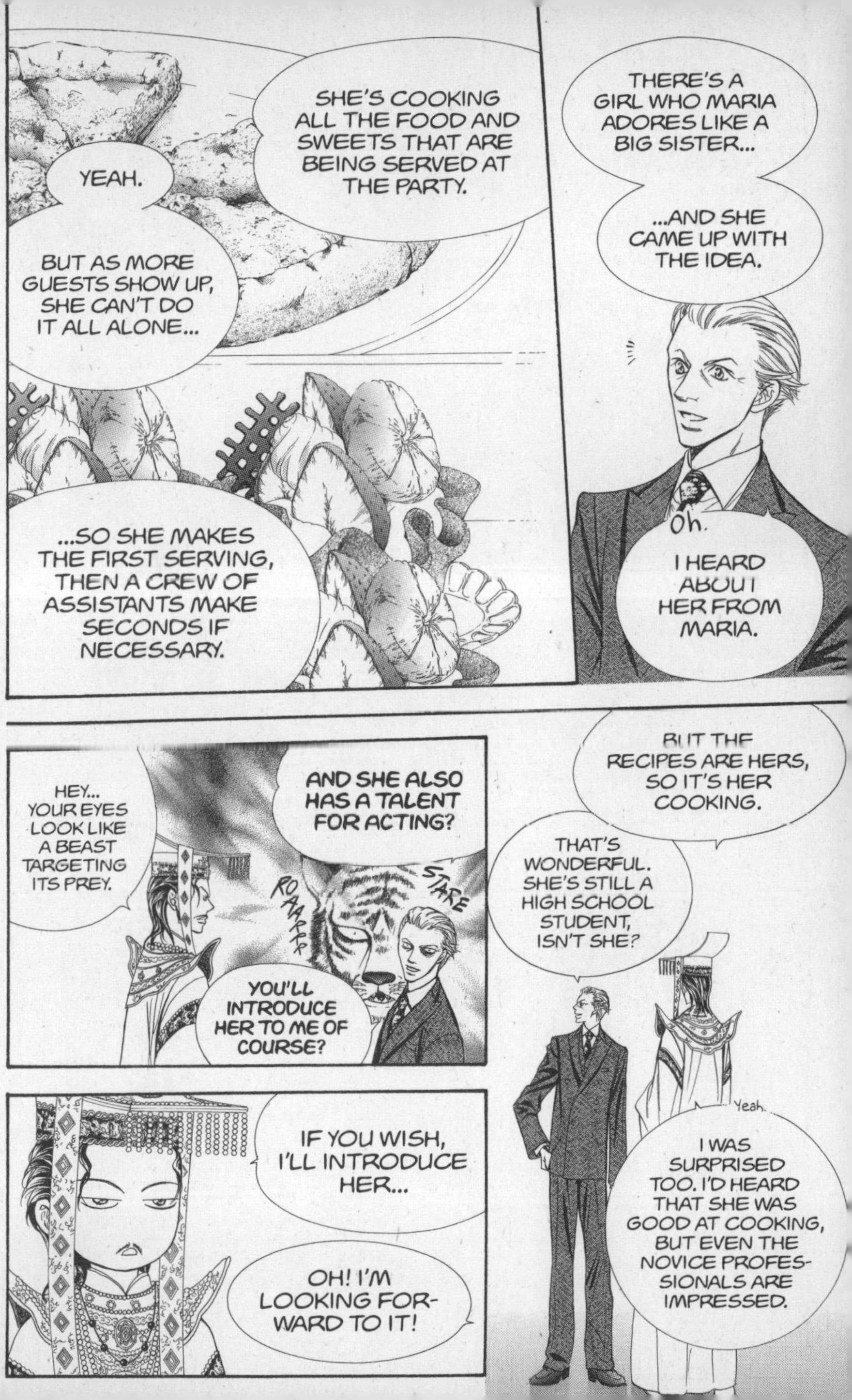
THERE'S A GIRL WHO MARIA ADORES LIKE A BIG SISTER...
...AND SHE CAME UP WITH THE IDEA.
Oh.
I HEARD ABOUT HER FROM MARIA.
SHE'S COOKING ALL THE FOOD AND SWEETS THAT ARE BEING SERVED AT THE PARTY.
YEAH.
BUT AS MORE GUESTS SHOW UP, SHE CAN'T DO IT ALL ALONE...
...SO SHE MAKES THE FIRST SERVING, THEN A CREW OF ASSISTANTS MAKE SECONDS IF NECESSARY.
BUT THE RECIPES ARE HERS, SO IT'S HER COOKING.
THAT'S WONDERFUL. SHE'S STILL A HIGH SCHOOL STUDENT, ISN'T SHE?
...Yeah...
I WAS SURPRISED TOO. I'D HEARD THAT SHE WAS GOOD AT COOKING, BUT EVEN THE NOVICE PROFES-SIONALS ARE IMPRESSED.
AND SHE ALSO HAS A TALENT FOR ACTING?
STARE
ROAARRR
HEY... YOUR EYES LOOK LIKE A BEAST TARGETING ITS PREY.
YOU'LL INTRODUCE HER TO ME OF COURSE?
IF YOU WISH, I'LL INTRODUCE HER...
OH! I'M LOOKING FOR-WARD TO IT!

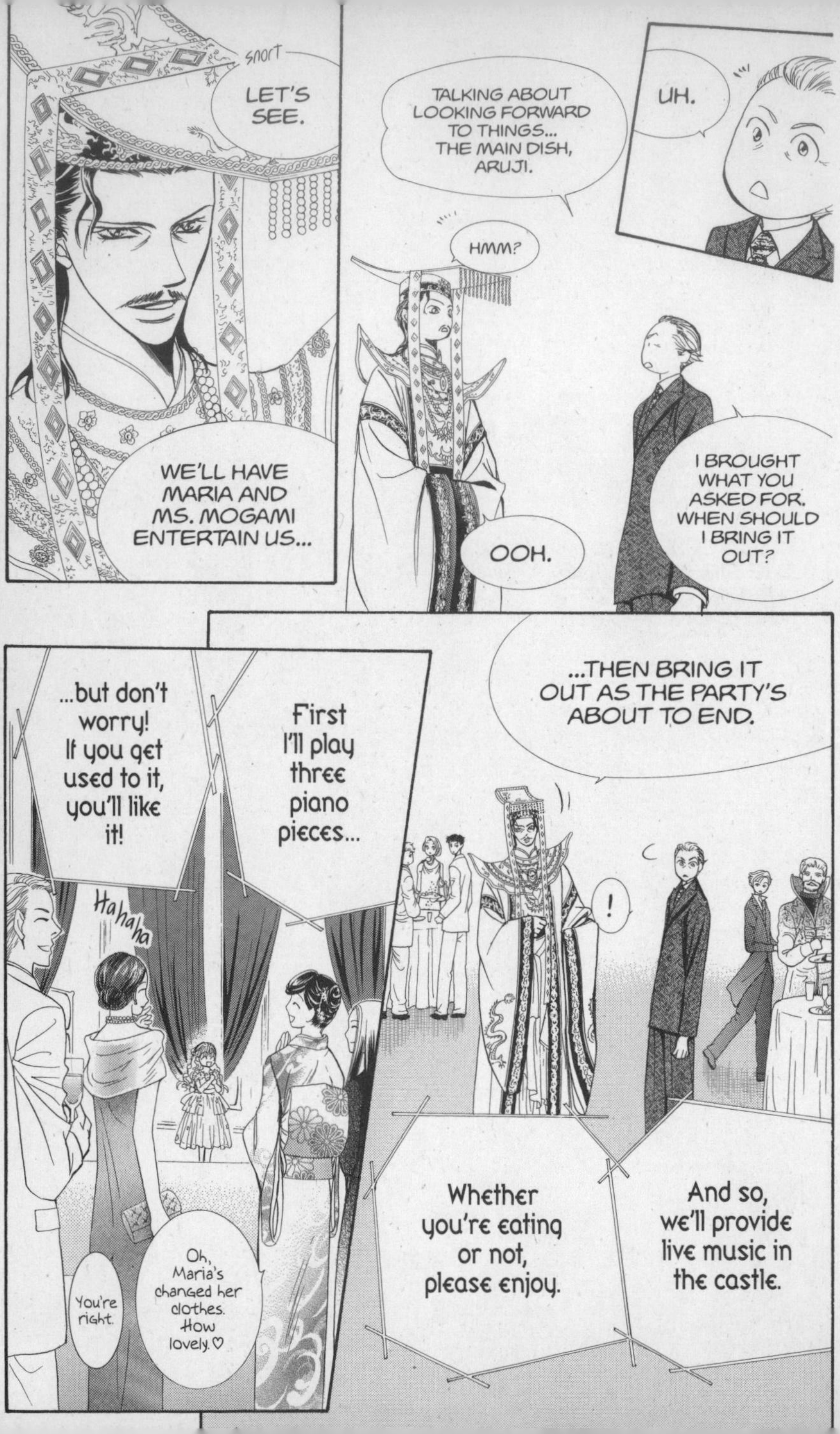
TALKING ABOUT LOOKING FORWARD TO THINGS... THE MAIN DISH, ARUJI.
UH.
HMM?
I BROUGHT WHAT YOU ASKED FOR. WHEN SHOULD I BRING IT OUT?
OOH.
snort
LET'S SEE.
WE'LL HAVE MARIA AND MS. MOGAMI ENTERTAIN US...
...THEN BRING IT OUT AS THE PARTY'S ABOUT TO END.
!
And so, we'll provide live music in the castle.
Whether you're eating or not, please enjoy.
First I'll play three piano pieces...
...but don't worry! If you get used to it, you'll like it!
Hahaha
Oh, Maria's changed her clothes. How lovely.♡
You're right.

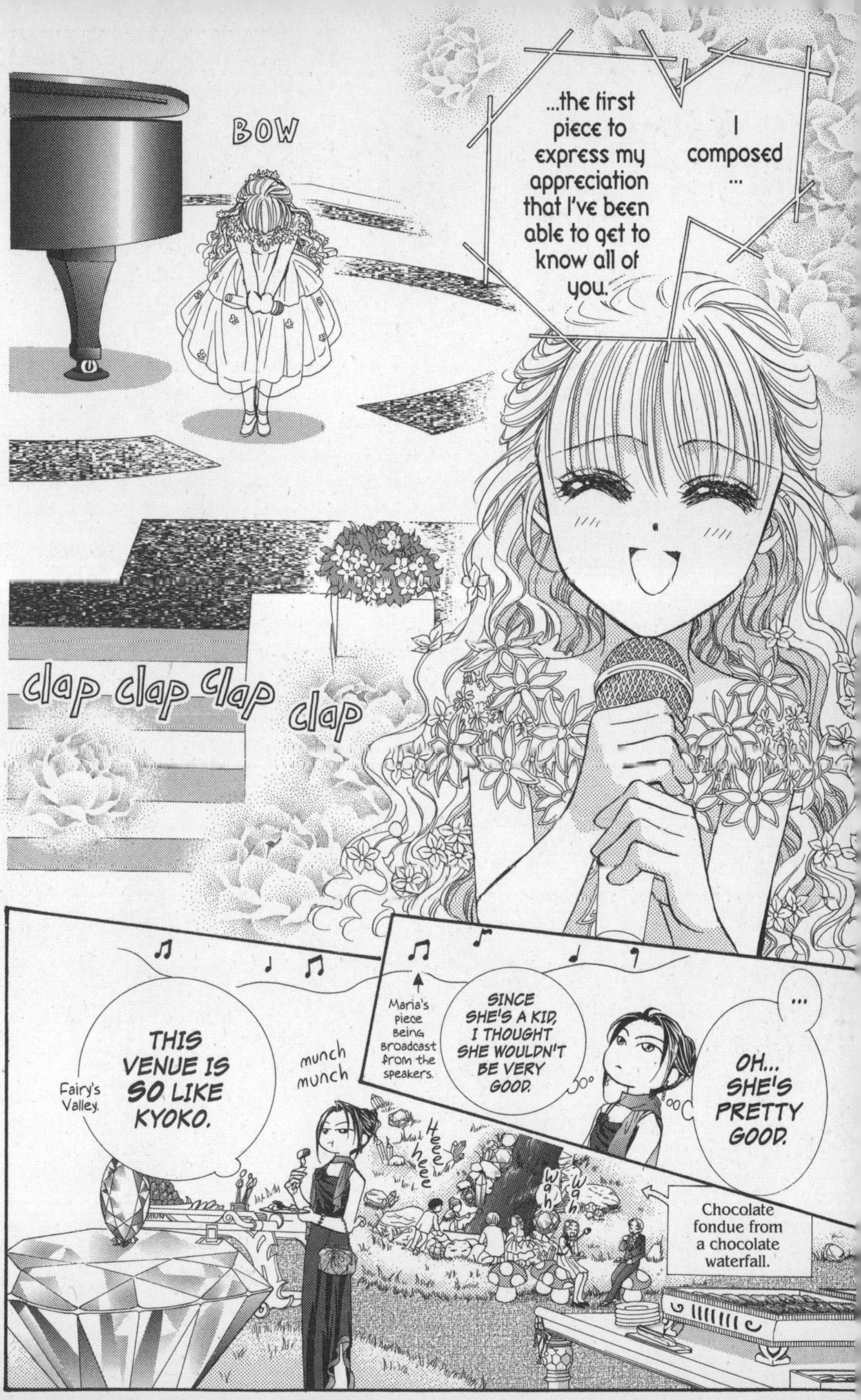
I composed ...
...the first piece to express my appreciation that I've been able to get to know all of you.
BOW
clap clap clap clap
...
OH... SHE'S PRETTY GOOD.
SINCE SHE'S A KID, I THOUGHT SHE WOULDN'T BE VERY GOOD.
Maria's piece Being Broadcast from the speakers.
Chocolate fondue from a chocolate waterfall.
Wah Wah
Heee heee
munch munch
THIS VENUE IS SO LIKE KYOKO.
Fairy's Valley.

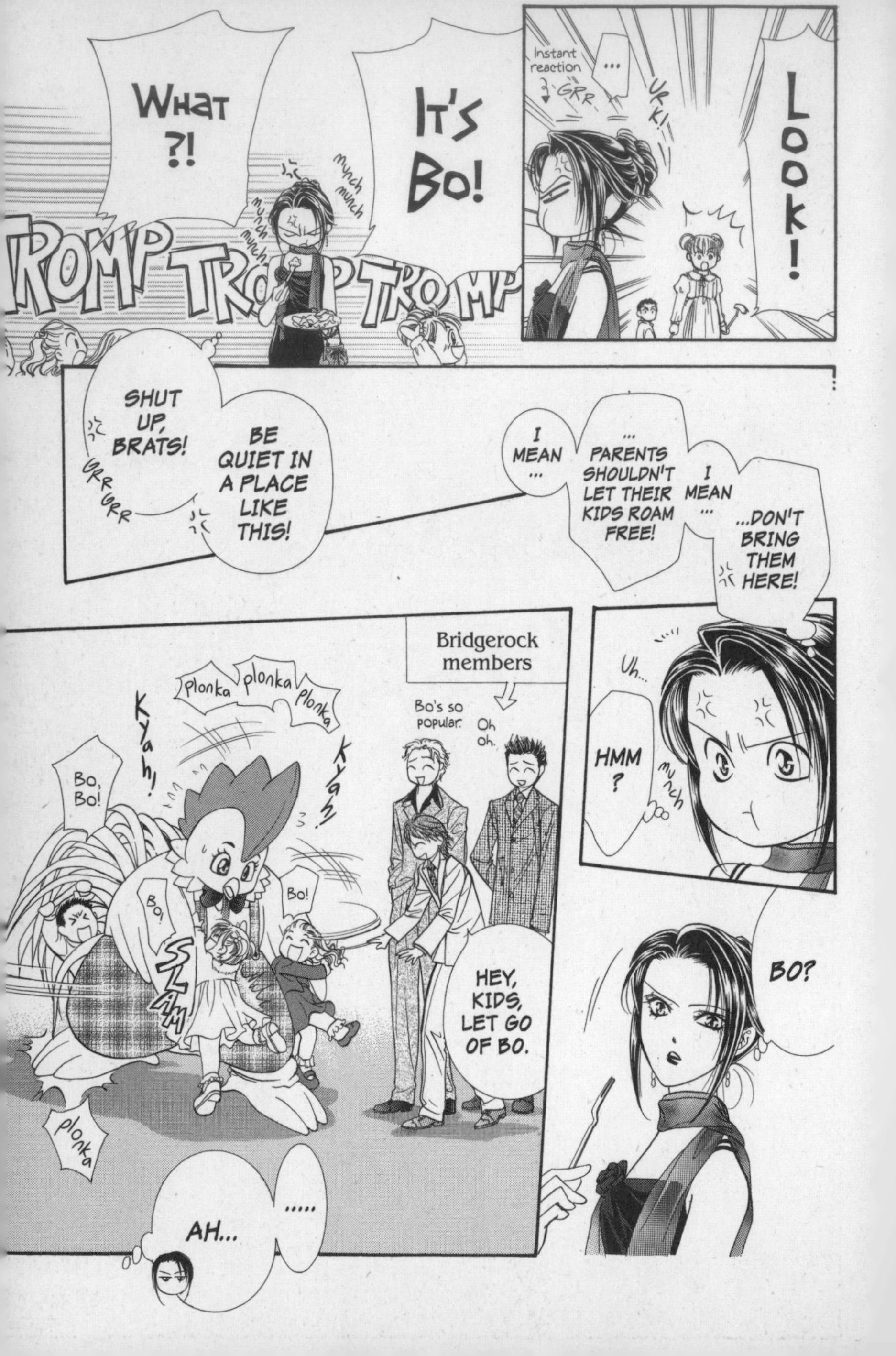

LOOK!
Instant reaction
GRR
...
URK!
IT'S BO!
WHAT?!
munch munch
munch munch
TROMP TROMP TROMP
...DON'T BRING THEM HERE!
I MEAN ...
... PARENTS SHOULDN'T LET THEIR KIDS ROAM FREE!
I MEAN ...
BE QUIET IN A PLACE LIKE THIS!
SHUT UP, BRATS!
GRR GRR
Uh...
HMM?
munch
BO?
Bridgerock members
Oh oh.
Bo's so popular.
plonka plonka plonka
Kyah!
Bo!
Kyah!
Bo, Bo!
Bo!
SLAM
HEY, KIDS, LET GO OF BO.
plonka
.....
AH...

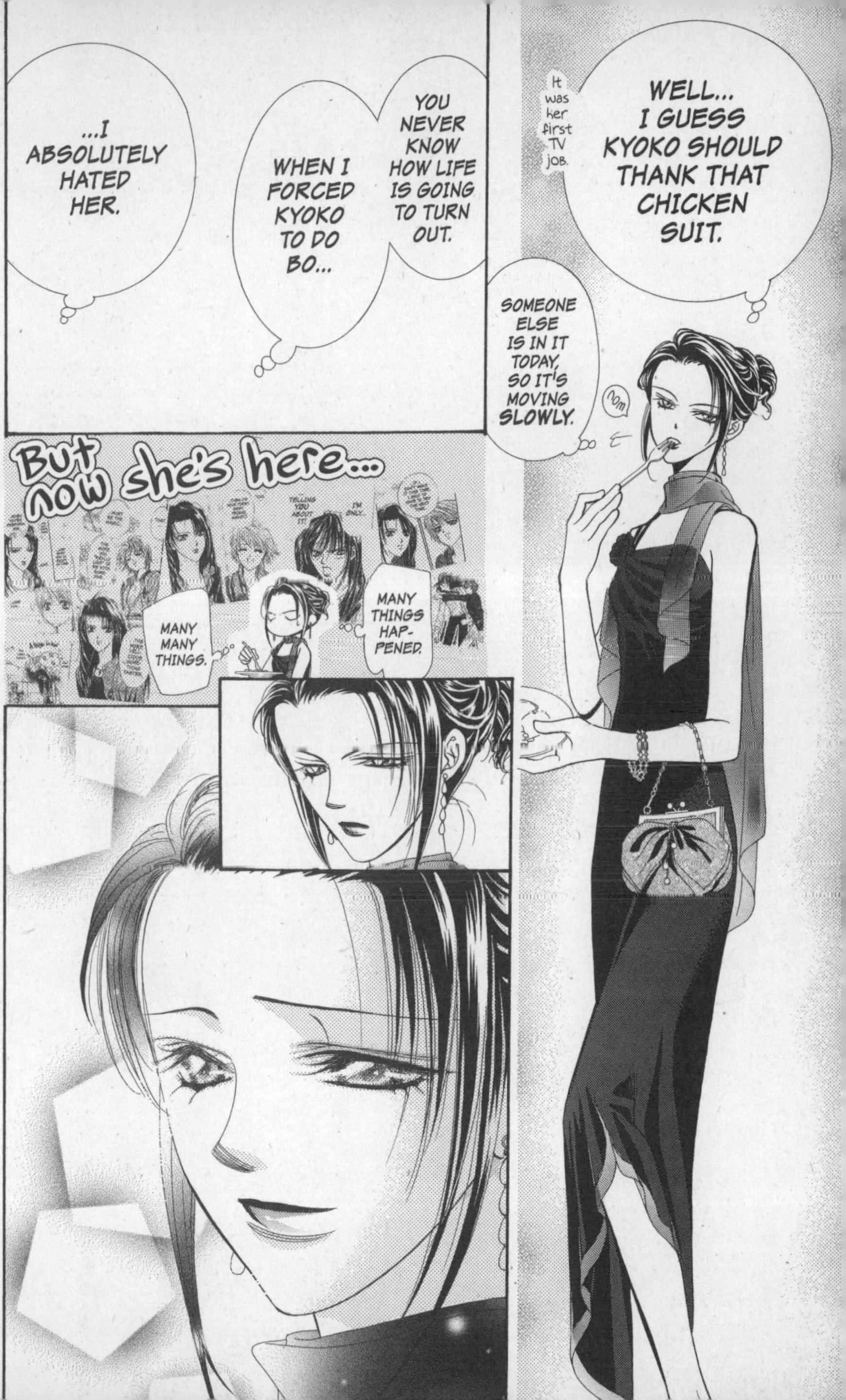
WELL... I GUESS KYOKO SHOULD THANK THAT CHICKEN SUIT.
It was her first TV job.
SOMEONE ELSE IS IN IT TODAY, SO IT'S MOVING SLOWLY.
nom
YOU NEVER KNOW HOW LIFE IS GOING TO TURN OUT.
WHEN I FORCED KYOKO TO DO BO...
...I ABSOLUTELY HATED HER.
But now she's here...
MANY THINGS HAP-PENED.
MANY MANY THINGS.

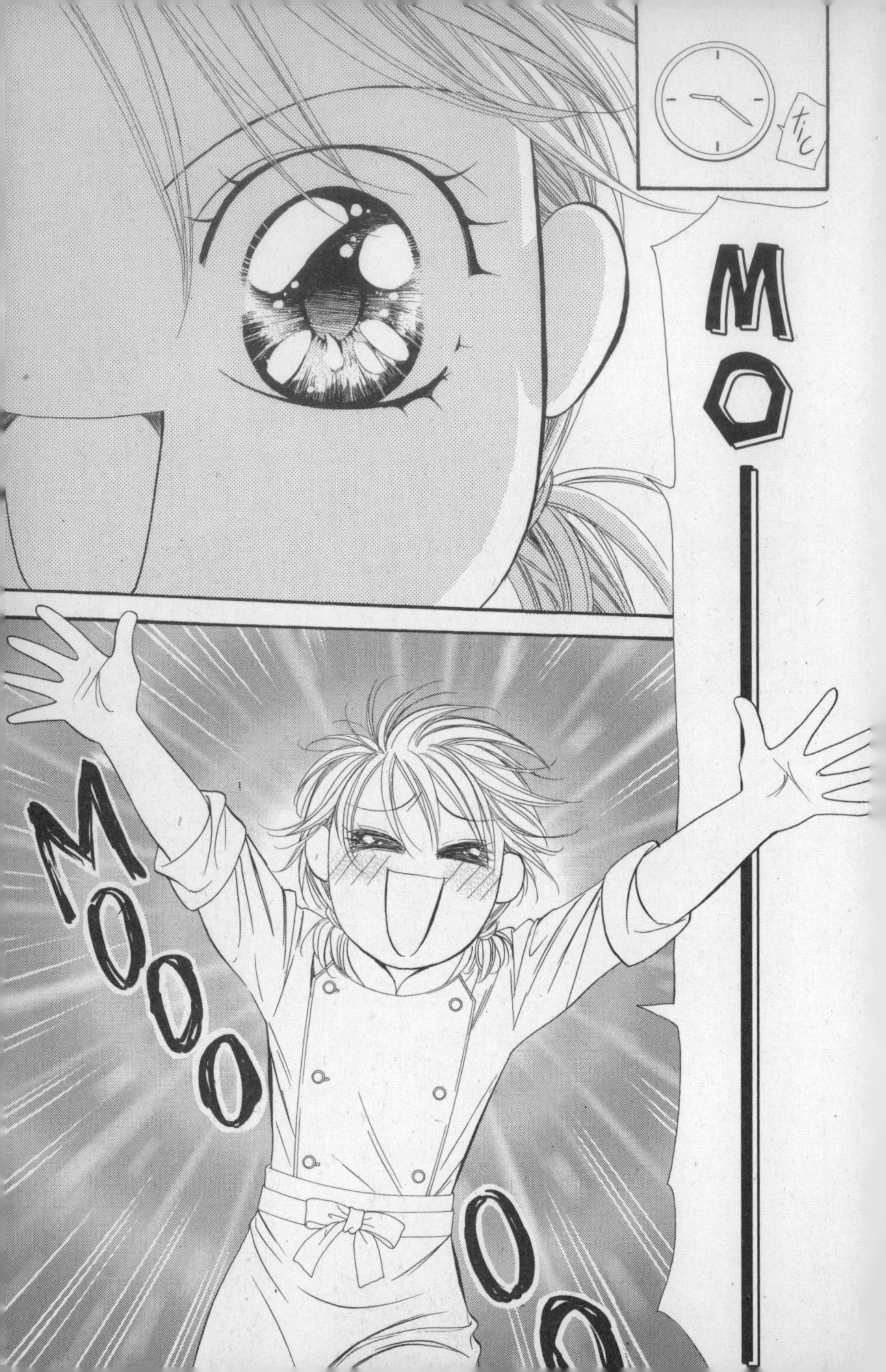
tic
MO—
MOOOO
OO

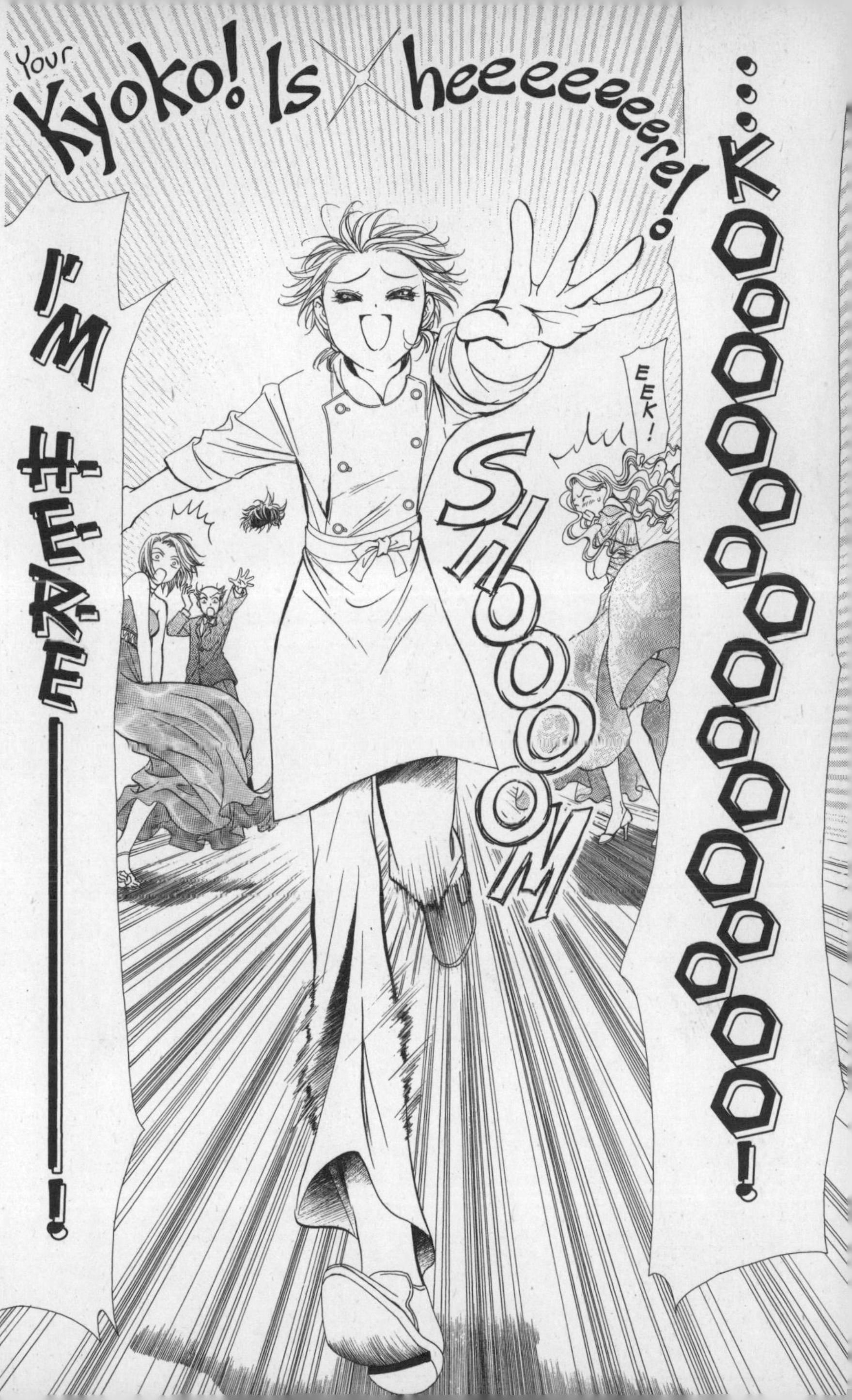
...KOOOOOOOOOOOOOOOO!
Your Kyoko! Is heeeeeeeere!
EEK!
SHOOOOOM
I'M H-E-R-E———!

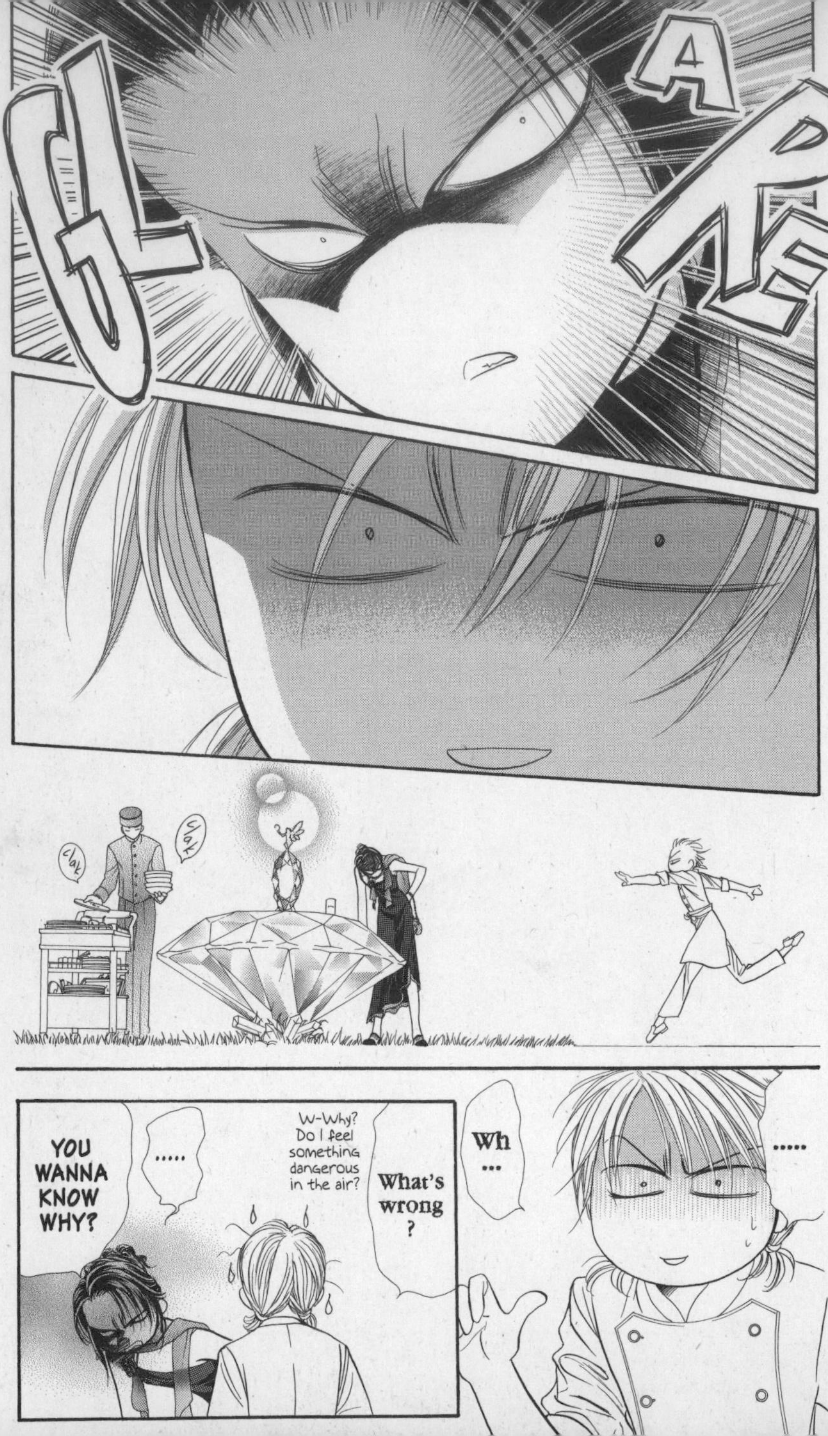
GLARE
clak
clak
.....
Wh ...
What's wrong ?
W-Why? Do I feel something dangerous in the air?
.....
YOU WANNA KNOW WHY?

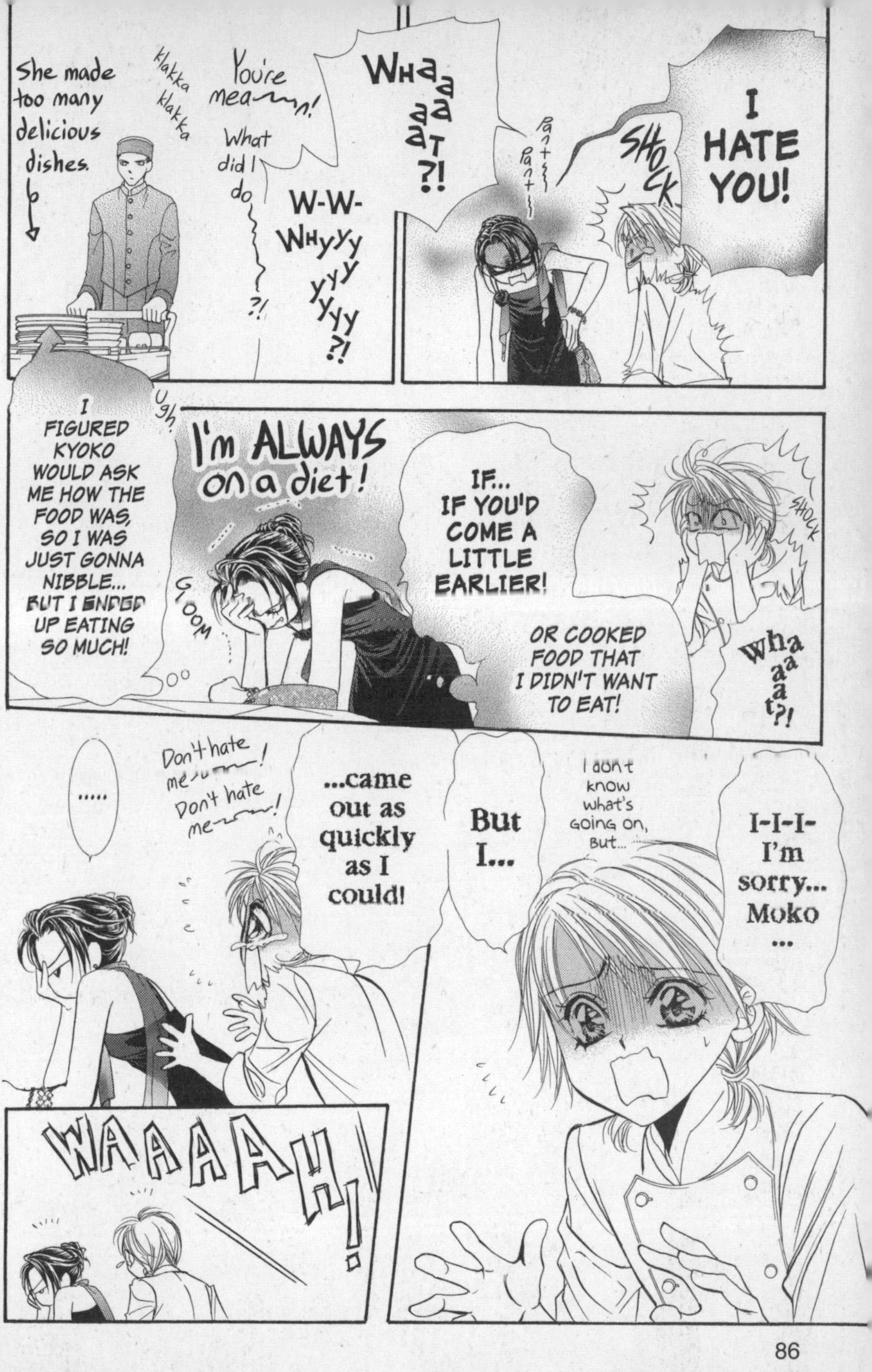
I HATE YOU!
SHOCK
Pant pant
WHAaaaaT?!
You're meaaan!
What did I do?!
W-W-WHYyyyyyyyy?!
klakka klakka
She made too many delicious dishes.
IF... IF YOU'D COME A LITTLE EARLIER!
OR COOKED FOOD THAT I DIDN'T WANT TO EAT!
SHOCK
Whaaaat?!
I'm ALWAYS on a diet!
GLOOM
I FIGURED KYOKO WOULD ASK ME HOW THE FOOD WAS, SO I WAS JUST GONNA NIBBLE... BUT I ENDED UP EATING SO MUCH!
Ugh
I-I-I-I'm sorry... Moko...
I don't know what's going on, but...
But I...
...came out as quickly as I could!
Don't hate meee! Don't hate meee!
.....
WAAAAH!

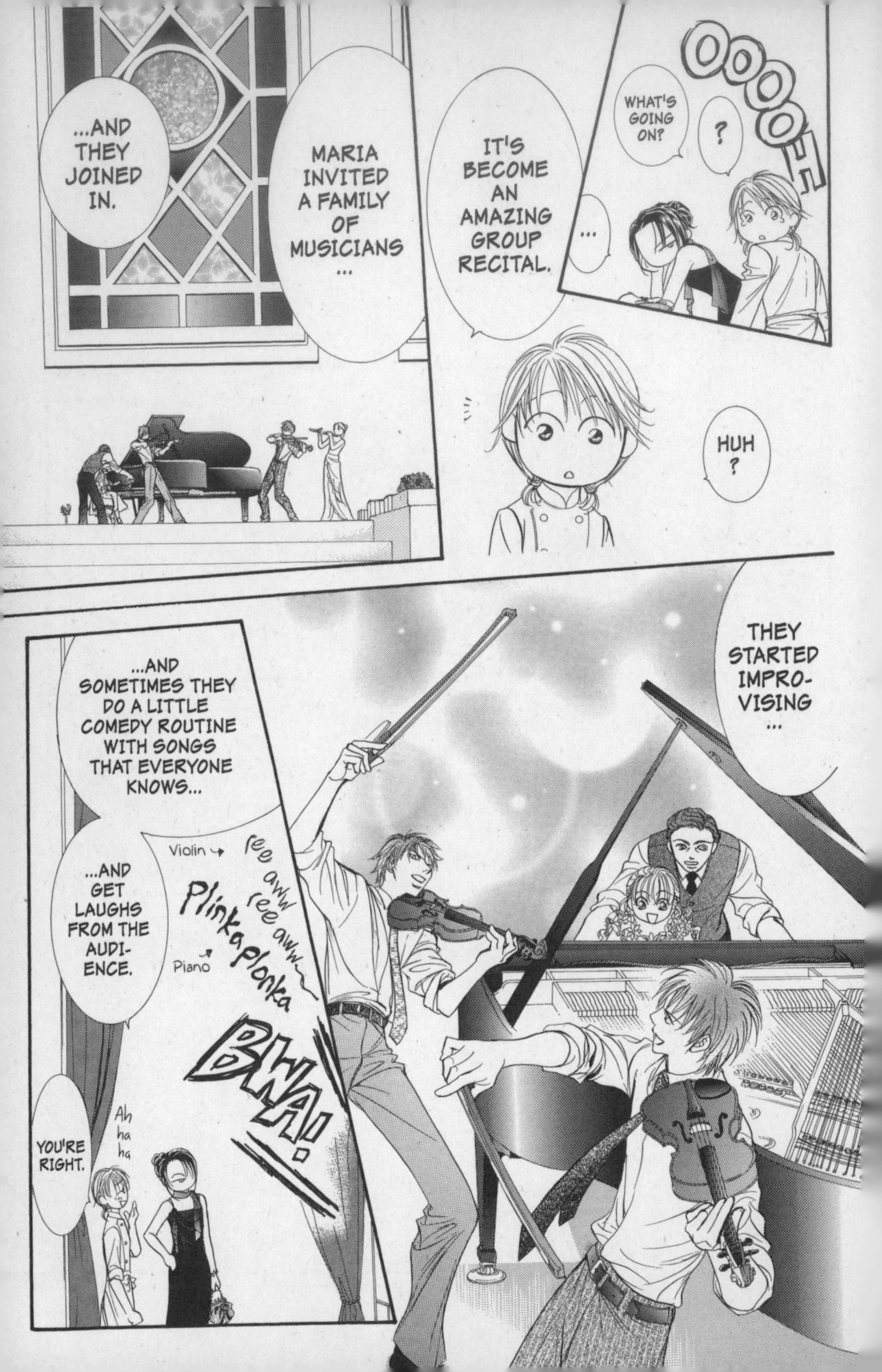
OOOO
?
WHAT'S GOING ON?
...
HUH?
IT'S BECOME AN AMAZING GROUP RECITAL.
MARIA INVITED A FAMILY OF MUSICIANS...
...AND THEY JOINED IN.
THEY STARTED IMPRO-VISING...
...AND SOMETIMES THEY DO A LITTLE COMEDY ROUTINE WITH SONGS THAT EVERYONE KNOWS...
Violin
ree aww ree aww
Plinka plonka
Piano
...AND GET LAUGHS FROM THE AUDI-ENCE.
BWAA!
Ah ha ha
YOU'RE RIGHT.

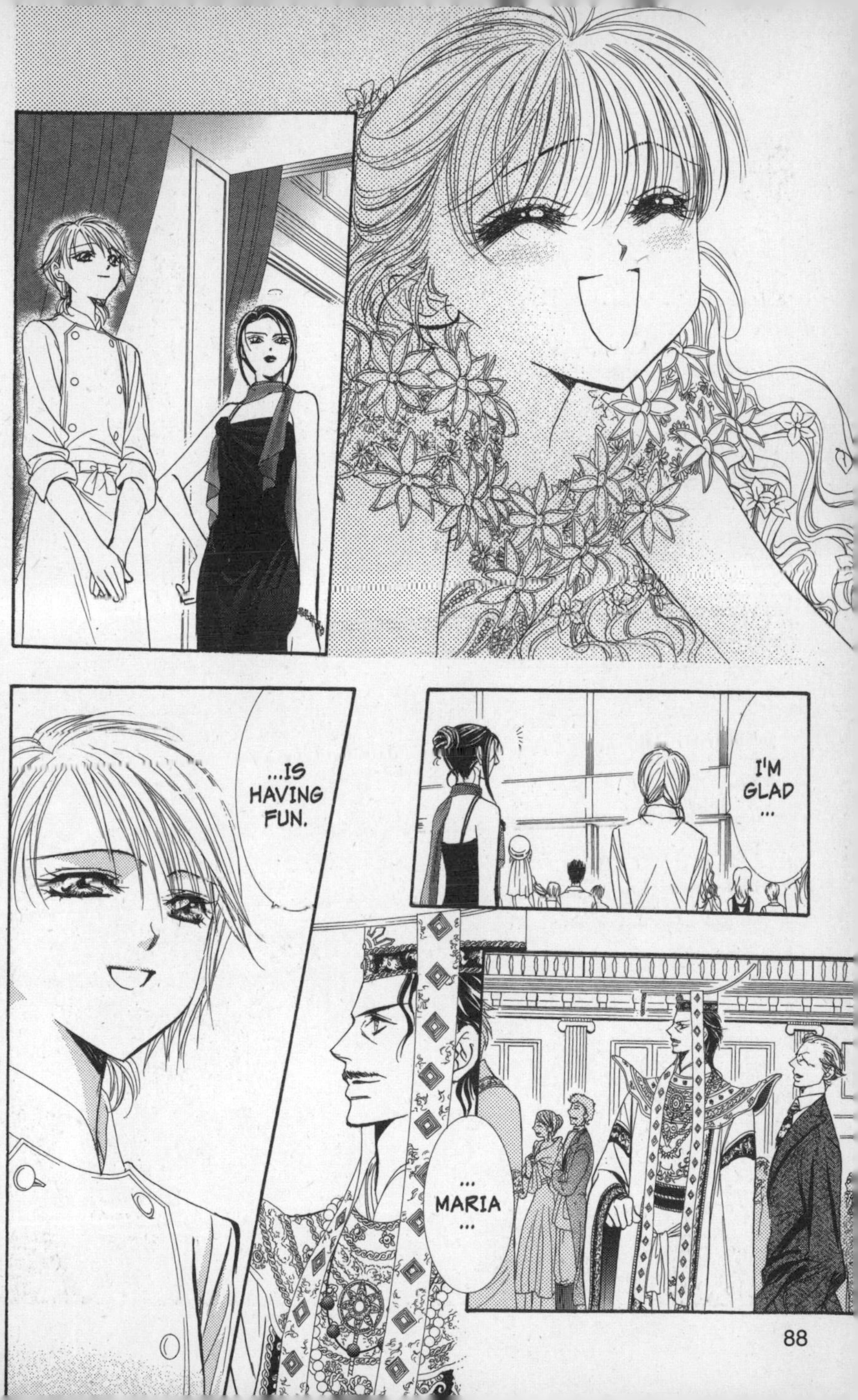
I'M GLAD ...
... MARIA ...
...IS HAVING FUN.

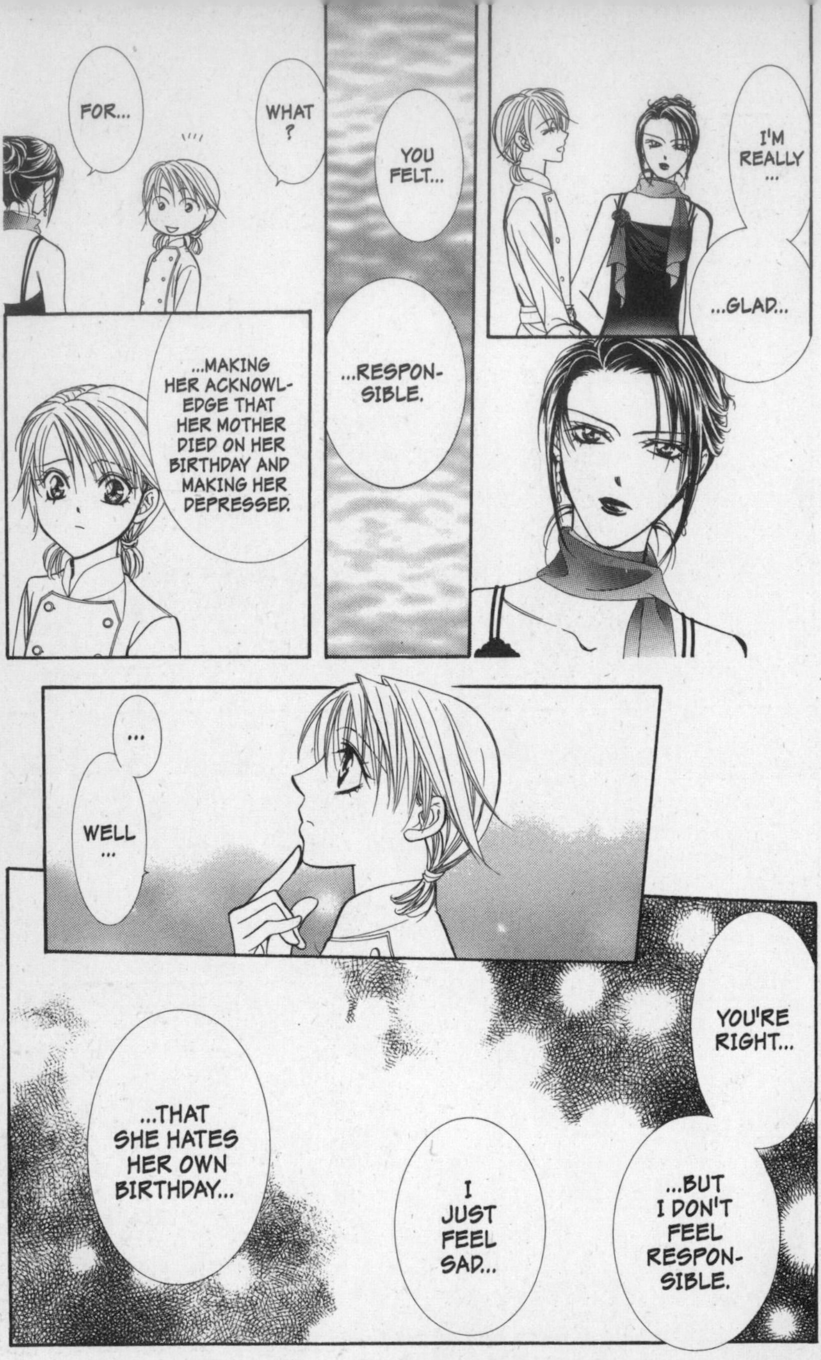
I'M REALLY...
...GLAD...
YOU FELT...
...RESPON-SIBLE.
WHAT?
FOR...
...MAKING HER ACKNOWL-EDGE THAT HER MOTHER DIED ON HER BIRTHDAY AND MAKING HER DEPRESSED.
...
WELL...
YOU'RE RIGHT...
...BUT I DON'T FEEL RESPON-SIBLE.
I JUST FEEL SAD...
...THAT SHE HATES HER OWN BIRTHDAY...

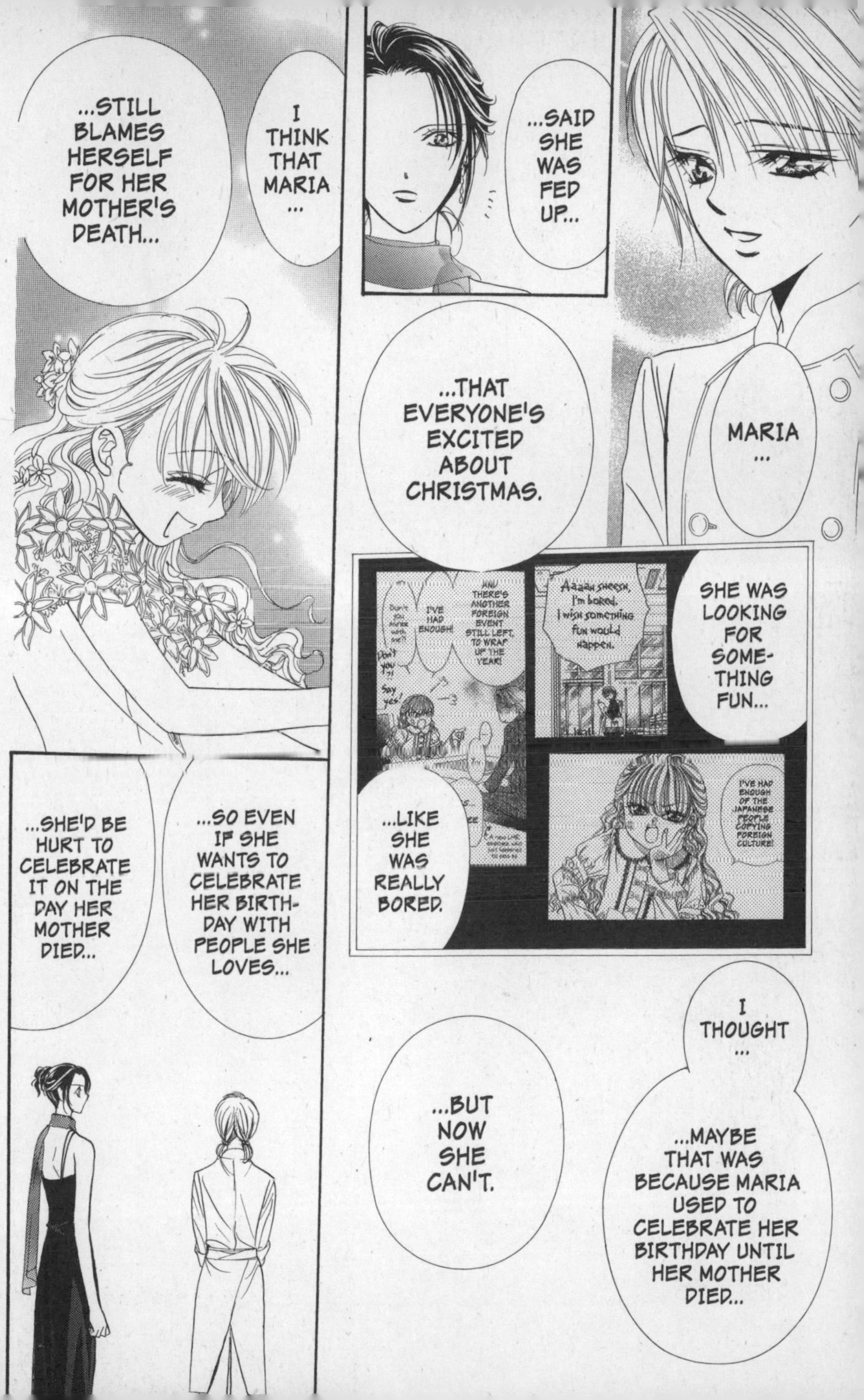
MARIA...
...SAID SHE WAS FED UP...
...THAT EVERYONE'S EXCITED ABOUT CHRISTMAS.
SHE WAS LOOKING FOR SOME-THING FUN...
Aaaah sheesh, I'm bored. I wish something fun would happen.
I'VE HAD ENOUGH OF THE JAPANESE PEOPLE COPYING FOREIGN CULTURE!
AND THERE'S ANOTHER FOREIGN EVENT STILL LEFT, TO WRAP UP THE YEAR!
I'VE HAD ENOUGH!
Don't you ?!
Say yes!
...LIKE SHE WAS REALLY BORED.
I THOUGHT...
...MAYBE THAT WAS BECAUSE MARIA USED TO CELEBRATE HER BIRTHDAY UNTIL HER MOTHER DIED...
...BUT NOW SHE CAN'T.
I THINK THAT MARIA...
...STILL BLAMES HERSELF FOR HER MOTHER'S DEATH...
...SO EVEN IF SHE WANTS TO CELEBRATE HER BIRTH-DAY WITH PEOPLE SHE LOVES...
...SHE'D BE HURT TO CELEBRATE IT ON THE DAY HER MOTHER DIED...

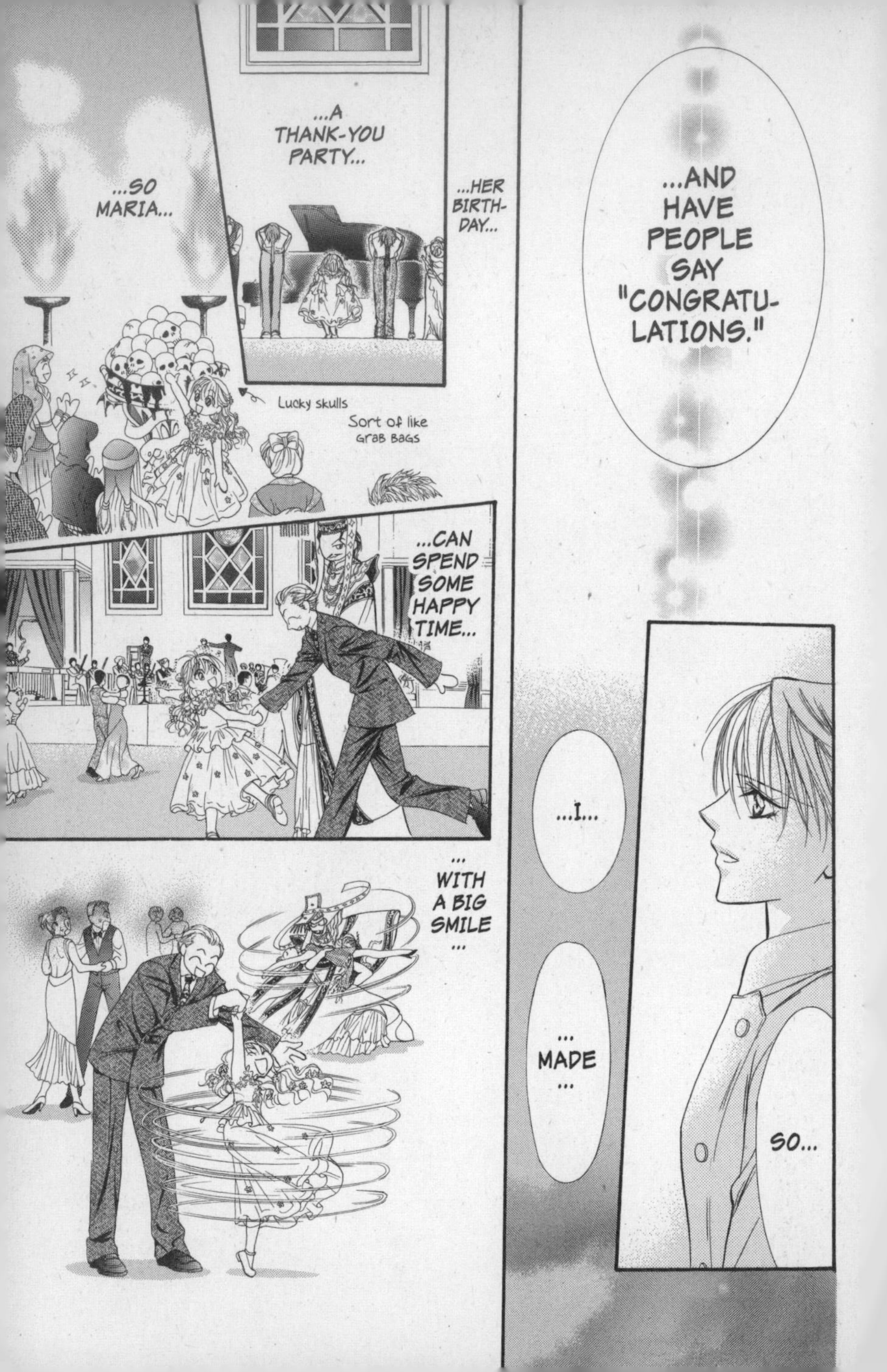
...AND HAVE PEOPLE SAY "CONGRATULATIONS."
...I...
...MADE...
SO...
...HER BIRTHDAY...
...A THANK-YOU PARTY...
...SO MARIA...
Lucky skulls
Sort of like Grab Bags
...CAN SPEND SOME HAPPY TIME...
...WITH A BIG SMILE...

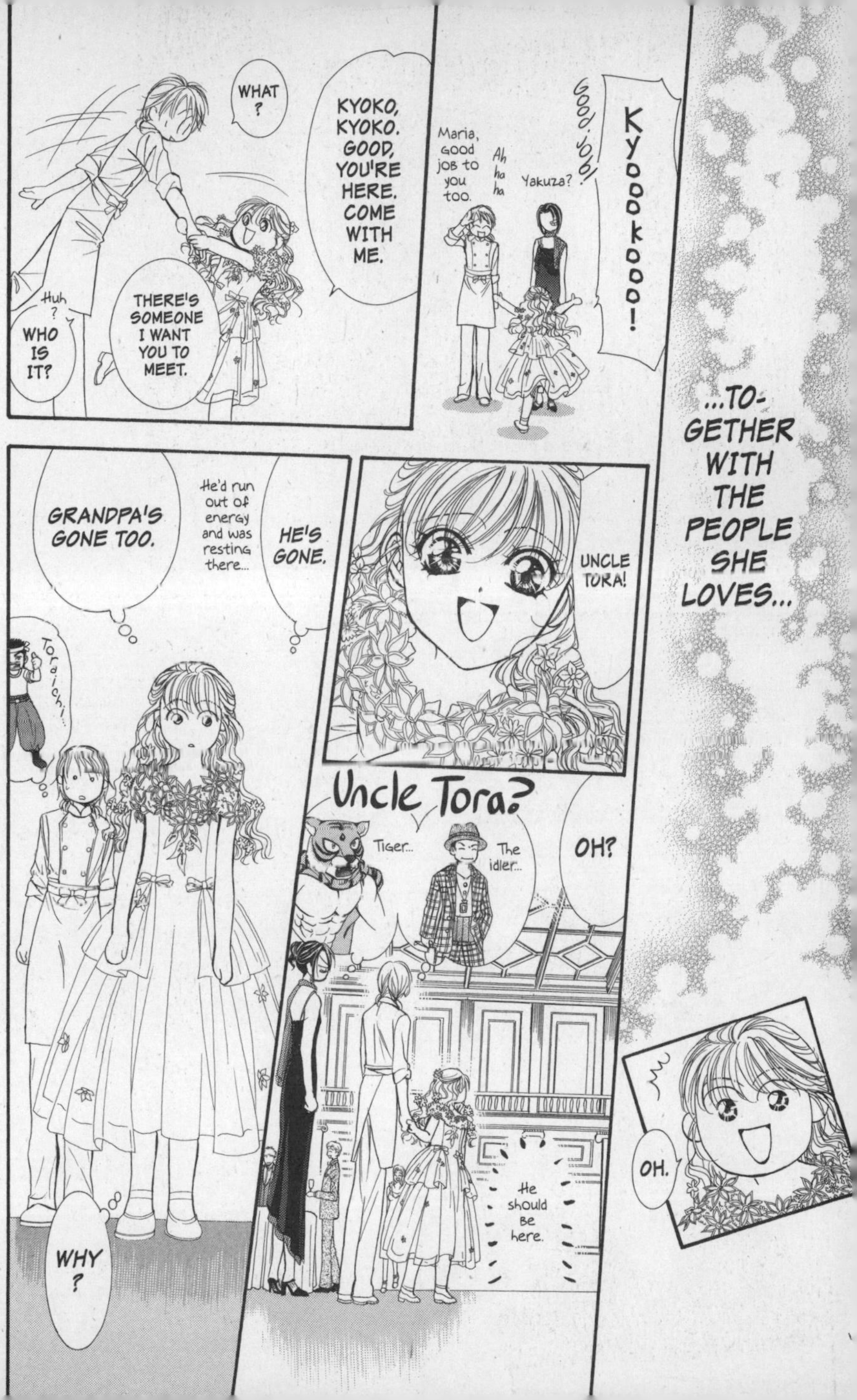

...TO-GETHER WITH THE PEOPLE SHE LOVES...
KYOOOKOOOO!
Good job!
Yakuza?
Ah ha ha
Maria, good job to you too.
KYOKO, KYOKO. GOOD, YOU'RE HERE. COME WITH ME.
WHAT?
THERE'S SOMEONE I WANT YOU TO MEET.
Huh?
WHO IS IT?
UNCLE TORA!
OH?
Uncle Tora?
The idler...
Tiger...
He should be here.
OH.
HE'S GONE.
He'd run out of energy and was resting there...
GRANDPA'S GONE TOO.
Toraichi...
WHY?

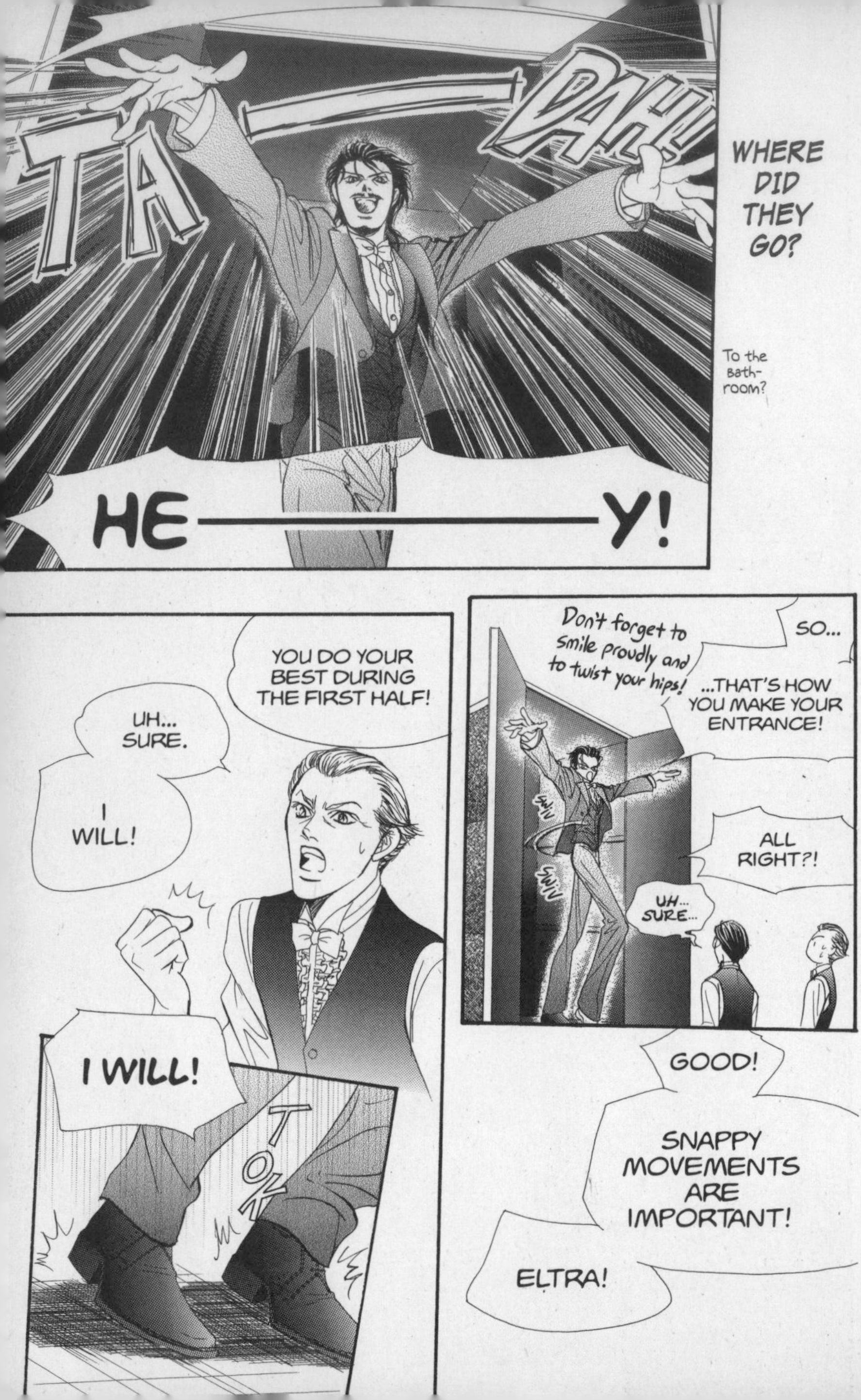
TA—DAH!
HE—Y!
WHERE DID THEY GO?
To the bathroom?
SO...
...THAT'S HOW YOU MAKE YOUR ENTRANCE!
Don't forget to smile proudly and to twist your hips!
ALL RIGHT?!
SWIV
SWIV
UH... SURE...
GOOD!
SNAPPY MOVEMENTS ARE IMPORTANT!
ELTRA!
YOU DO YOUR BEST DURING THE FIRST HALF!
UH... SURE.
I WILL!
I WILL!
TOK

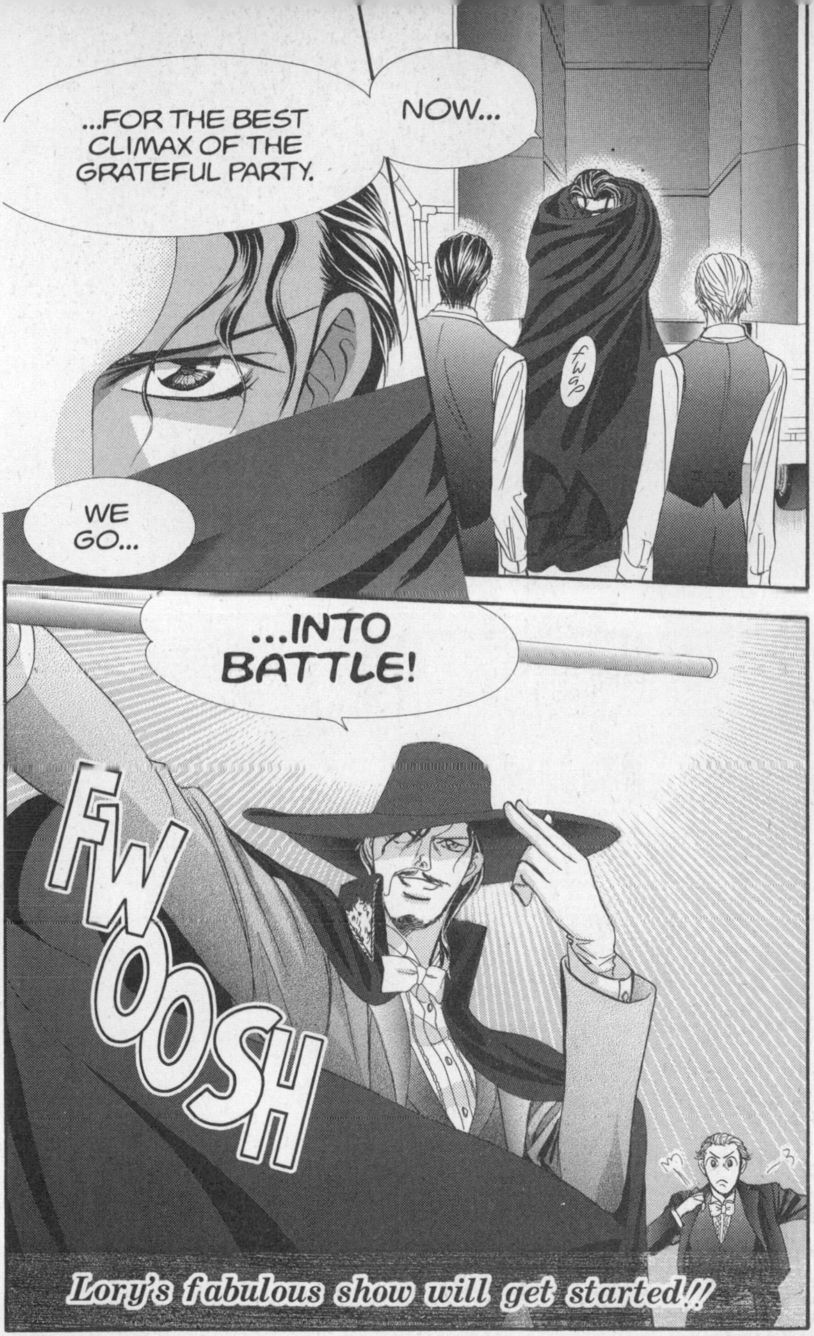
NOW...
...FOR THE BEST CLIMAX OF THE GRATEFUL PARTY.
fwsp
WE GO...
...INTO BATTLE!
FWOOSH
Lory's fabulous show will get started!!

End of Act 117

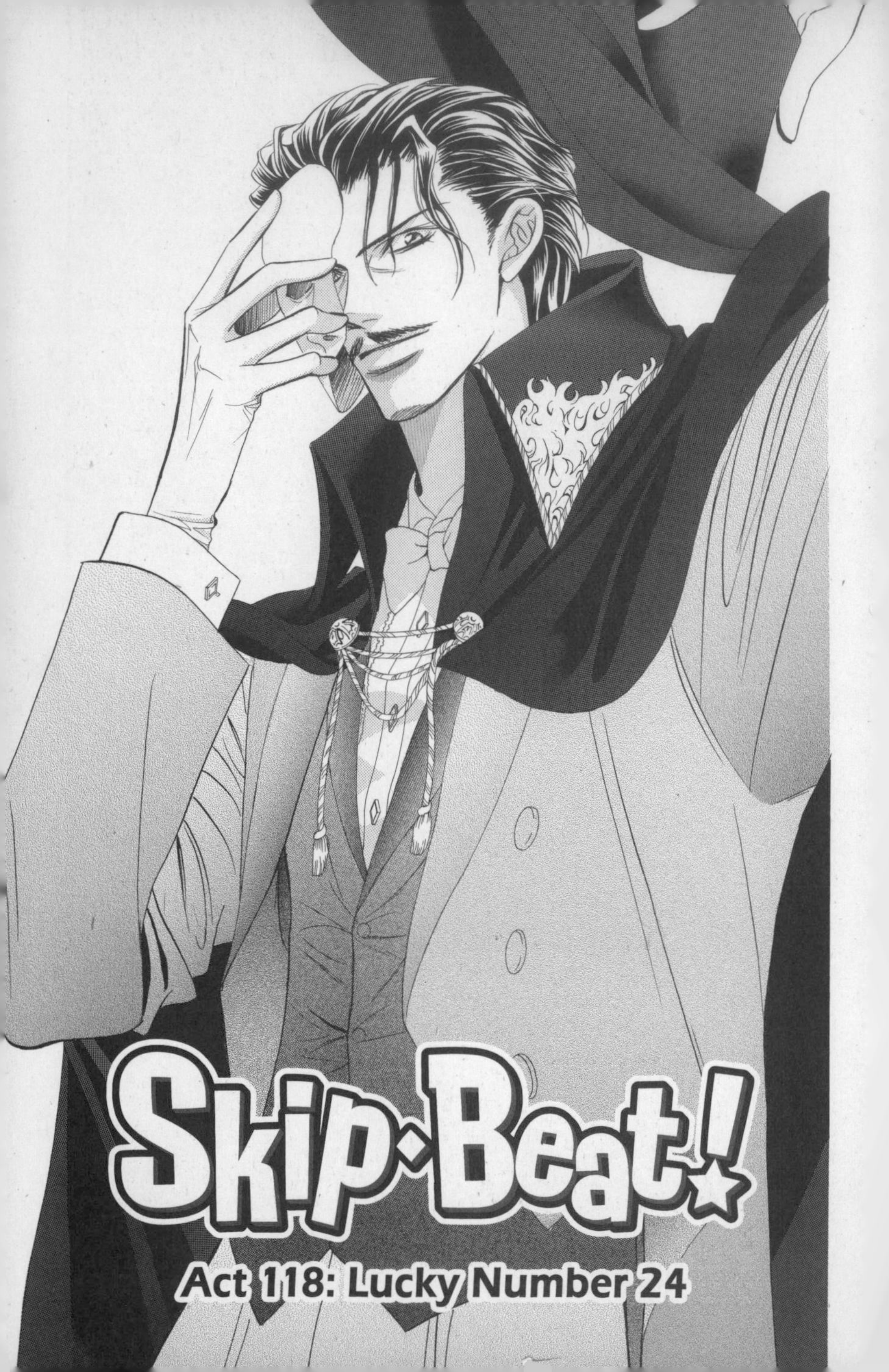
Skip·Beat!
Act 118: Lucky Number 24

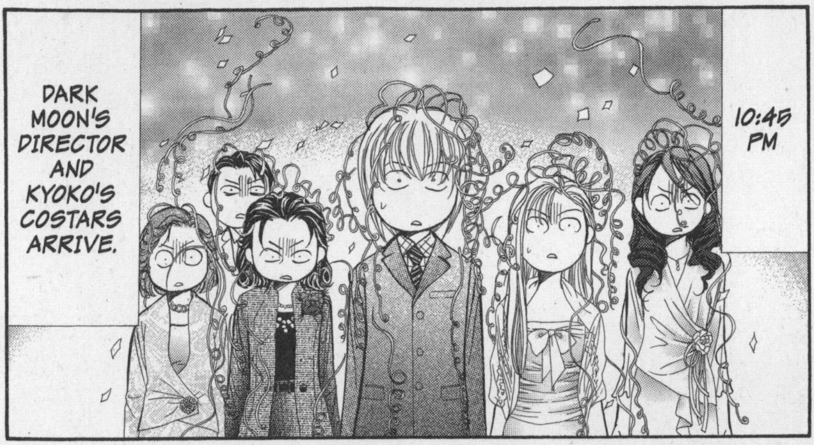
10:45 PM
DARK MOON'S DIRECTOR AND KYOKO'S COSTARS ARRIVE.
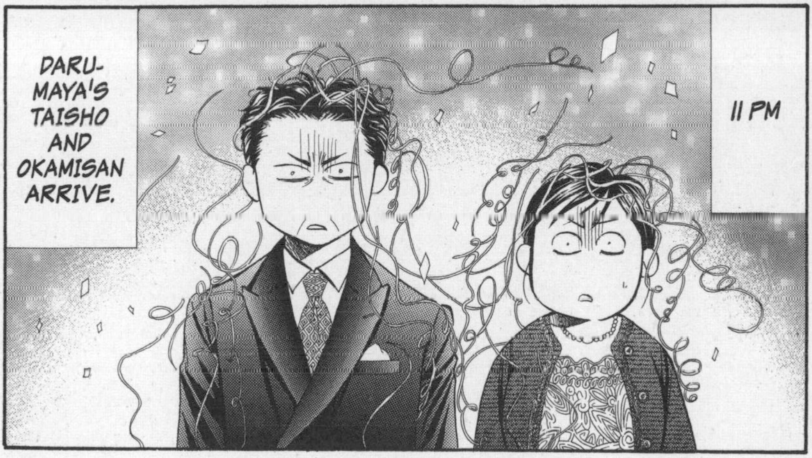
11 PM
DARU-MAYA'S TAISHO AND OKAMISAN ARRIVE.
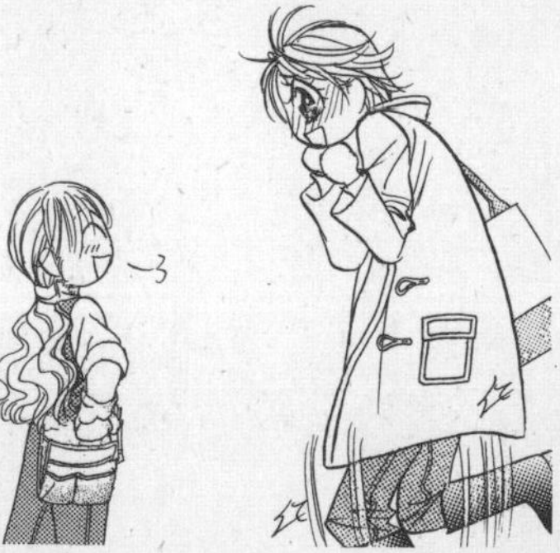

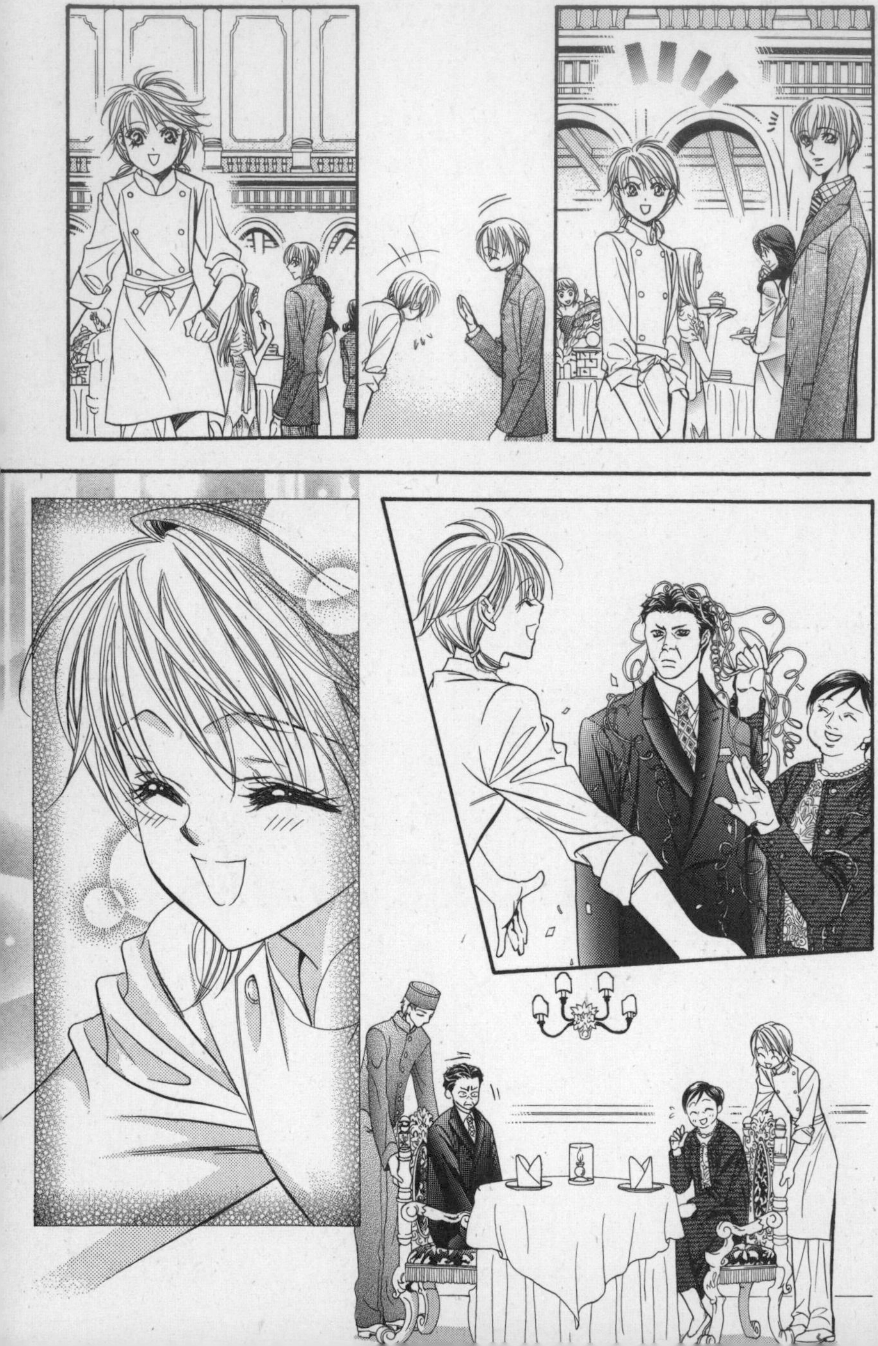

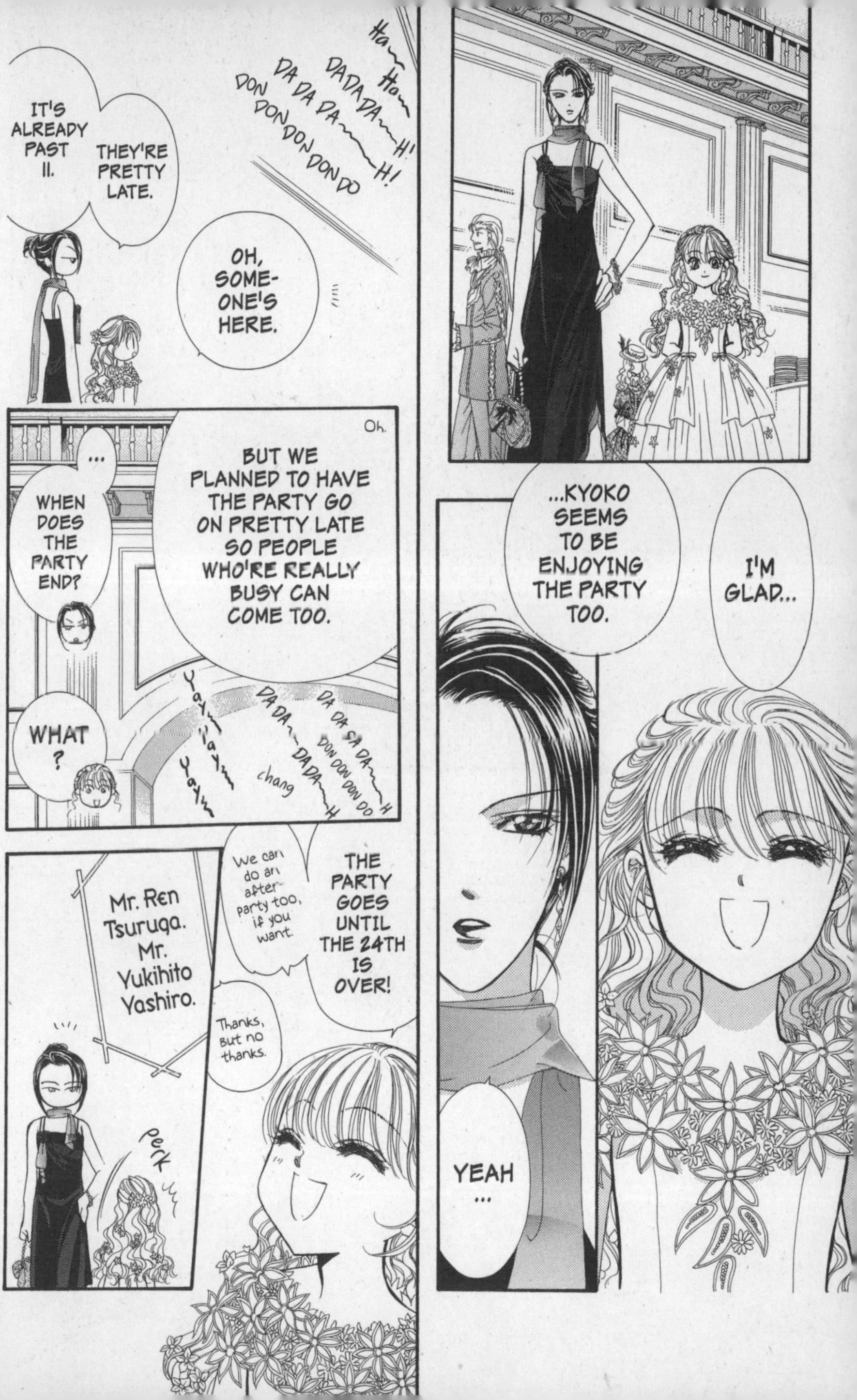
IT'S ALREADY PAST 11.
THEY'RE PRETTY LATE.
Ha~ Ha~ DADADA~H! DA DA DA~H! DON DON DON DON DO
OH, SOME-ONE'S HERE.
...KYOKO SEEMS TO BE ENJOYING THE PARTY TOO.
I'M GLAD...
YEAH ...
Oh.
BUT WE PLANNED TO HAVE THE PARTY GO ON PRETTY LATE SO PEOPLE WHO'RE REALLY BUSY CAN COME TOO.
...
WHEN DOES THE PARTY END?
WHAT ?
DA DA SA DA~H DON DON DON DO
DA DA~ DADA~H
Yay~ Yay~ Yay~
chang
THE PARTY GOES UNTIL THE 24TH IS OVER!
We can do an after-party too, if you want.
Mr. Ren Tsuruga. Mr. Yukihito Yashiro.
Thanks, but no thanks.
perk

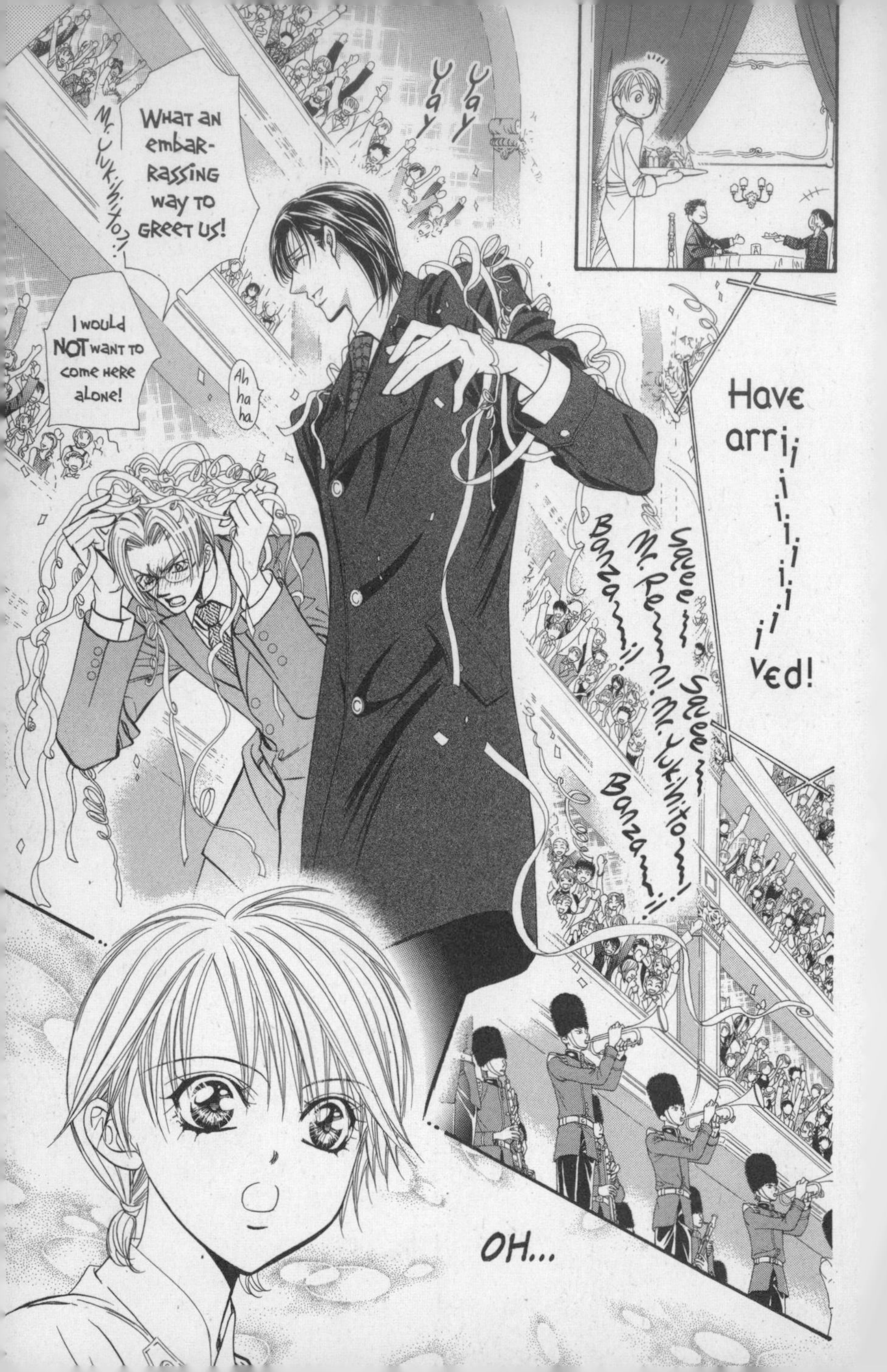
Have arriiiiiiiiived!
Sqeee~ Sqeee~
Mr. Ren~!! Mr. Yukihito~!
Banza~i!! Banza~i!!
Yay Yay
Mr. Yukihito?!
What an embarrassing way to greet us!
Ah ha ha.
I would NOT want to come here alone!
...
...
OH...

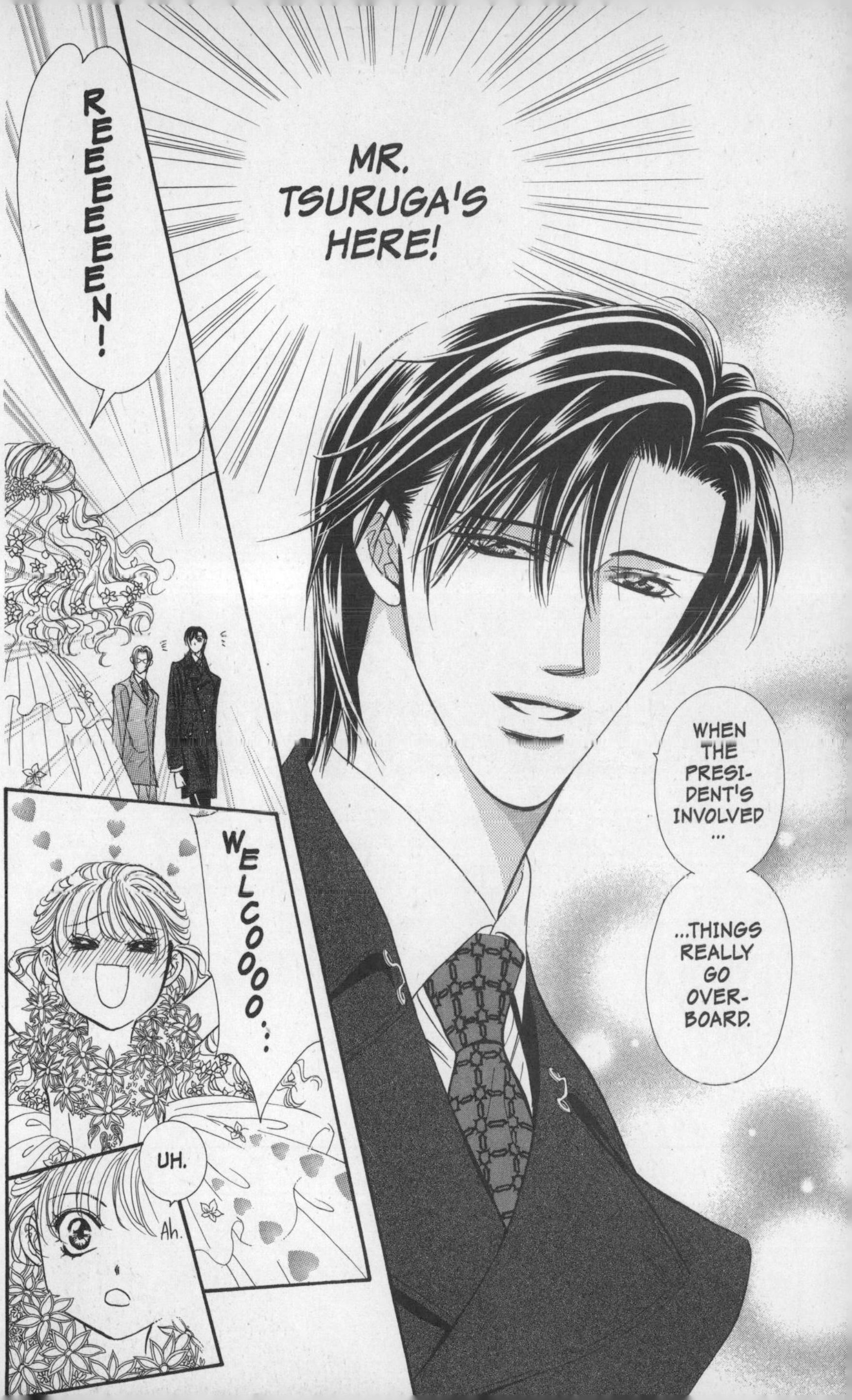
MR. TSURUGA'S HERE!
WHEN THE PRESIDENT'S INVOLVED...
...THINGS REALLY GO OVERBOARD.
REEEEEEEN!
WELCOOOOO...
UH.
Ah.

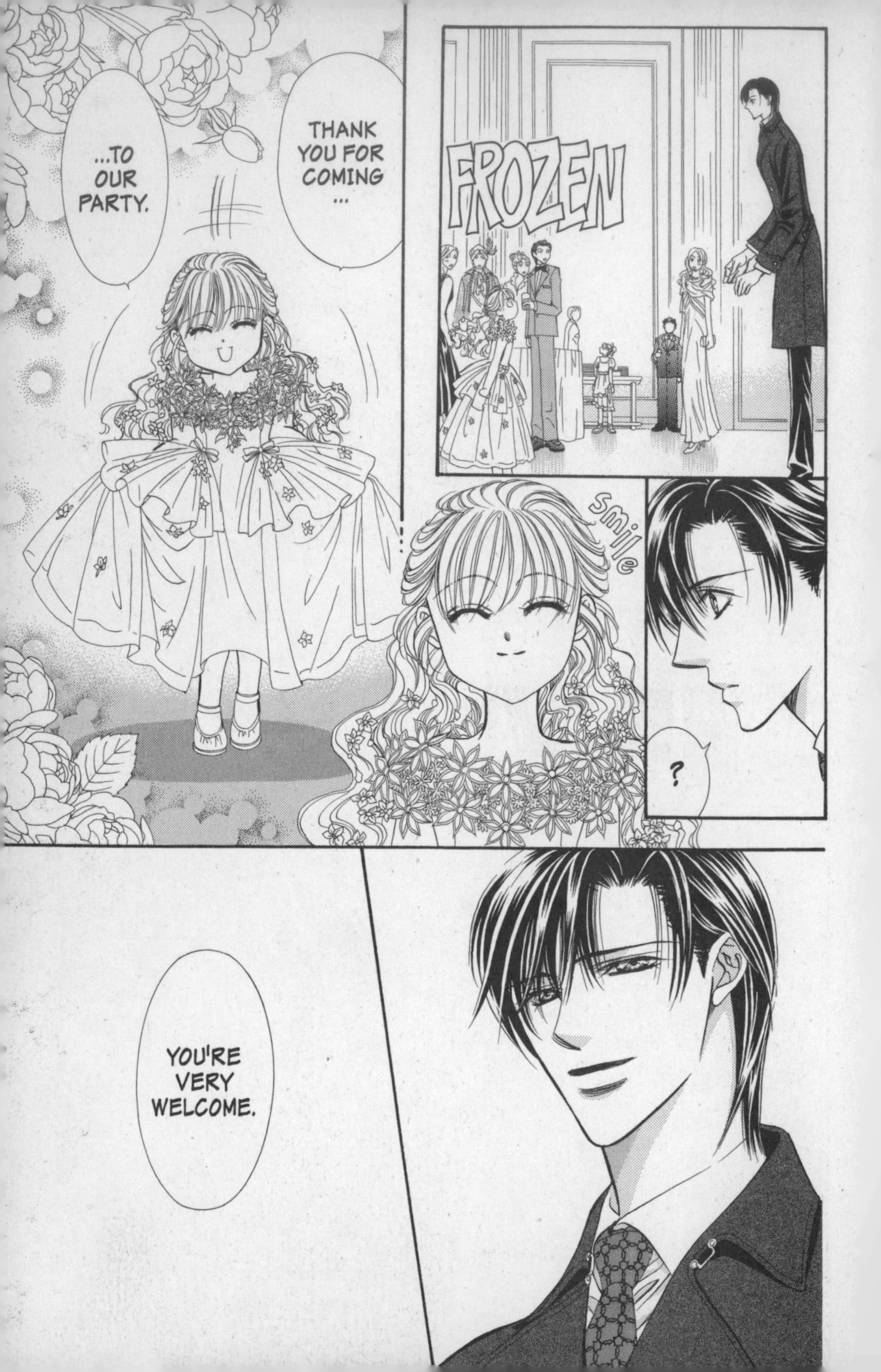
FROZEN
?
smile
THANK YOU FOR COMING ...
...TO OUR PARTY.
YOU'RE VERY WELCOME.

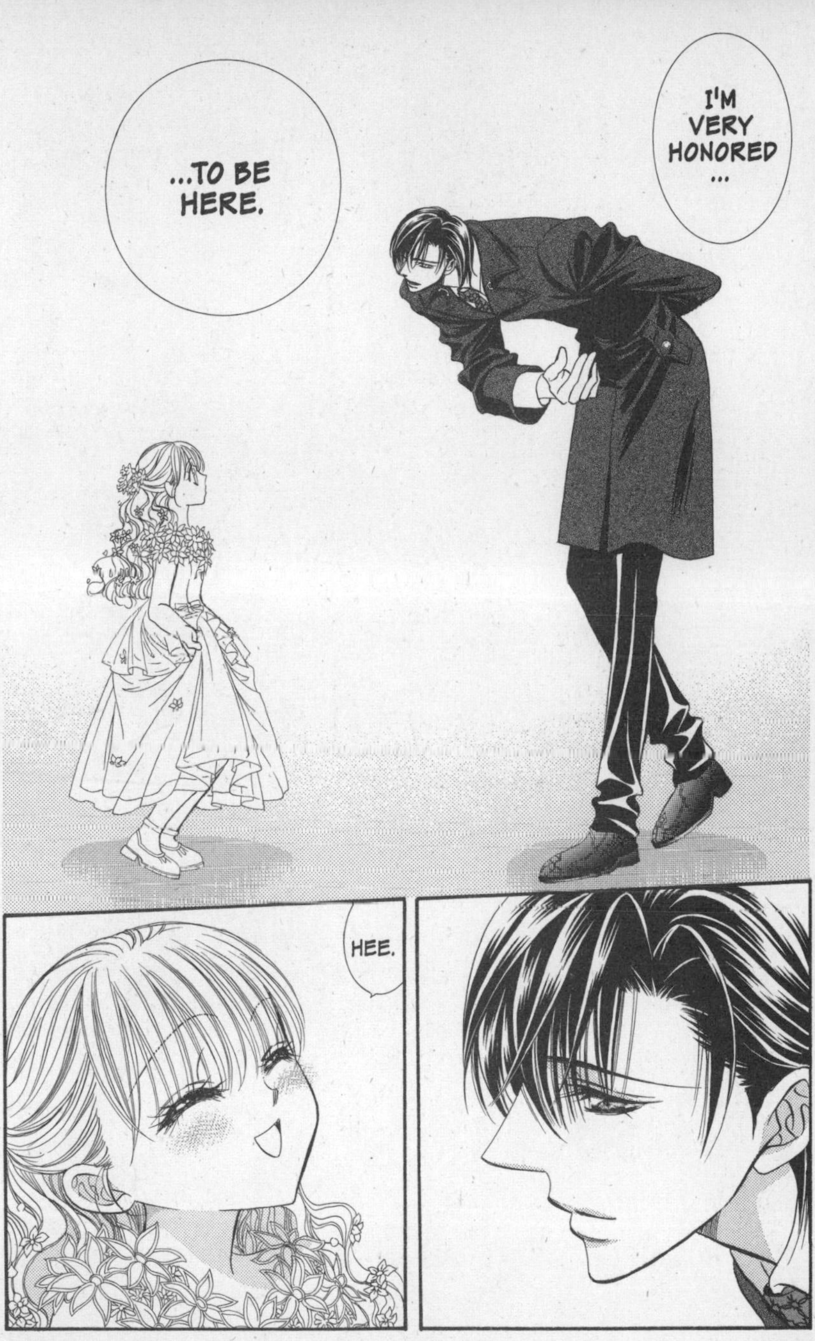
I'M VERY HONORED ...
...TO BE HERE.
HEE.

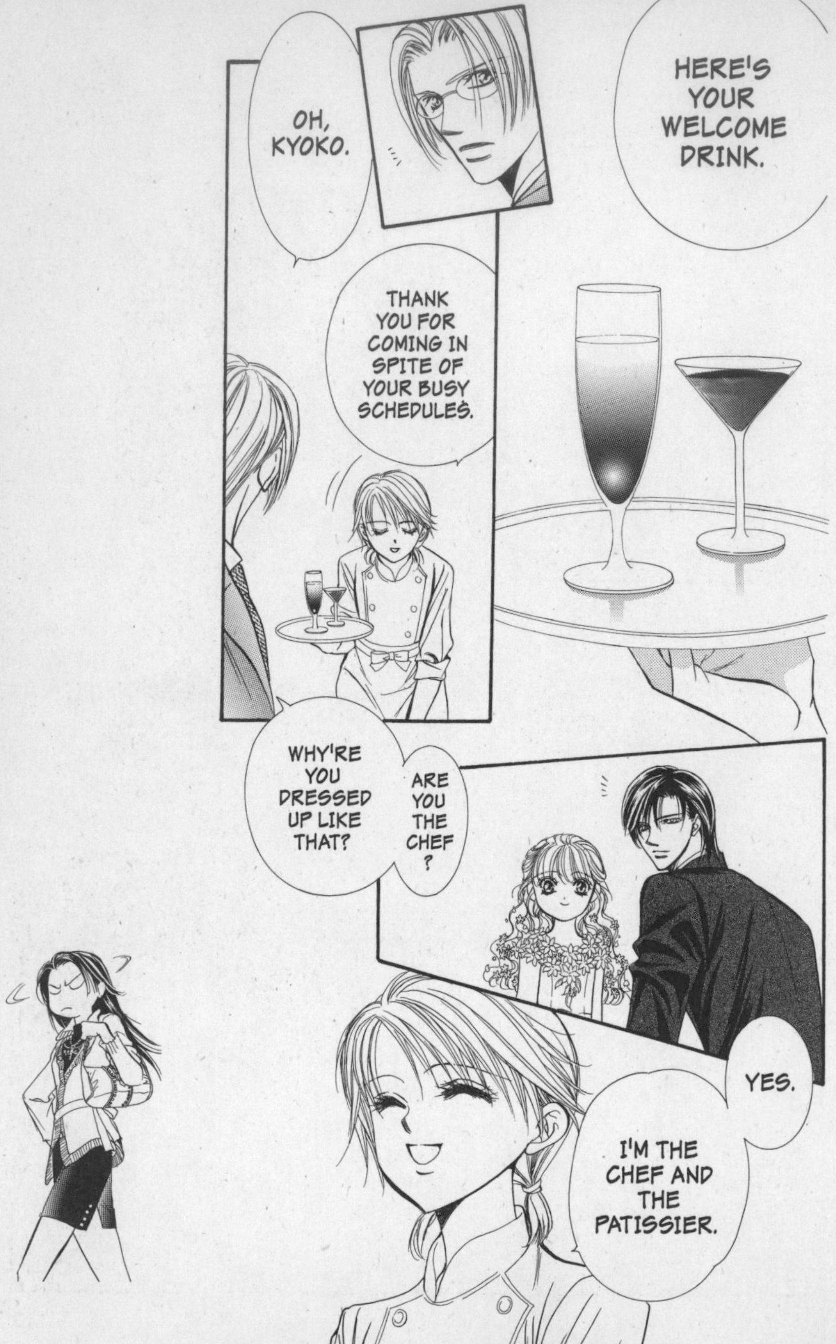
HERE'S YOUR WELCOME DRINK.
OH, KYOKO.
THANK YOU FOR COMING IN SPITE OF YOUR BUSY SCHEDULES.
ARE YOU THE CHEF ?
WHY'RE YOU DRESSED UP LIKE THAT?
YES.
I'M THE CHEF AND THE PATISSIER.

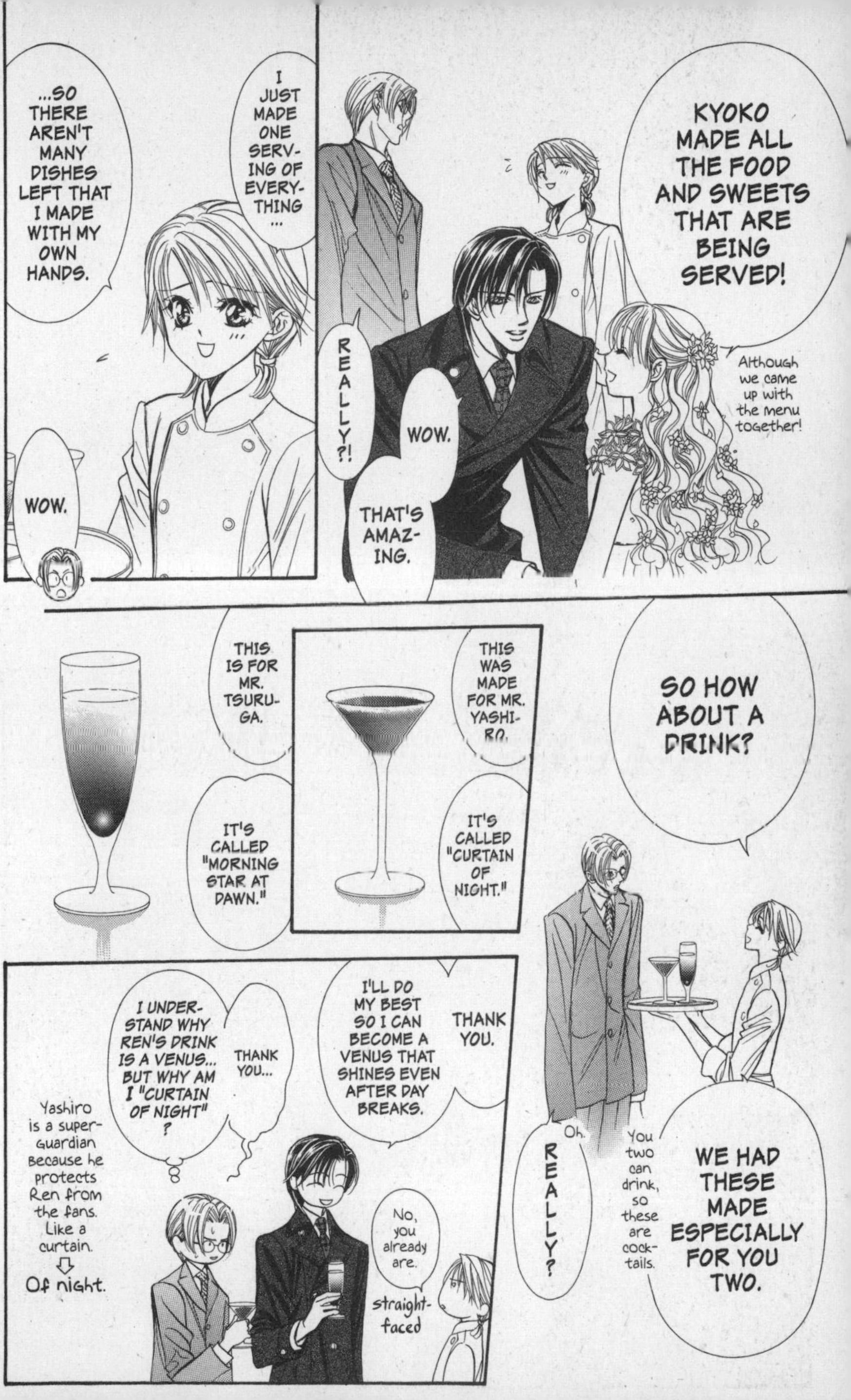
KYOKO MADE ALL THE FOOD AND SWEETS THAT ARE BEING SERVED!
Although we came up with the menu together!
REALLY?!
WOW.
THAT'S AMAZING.
I JUST MADE ONE SERVING OF EVERYTHING...
...SO THERE AREN'T MANY DISHES LEFT THAT I MADE WITH MY OWN HANDS.
WOW.
SO HOW ABOUT A DRINK?
WE HAD THESE MADE ESPECIALLY FOR YOU TWO.
You two can drink, so these are cocktails.
REALLY?
Oh.
THIS WAS MADE FOR MR. YASHIRO.
IT'S CALLED "CURTAIN OF NIGHT."
THIS IS FOR MR. TSURUGA.
IT'S CALLED "MORNING STAR AT DAWN."
THANK YOU.
I'LL DO MY BEST SO I CAN BECOME A VENUS THAT SHINES EVEN AFTER DAY BREAKS.
No, you already are.
straight-faced
THANK YOU...
I UNDERSTAND WHY REN'S DRINK IS A VENUS... BUT WHY AM I "CURTAIN OF NIGHT"?
Yashiro is a super-guardian because he protects Ren from the fans. Like a curtain.
Of night.

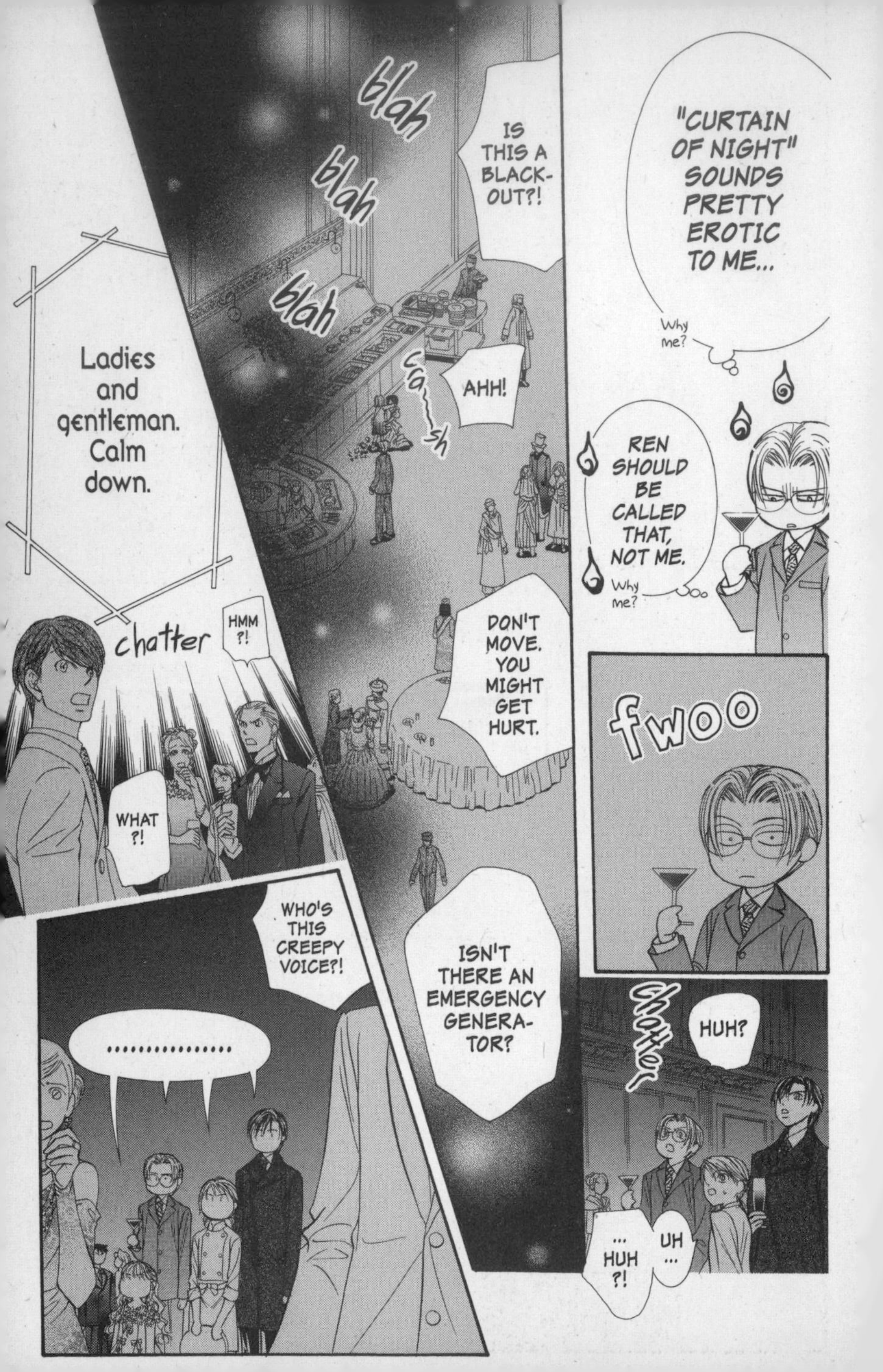

"CURTAIN OF NIGHT" SOUNDS PRETTY EROTIC TO ME...
Why me?
REN SHOULD BE CALLED THAT, NOT ME.
Why me?
blah blah blah
IS THIS A BLACK-OUT?!
crash
AHH!
DON'T MOVE. YOU MIGHT GET HURT.
ISN'T THERE AN EMERGENCY GENERA-TOR?
Ladies and gentleman. Calm down.
chatter
HMM ?!
WHAT ?!
fwoo
chatter
HUH?
UH ...
... HUH ?!
WHO'S THIS CREEPY VOICE?!
....

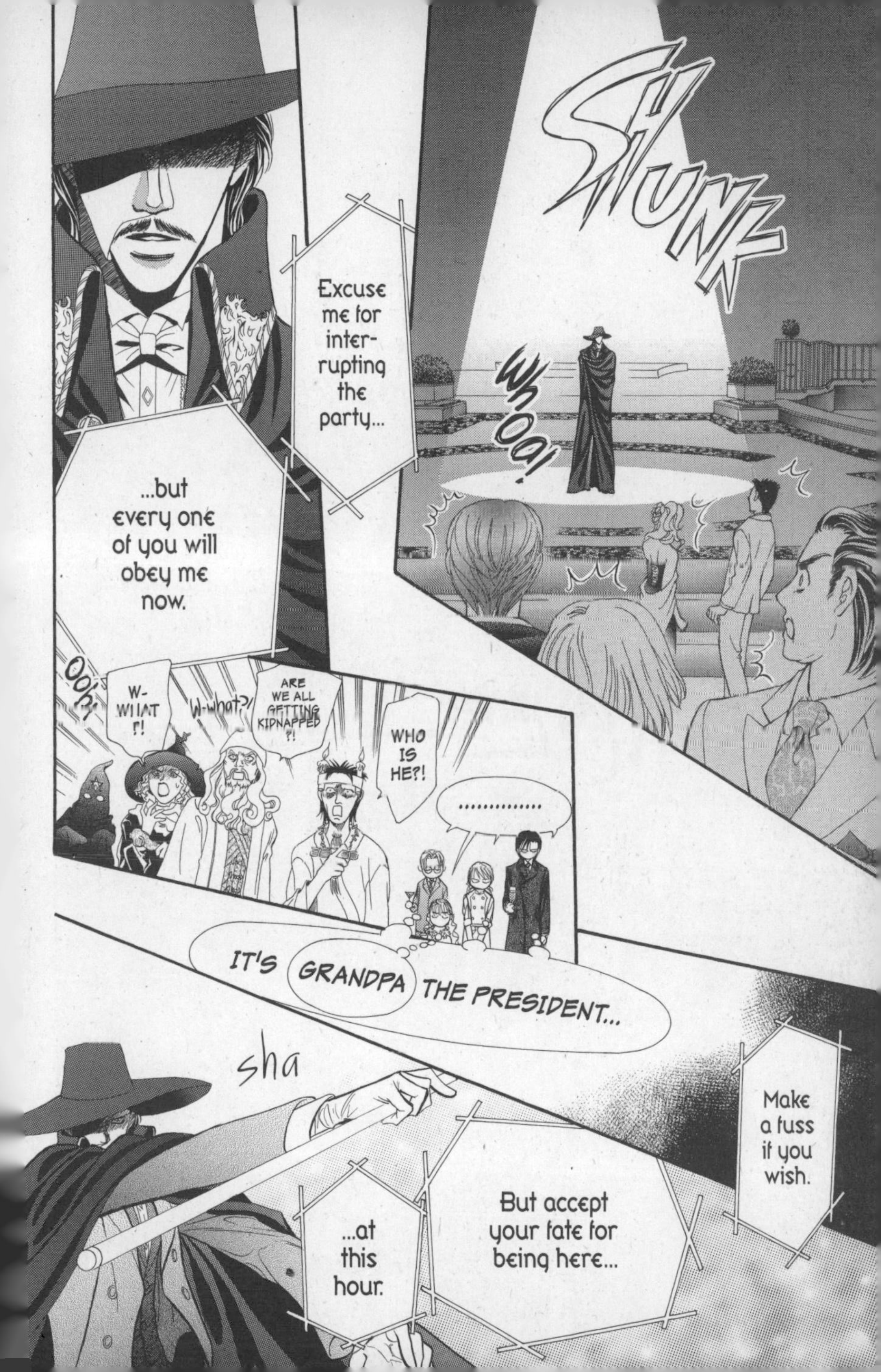
SHUNK
Whoa!
Excuse me for interrupting the party...
...but every one of you will obey me now.
WHO IS HE?!
....
IT'S GRANDPA THE PRESIDENT...
ARE WE ALL GETTING KIDNAPPED?!
W-what?!
W-WHAT?!
Ooh
sha
Make a fuss if you wish.
But accept your fate for being here...
...at this hour.

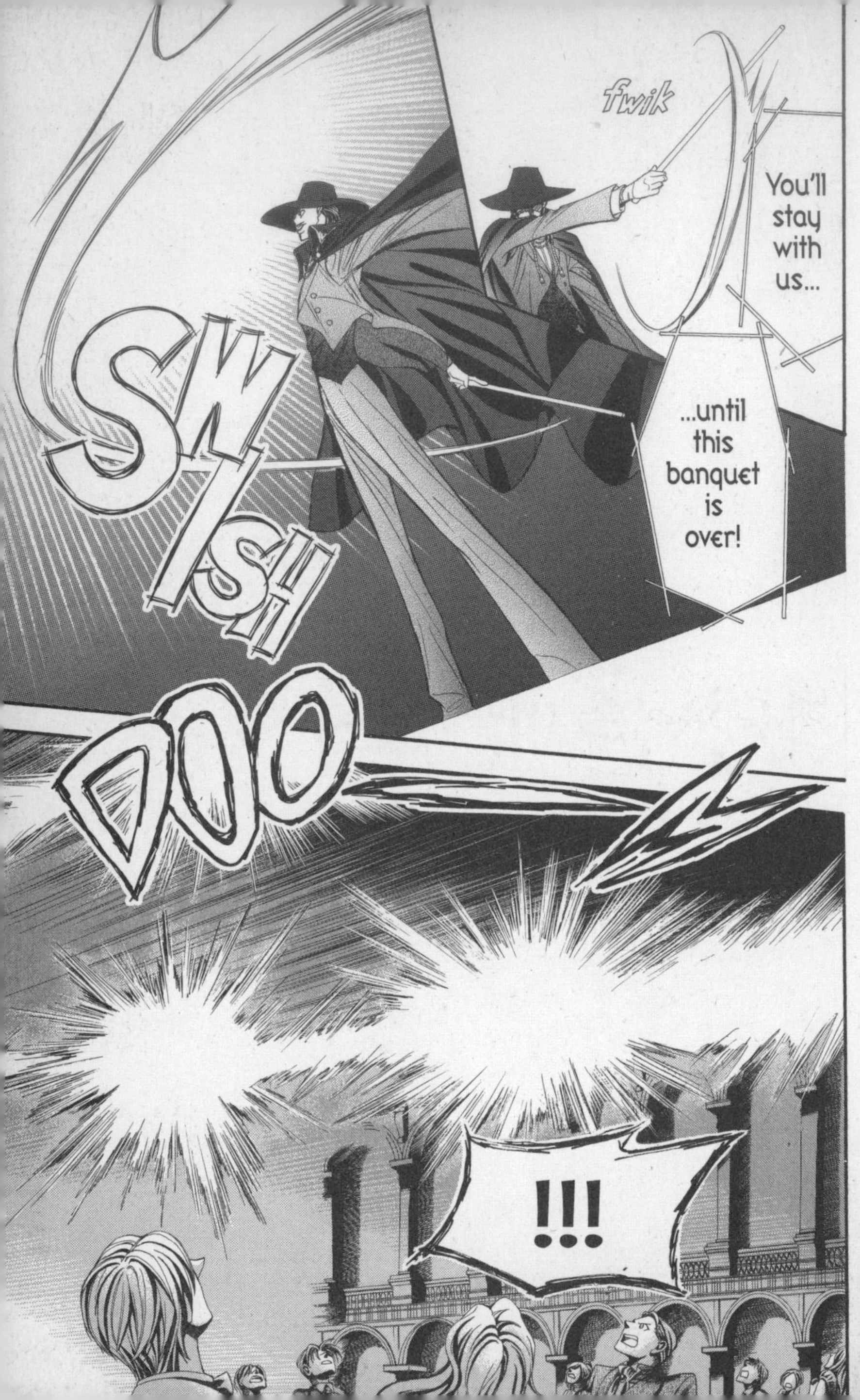
fwik
You'll stay with us...
...until this banquet is over!
SWISH
DOO
!!!

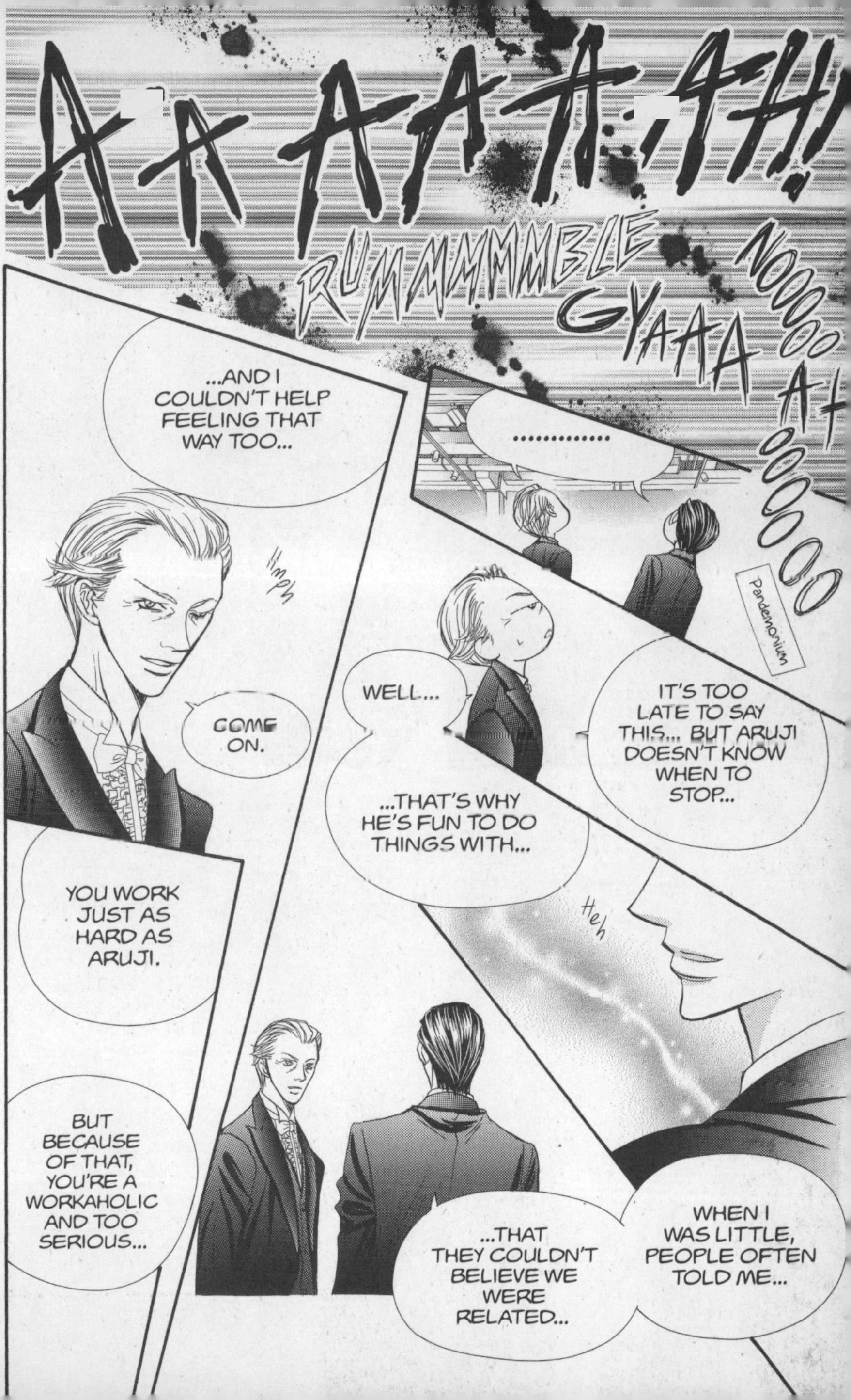
AAAA-AH!!
RUMMMMMMBLE
GYAAA
NOOOOOO
AH
OOOOOOO
....
Pandemonium
IT'S TOO LATE TO SAY THIS... BUT ARUJI DOESN'T KNOW WHEN TO STOP...
WELL...
...THAT'S WHY HE'S FUN TO DO THINGS WITH...
Heh
WHEN I WAS LITTLE, PEOPLE OFTEN TOLD ME...
...THAT THEY COULDN'T BELIEVE WE WERE RELATED...
...AND I COULDN'T HELP FEELING THAT WAY TOO...
Hmph
COME ON.
YOU WORK JUST AS HARD AS ARUJI.
BUT BECAUSE OF THAT, YOU'RE A WORKAHOLIC AND TOO SERIOUS...

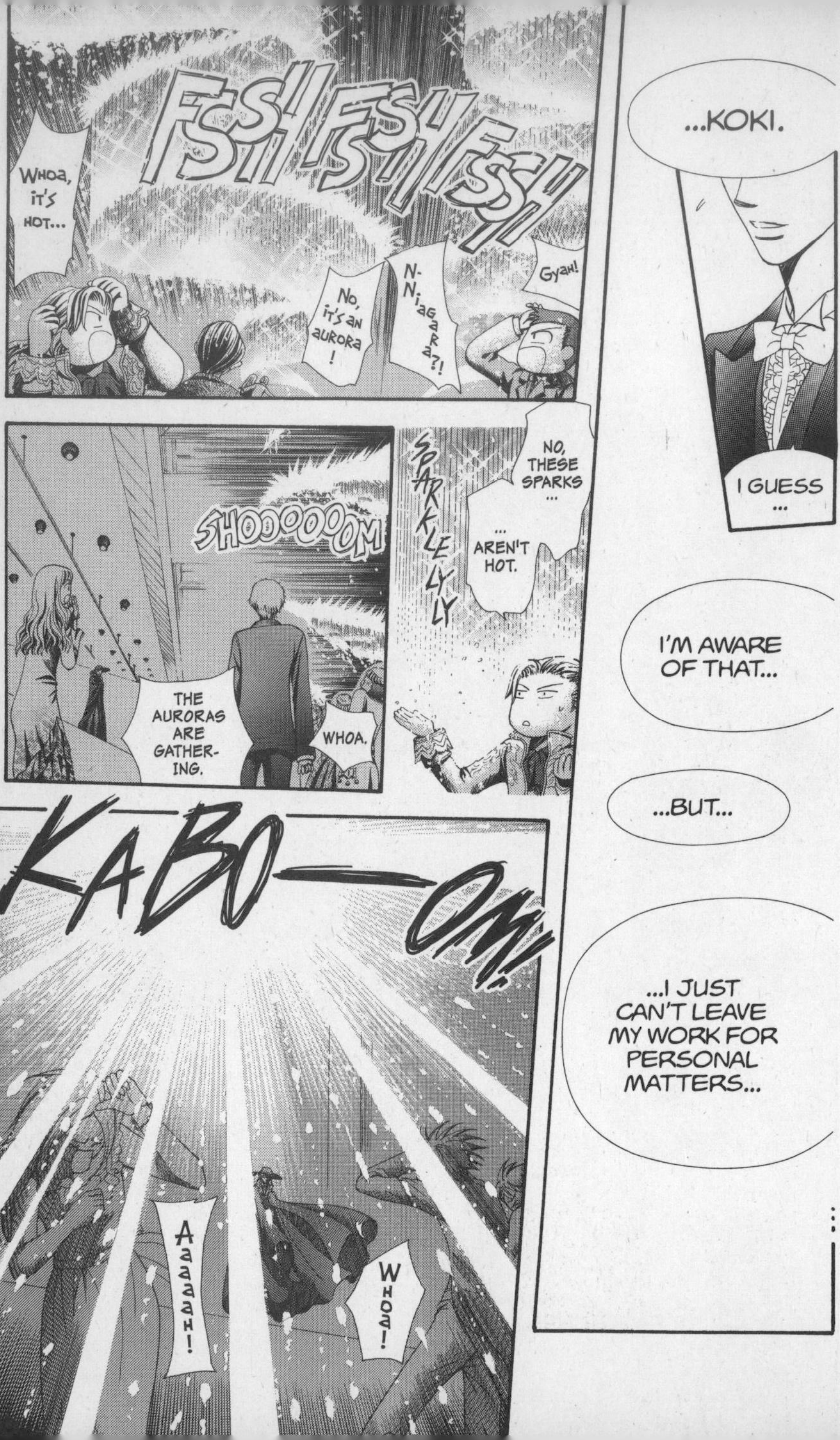
...KOKI.
I GUESS...
I'M AWARE OF THAT...
...BUT...
...I JUST CAN'T LEAVE MY WORK FOR PERSONAL MATTERS...
...
FSSH FSSH FSSH
Gyah!
N-Niagara?!
No, it's an aurora!
Whoa, it's hot...
SPARKLELYLY
NO, THESE SPARKS...
...AREN'T HOT.
SHOOOOOOM
WHOA.
THE AURORAS ARE GATHERING.
KABO—OM!
Whoa!
Aaaaah!

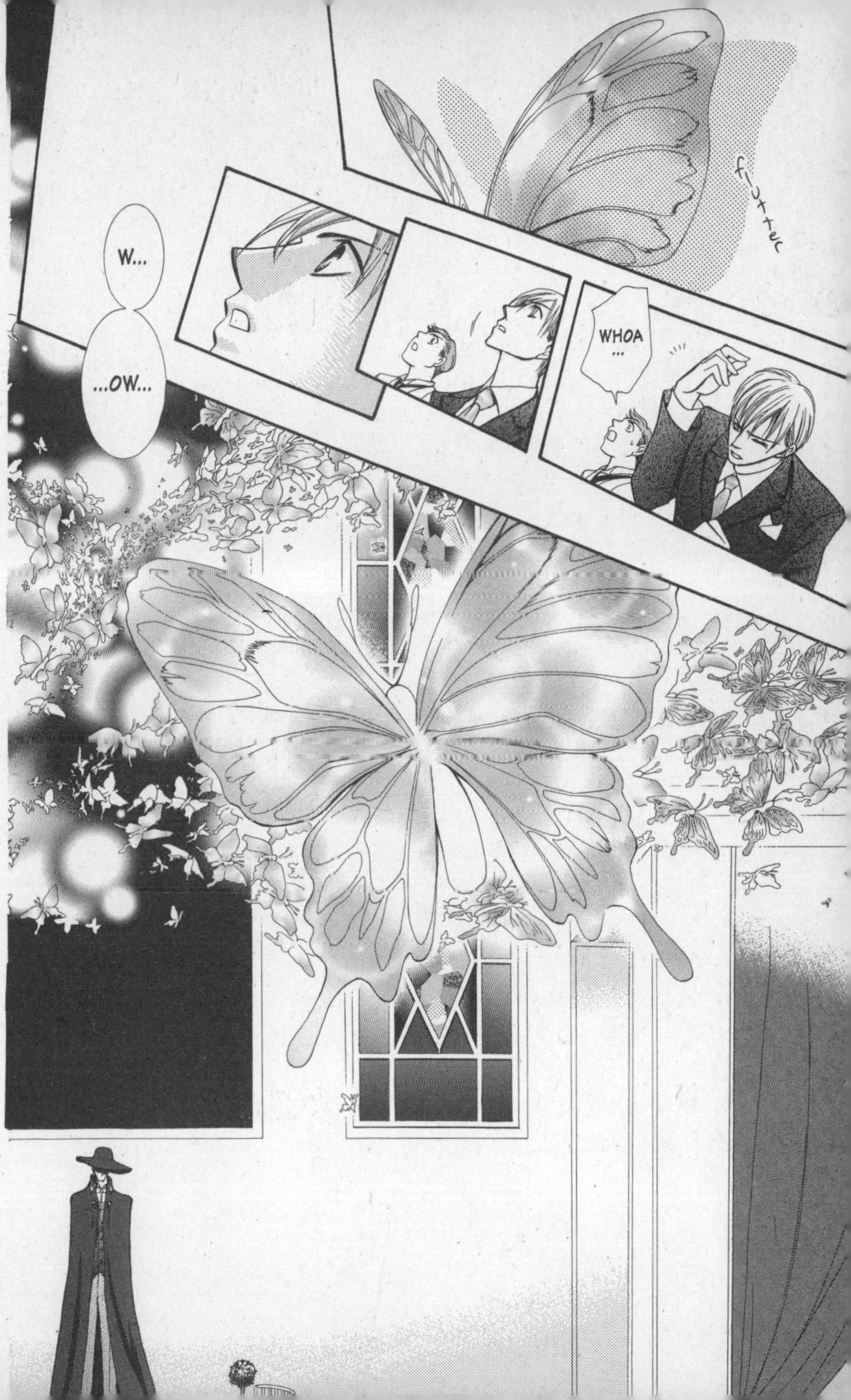
flutter
WHOA ...
W...
...OW...

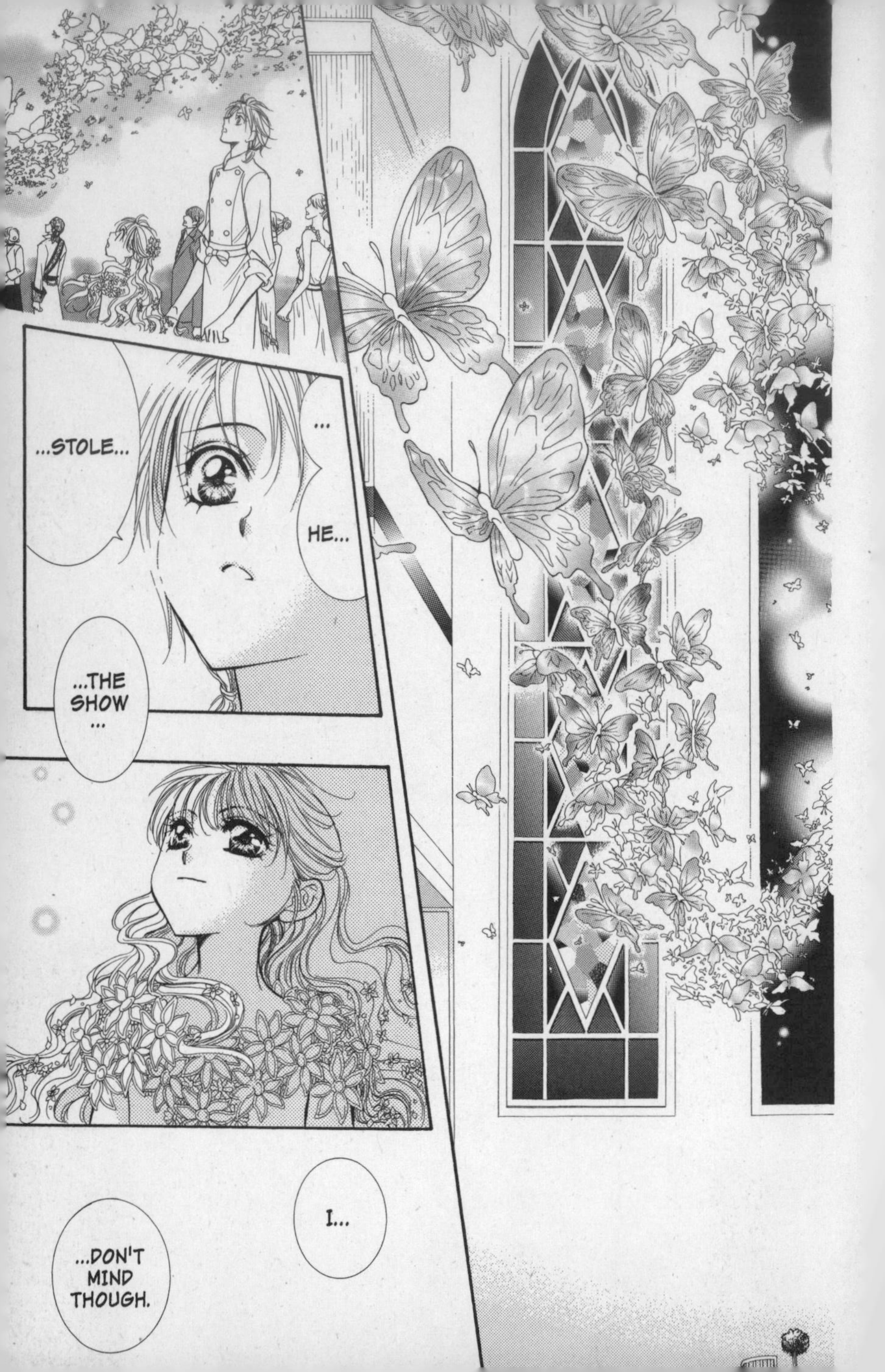
...
HE...
...STOLE...
...THE SHOW ...
I...
...DON'T MIND THOUGH.

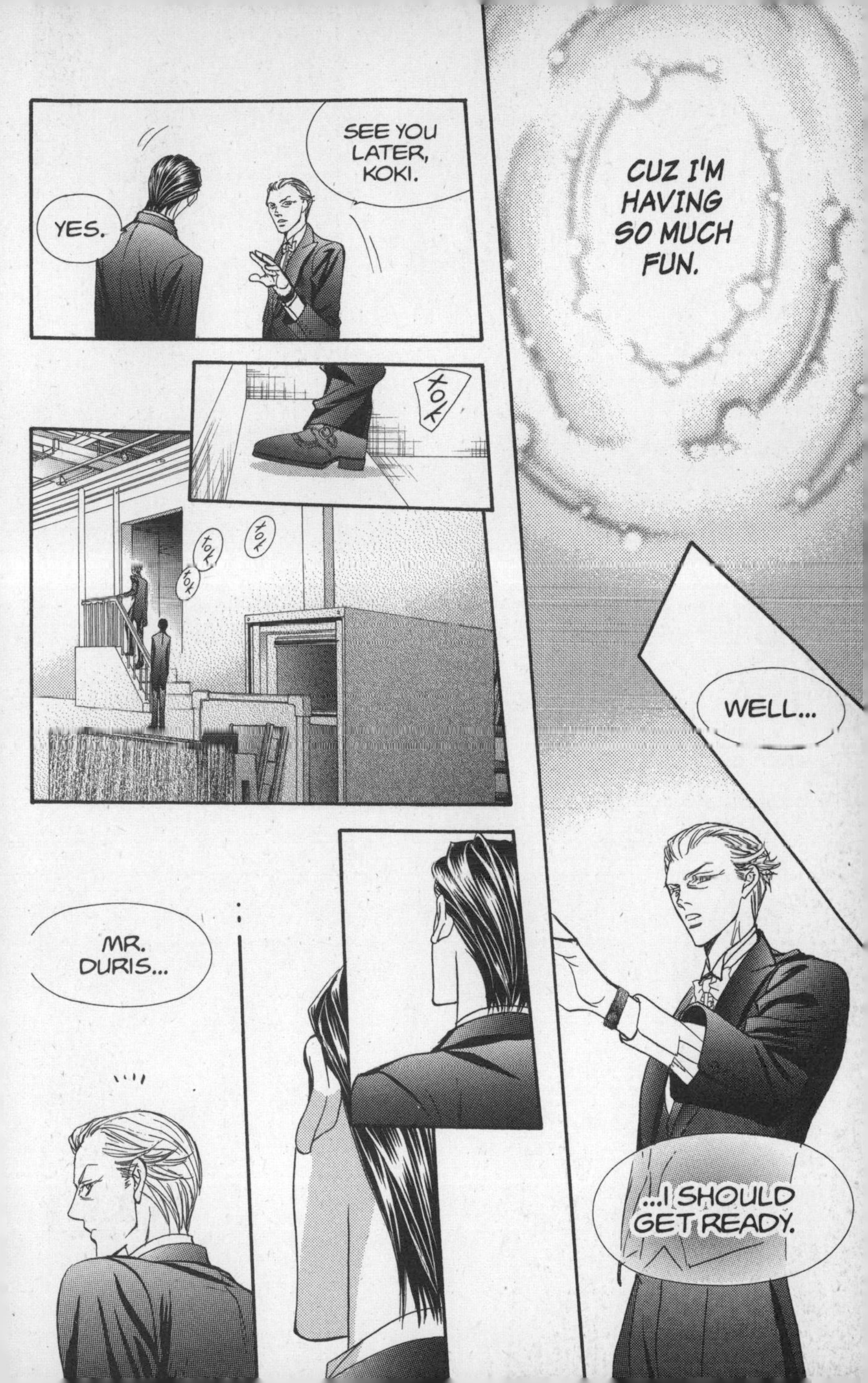
CUZ I'M HAVING SO MUCH FUN.
WELL...
...I SHOULD GET READY.
SEE YOU LATER, KOKI.
YES.
KOK
KOK
KOK
KOK
MR. DURIS...

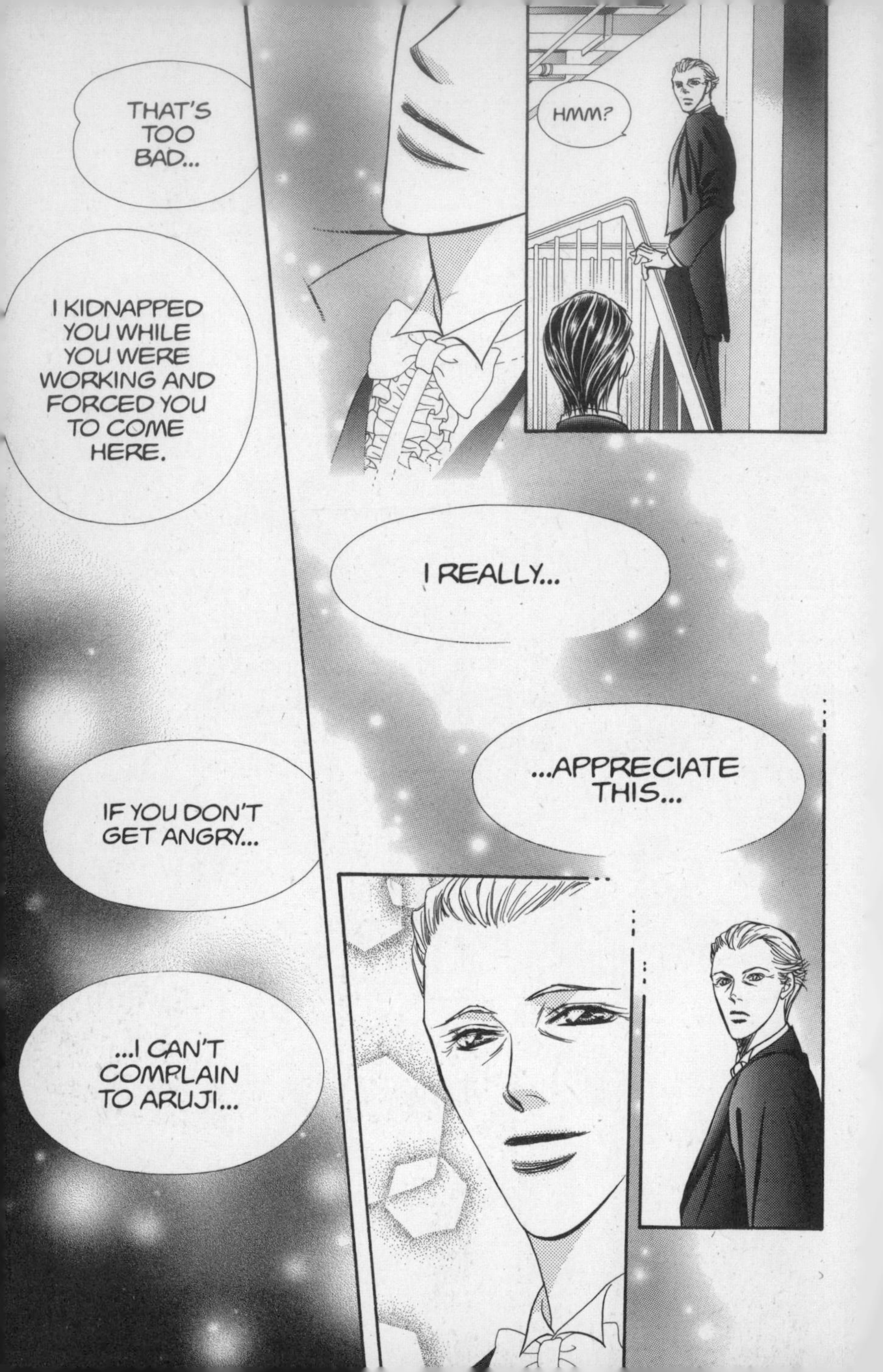
HMM?
THAT'S TOO BAD...
I KIDNAPPED YOU WHILE YOU WERE WORKING AND FORCED YOU TO COME HERE.
I REALLY...
...APPRECIATE THIS...
IF YOU DON'T GET ANGRY...
...I CAN'T COMPLAIN TO ARUJI...

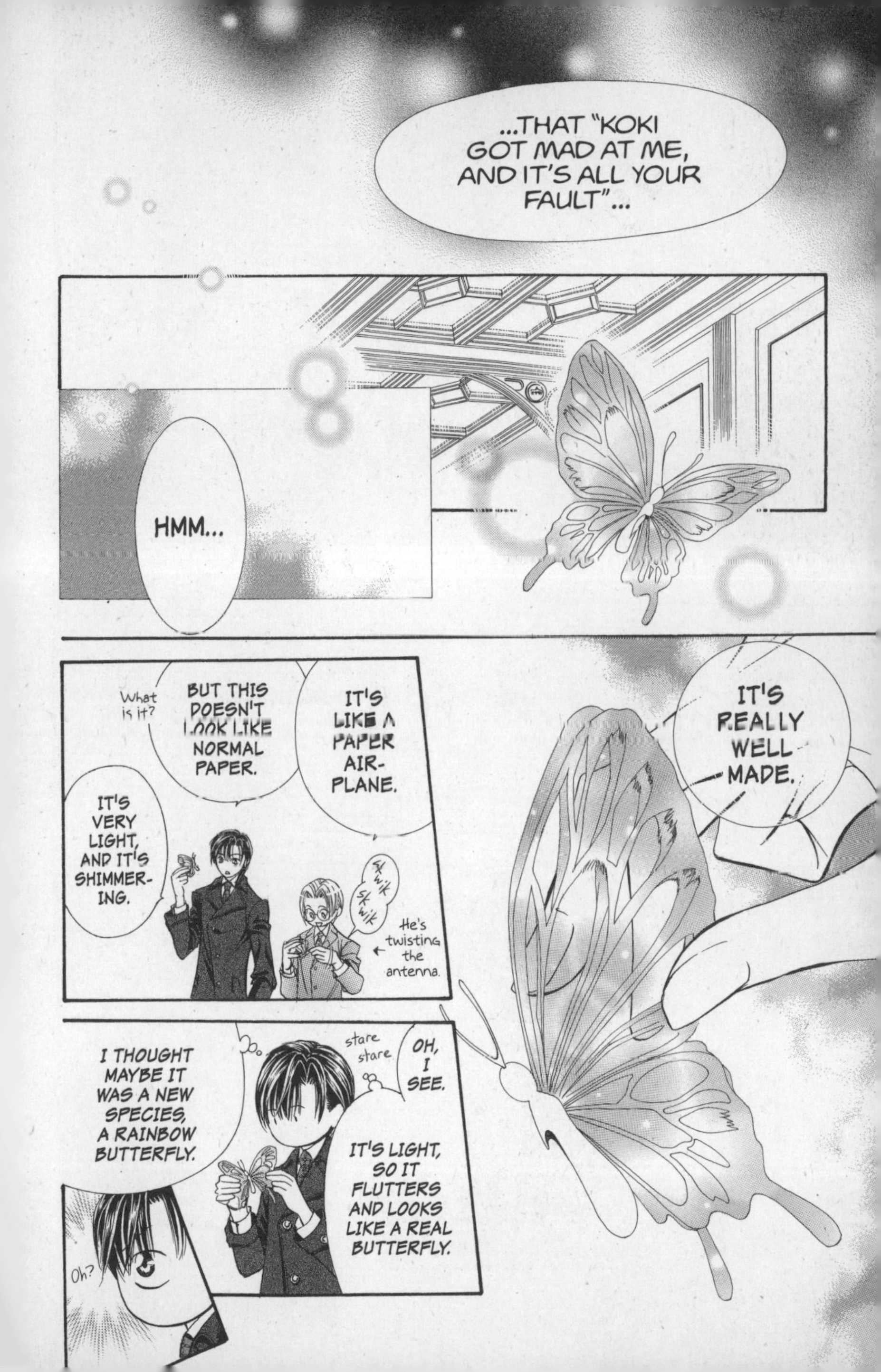
...THAT "KOKI GOT MAD AT ME, AND IT'S ALL YOUR FAULT"...
HMM...
IT'S REALLY WELL MADE.
IT'S LIKE A PAPER AIRPLANE.
BUT THIS DOESN'T LOOK LIKE NORMAL PAPER.
What is it?
IT'S VERY LIGHT, AND IT'S SHIMMERING.
sk wik sk wik
He's twisting the antenna.
OH, I SEE.
stare stare
I THOUGHT MAYBE IT WAS A NEW SPECIES, A RAINBOW BUTTERFLY.
IT'S LIGHT, SO IT FLUTTERS AND LOOKS LIKE A REAL BUTTERFLY.
Oh?

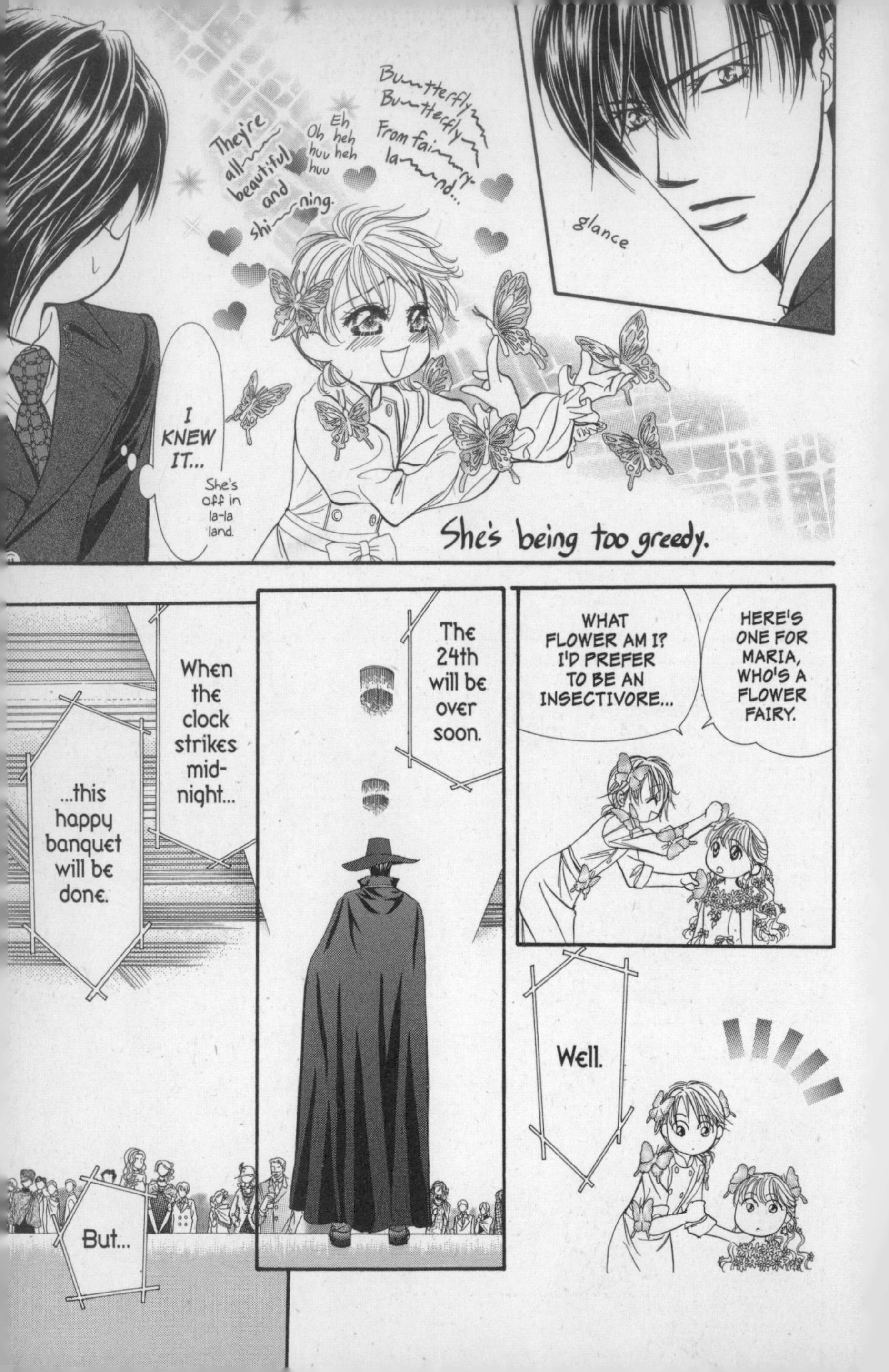
glance
Bu~tterfly
Bu~tterfly~
From fai~ry-la~nd...
Eh
Oh heh huu heh huu
They're all~ beautiful and shi~ning.
I KNEW IT...
She's off in la-la land.
She's being too greedy.
HERE'S ONE FOR MARIA, WHO'S A FLOWER FAIRY.
WHAT FLOWER AM I? I'D PREFER TO BE AN INSECTIVORE...
Well.
The 24th will be over soon.
When the clock strikes mid-night...
...this happy banquet will be done.
But...

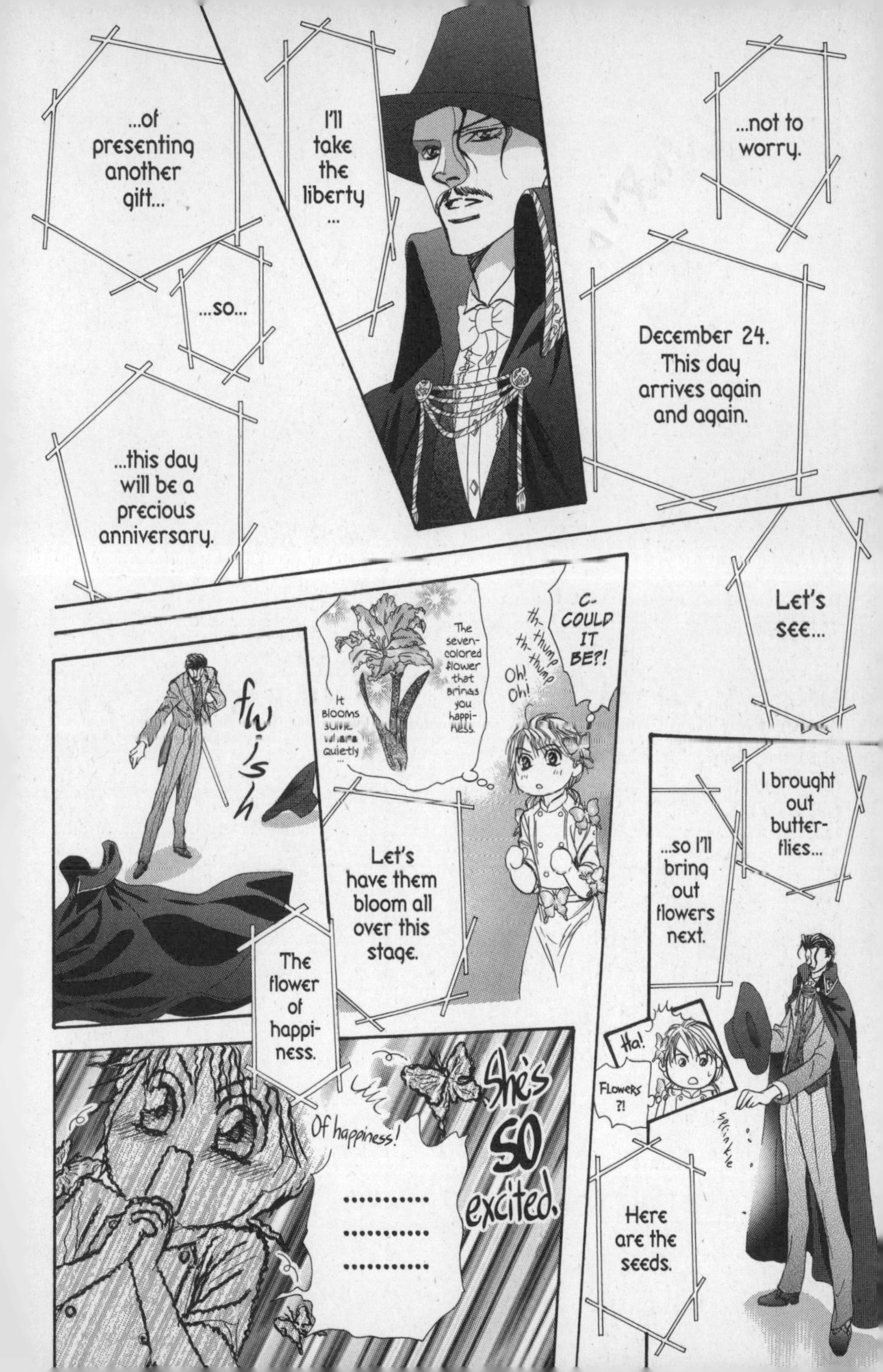
...not to worry.
December 24. This day arrives again and again.
I'll take the liberty...
...of presenting another gift...
...so...
...this day will be a precious anniversary.
Let's see...
I brought out butterflies...
...so I'll bring out flowers next.
Ha!
Flowers?!
sprinkle
Here are the seeds.
C-COULD IT BE?!
th-thump th-thump
Oh! Oh!
The seven-colored flower that brings you happiness.
It blooms some where quietly...
Let's have them bloom all over this stage.
fwish
The flower of happiness.
Of happiness!
She's SO excited.
....
....
....

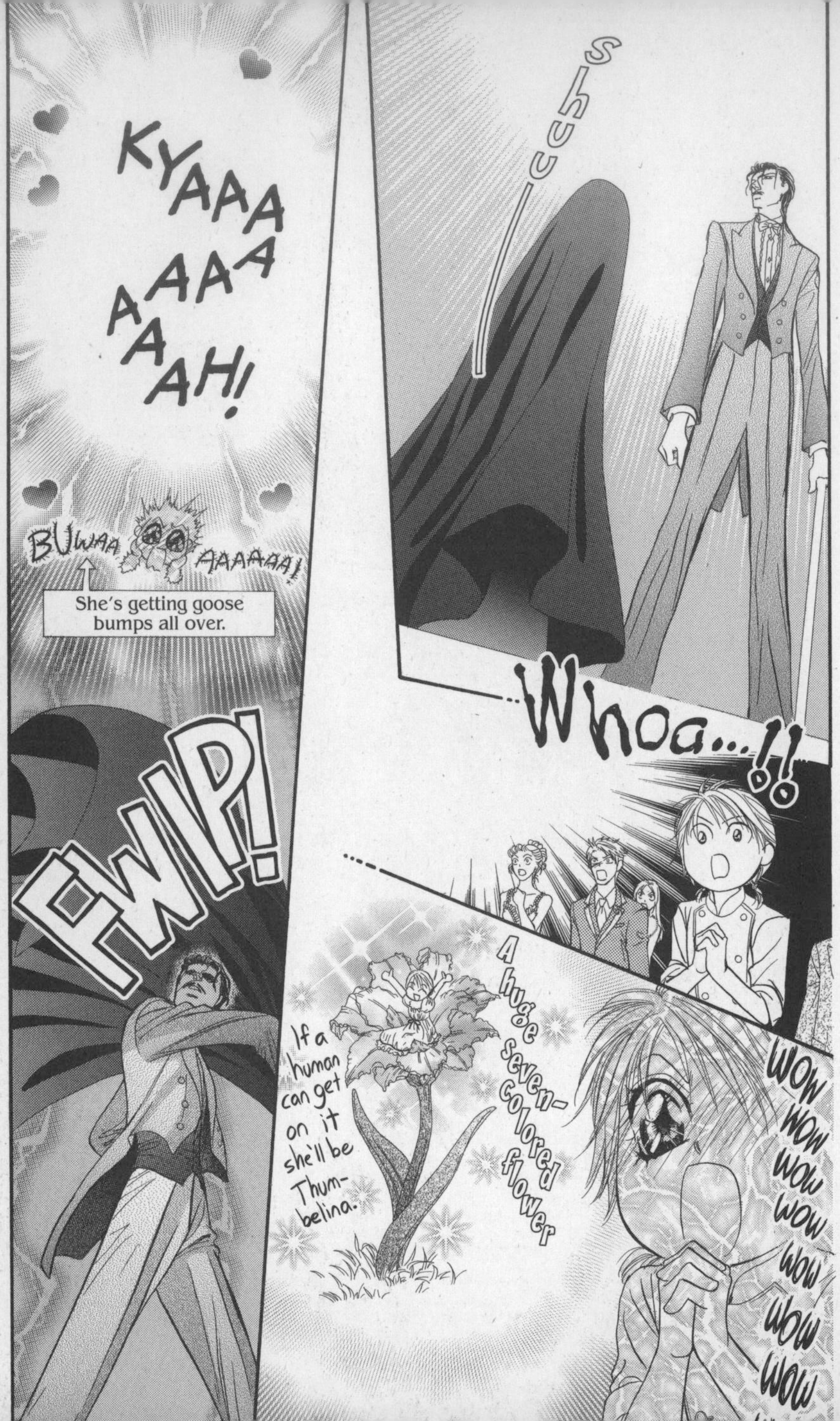
Shuuu
KYAAAAAAAAH!
BUWAA AAAAAA!
She's getting goose bumps all over.
Whoa...!!
WOW WOW WOW WOW WOW WOW WOW WOW WOW WOW
A huge seven-colored flower
If a human can get on it she'll be Thumbelina.
FWIP!!

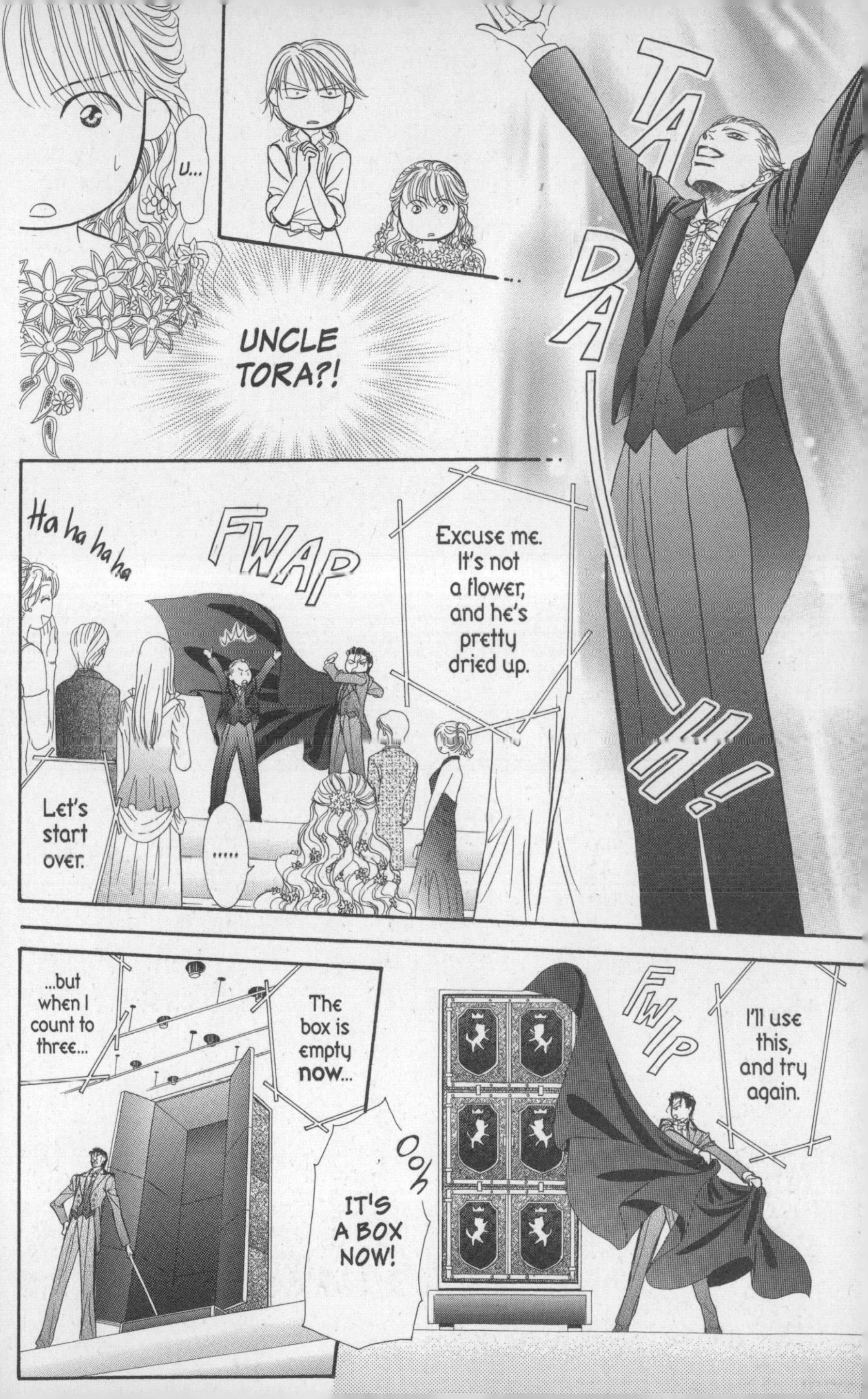
TA DA H!
U...
UNCLE TORA?!
Excuse me. It's not a flower, and he's pretty dried up.
FWAP
Ha ha ha ha
Let's start over.
.....
FWIP
I'll use this, and try again.
The box is empty now...
...but when I count to three...
Ooh
IT'S A BOX NOW!

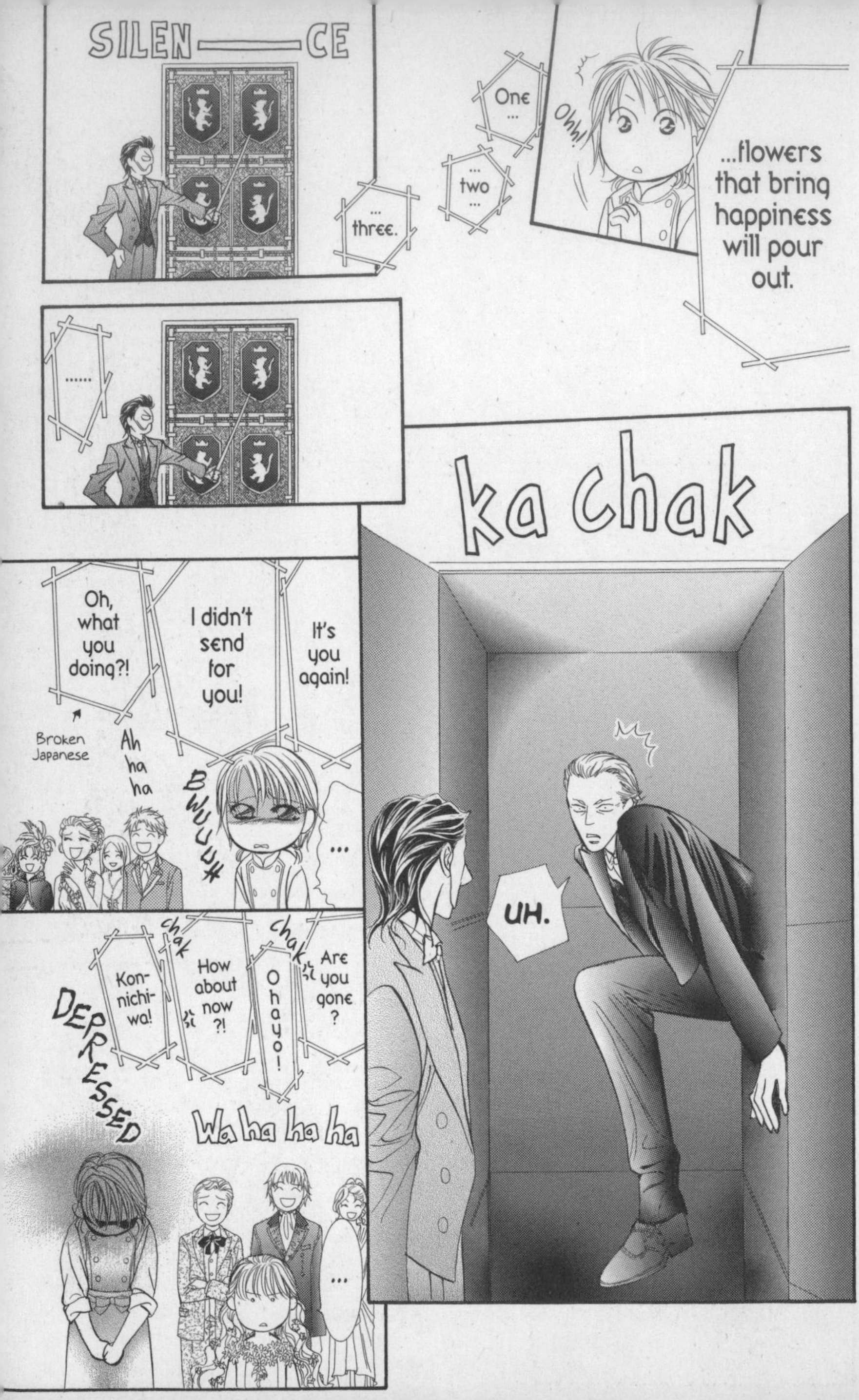
...flowers that bring happiness will pour out.
Ohh!
One ...
... two ...
... three.
SILEN——CE
......
ka chak
UH.
It's you again!
I didn't send for you!
Oh, what you doing?!
Broken Japanese
Ah ha ha
BWUUUH
...
Are you gone?
chak
Ohayo!
How about now?!
chak
Kon-nichi-wa!
DEPRESSED
Wa ha ha ha
...

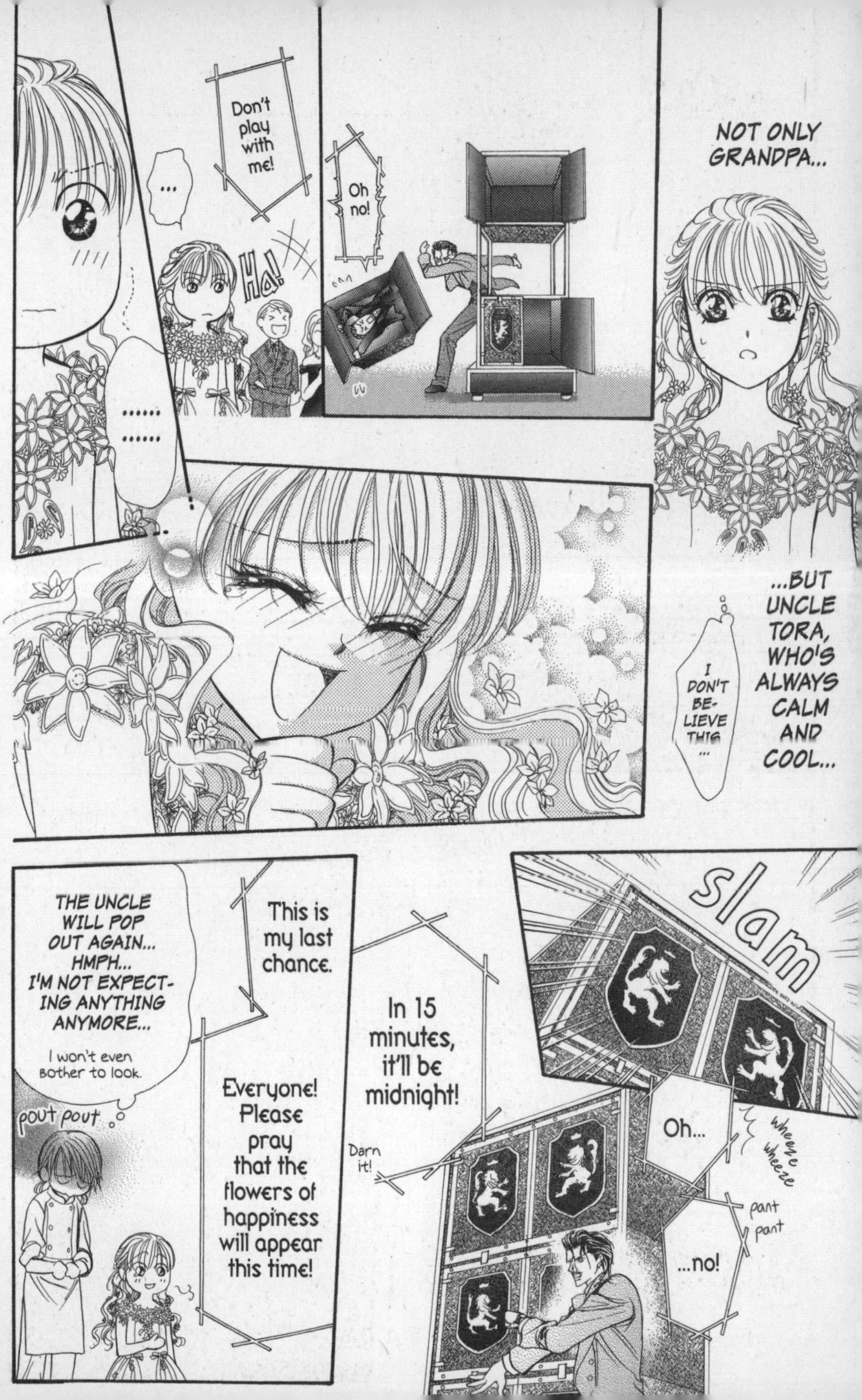
NOT ONLY GRANDPA...
...BUT UNCLE TORA, WHO'S ALWAYS CALM AND COOL...
I DON'T BE-LIEVE THIS...
Oh no!
Don't play with me!
...
Ha!
......
......
slam
Oh...
wheeze wheeze
pant pant
...no!
Darn it!
In 15 minutes, it'll be midnight!
This is my last chance.
Everyone! Please pray that the flowers of happiness will appear this time!
THE UNCLE WILL POP OUT AGAIN... HMPH... I'M NOT EXPECTING ANYTHING ANYMORE...
I won't even bother to look.
pout pout

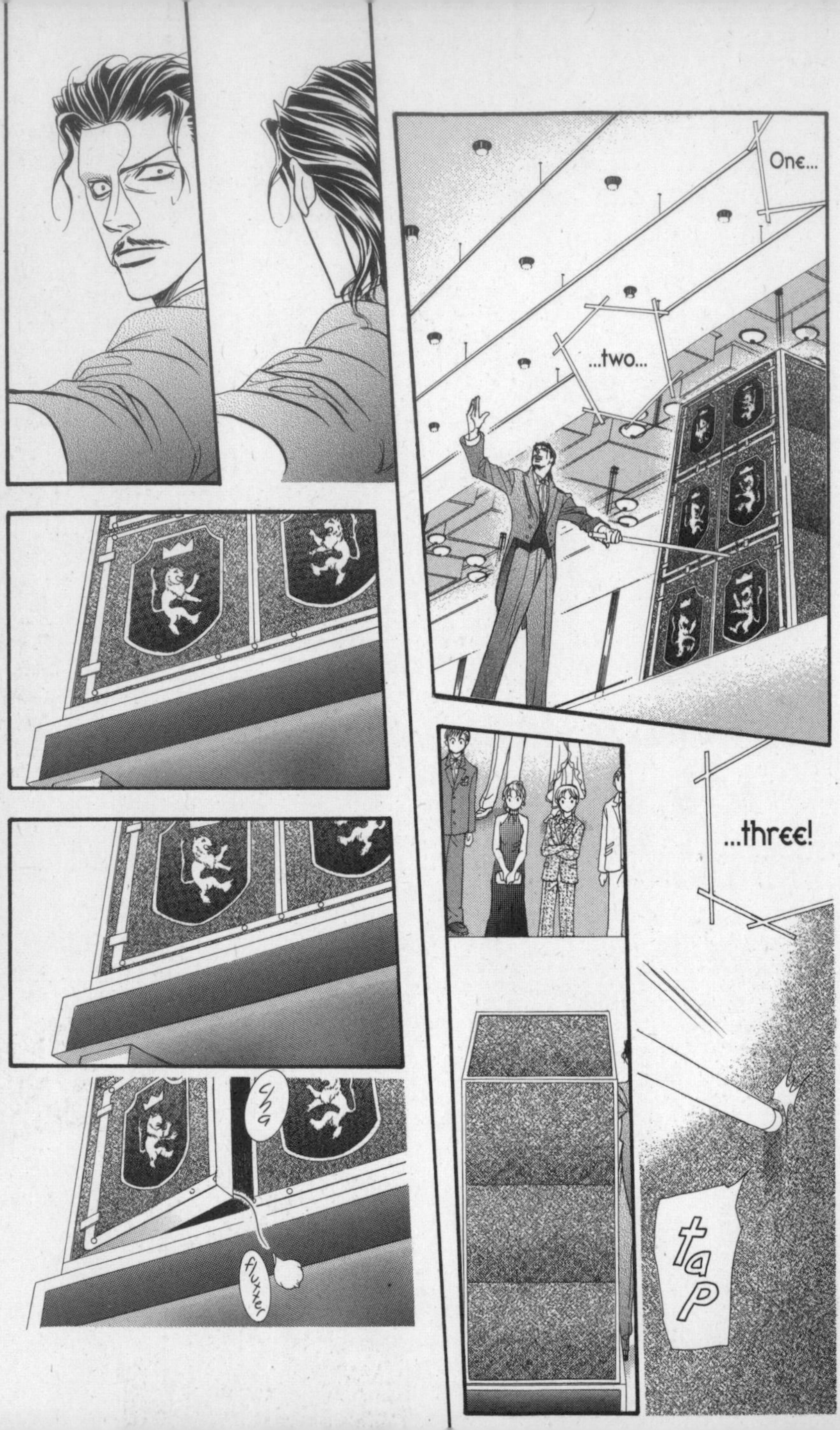
One...
...two...
...three!
tap
cha
fluxxer

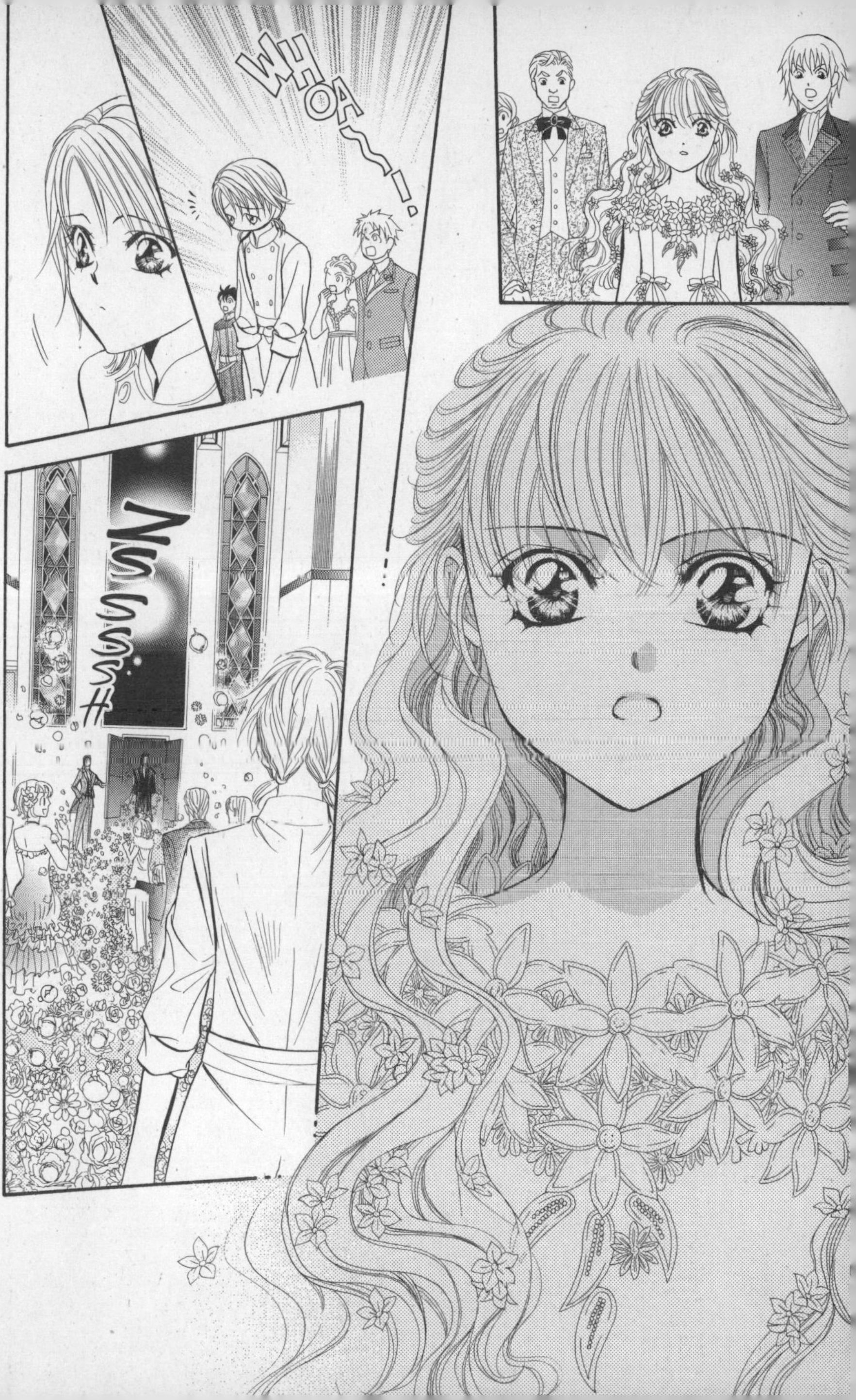
WHOA~~~!

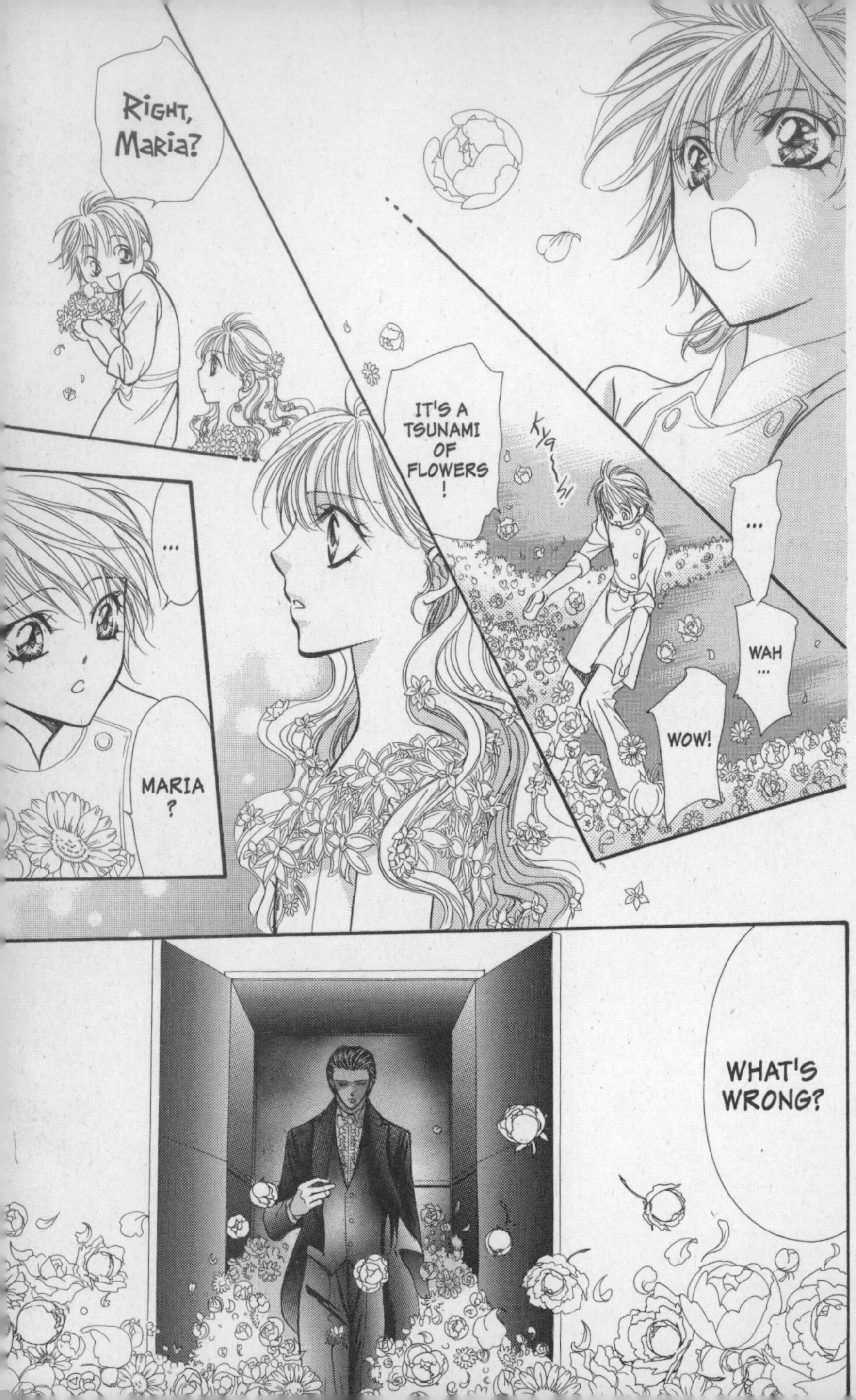
...
WAH ...
WOW!
Kya~~!
IT'S A TSUNAMI OF FLOWERS!
Right, Maria?
...
MARIA?
WHAT'S WRONG?

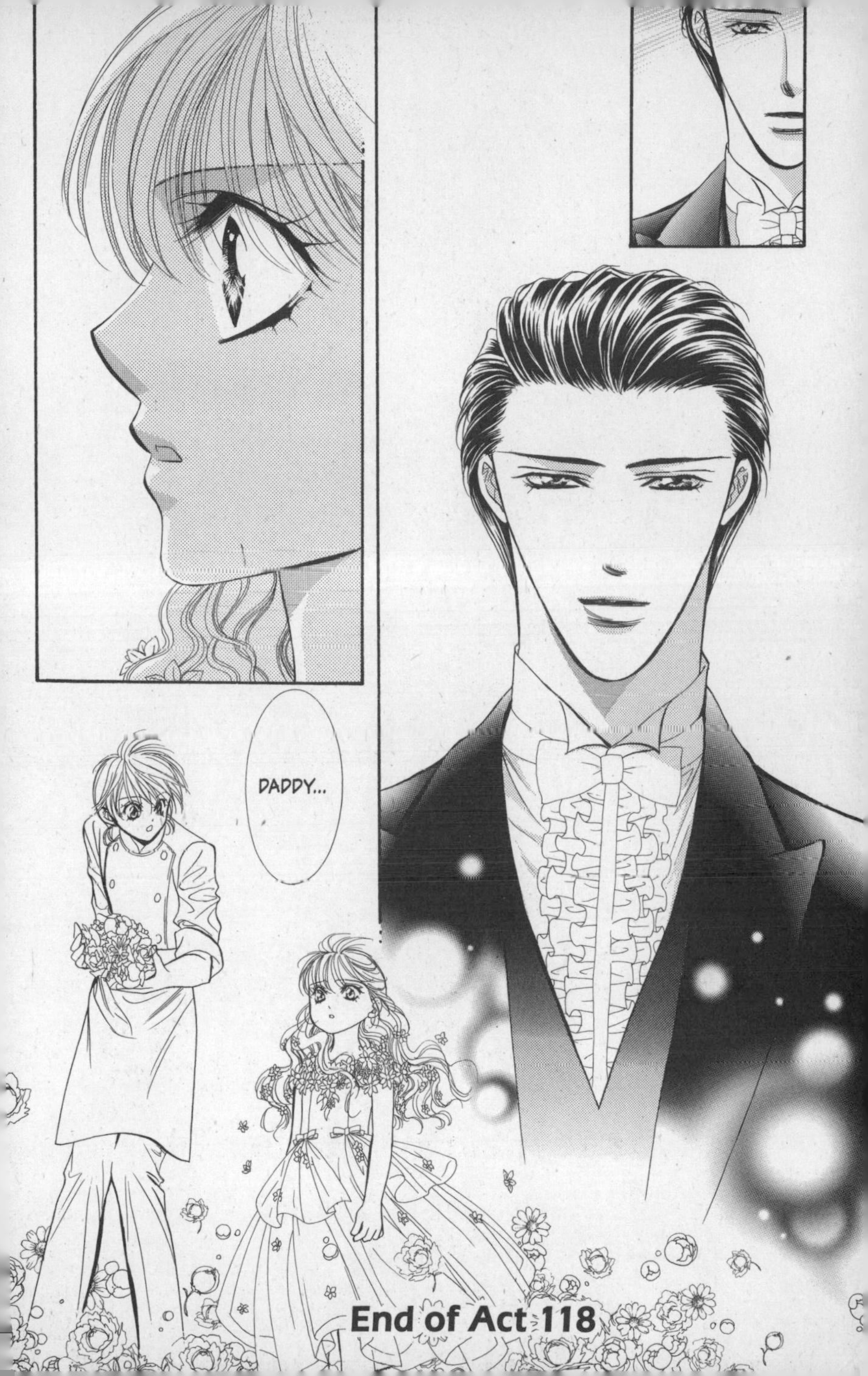
DADDY...
End of Act 118

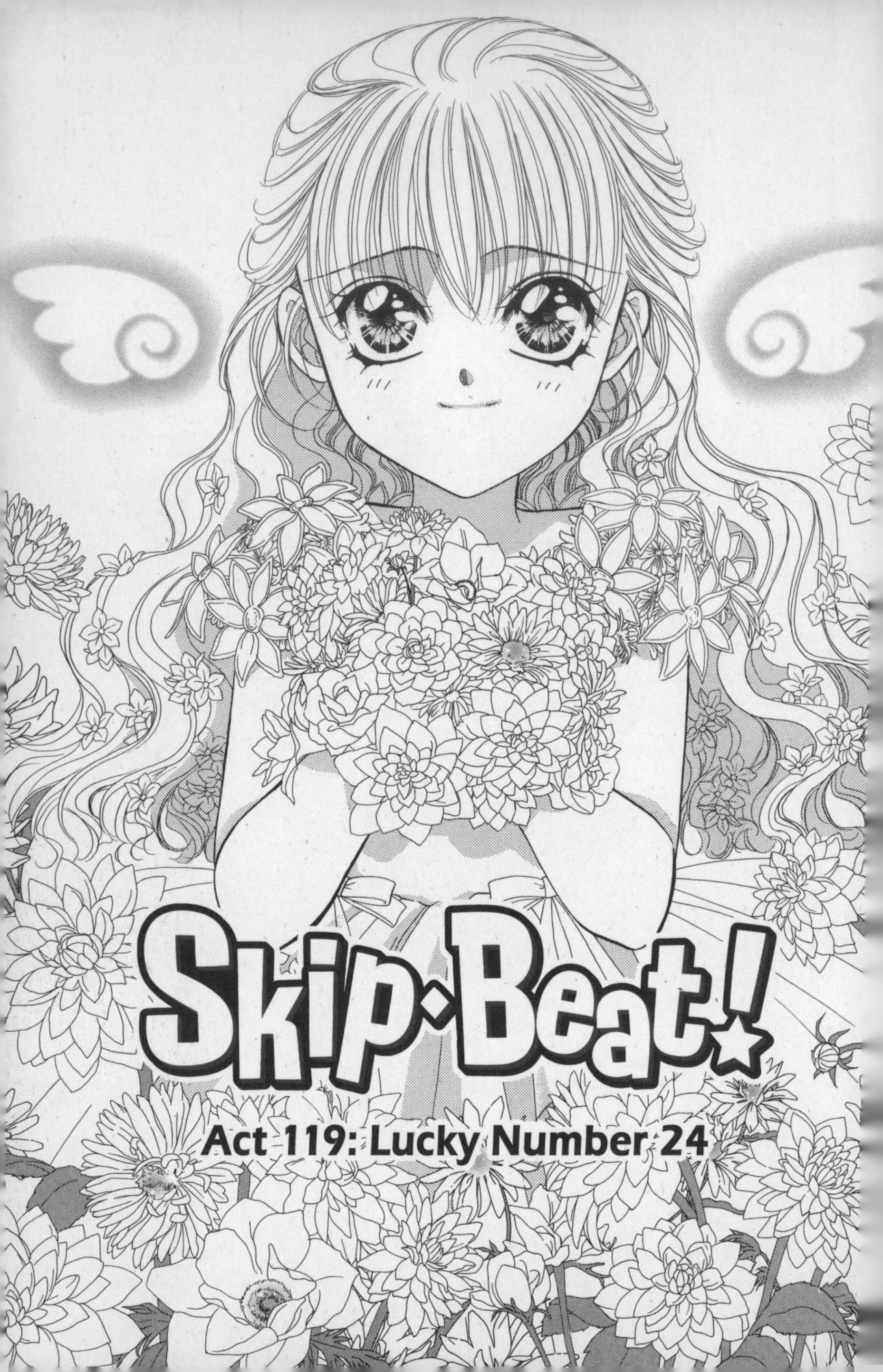
Skip·Beat!
Act 119: Lucky Number 24

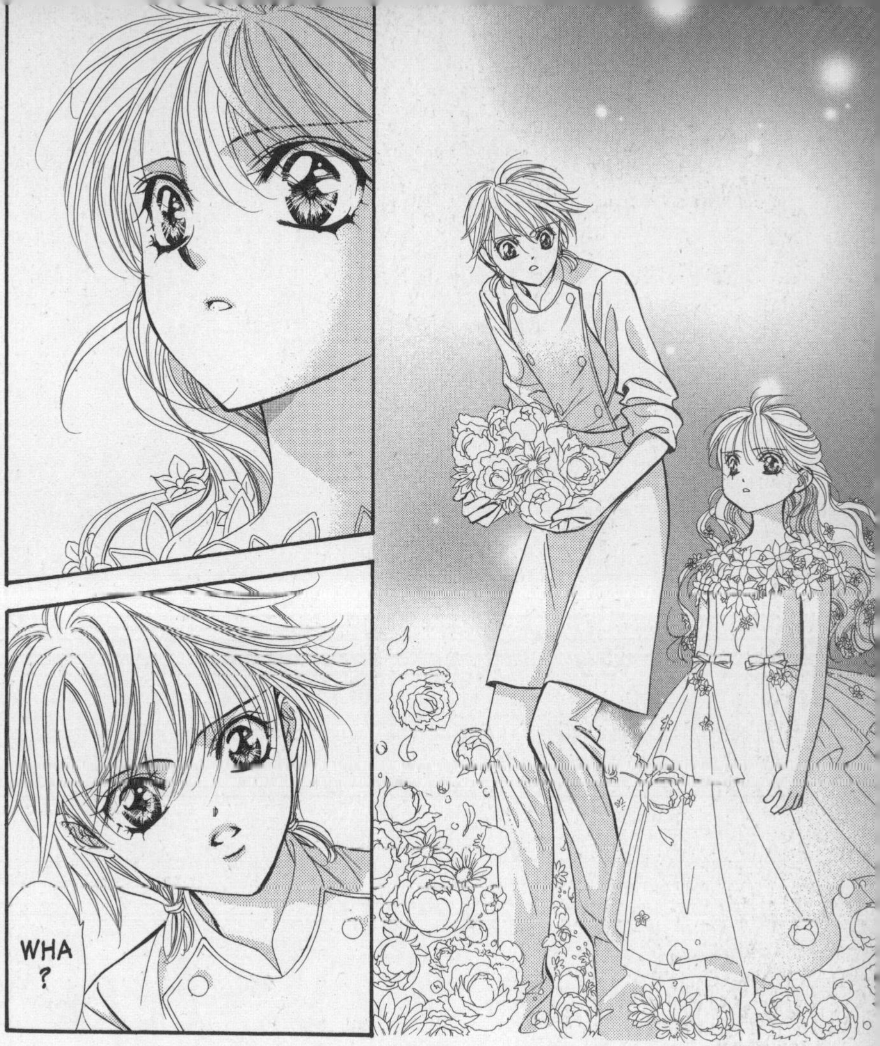
WHA ?
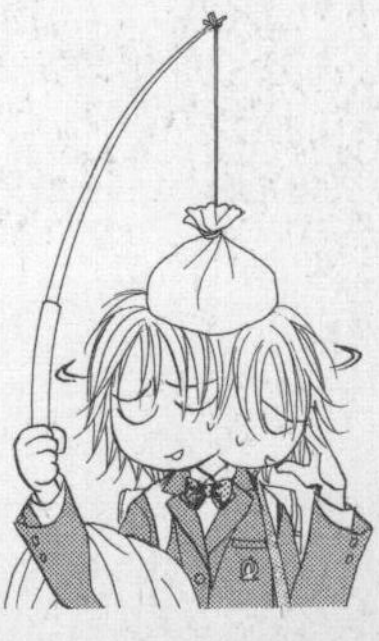

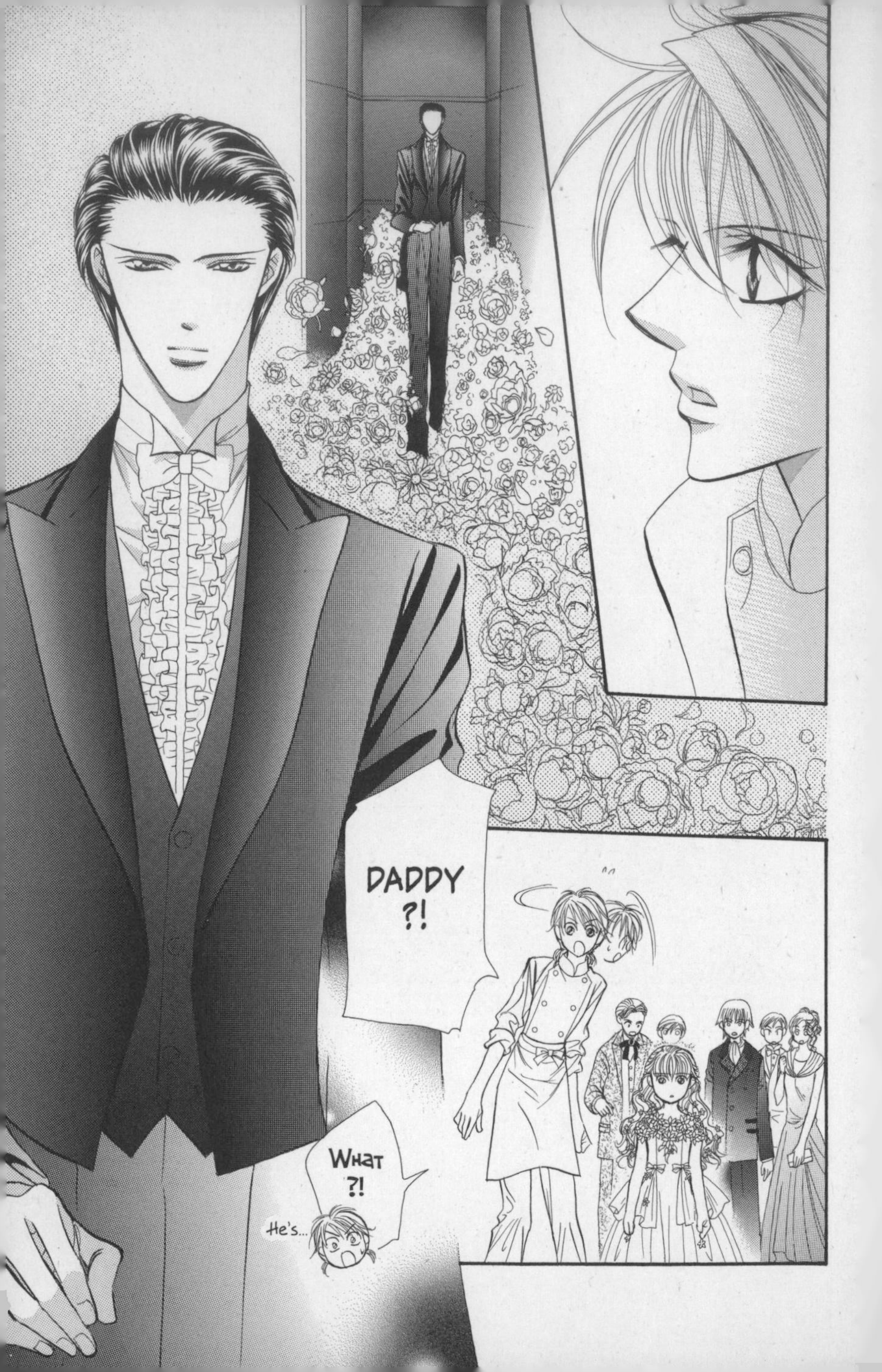
DADDY ?!
WHAT ?!
He's...

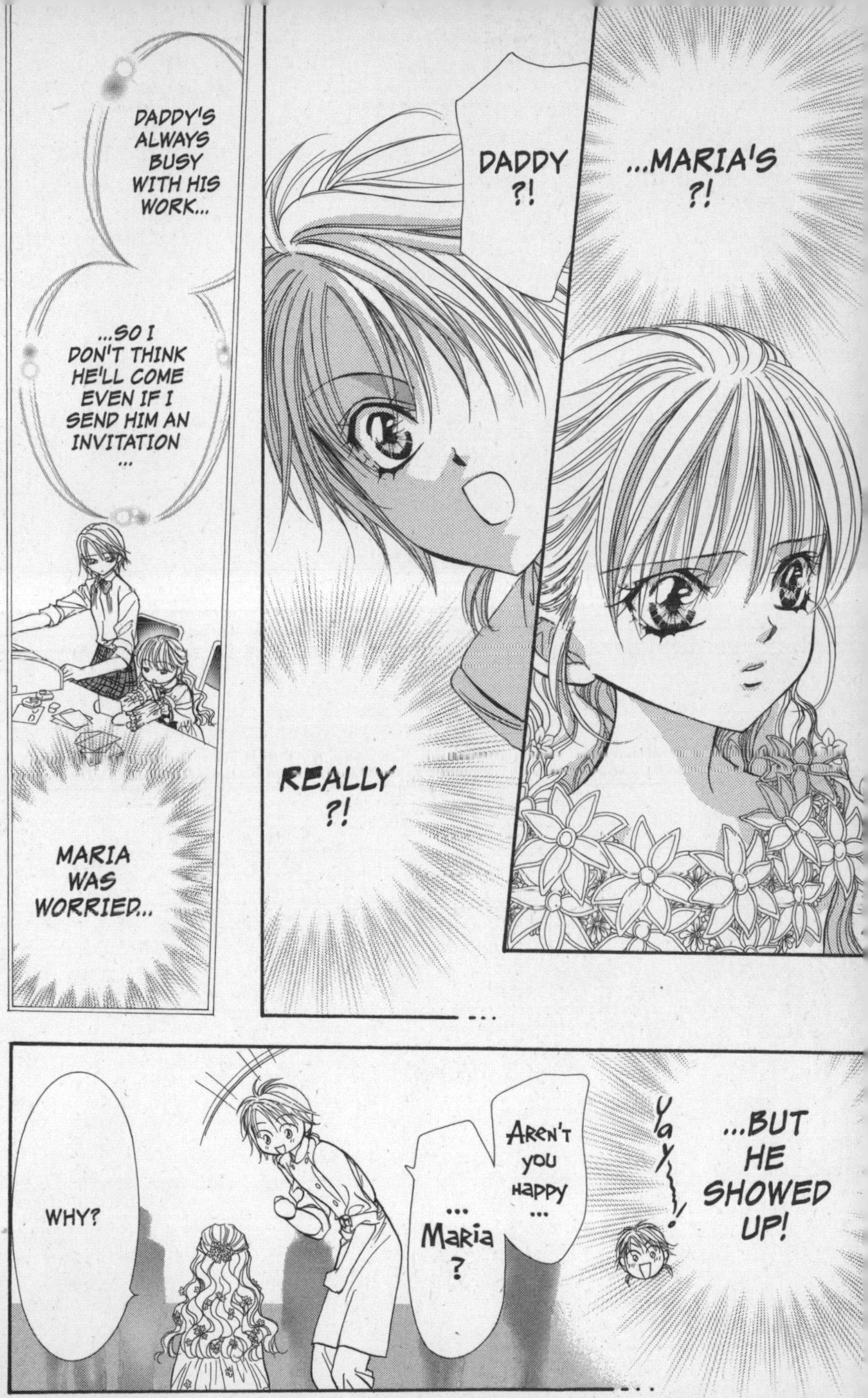
...MARIA'S ?!
DADDY ?!
REALLY ?!
DADDY'S ALWAYS BUSY WITH HIS WORK...
...SO I DON'T THINK HE'LL COME EVEN IF I SEND HIM AN INVITATION ...
MARIA WAS WORRIED...
...
...BUT HE SHOWED UP!
Yay~!
Aren't you happy ...
... Maria ?
WHY?
...

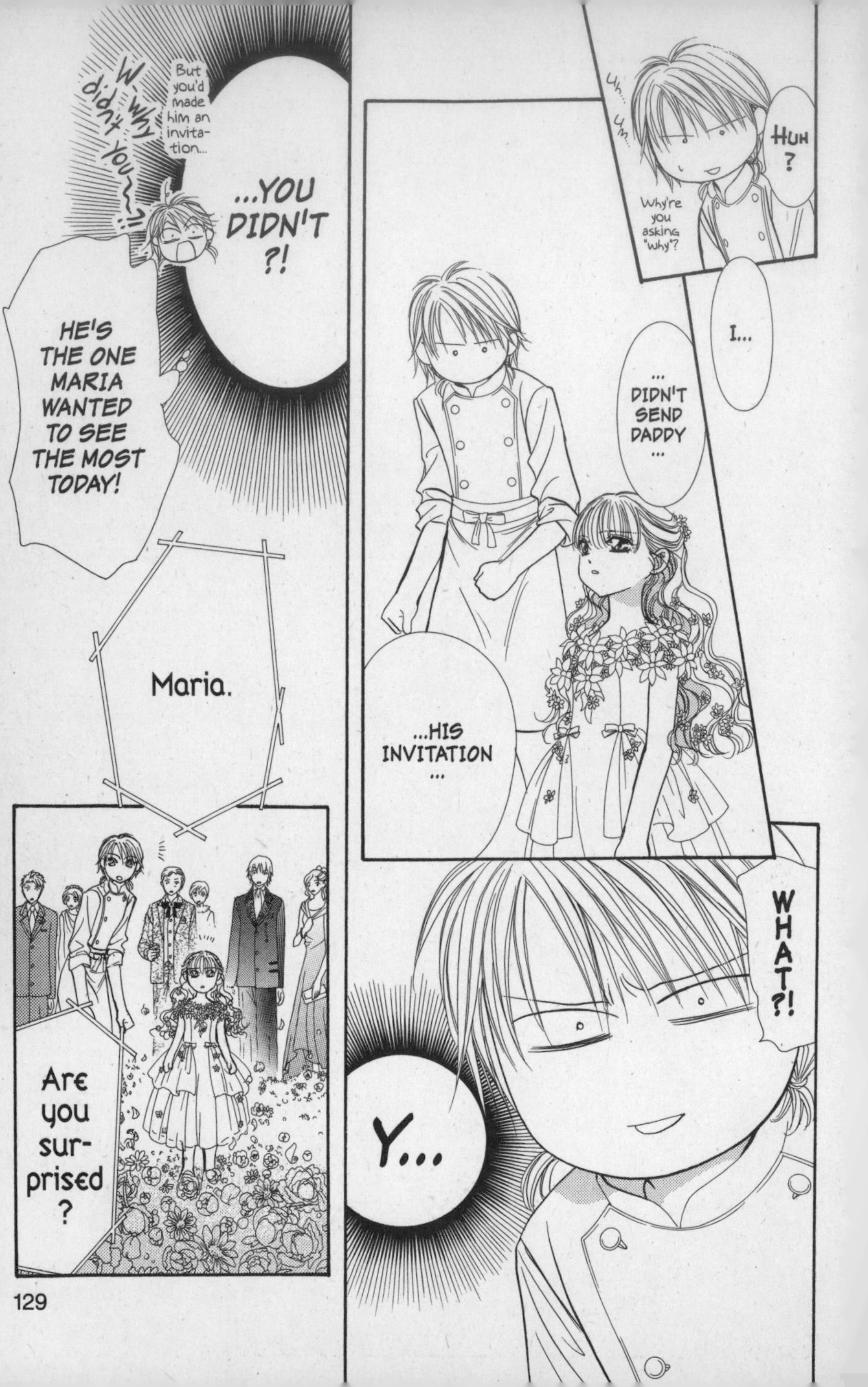
HUH?
Uh... Um...
Why're you asking "why"?
I...
...DIDN'T SEND DADDY...
...HIS INVITATION...
WHAT?!
Y...
...YOU DIDN'T?!
But you'd made him an invitation...
W-why didn't you~?!
HE'S THE ONE MARIA WANTED TO SEE THE MOST TODAY!
Maria.
Are you sur-prised?

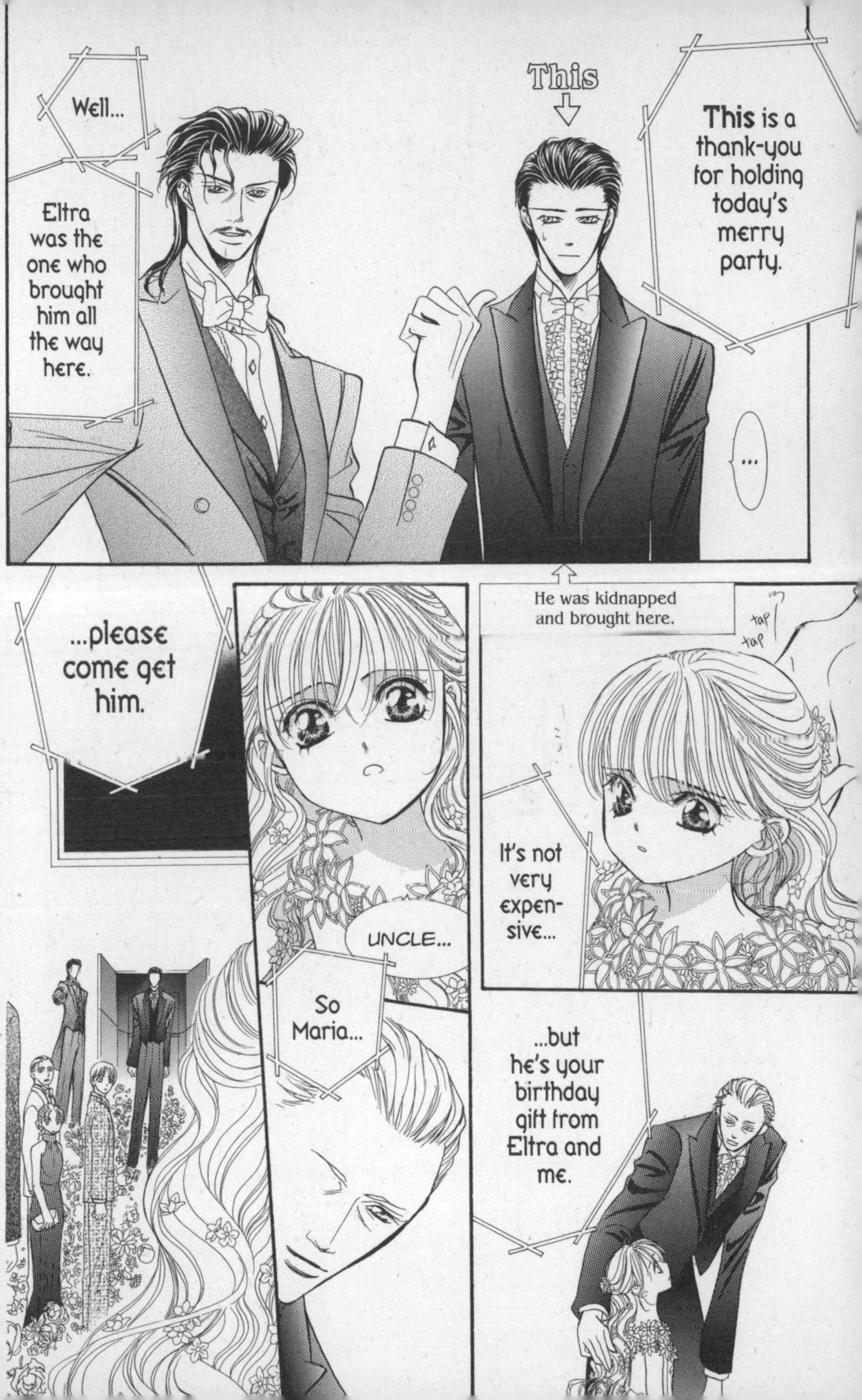
This
This is a thank-you for holding today's merry party.
...
Well...
Eltra was the one who brought him all the way here.
He was kidnapped and brought here.
tap tap
It's not very expensive...
UNCLE...
...please come get him.
...but he's your birthday gift from Eltra and me.
So Maria...

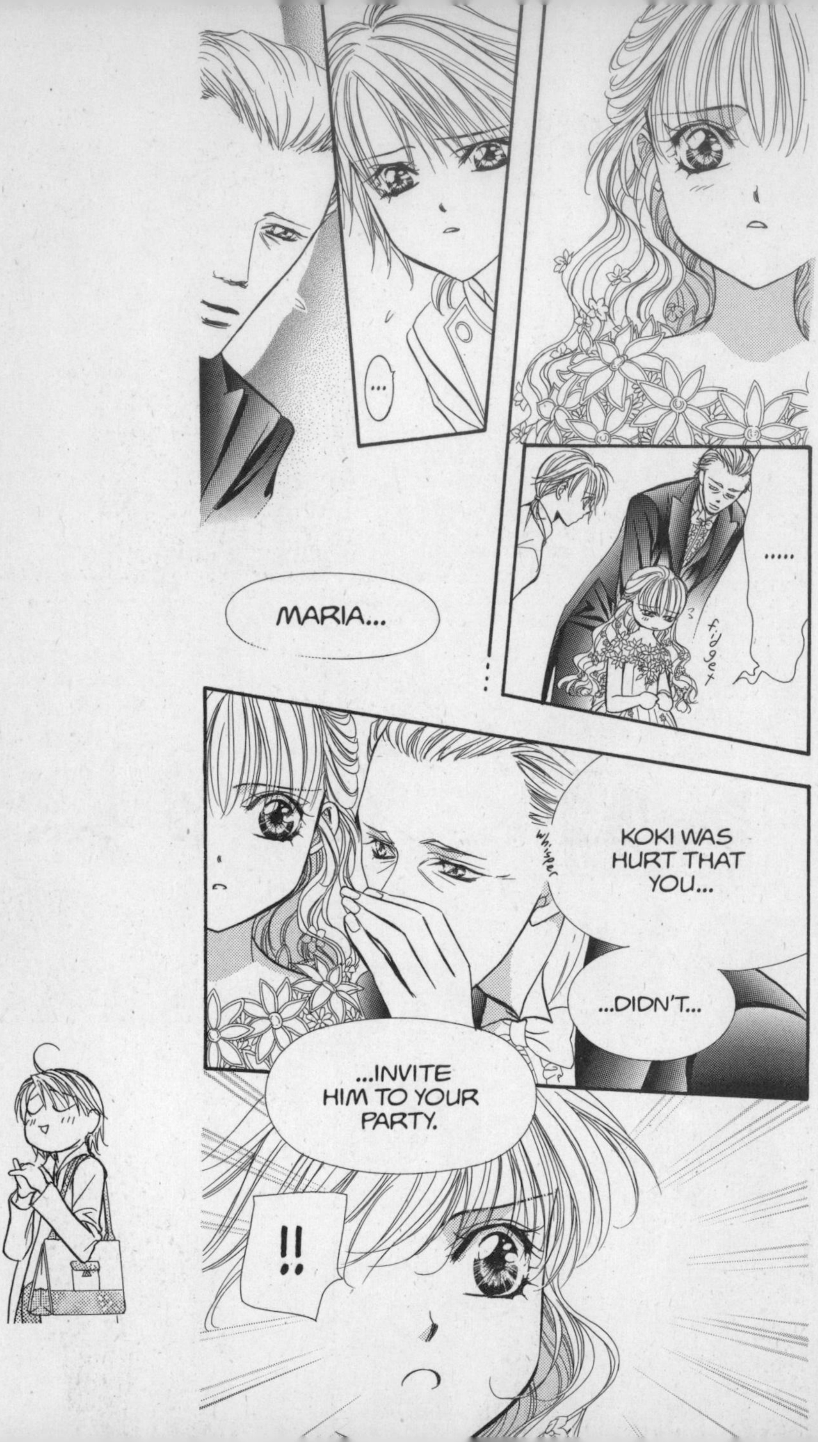
...
.....
fidget
MARIA...
whisper
KOKI WAS HURT THAT YOU...
...DIDN'T...
...INVITE HIM TO YOUR PARTY.
!!

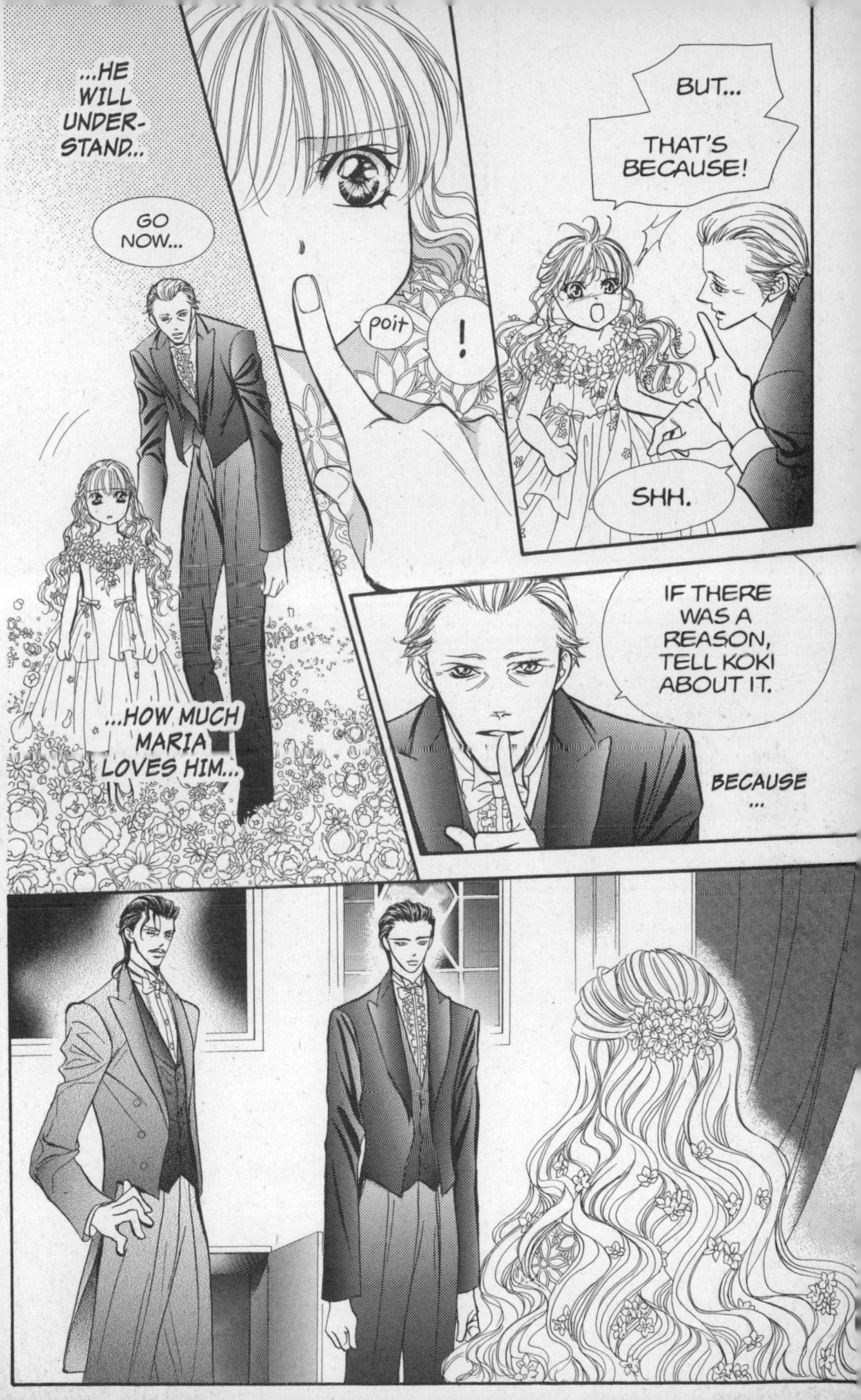

BUT...
THAT'S BECAUSE!
SHH.
poit
!
IF THERE WAS A REASON, TELL KOKI ABOUT IT.
BECAUSE ...
...HE WILL UNDER-STAND...
GO NOW...
...HOW MUCH MARIA LOVES HIM...

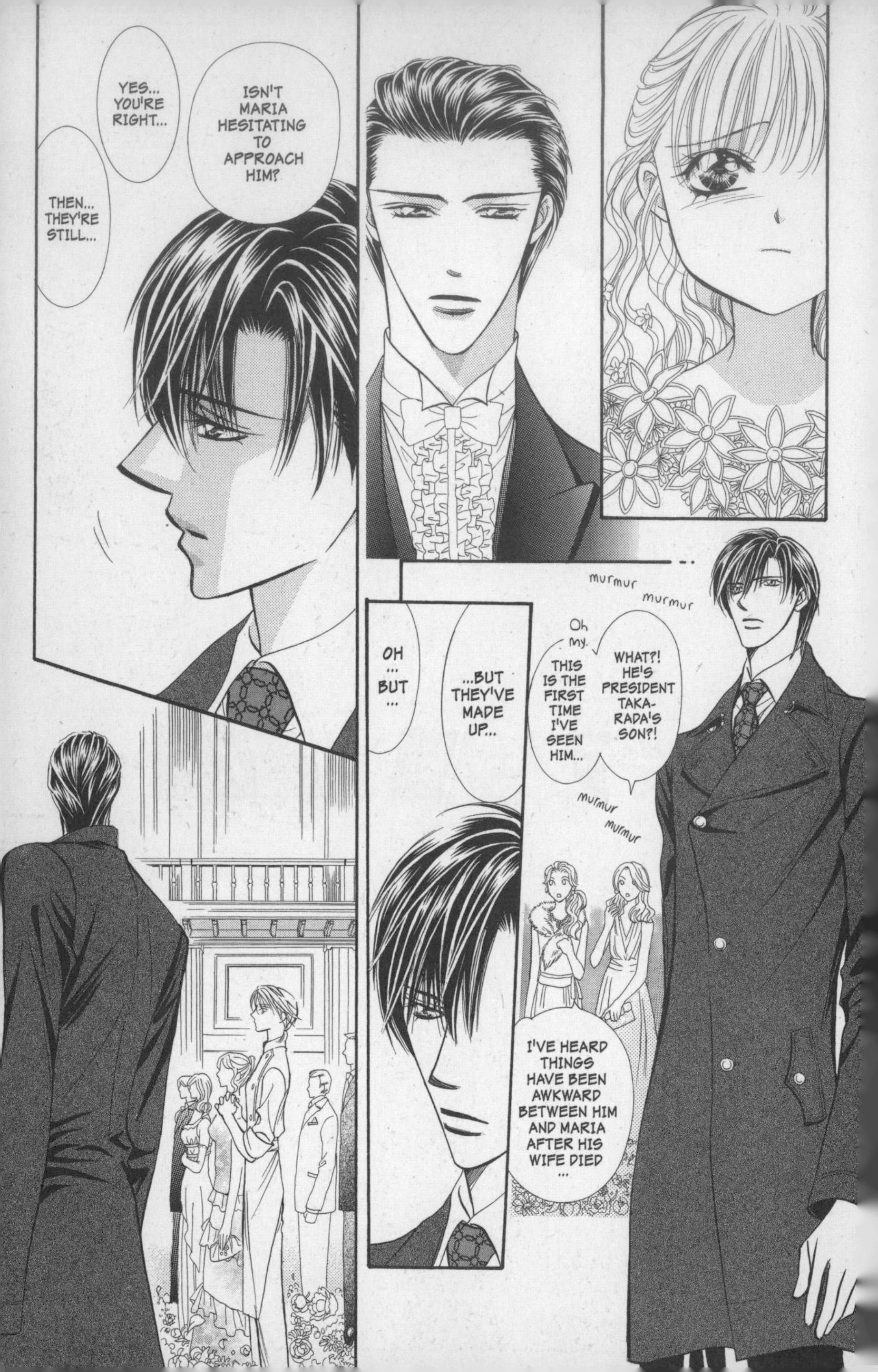
ISN'T MARIA HESITATING TO APPROACH HIM?
YES... YOU'RE RIGHT...
THEN... THEY'RE STILL...
murmur murmur
WHAT?! HE'S PRESIDENT TAKARADA'S SON?!
Oh my. THIS IS THE FIRST TIME I'VE SEEN HIM...
murmur murmur
I'VE HEARD THINGS HAVE BEEN AWKWARD BETWEEN HIM AND MARIA AFTER HIS WIFE DIED ...
...BUT THEY'VE MADE UP...
OH ... BUT ...

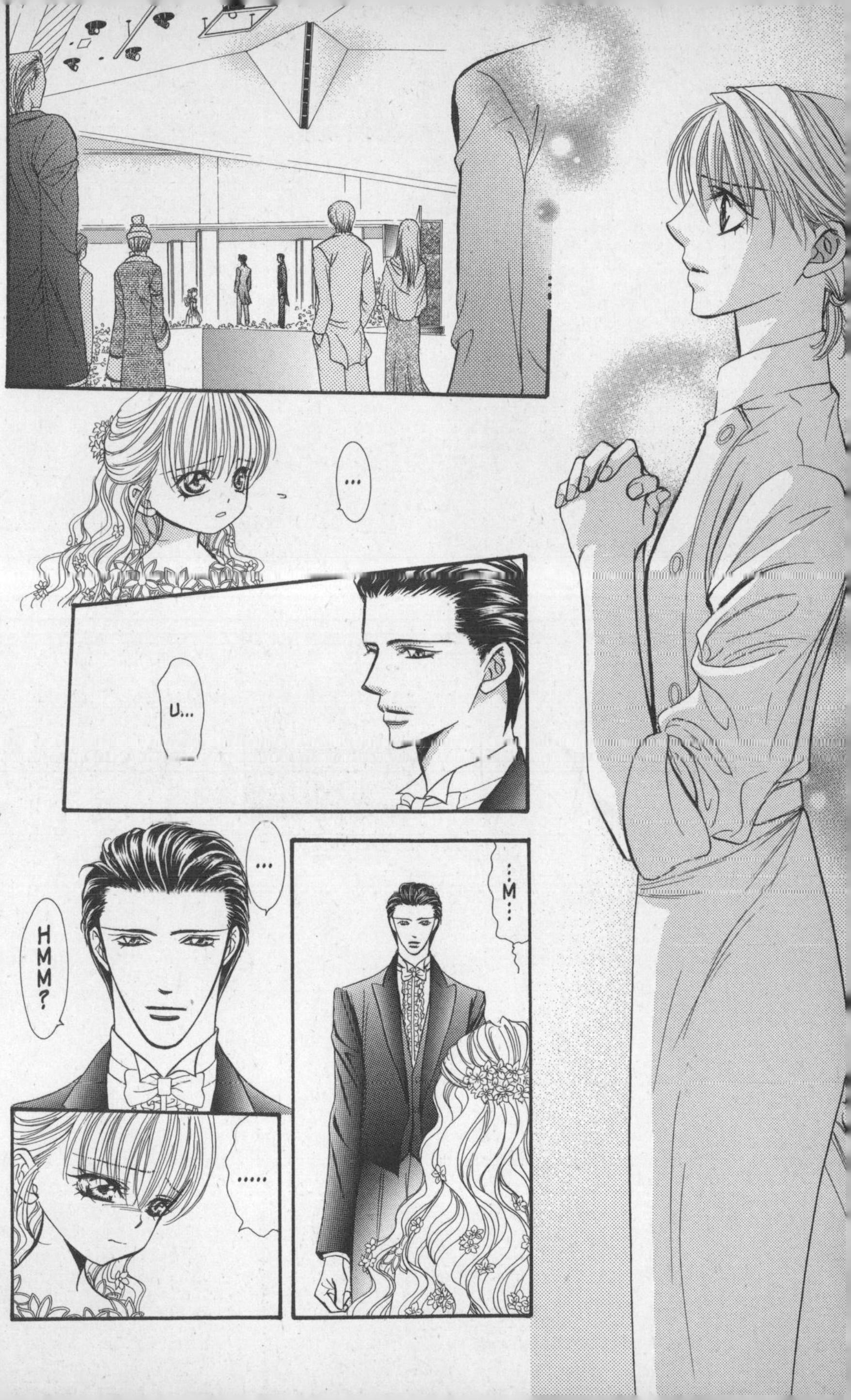
...
U...
...M...
...
HMM?
......

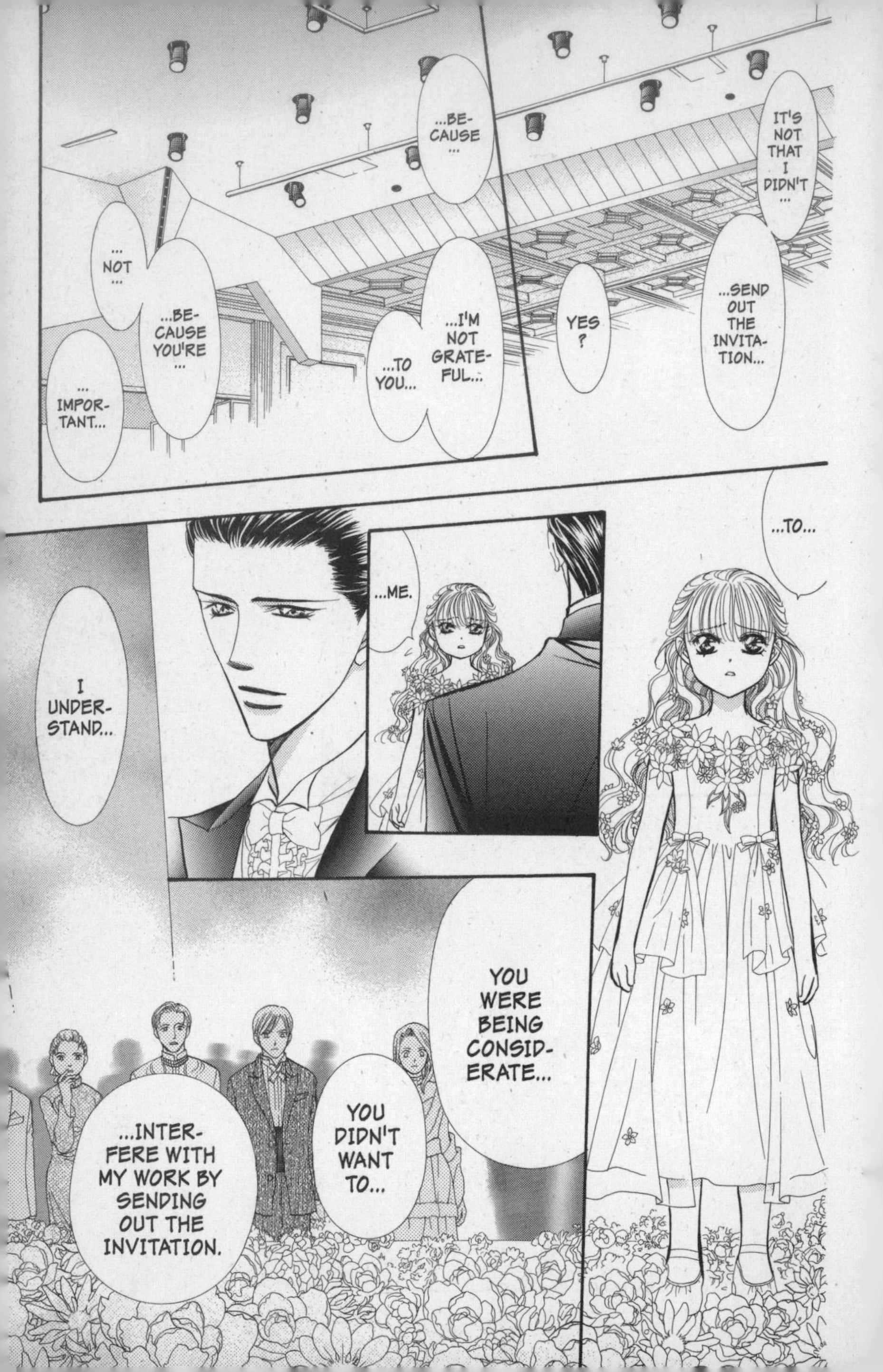
IT'S NOT THAT I DIDN'T ...
...SEND OUT THE INVITATION...
YES?
...BE-CAUSE ...
...I'M NOT GRATE-FUL...
...TO YOU...
...BE-CAUSE YOU'RE ...
... NOT ...
... IMPOR-TANT...
...TO...
...ME.
I UNDER-STAND...
YOU WERE BEING CONSID-ERATE...
YOU DIDN'T WANT TO...
...INTER-FERE WITH MY WORK BY SENDING OUT THE INVITATION.

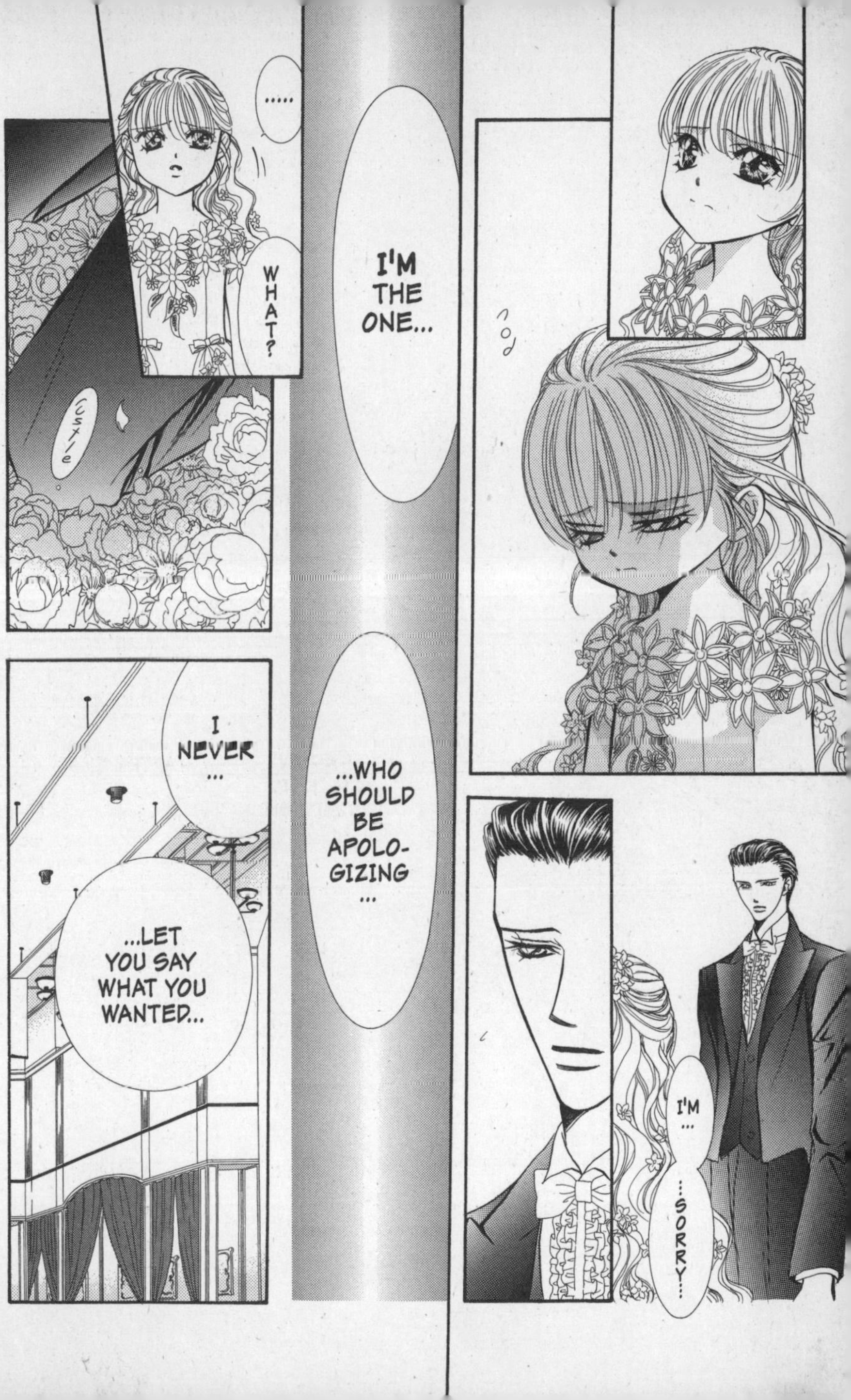
I'M ...
...SORRY...
I'M THE ONE...
...WHO SHOULD BE APOLOGIZING...
......
WHAT?
rustle
I NEVER ...
...LET YOU SAY WHAT YOU WANTED...

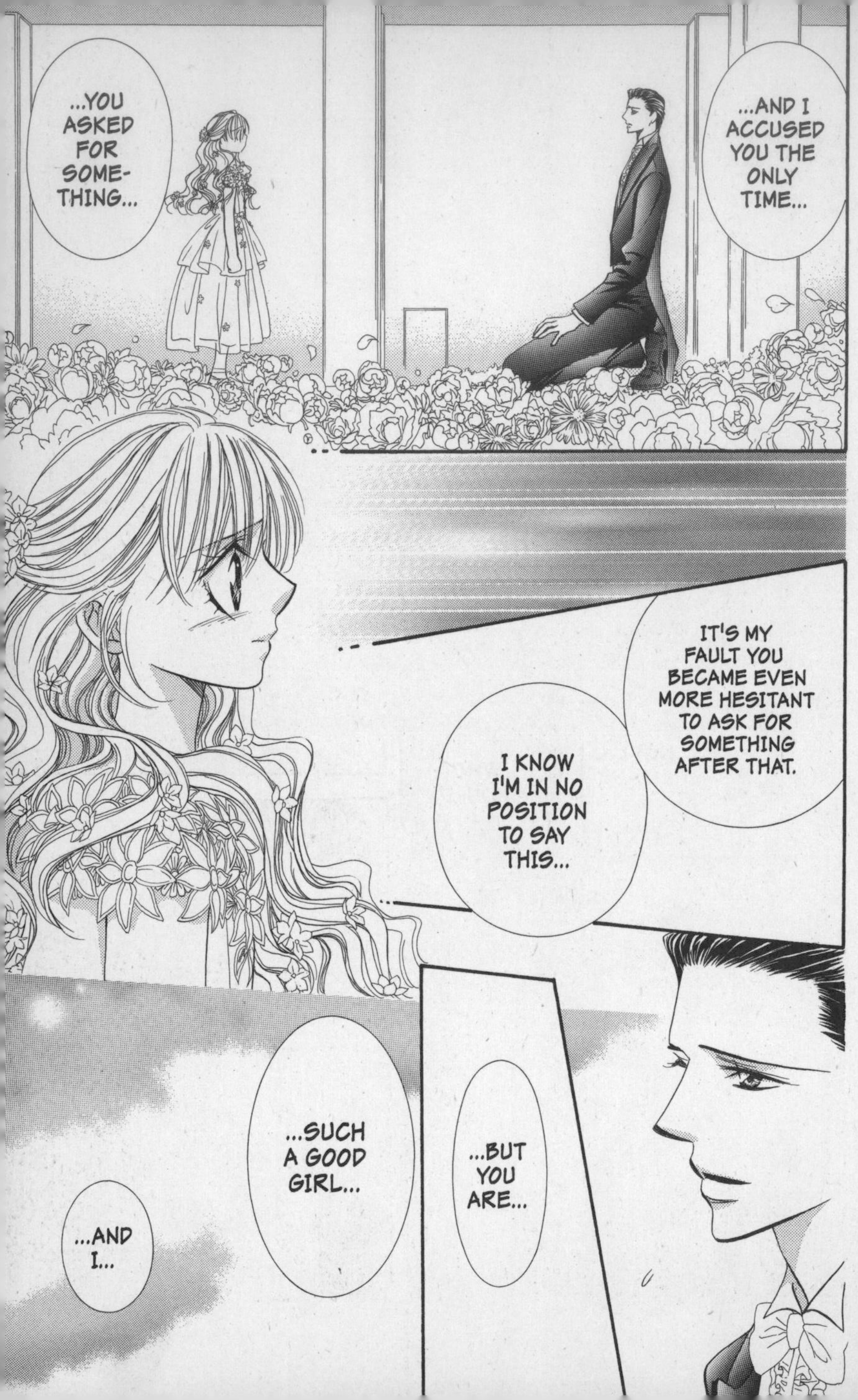
...AND I ACCUSED YOU THE ONLY TIME...
...YOU ASKED FOR SOME-THING...
IT'S MY FAULT YOU BECAME EVEN MORE HESITANT TO ASK FOR SOMETHING AFTER THAT.
I KNOW I'M IN NO POSITION TO SAY THIS...
...BUT YOU ARE...
...SUCH A GOOD GIRL...
...AND I...

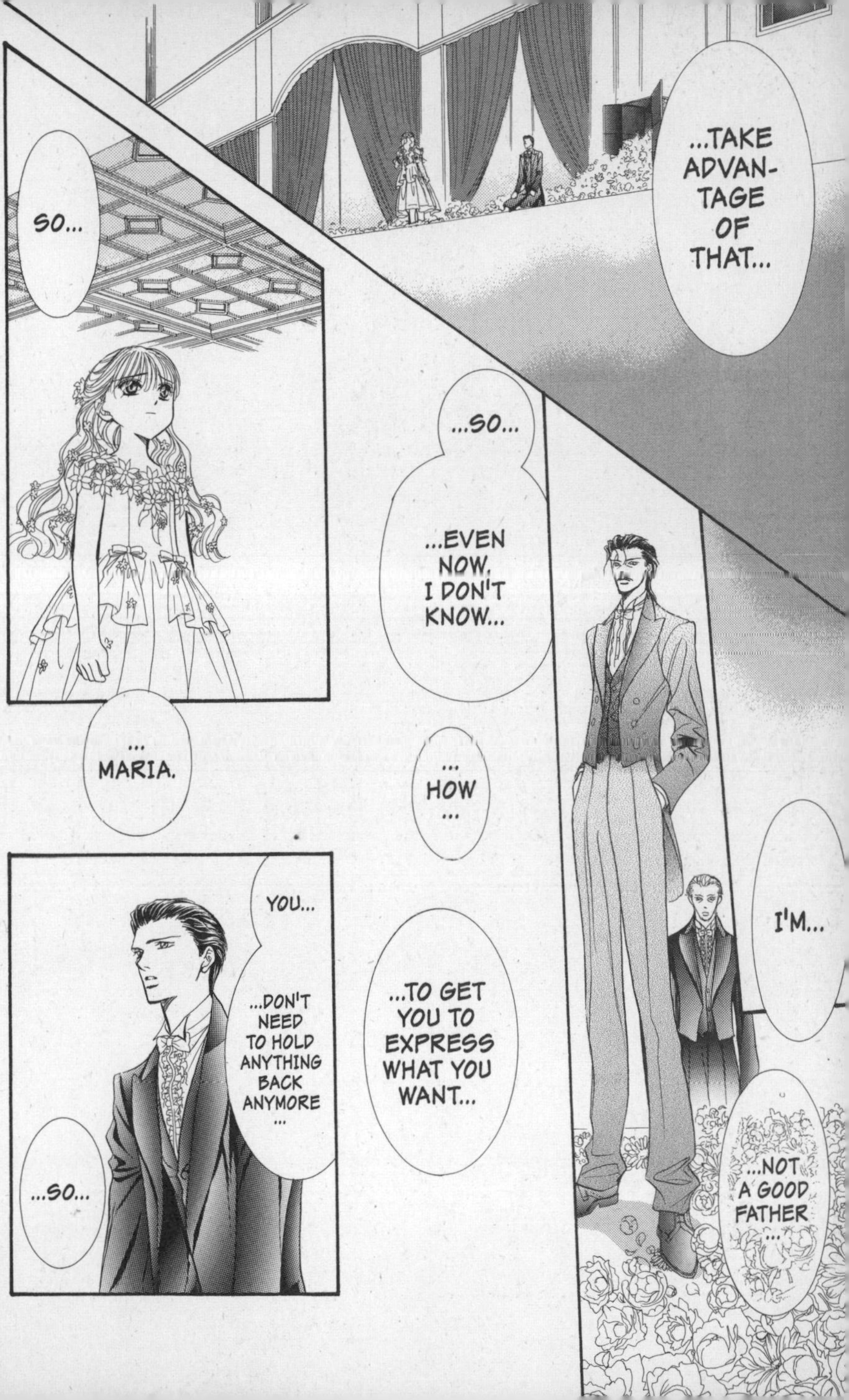
...TAKE ADVAN-TAGE OF THAT...
I'M...
...NOT A GOOD FATHER...
...SO...
...EVEN NOW, I DON'T KNOW...
...HOW...
...TO GET YOU TO EXPRESS WHAT YOU WANT...
SO...
...MARIA.
YOU...
...DON'T NEED TO HOLD ANYTHING BACK ANYMORE...
...SO...

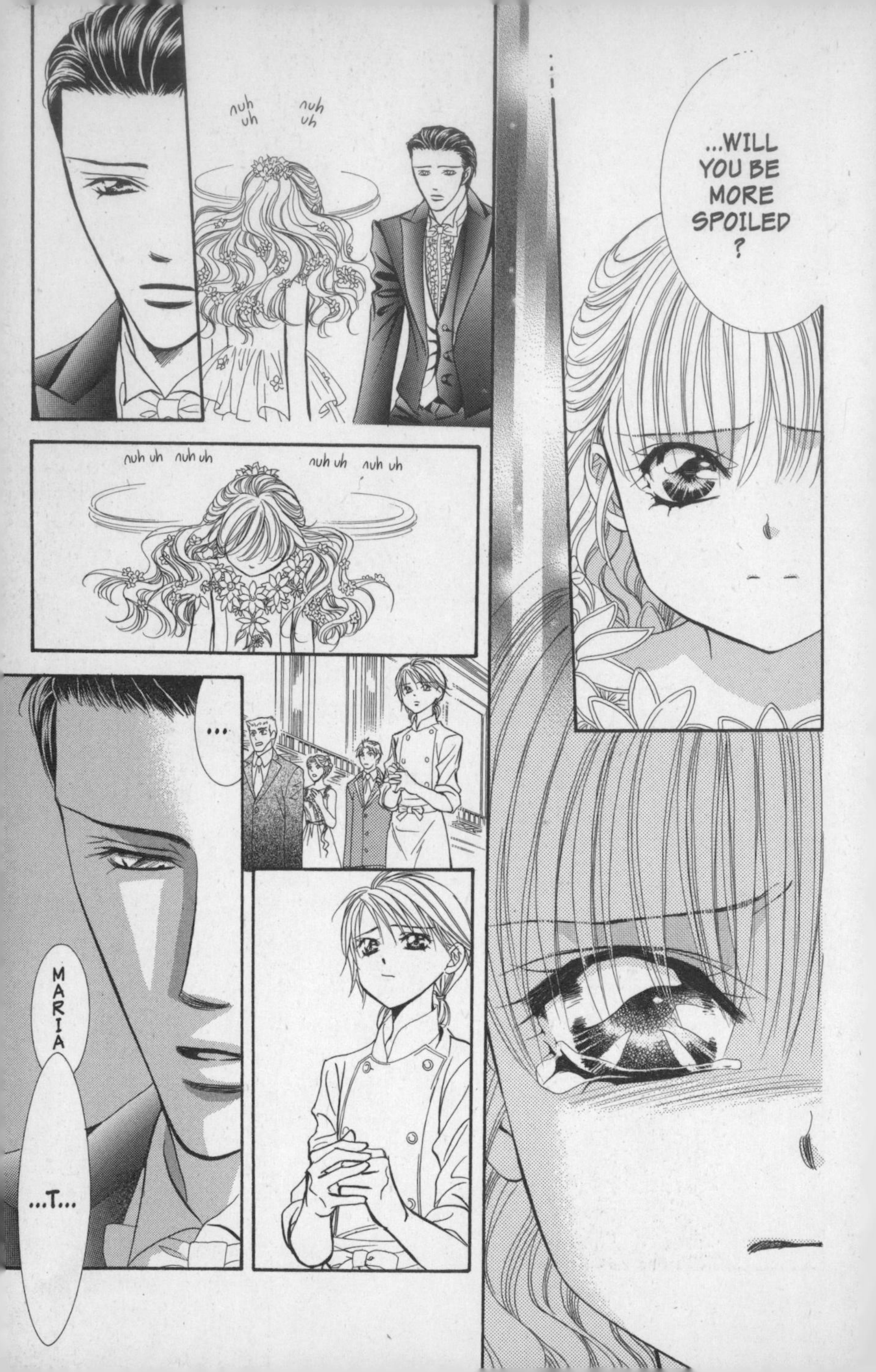
...WILL YOU BE MORE SPOILED?
nuh uh nuh uh
nuh uh nuh uh
nuh uh nuh uh
...
MARIA
...T...

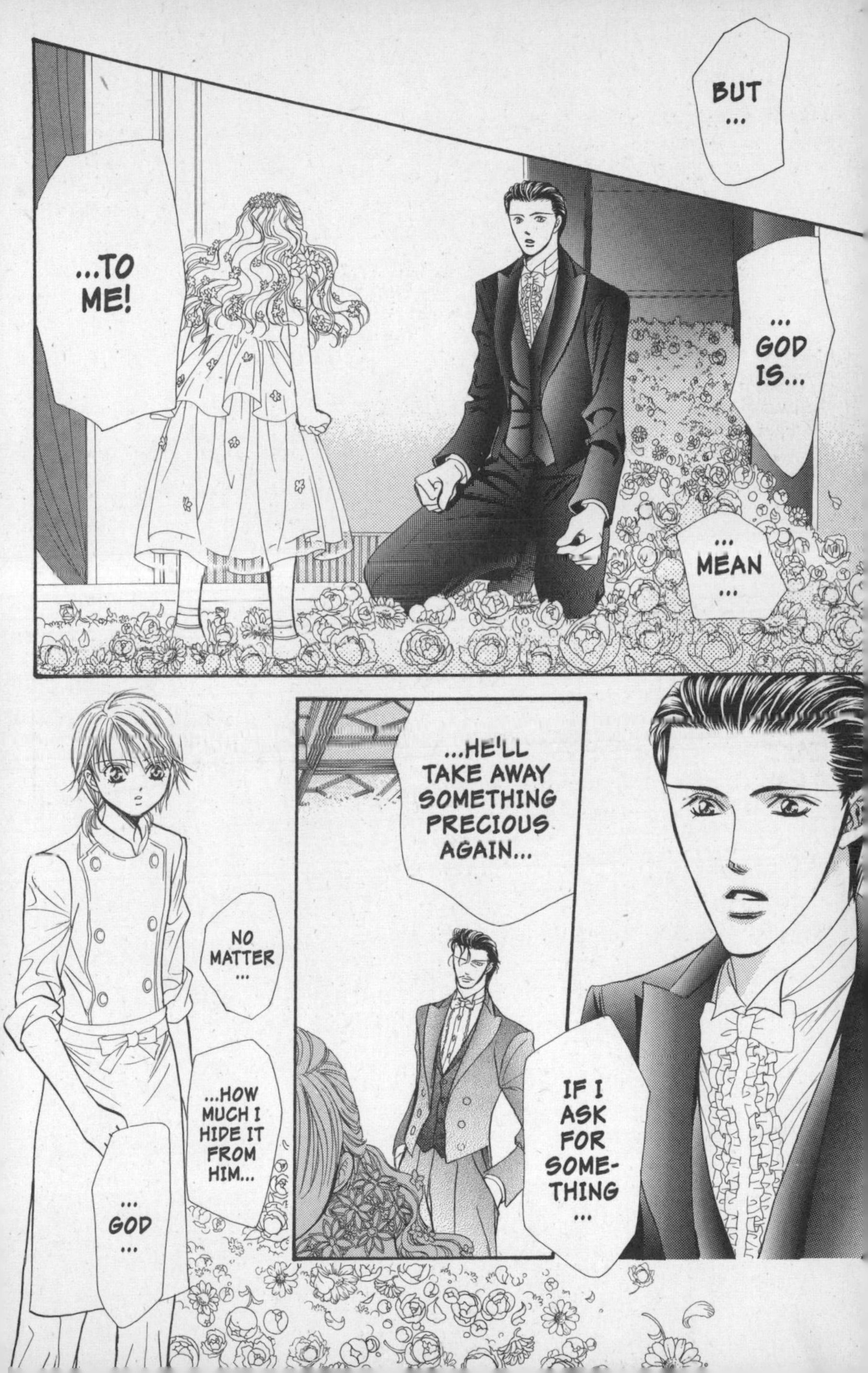
BUT ...
... GOD IS...
... MEAN ...
...TO ME!
IF I ASK FOR SOME-THING ...
...HE'LL TAKE AWAY SOMETHING PRECIOUS AGAIN...
NO MATTER ...
...HOW MUCH I HIDE IT FROM HIM...
... GOD ...

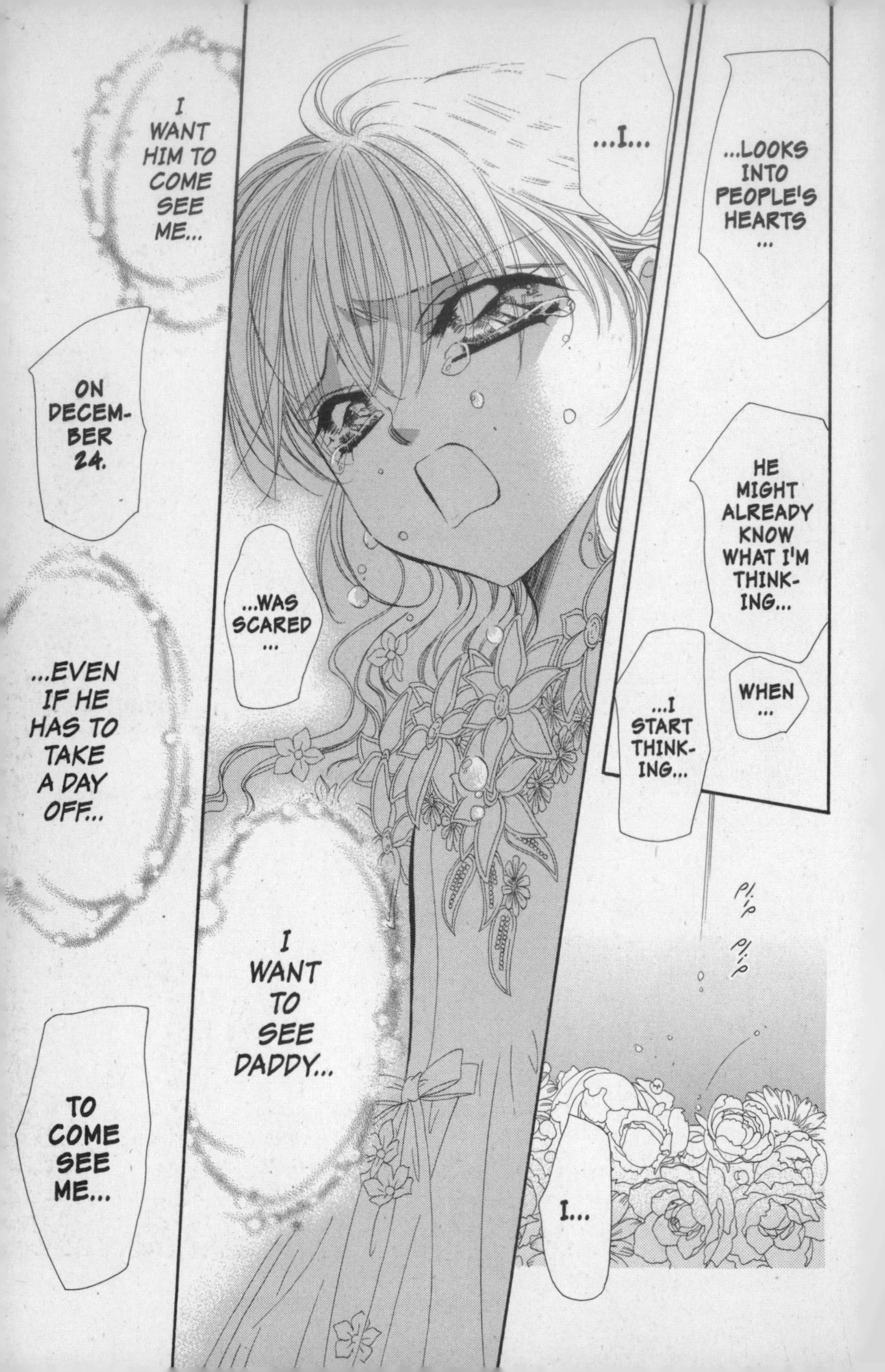
...LOOKS INTO PEOPLE'S HEARTS ...
HE MIGHT ALREADY KNOW WHAT I'M THINKING...
WHEN ...
...I START THINKING...
...I...
...WAS SCARED ...
Plip
Plip
I...
I WANT TO SEE DADDY...
I WANT HIM TO COME SEE ME...
ON DECEMBER 24.
...EVEN IF HE HAS TO TAKE A DAY OFF...
TO COME SEE ME...

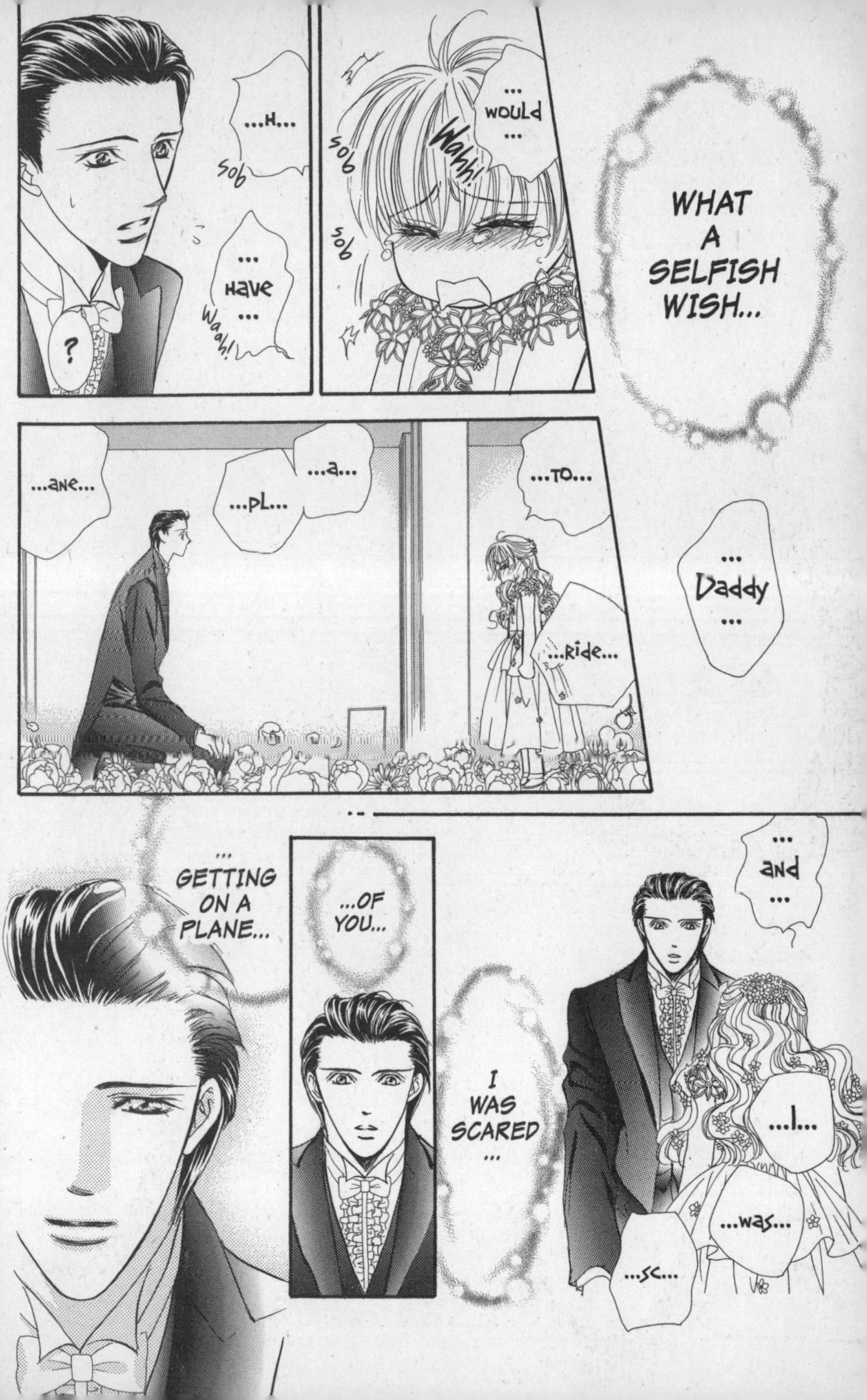
WHAT A SELFISH WISH...
...would...
Wahh!
sob
sob
...H...
sob
...have...
Waah!
?
...Daddy...
...TO...
...ride...
...a...
...pL...
...ane...
...and...
...I...
...was...
...sc...
I WAS SCARED...
...OF YOU...
...GETTING ON A PLANE...

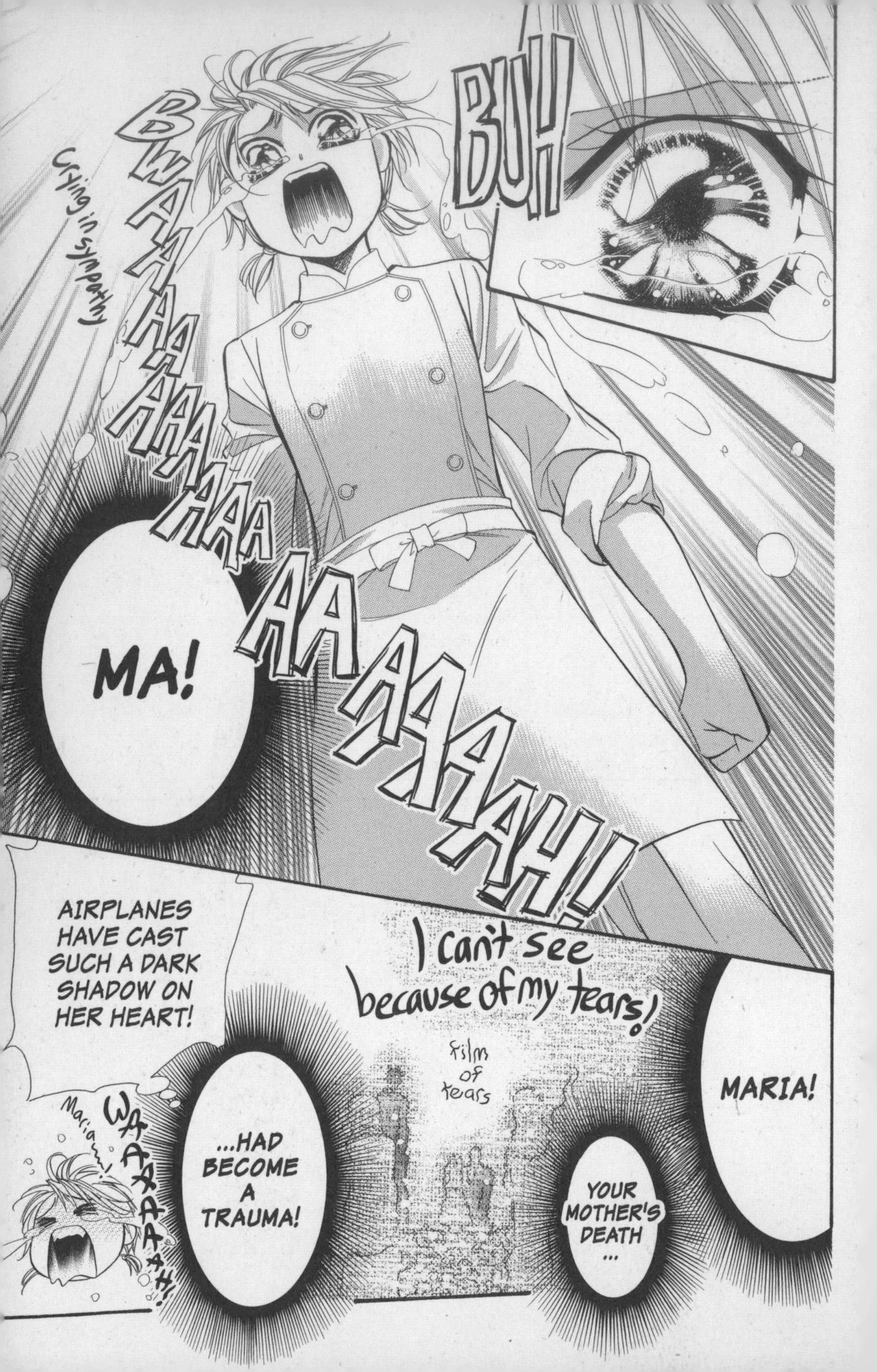
BUH
BWAAAAAAAAAAAAAAAAAAAH!!
Crying in sympathy
MA!
MARIA!
YOUR MOTHER'S DEATH ...
I can't see because of my tears!
Film of tears
...HAD BECOME A TRAUMA!
AIRPLANES HAVE CAST SUCH A DARK SHADOW ON HER HEART!
WAAAAAAH!!
Maria~!

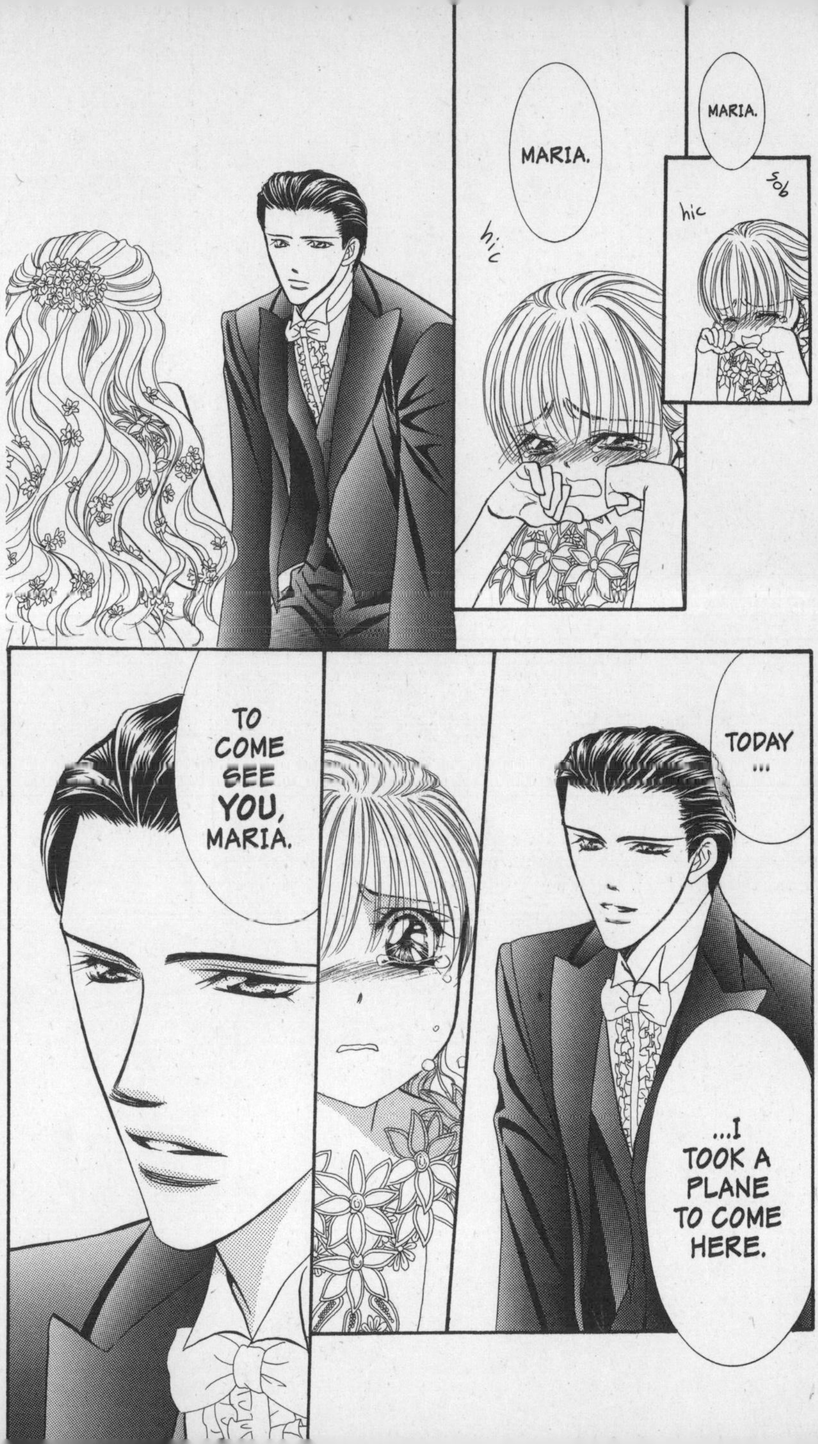
MARIA.
sob
hic
MARIA.
hic
TODAY ...
...I TOOK A PLANE TO COME HERE.
TO COME SEE YOU, MARIA.

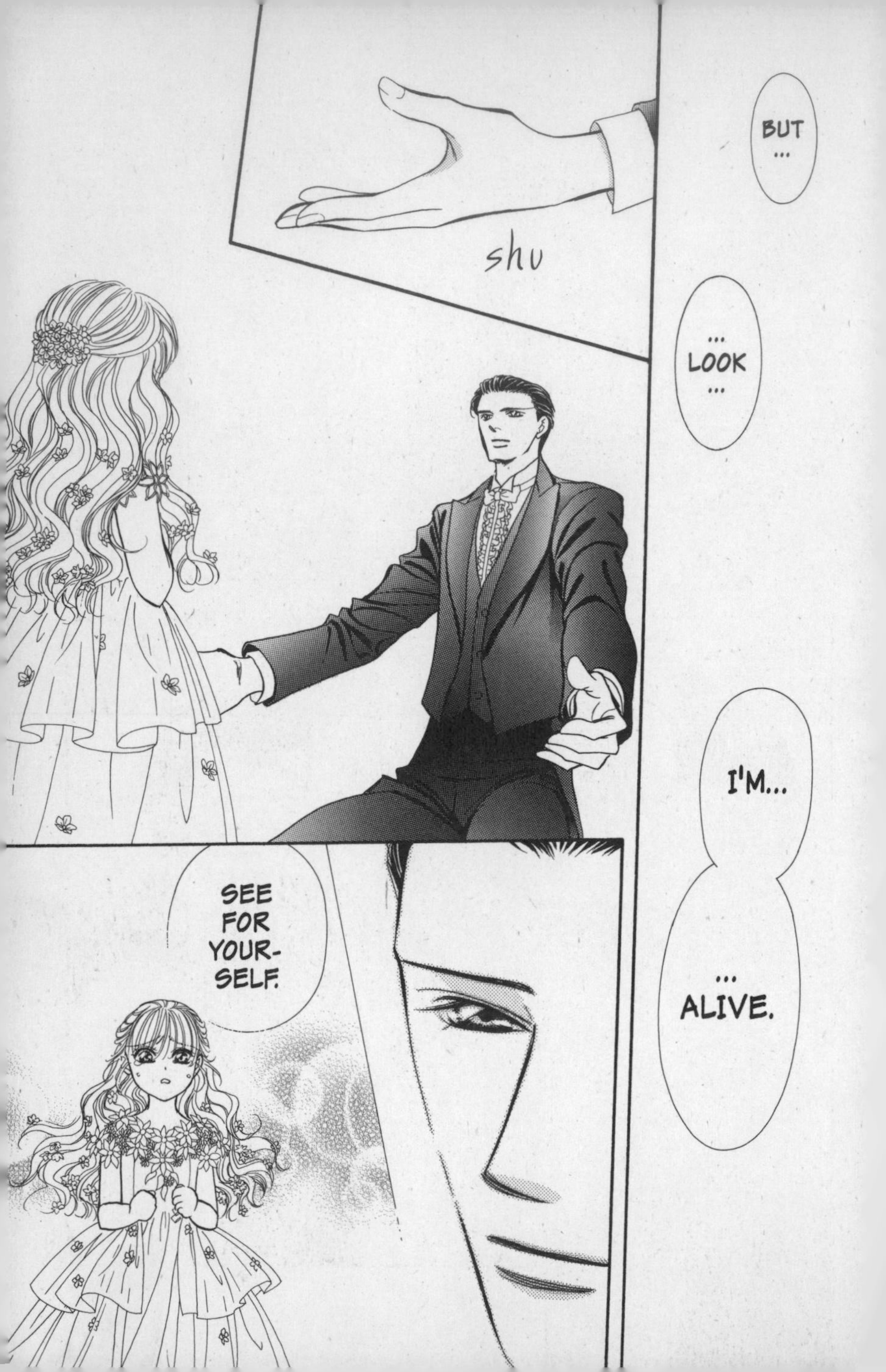
BUT ...
... LOOK ...
I'M...
... ALIVE.
shu
SEE FOR YOUR-SELF.

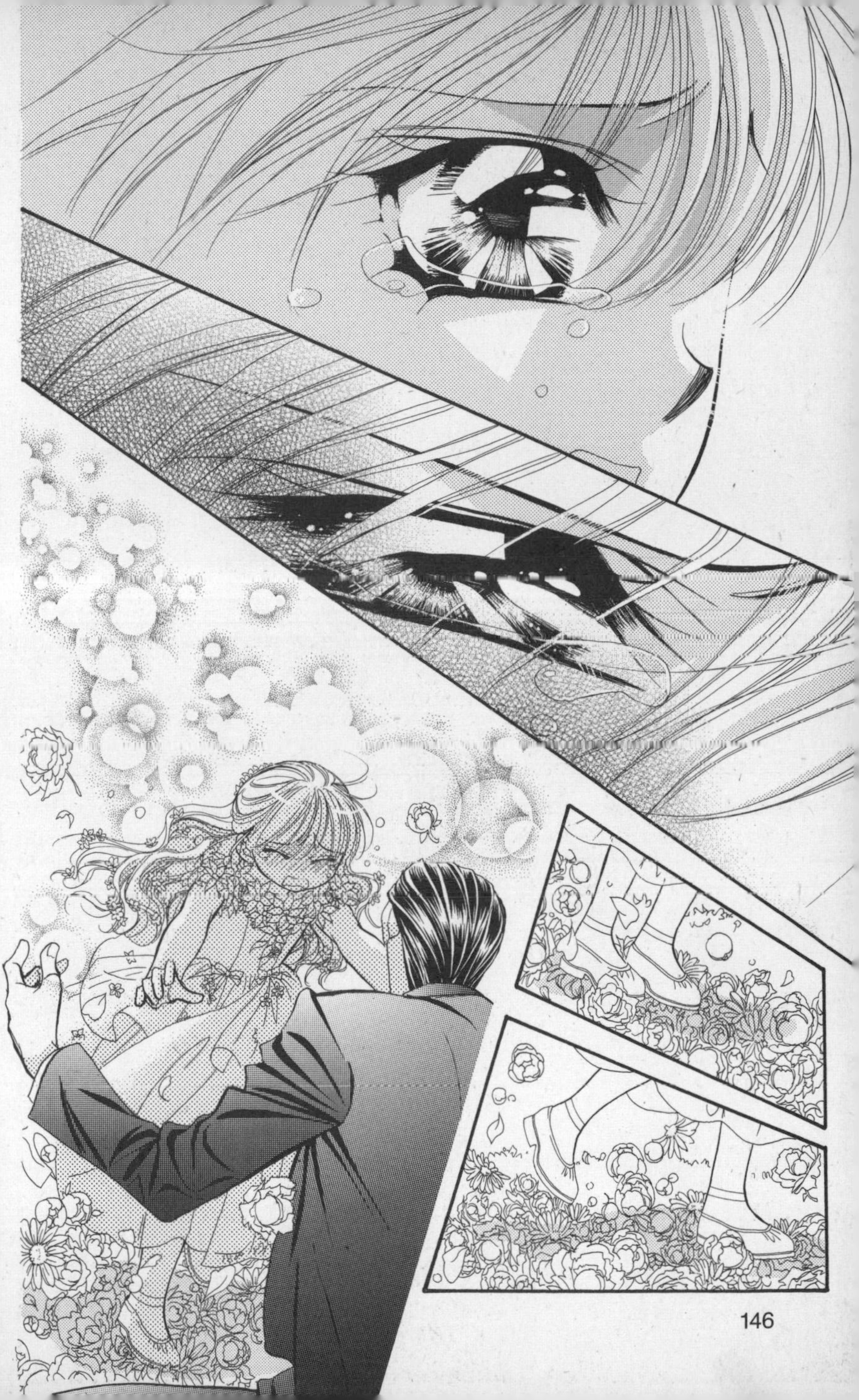

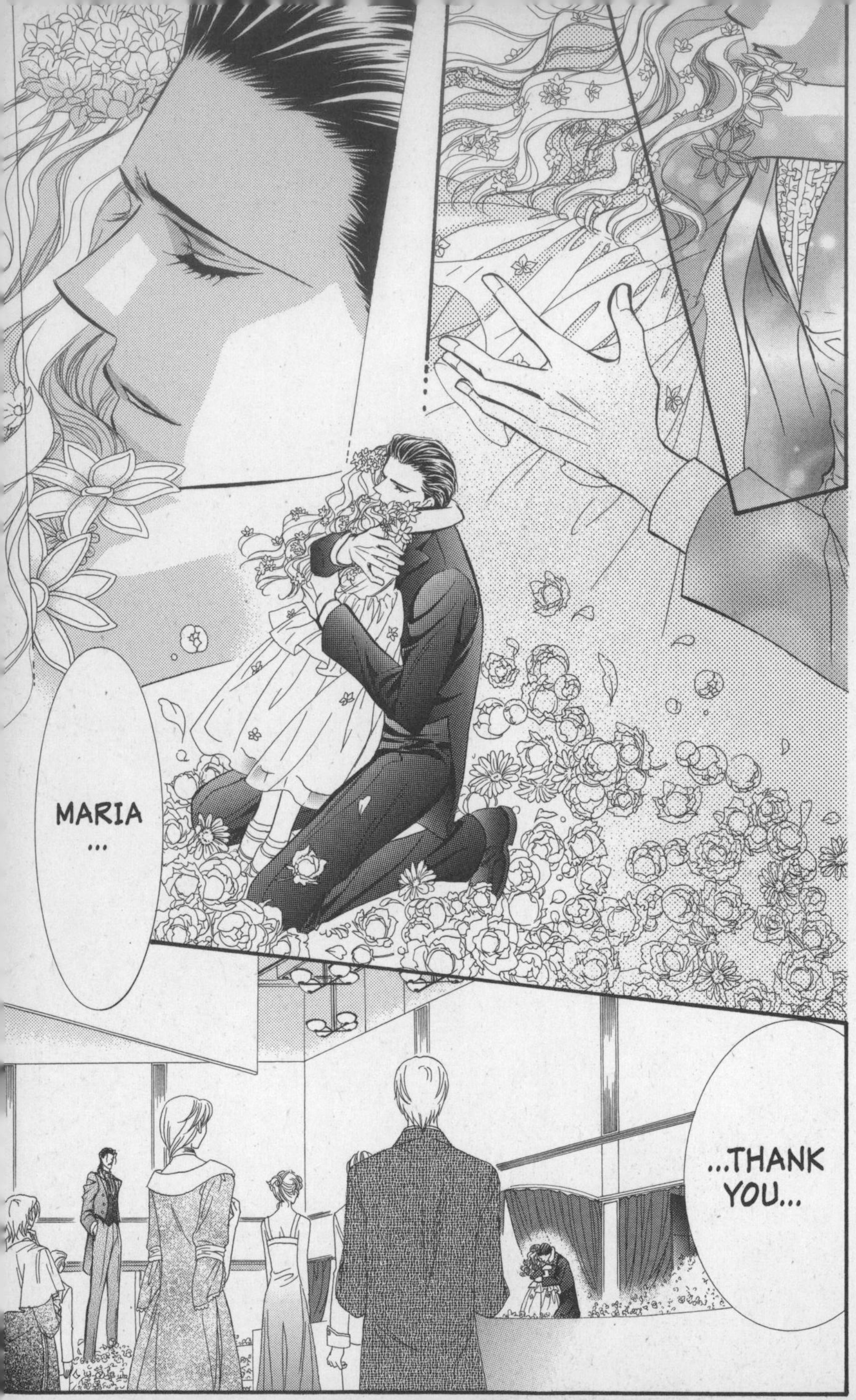
MARIA ...
...THANK YOU...

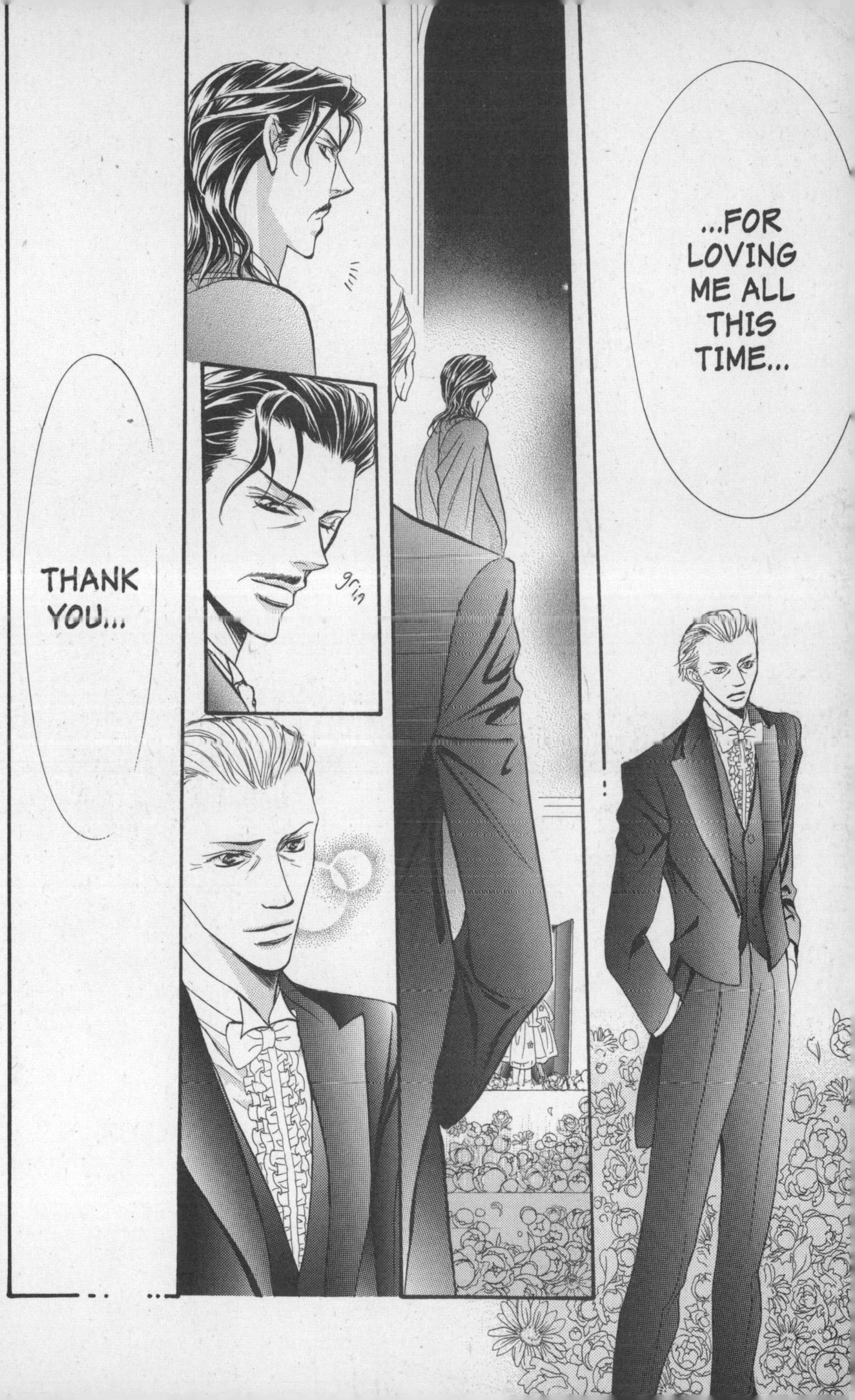
THANK YOU...
grin
...FOR LOVING ME ALL THIS TIME...

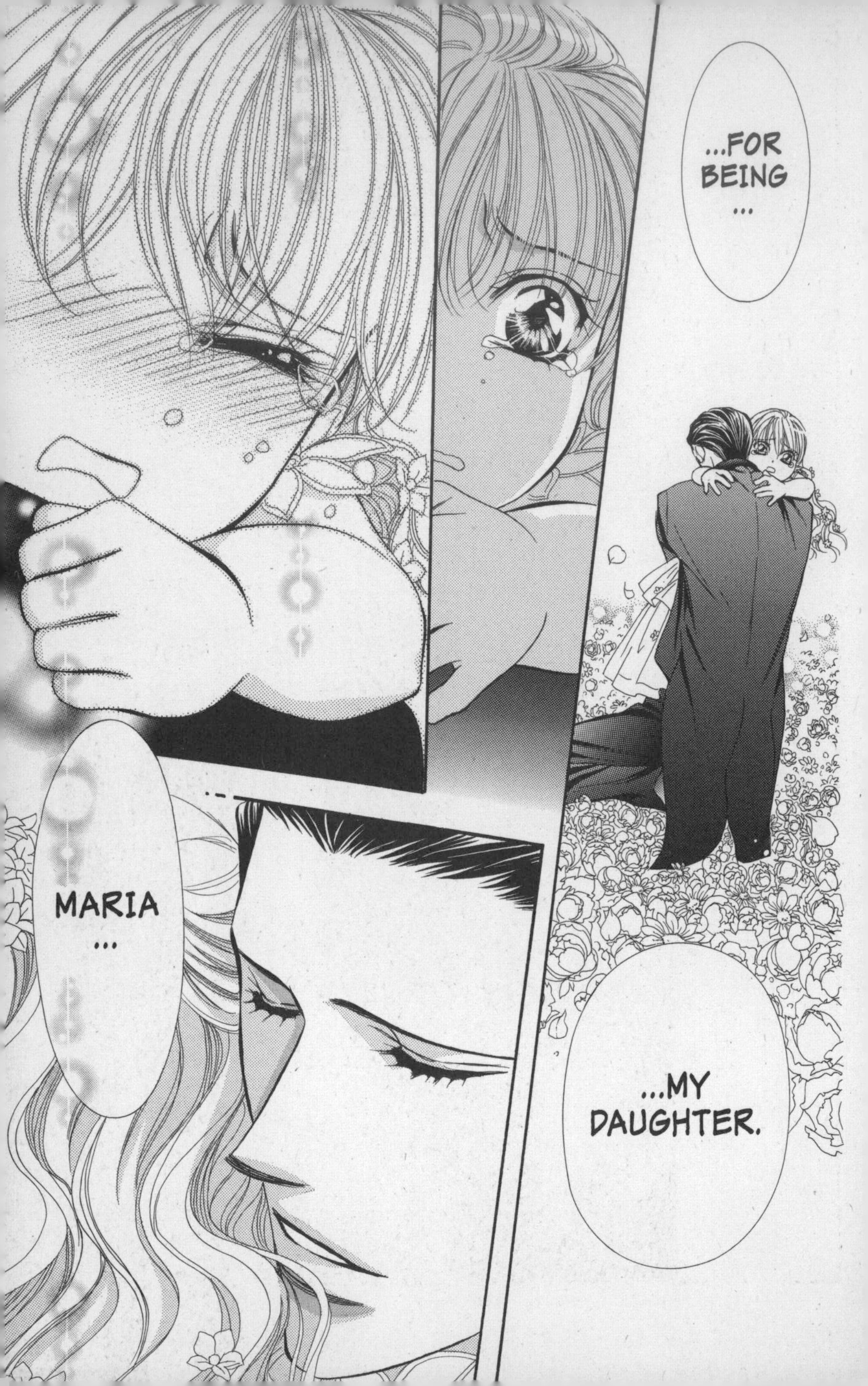
...FOR BEING ...
...MY DAUGHTER.
MARIA ...

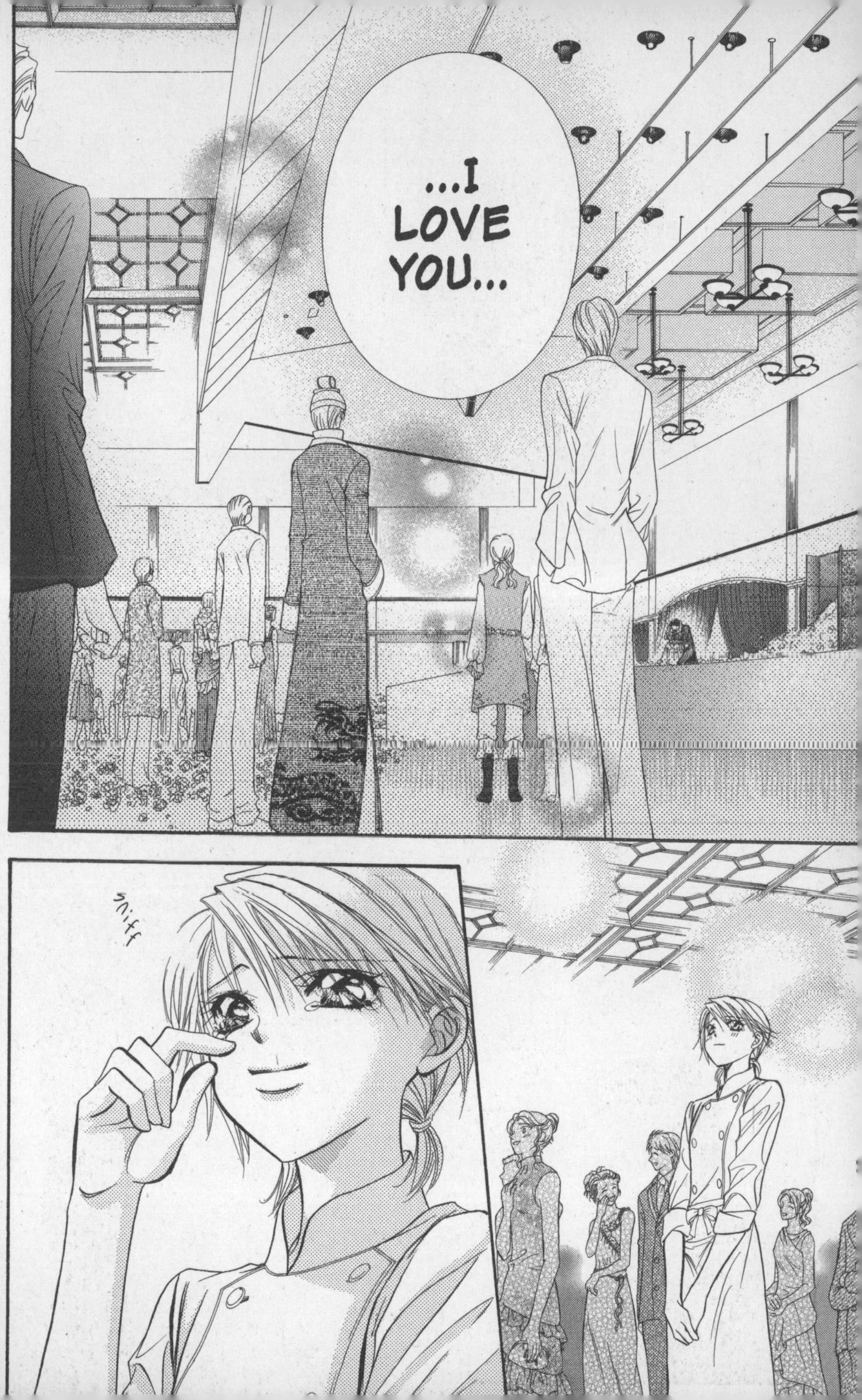
...I LOVE YOU...
sniff

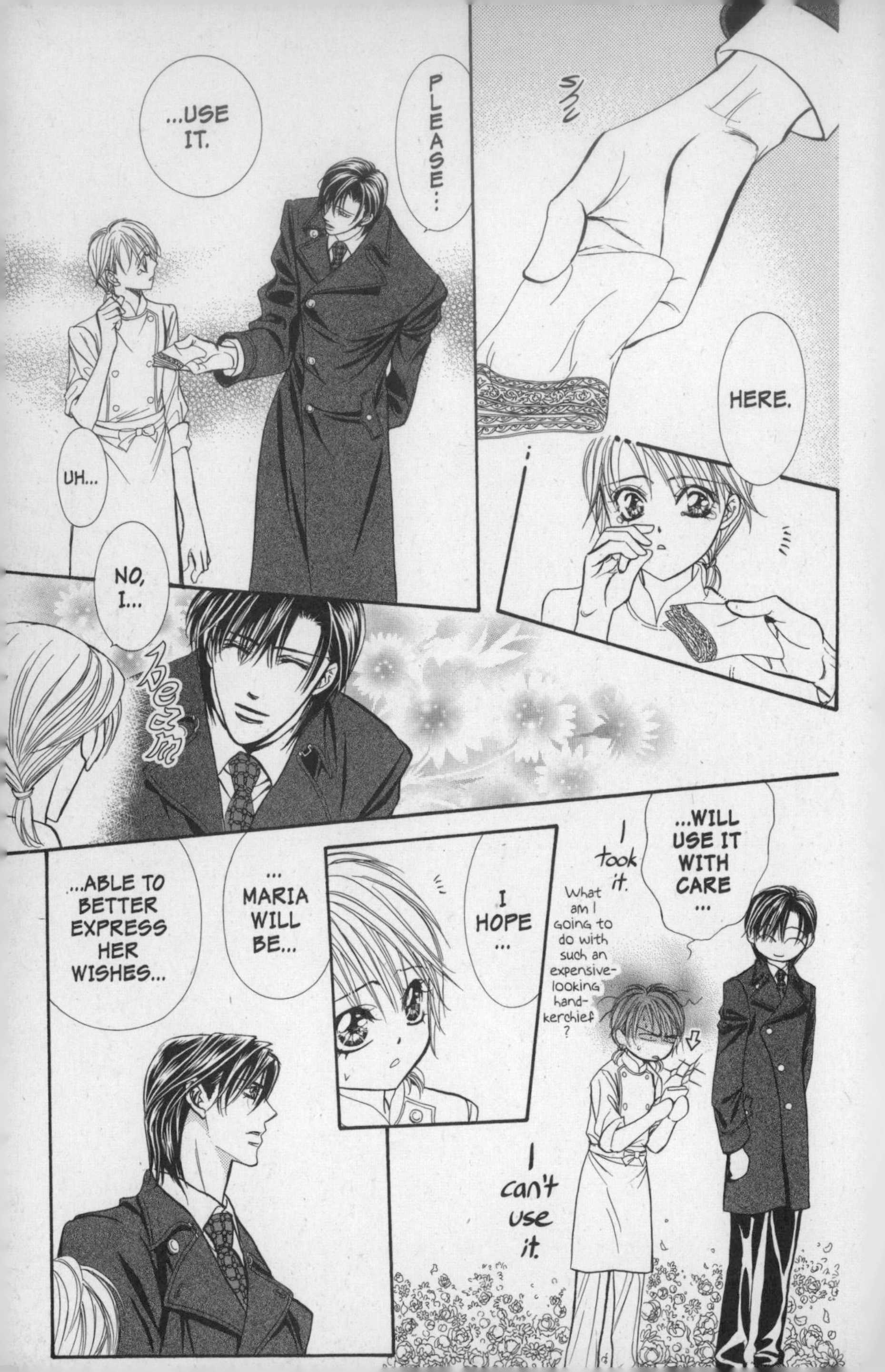
HERE.
PLEASE...
...USE IT.
UH...
NO, I...
beam
...WILL USE IT WITH CARE...
I took it.
What am I going to do with such an expensive-looking handkerchief?
I can't use it.
I HOPE...
...MARIA WILL BE...
...ABLE TO BETTER EXPRESS HER WISHES...

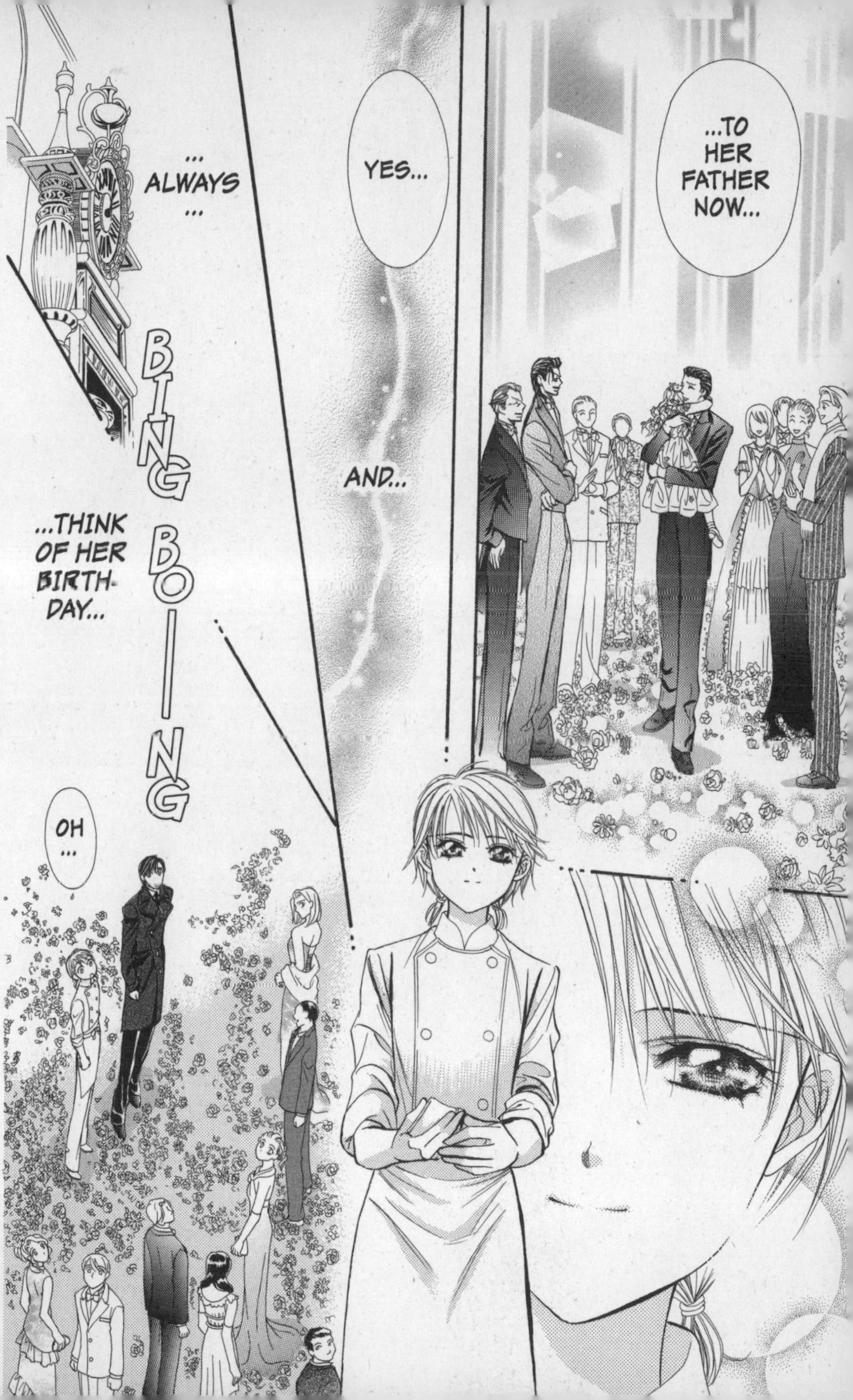
...TO HER FATHER NOW...
YES...
AND...
... ALWAYS ...
BING BOING
...THINK OF HER BIRTHDAY...
OH ...

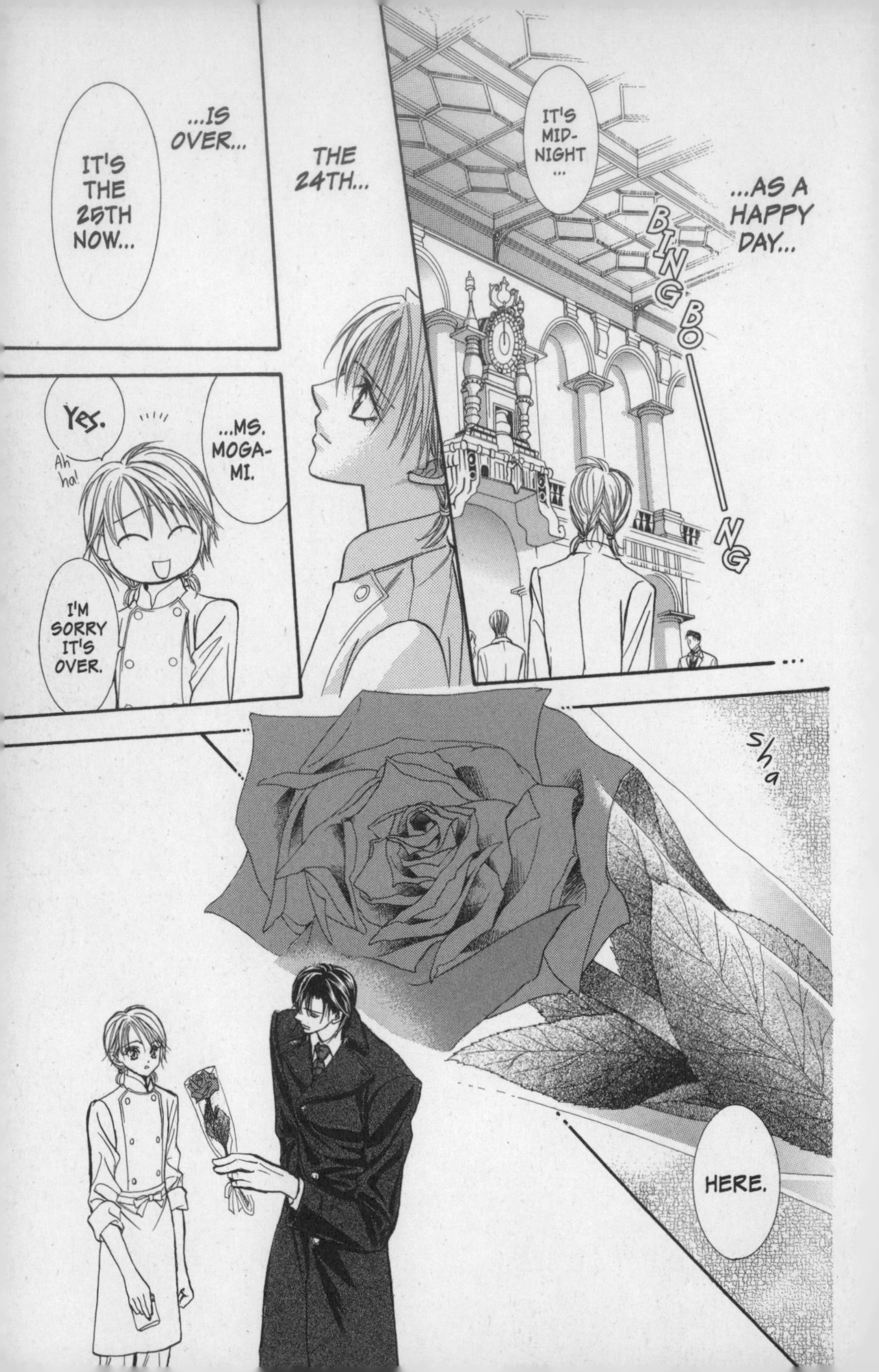
IT'S MID-NIGHT ...
BINGBONG
...AS A HAPPY DAY...
THE 24TH...
...IS OVER...
IT'S THE 25TH NOW...
...MS. MOGA-MI.
Yes.
Ah ha!
I'M SORRY IT'S OVER.
...
Sha
HERE.

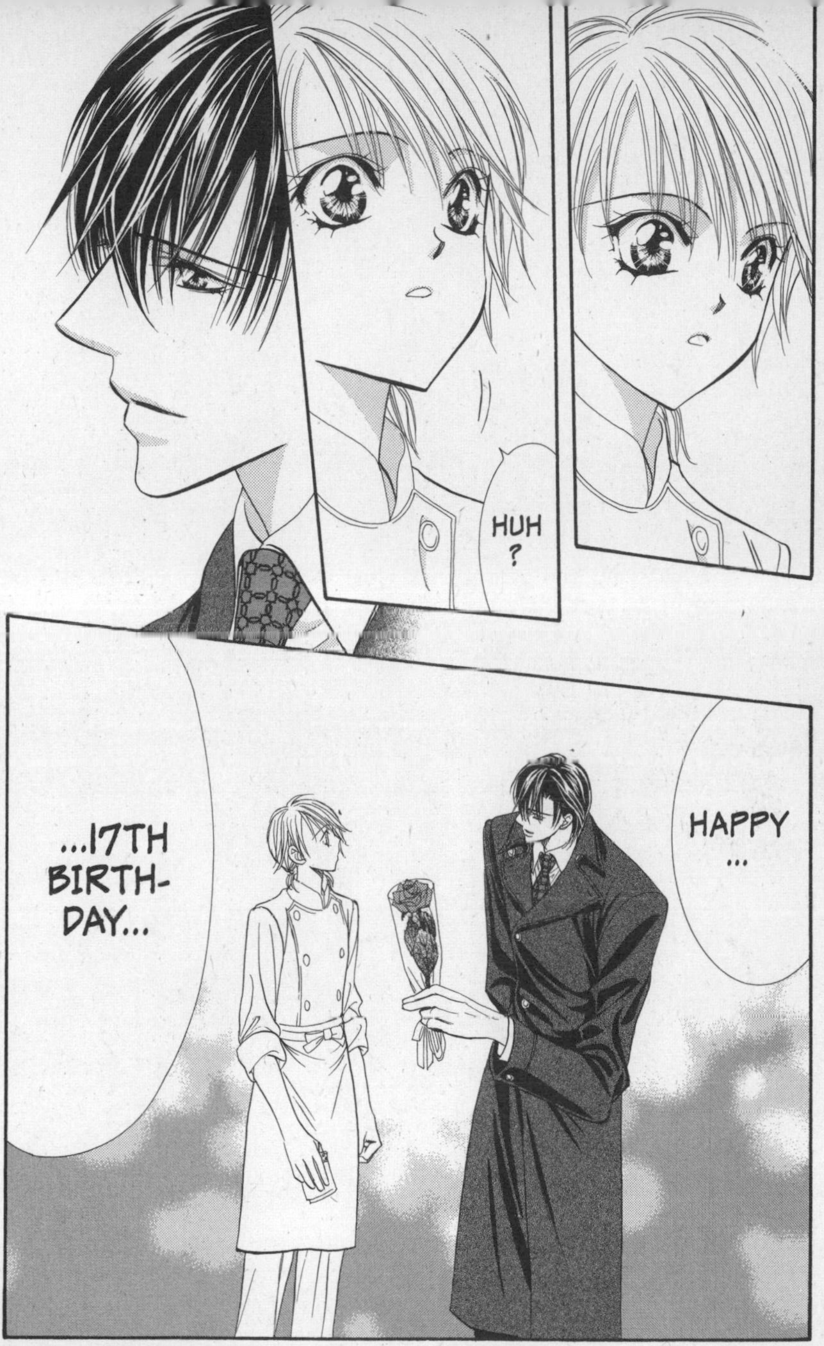
HUH?
HAPPY...
...17TH BIRTH-DAY...

End of Act 119

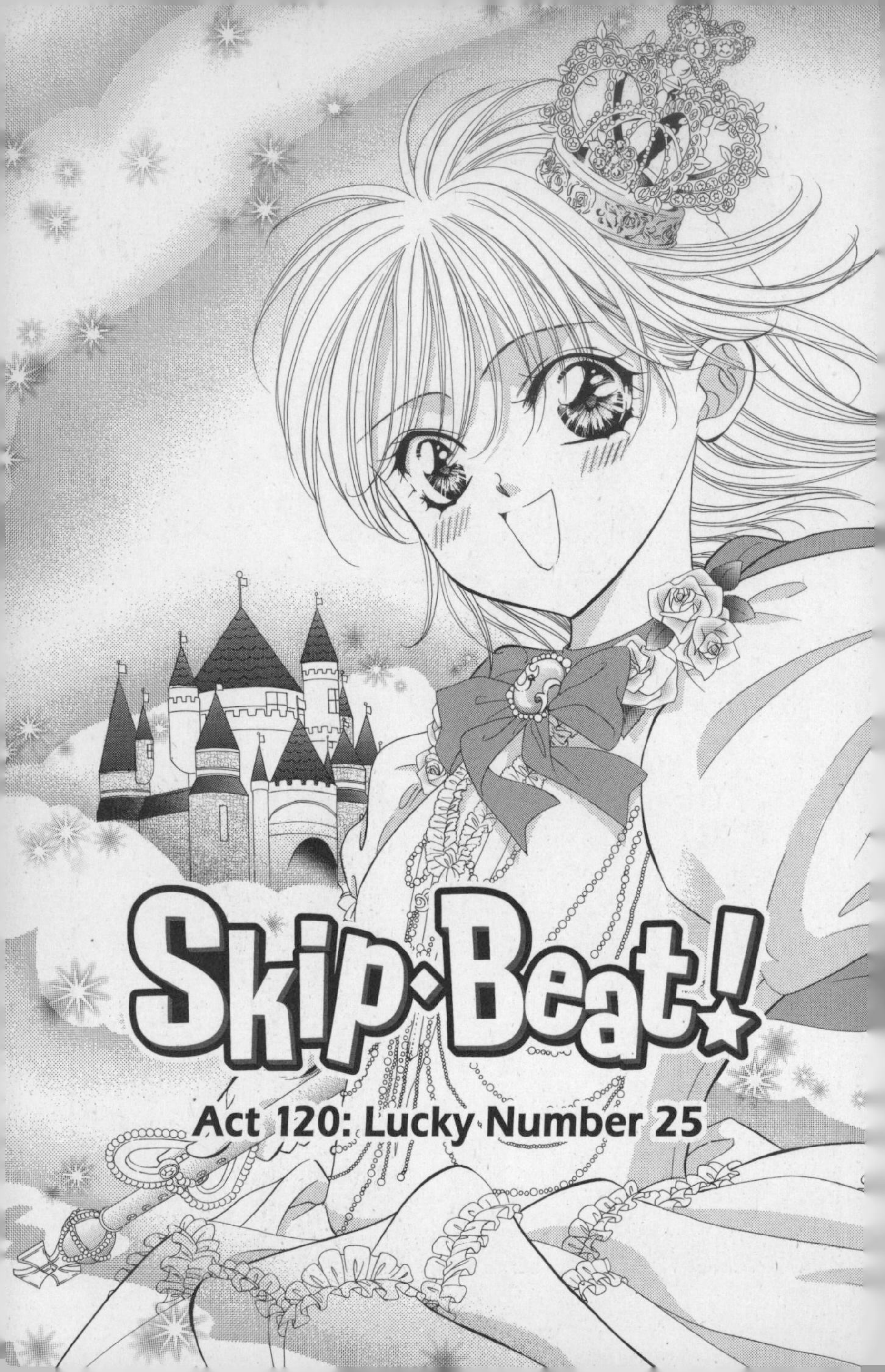
Skip·Beat!
Act 120: Lucky Number 25

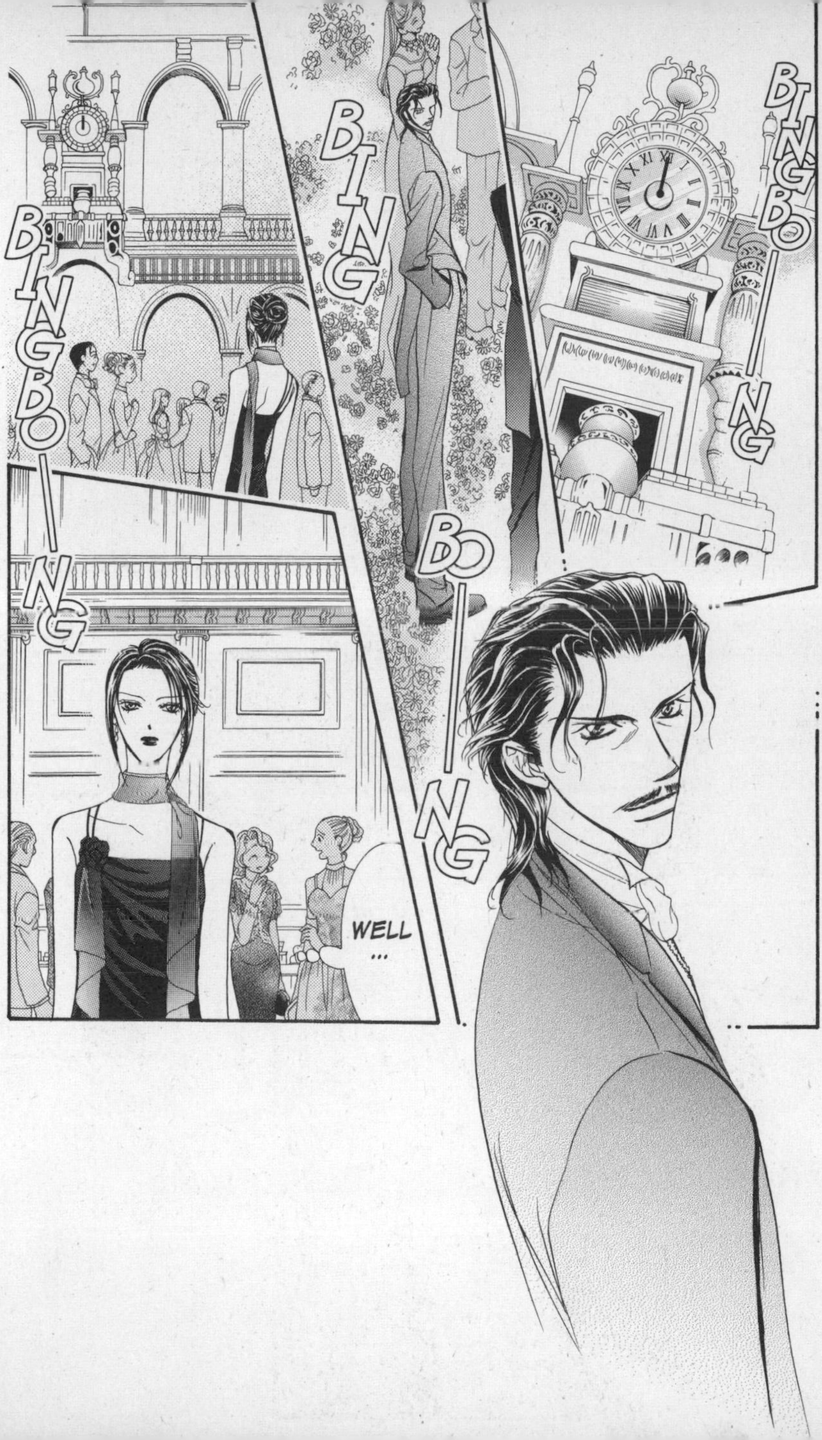
BINGBO-ING
BING
BINGBO-I-NG
BO-I-NG
WELL ...

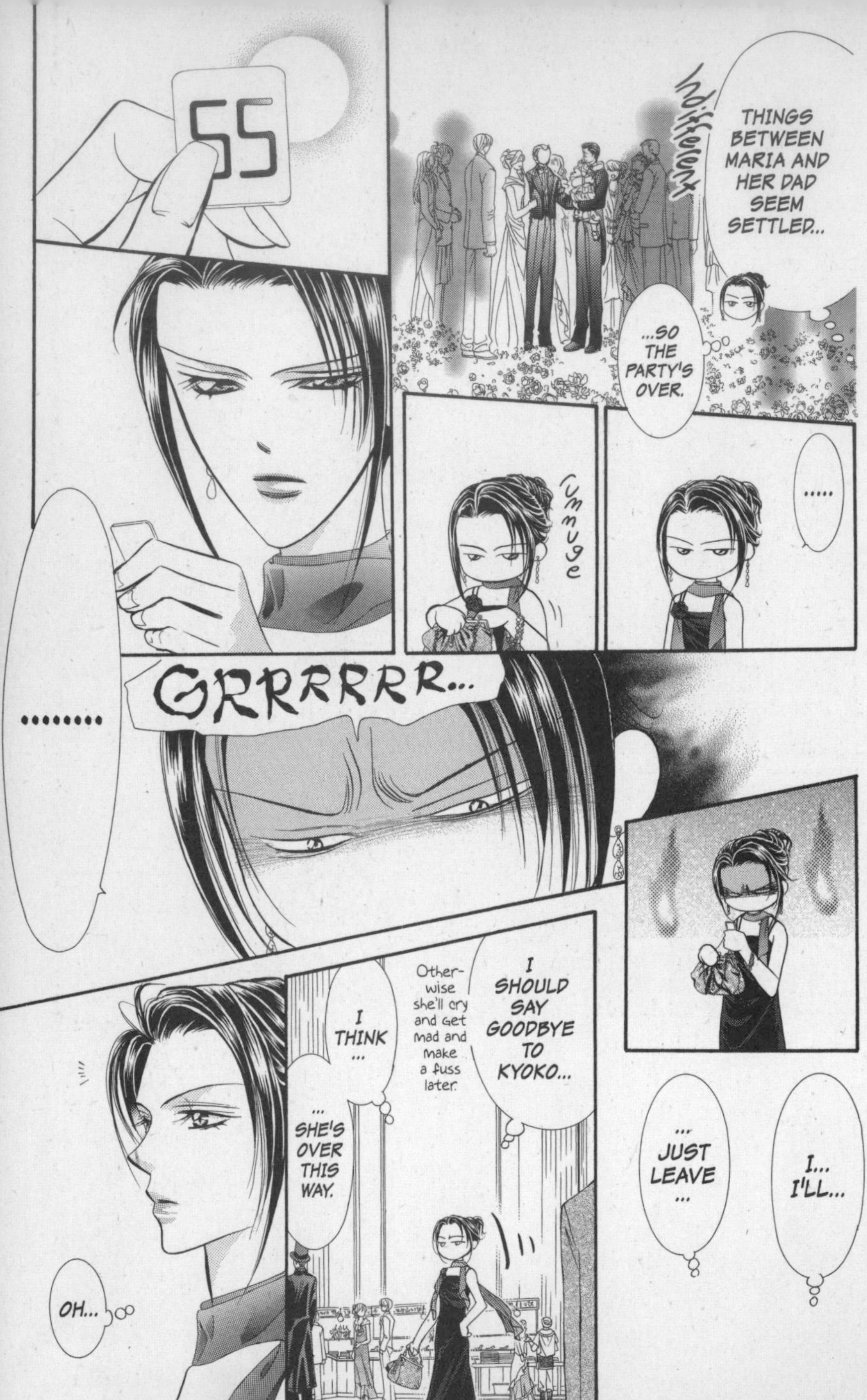
indifferent
THINGS BETWEEN MARIA AND HER DAD SEEM SETTLED...
...SO THE PARTY'S OVER.
55
.....
rummage
....
GRRRRRR...
I... I'LL...
... JUST LEAVE ...
I SHOULD SAY GOODBYE TO KYOKO...
Other-wise she'll cry and get mad and make a fuss later.
I THINK ...
... SHE'S OVER THIS WAY.
OH...

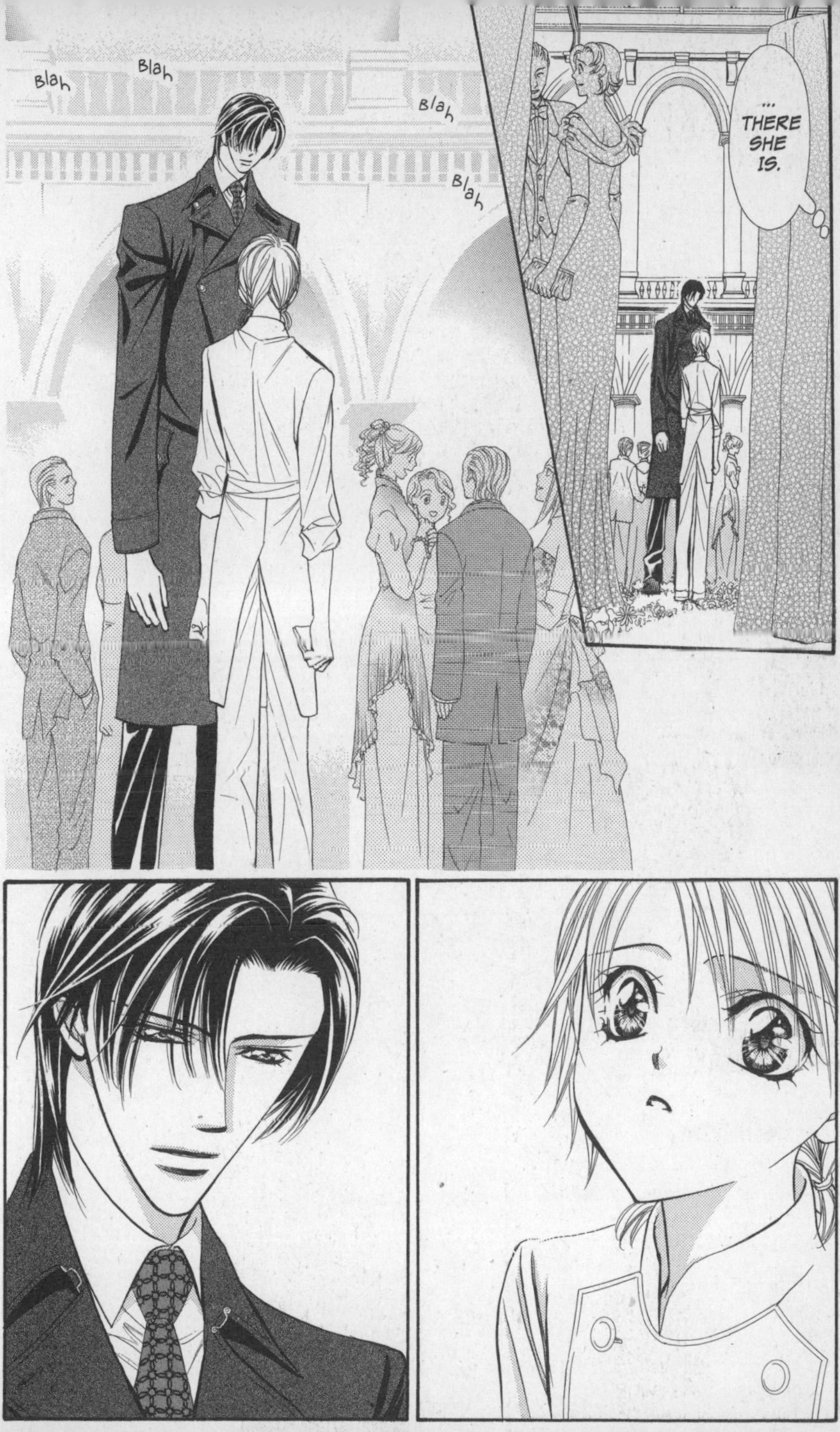
... THERE SHE IS.
Blah
Blah
Blah
Blah

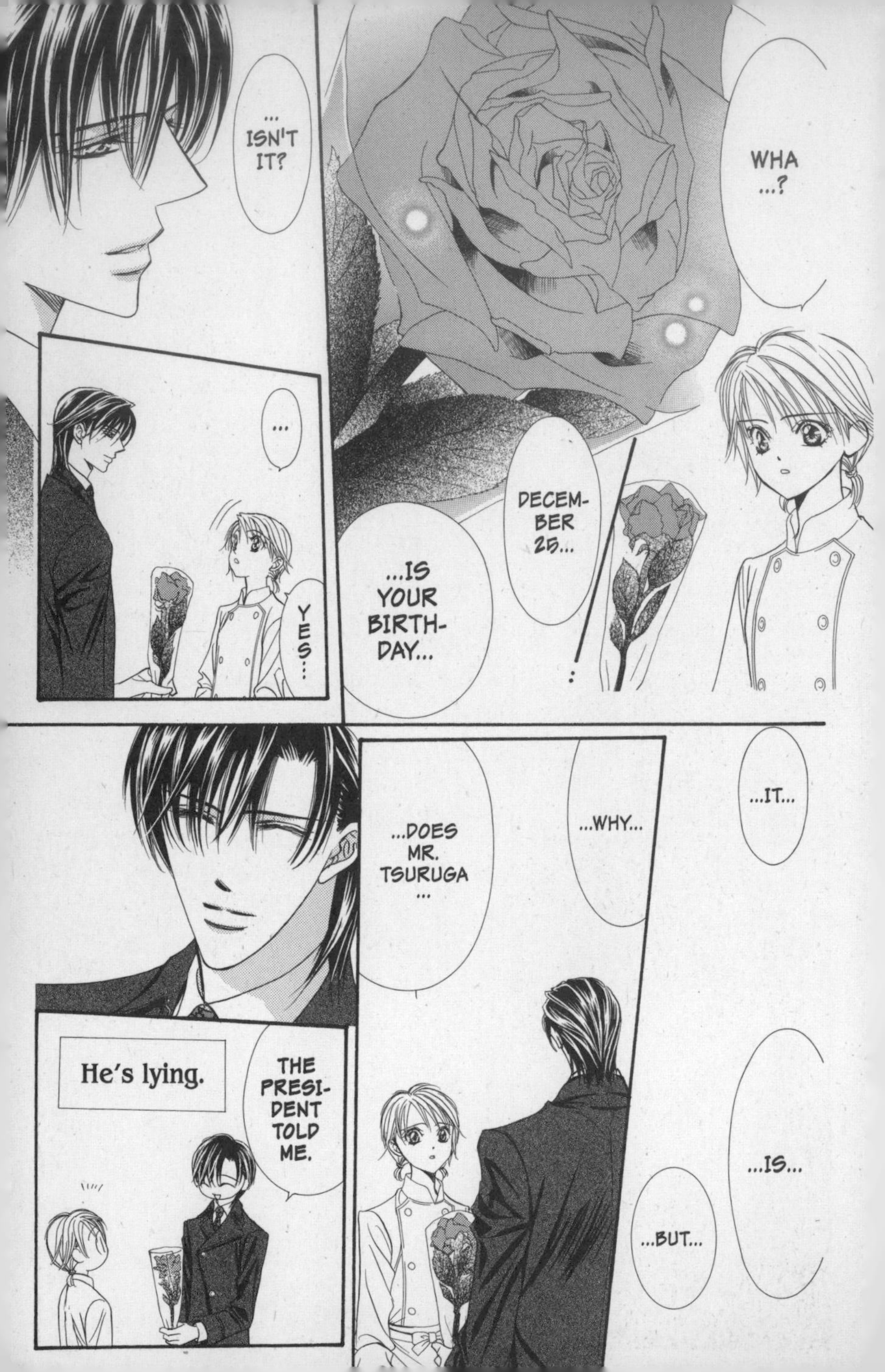
WHA ...?
DECEMBER 25...
...IS YOUR BIRTHDAY...
... ISN'T IT?
...
YES...
...IT...
...IS...
...BUT...
...WHY...
...DOES MR. TSURUGA ...
THE PRESIDENT TOLD ME.
He's lying.

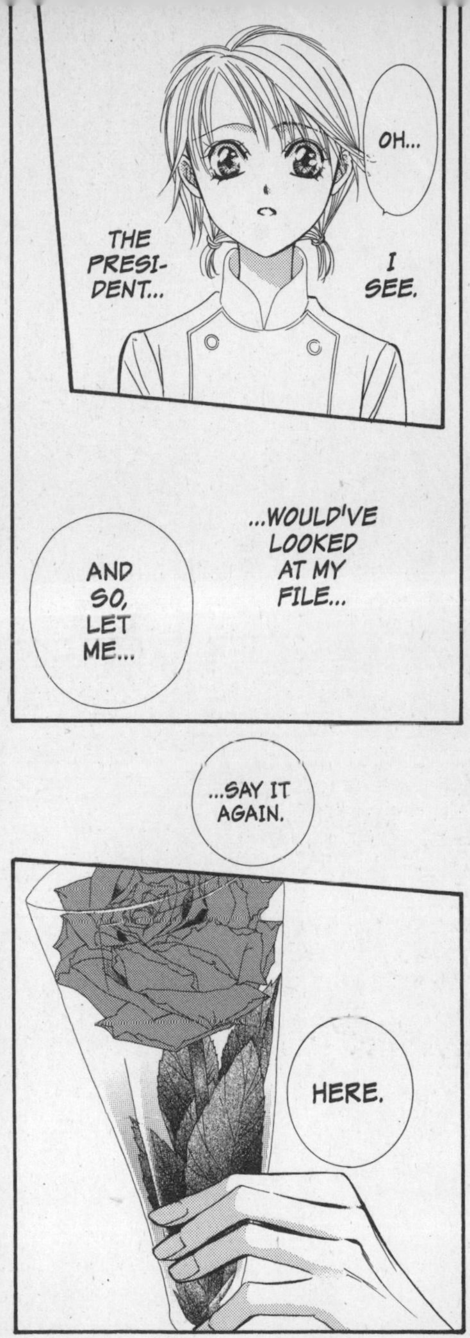
OH... I SEE.
THE PRESIDENT...
...WOULD'VE LOOKED AT MY FILE...
AND SO, LET ME...
...SAY IT AGAIN.
HERE.
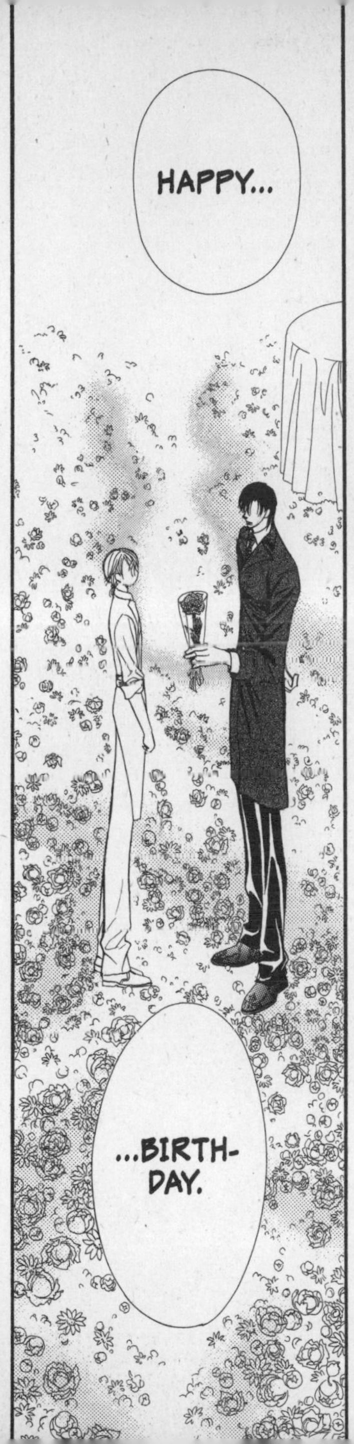
HAPPY...
...BIRTH-DAY.

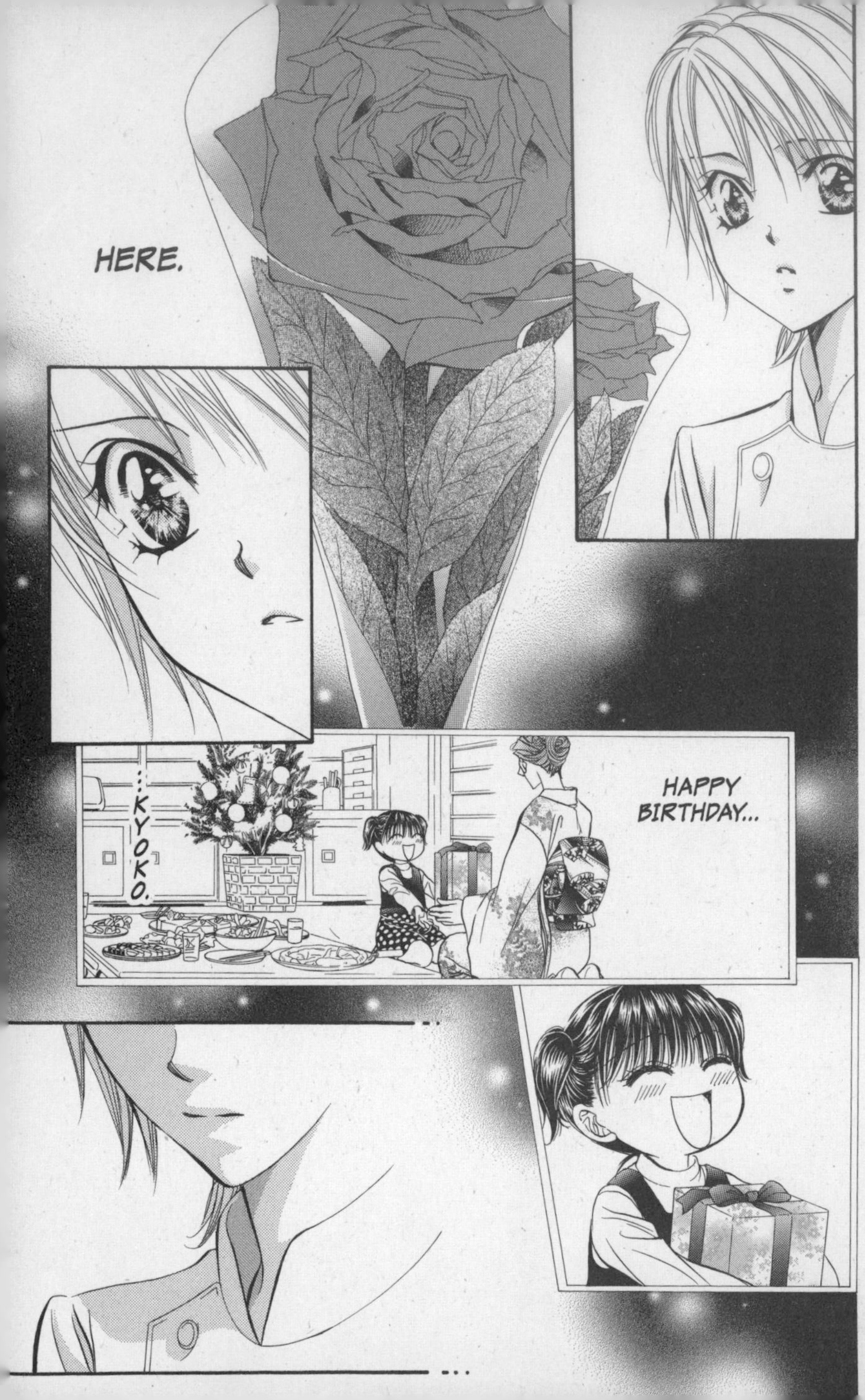
HERE.
HAPPY BIRTHDAY...
...KYOKO.

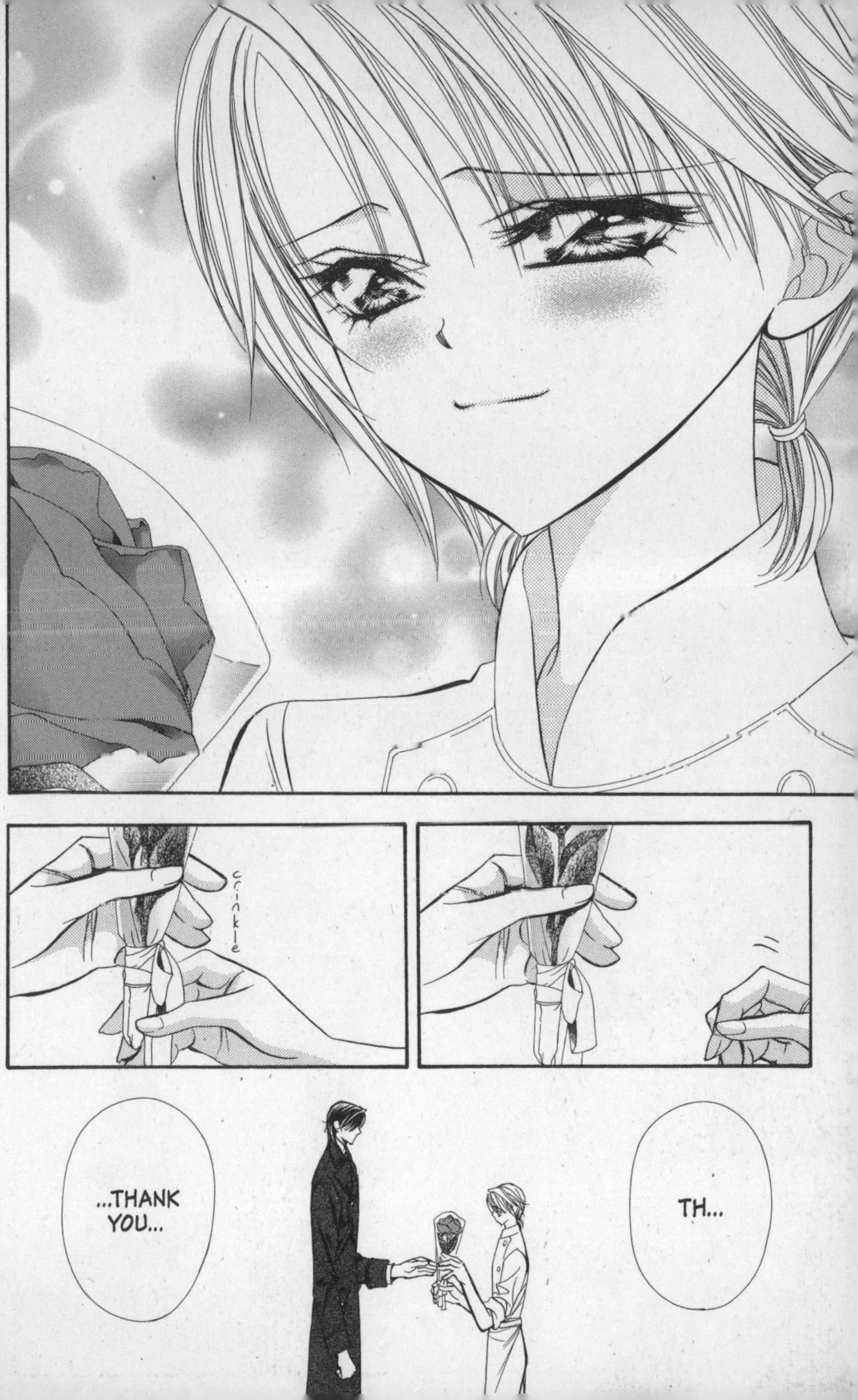
crinkle
TH...
...THANK YOU...

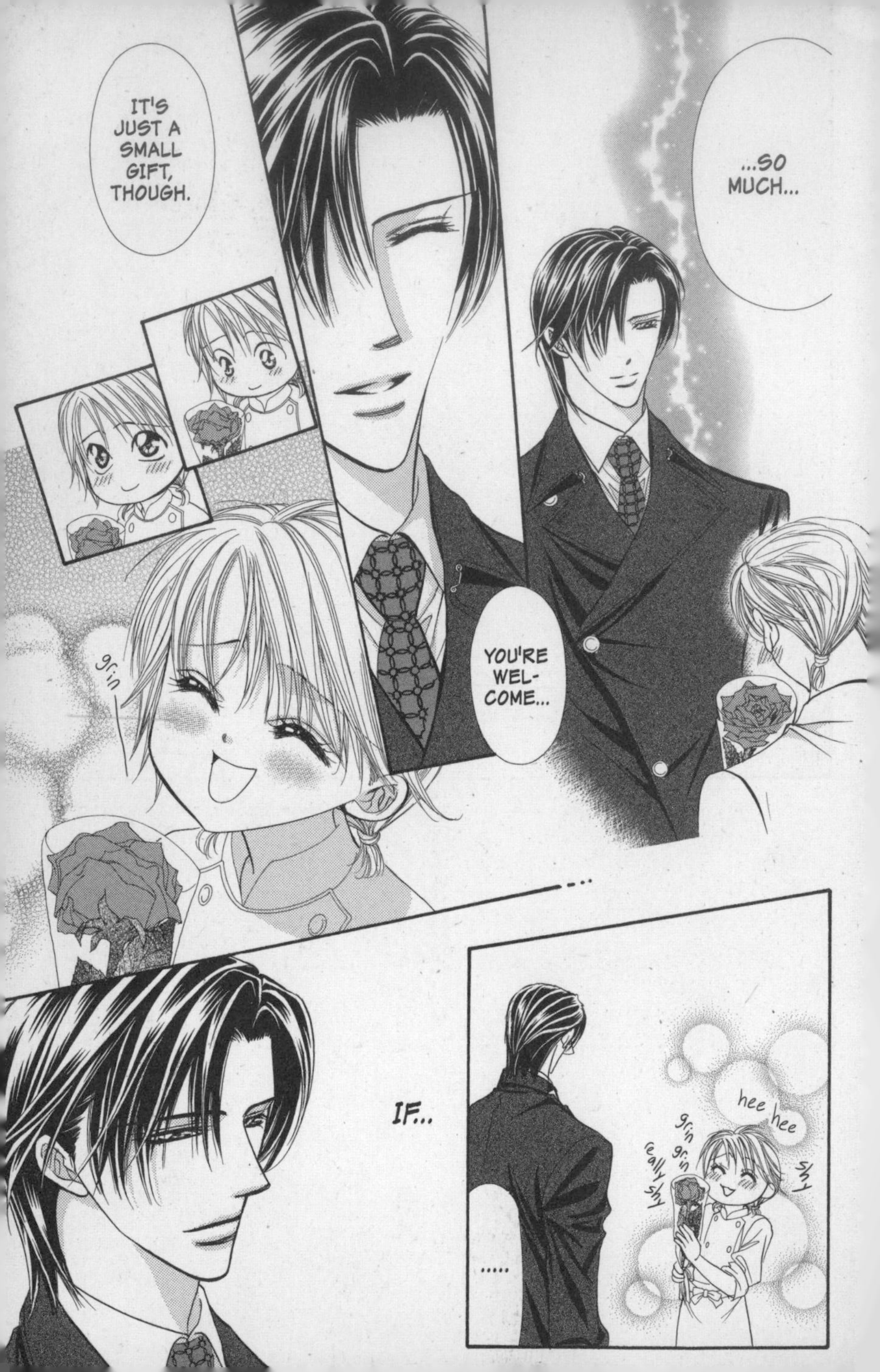
...SO MUCH...
YOU'RE WEL-COME...
IT'S JUST A SMALL GIFT, THOUGH.
grin
—...
hee hee
grin grin
really shy
shy
......
IF...

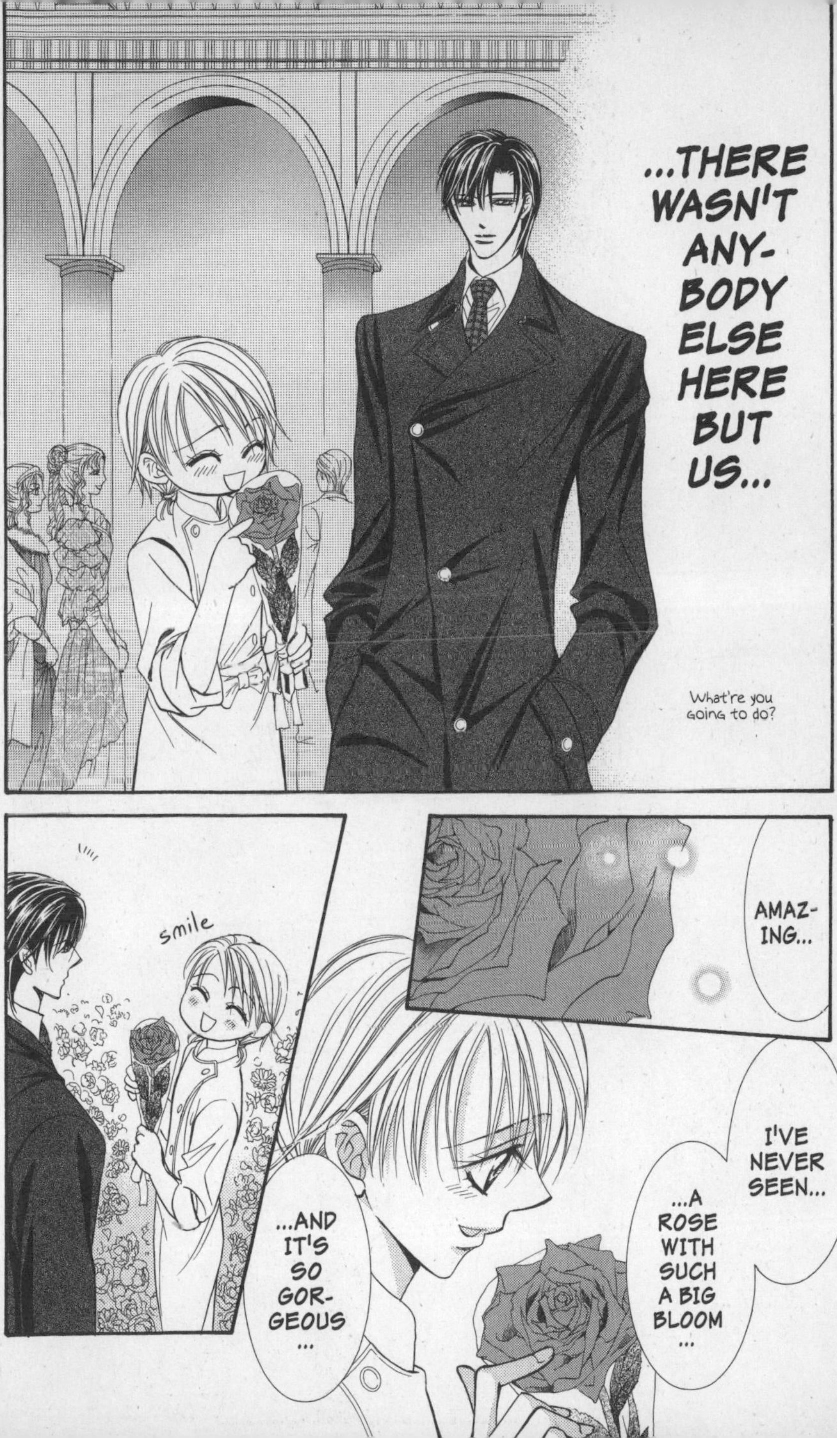
...THERE WASN'T ANY-BODY ELSE HERE BUT US...
What're you going to do?
AMAZ-ING...
I'VE NEVER SEEN...
...A ROSE WITH SUCH A BIG BLOOM...
...AND IT'S SO GOR-GEOUS...
smile

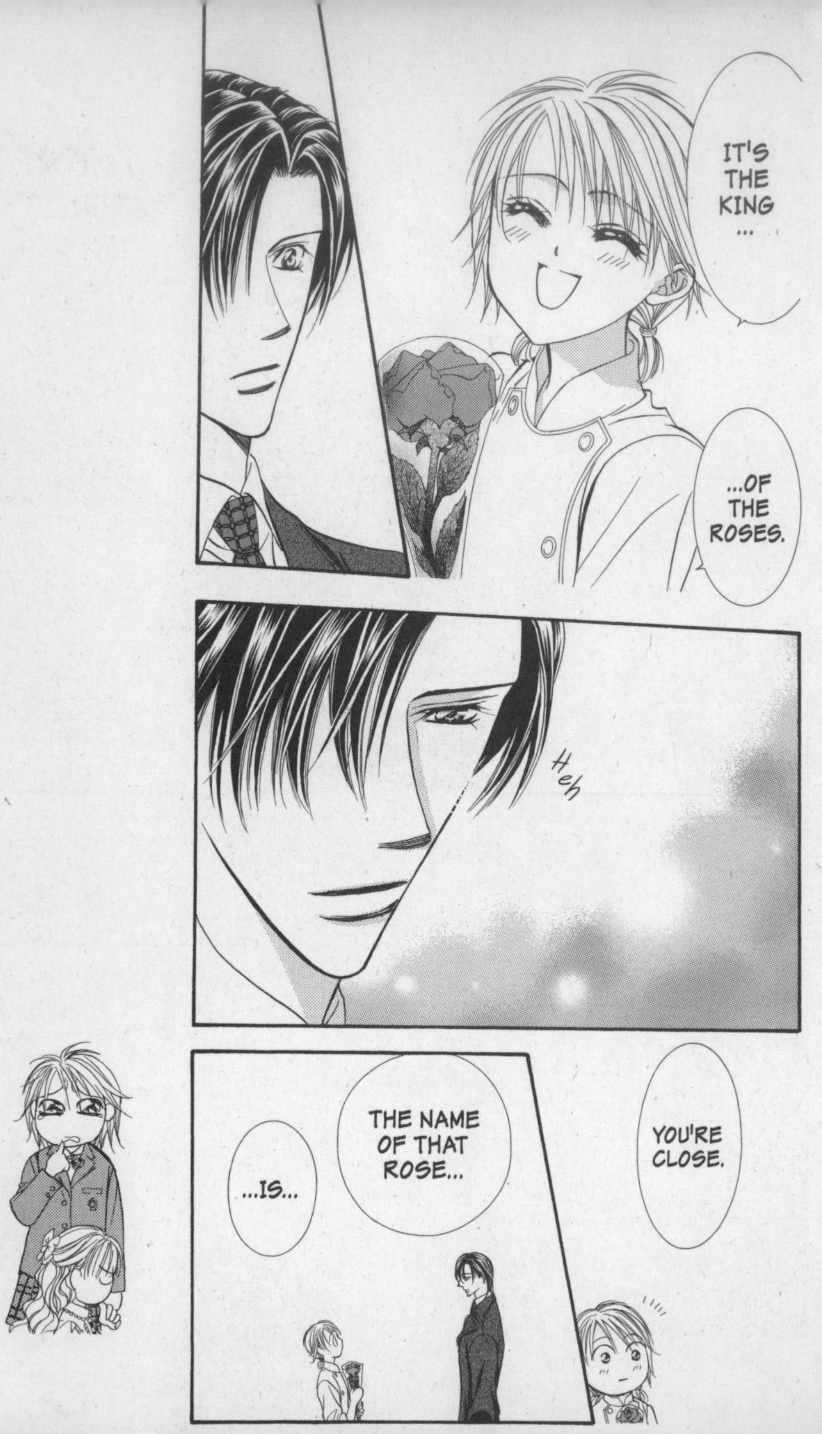
IT'S THE KING ...
...OF THE ROSES.
Heh
YOU'RE CLOSE.
THE NAME OF THAT ROSE...
...IS...

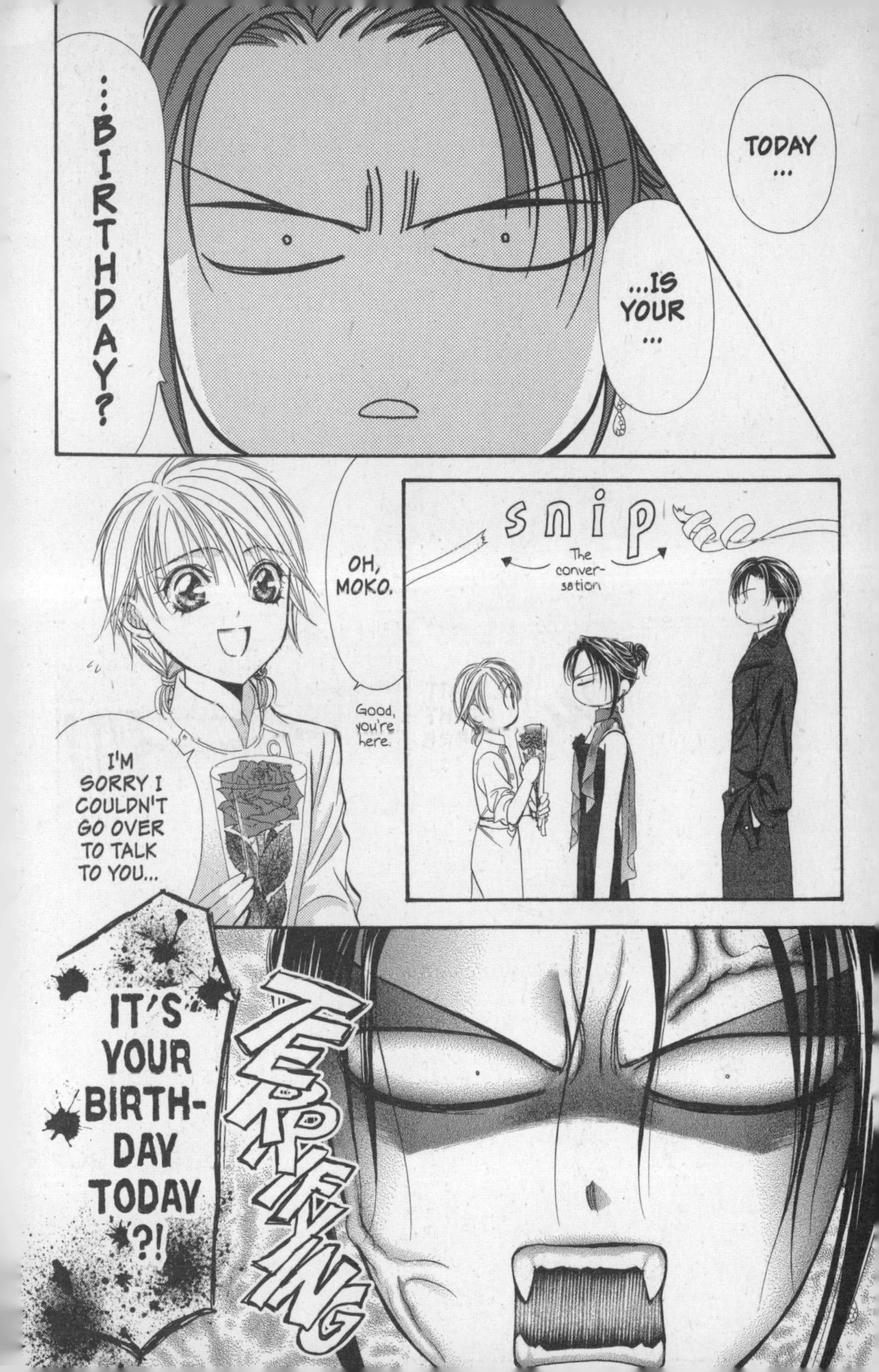
TODAY ...
...IS YOUR ...
...BIRTHDAY?
snip
The conversation
OH, MOKO.
Good, you're here.
I'M SORRY I COULDN'T GO OVER TO TALK TO YOU...
TERRIFYING
IT'S YOUR BIRTHDAY TODAY?!

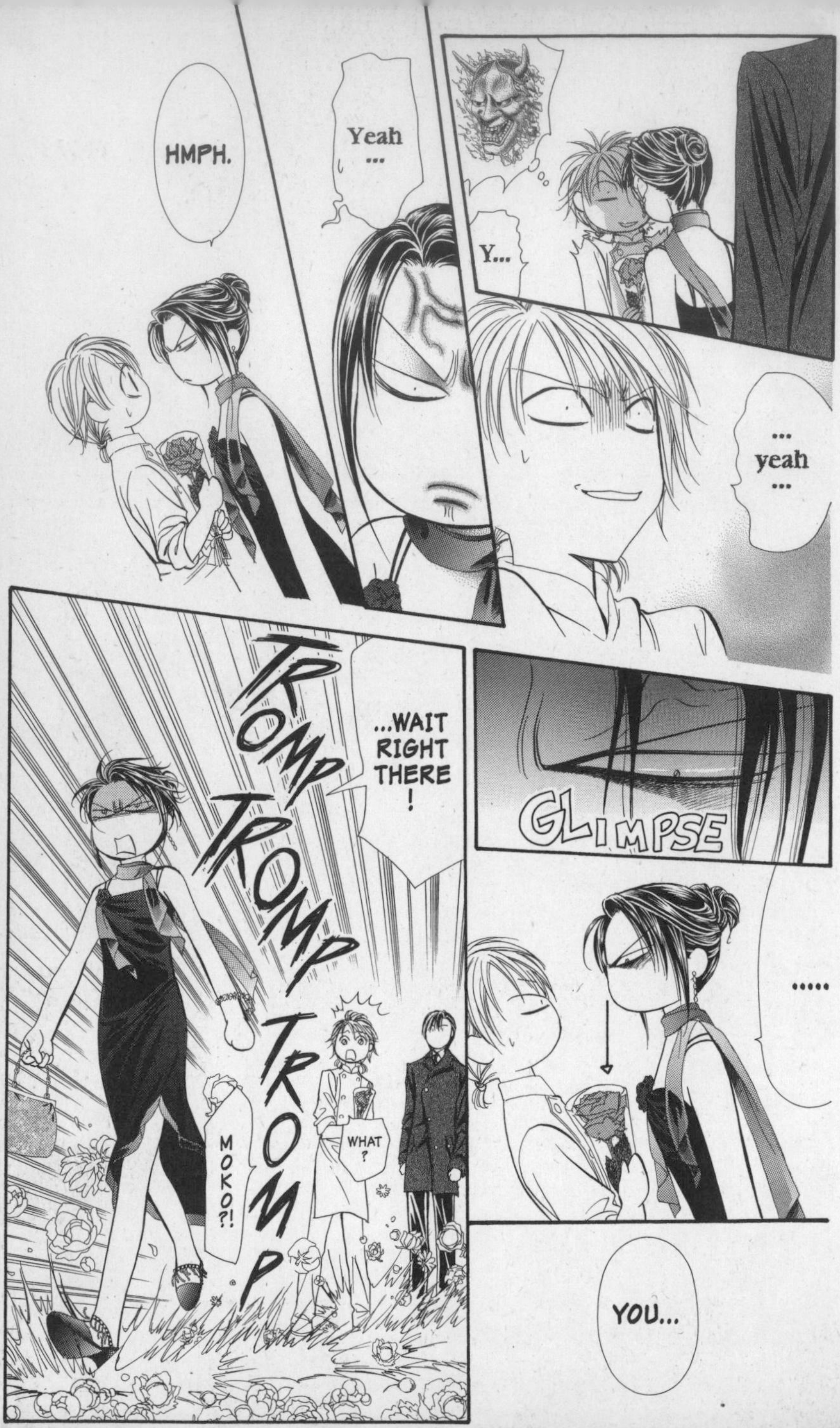
Y...
... yeah ...
Yeah ...
HMPH.
GLIMPSE
.....
YOU...
...WAIT RIGHT THERE!
TROMP TROMP TROMP
MOKO?!
WHAT?

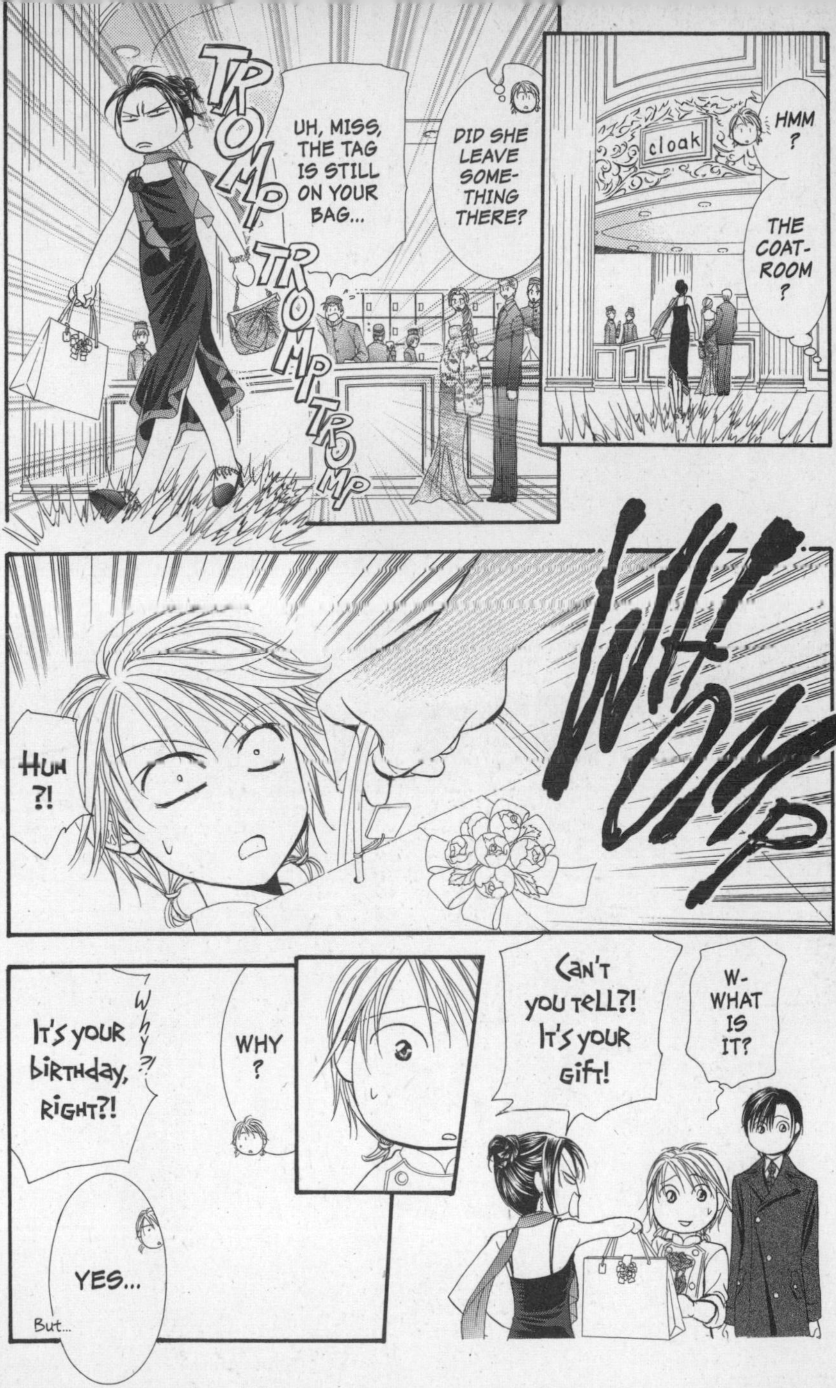
HMM?
cloak
THE COAT-ROOM?
DID SHE LEAVE SOME-THING THERE?
UH, MISS, THE TAG IS STILL ON YOUR BAG...
TROMP
TROMP
TROMP
TROMP
WHOMP
HUH?!
W-WHAT IS IT?
CAN'T YOU TELL?! IT'S YOUR GIFT!
WHY?
WHY?!
IT'S YOUR BIRTHDAY, RIGHT?!
YES...
But...

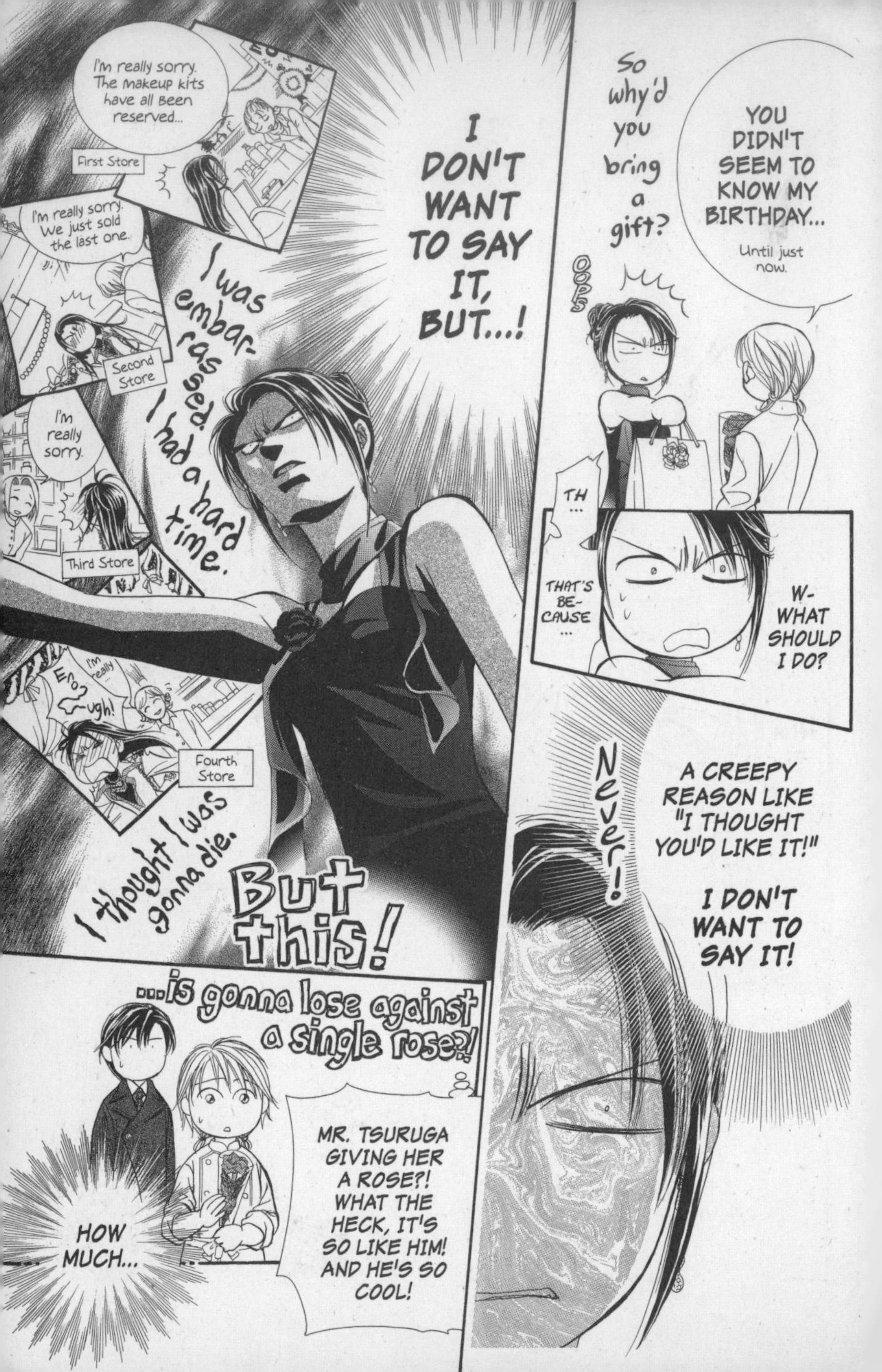
YOU DIDN'T SEEM TO KNOW MY BIRTHDAY...
Until just now.
So why'd you bring a gift?
OOPS
TH...
THAT'S BE-CAUSE...
W-WHAT SHOULD I DO?
Never!
A CREEPY REASON LIKE "I THOUGHT YOU'D LIKE IT!"
I DON'T WANT TO SAY IT!
I DON'T WANT TO SAY IT, BUT...!
I was embar-rassed. I had a hard time.
I'm really sorry. The makeup kits have all been reserved...
First Store
I'm really sorry. We just sold the last one.
Second Store
I'm really sorry.
Third Store
I'm really
Er...ugh!
Fourth Store
I thought I was gonna die.
But this!
...is gonna lose against a single rose?!
MR. TSURUGA GIVING HER A ROSE?! WHAT THE HECK, IT'S SO LIKE HIM! AND HE'S SO COOL!
HOW MUCH...

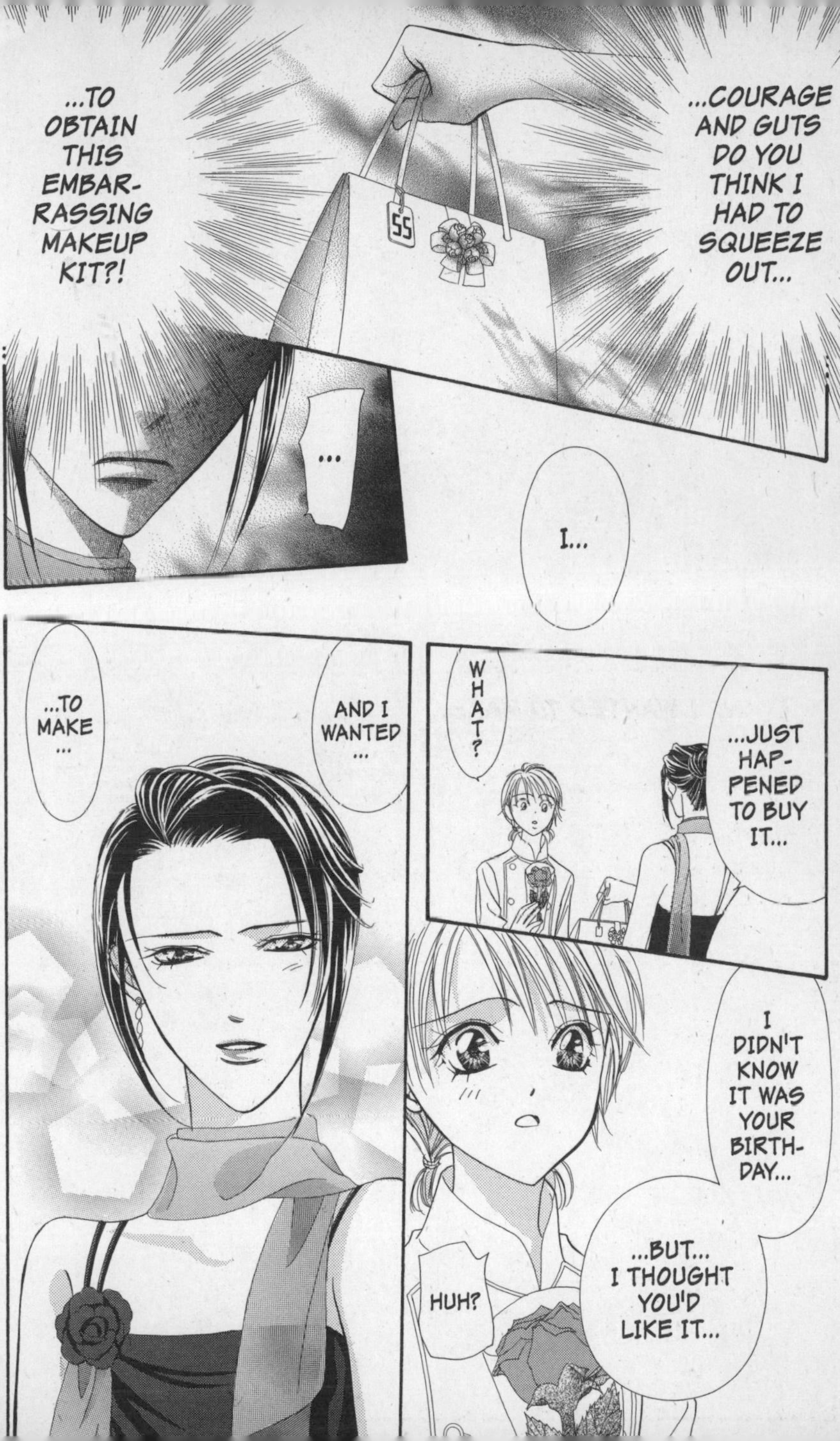
...COURAGE AND GUTS DO YOU THINK I HAD TO SQUEEZE OUT...
...TO OBTAIN THIS EMBARRASSING MAKEUP KIT?!
I...
...
...JUST HAPPENED TO BUY IT...
WHAT?
I DIDN'T KNOW IT WAS YOUR BIRTHDAY...
...BUT... I THOUGHT YOU'D LIKE IT...
HUH?
AND I WANTED...
...TO MAKE...

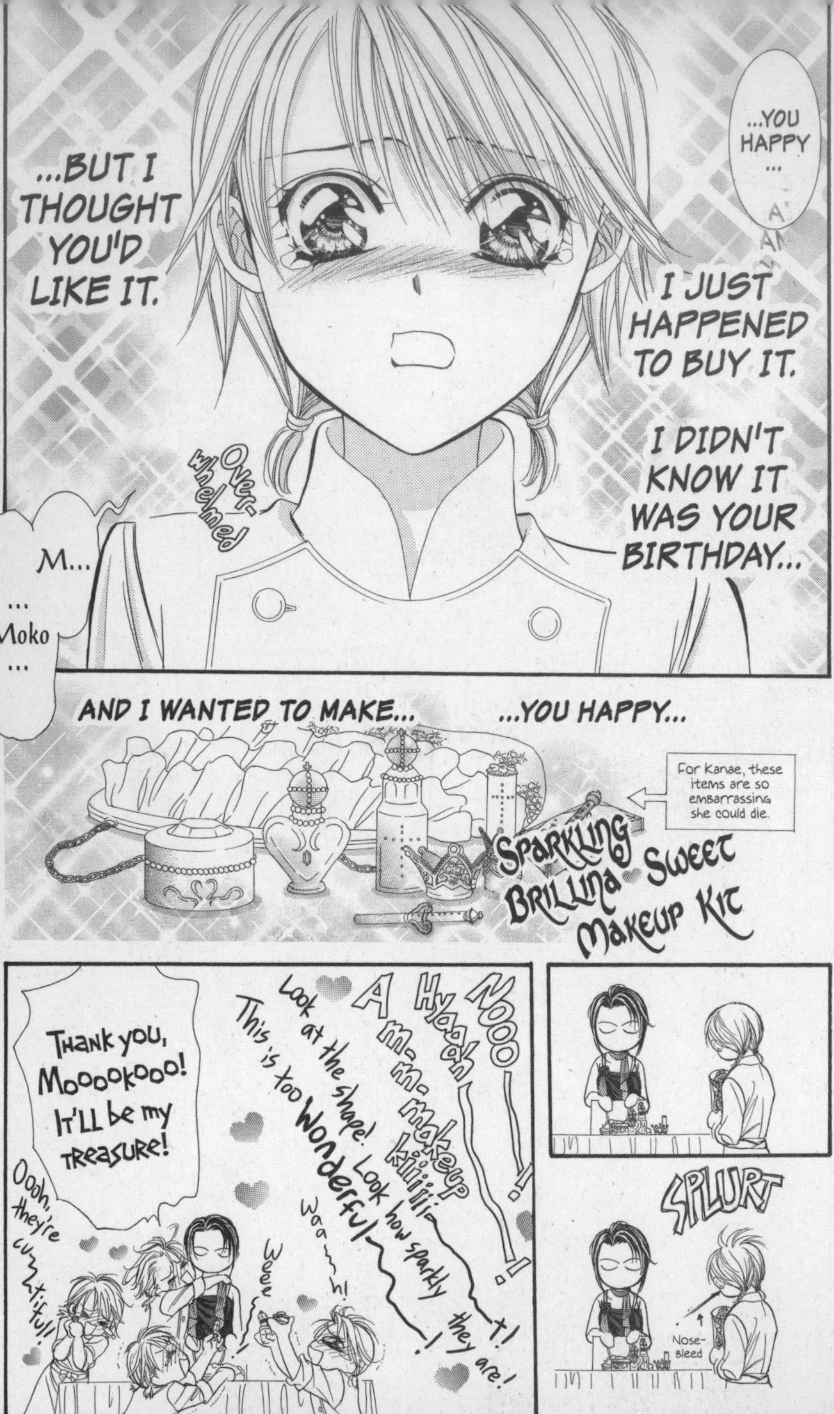
...YOU HAPPY ...
I JUST HAPPENED TO BUY IT.
I DIDN'T KNOW IT WAS YOUR BIRTHDAY...
...BUT I THOUGHT YOU'D LIKE IT.
Over-whelmed
M... ... Moko ...
AND I WANTED TO MAKE...
...YOU HAPPY...
For Kanae, these items are so embarrassing she could die.
Sparkling Brilluna Sweet Makeup Kit
SPLURT
Nose-Bleed
NOOO—!
Hyaaah
A m-m-makeup kiiiiit!
Look at the shape! Look how sparkly they are!
This is too wonderful—!
Waa—h!
Weee
Thank you, Mooookooo! It'll be my treasure!
Oooh, they're cu—tiful!

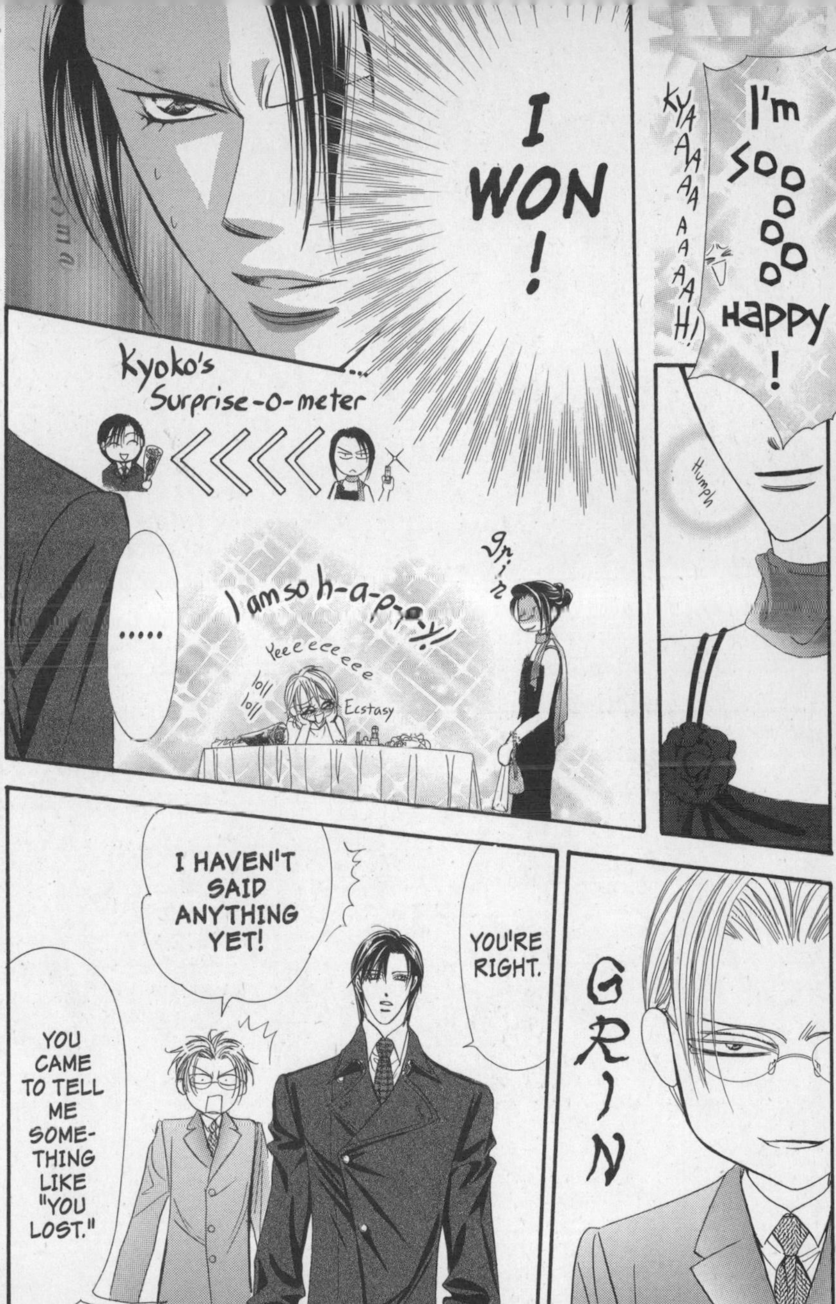
I'm sooooooo happy!
KYAAAAAAAAAH!
I WON!
Humph
Kyoko's Surprise-o-meter
.....
I am so h-a-p-p-y!!
grin
Yeeeeeeeee
loll loll
Ecstasy
GRIN
YOU'RE RIGHT.
I HAVEN'T SAID ANYTHING YET!
YOU CAME TO TELL ME SOMETHING LIKE "YOU LOST."

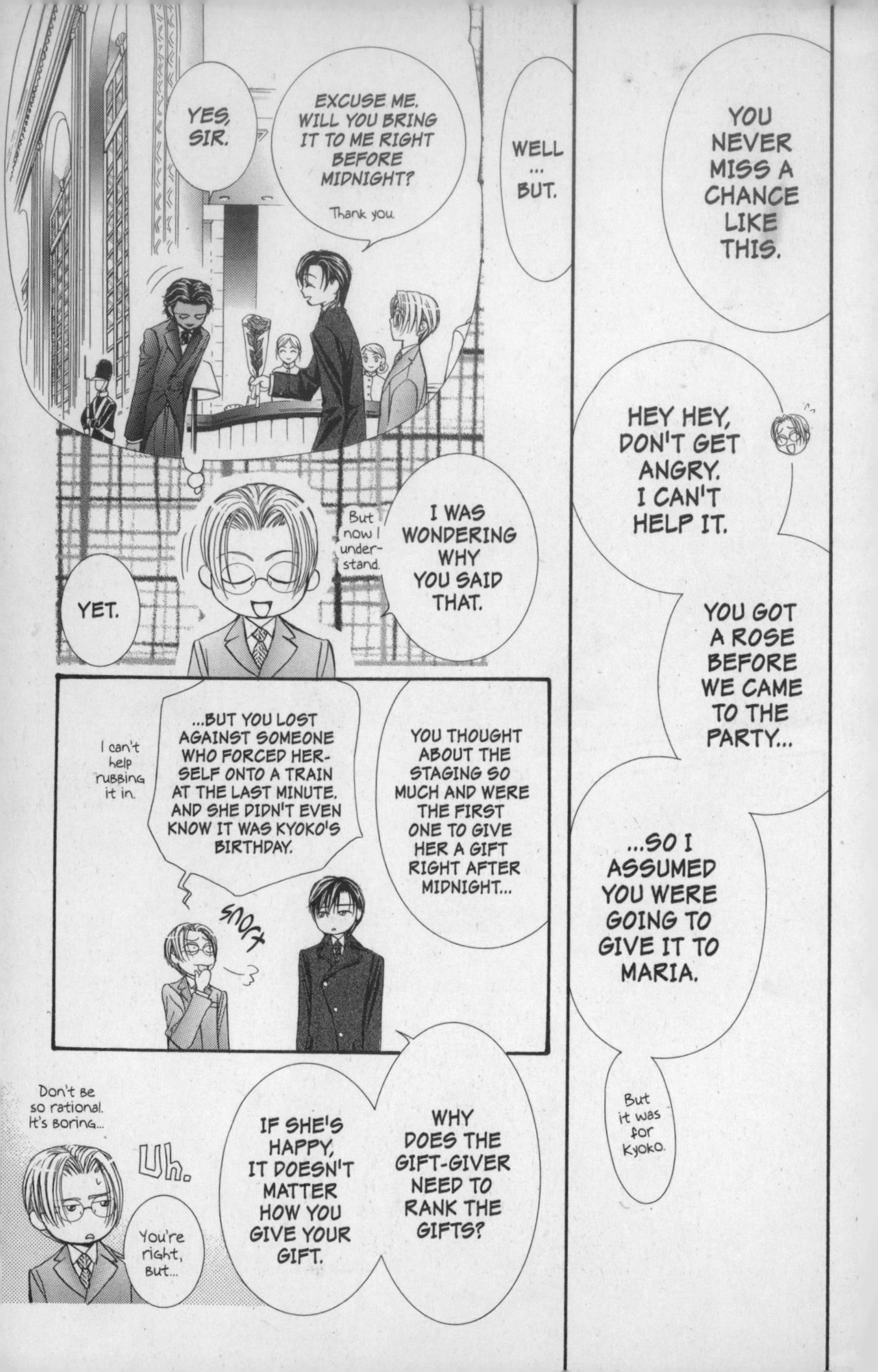
YOU NEVER MISS A CHANCE LIKE THIS.
HEY HEY, DON'T GET ANGRY. I CAN'T HELP IT.
YOU GOT A ROSE BEFORE WE CAME TO THE PARTY...
...SO I ASSUMED YOU WERE GOING TO GIVE IT TO MARIA.
But it was for Kyoko.
WELL ... BUT.
EXCUSE ME. WILL YOU BRING IT TO ME RIGHT BEFORE MIDNIGHT?
Thank you.
YES, SIR.
I WAS WONDERING WHY YOU SAID THAT.
But now I under-stand.
YET.
YOU THOUGHT ABOUT THE STAGING SO MUCH AND WERE THE FIRST ONE TO GIVE HER A GIFT RIGHT AFTER MIDNIGHT...
...BUT YOU LOST AGAINST SOMEONE WHO FORCED HER-SELF ONTO A TRAIN AT THE LAST MINUTE. AND SHE DIDN'T EVEN KNOW IT WAS KYOKO'S BIRTHDAY.
I can't help rubbing it in.
snort
WHY DOES THE GIFT-GIVER NEED TO RANK THE GIFTS?
IF SHE'S HAPPY, IT DOESN'T MATTER HOW YOU GIVE YOUR GIFT.
Uh.
Don't be so rational. It's boring...
You're right, but...

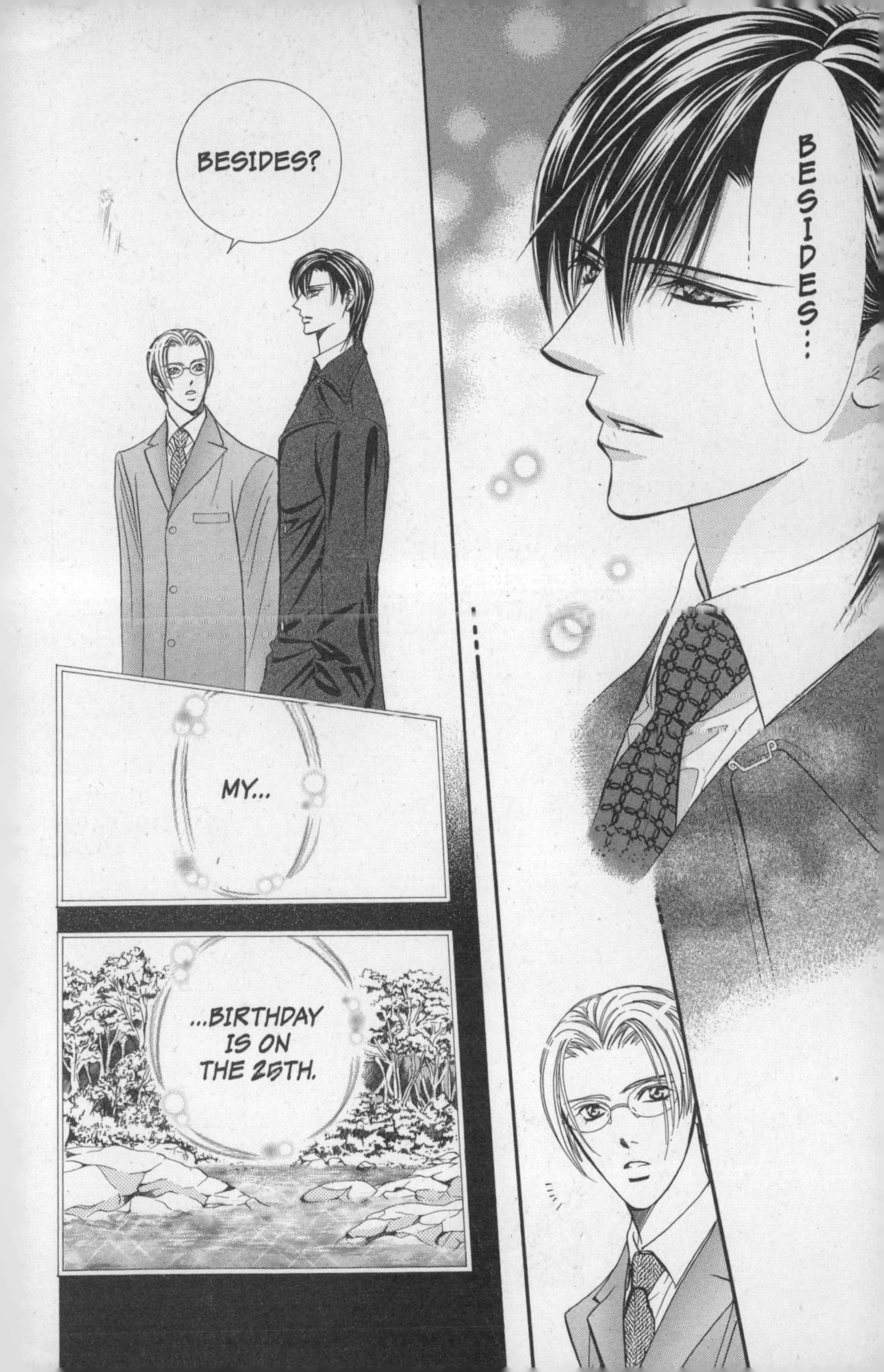
BESIDES...
BESIDES?
MY...
...BIRTHDAY IS ON THE 25TH.

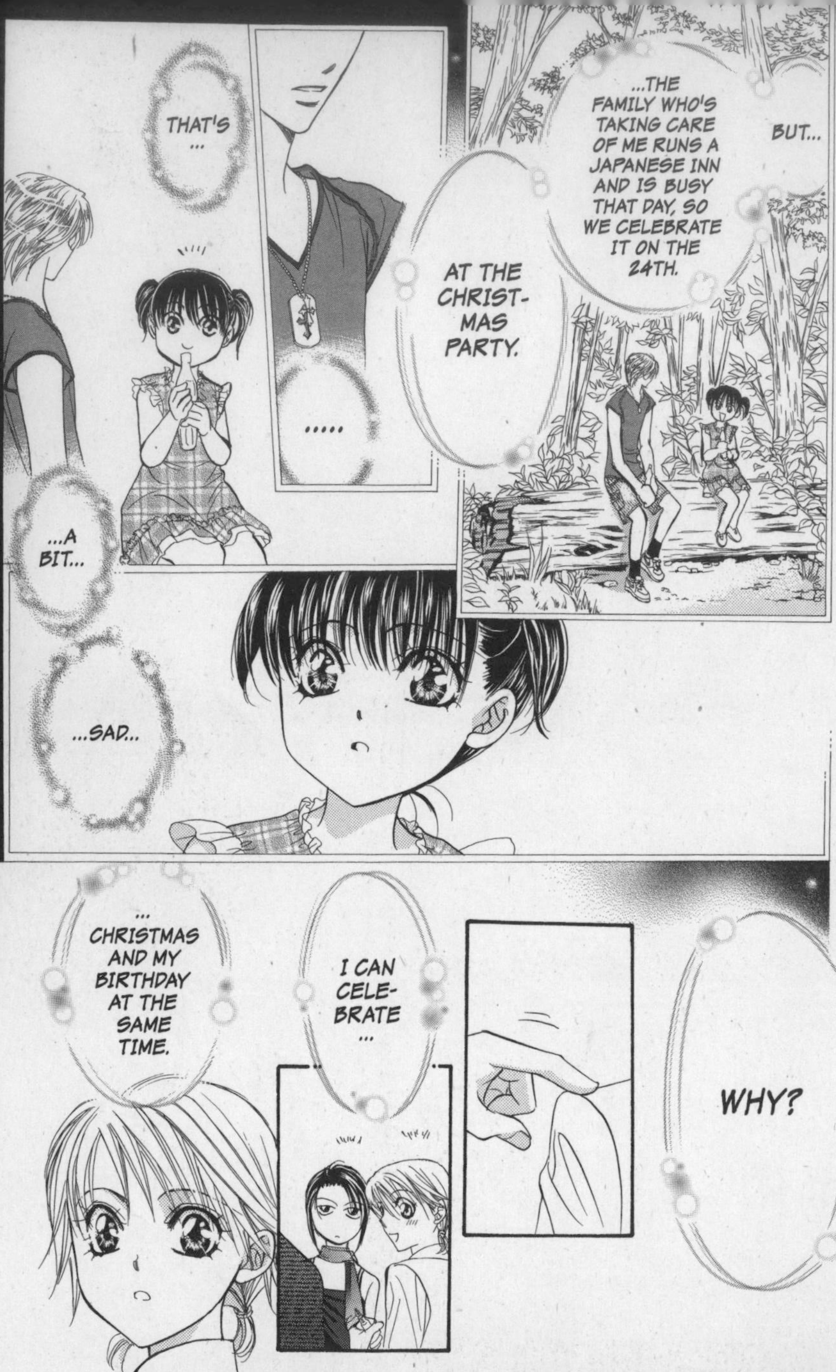
BUT...
...THE FAMILY WHO'S TAKING CARE OF ME RUNS A JAPANESE INN AND IS BUSY THAT DAY, SO WE CELEBRATE IT ON THE 24TH.
AT THE CHRIST-MAS PARTY.
.....
THAT'S ...
...A BIT...
...SAD...
WHY?
I CAN CELE-BRATE ...
... CHRISTMAS AND MY BIRTHDAY AT THE SAME TIME.

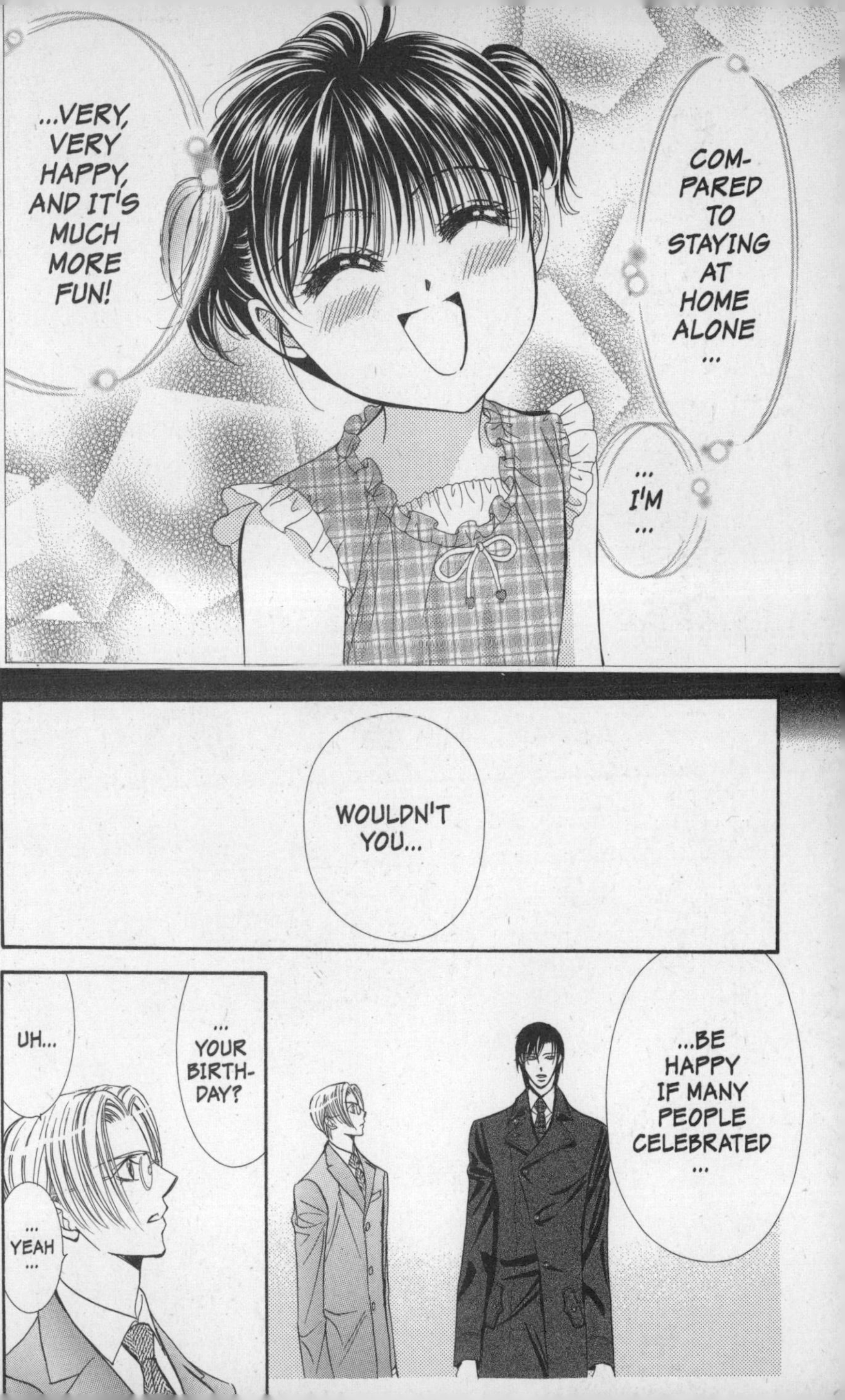
COM-PARED TO STAYING AT HOME ALONE ...
... I'M ...
...VERY, VERY HAPPY, AND IT'S MUCH MORE FUN!
WOULDN'T YOU...
...BE HAPPY IF MANY PEOPLE CELEBRATED ...
... YOUR BIRTH-DAY?
UH...
... YEAH ...

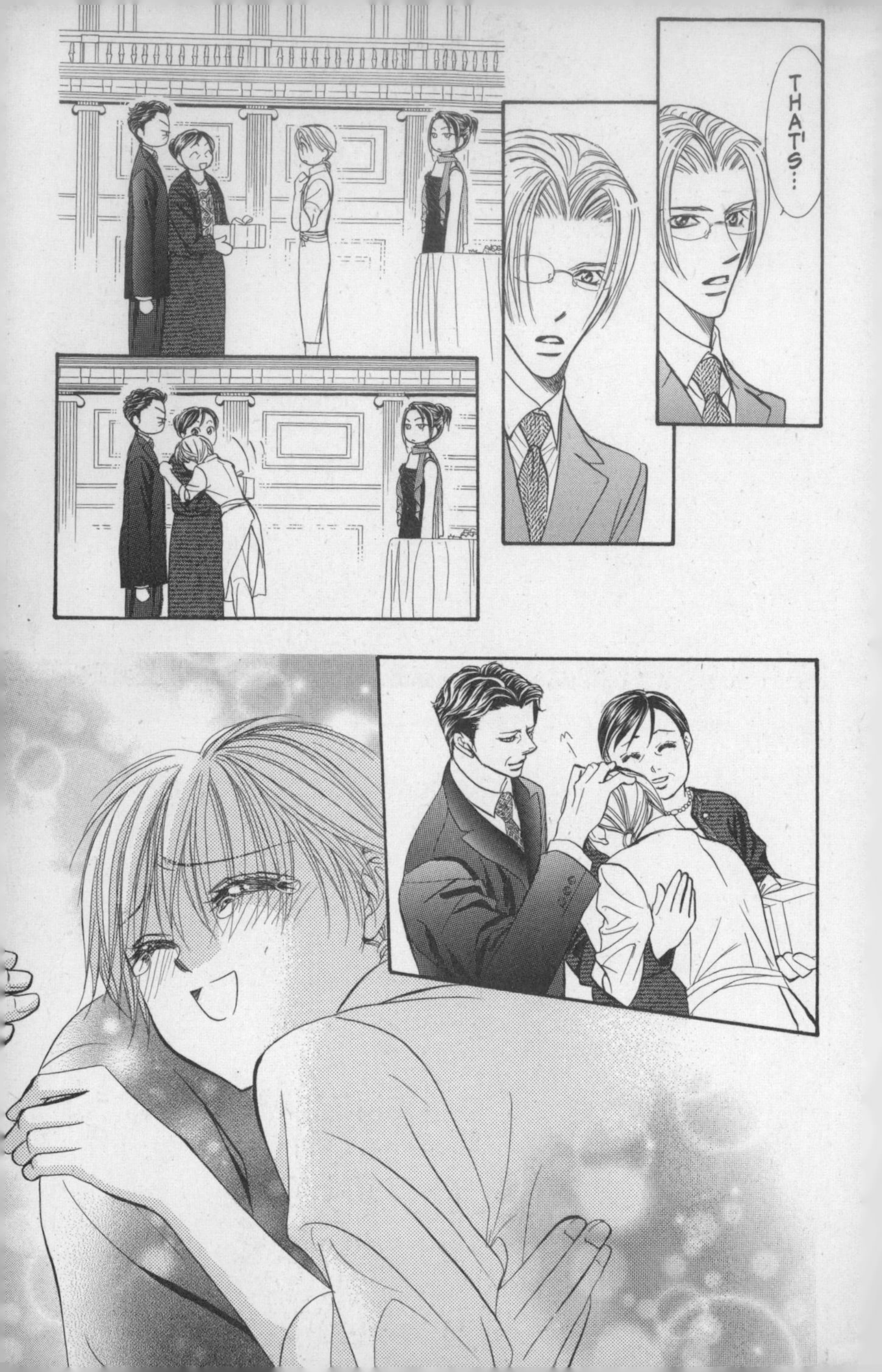
THAT'S...

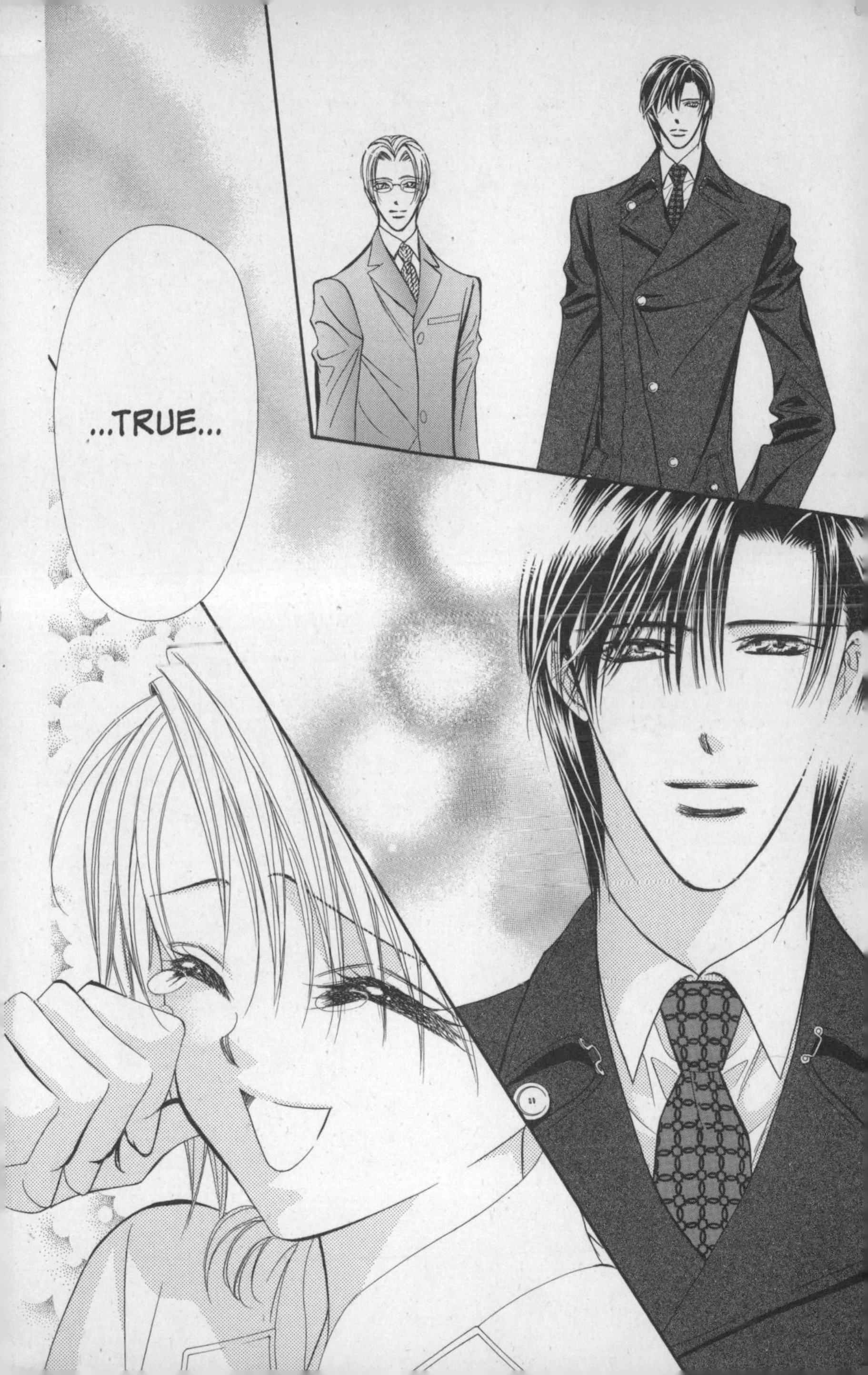
...TRUE...

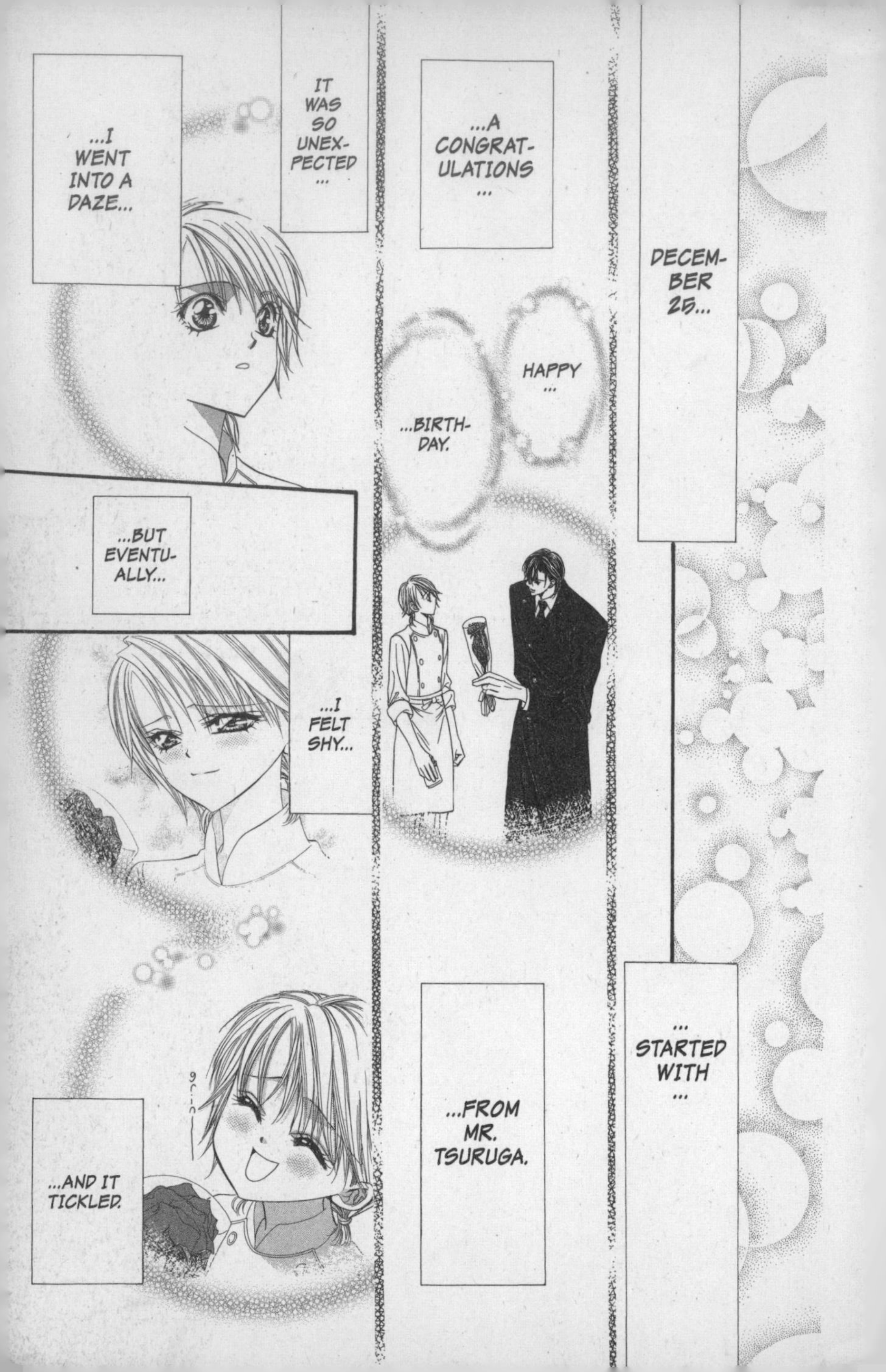
DECEMBER 25...
... STARTED WITH ...
...A CONGRATULATIONS ...
HAPPY ...
...BIRTHDAY.
...FROM MR. TSURUGA.
IT WAS SO UNEXPECTED ...
...I WENT INTO A DAZE...
...BUT EVENTUALLY...
...I FELT SHY...
...AND IT TICKLED.

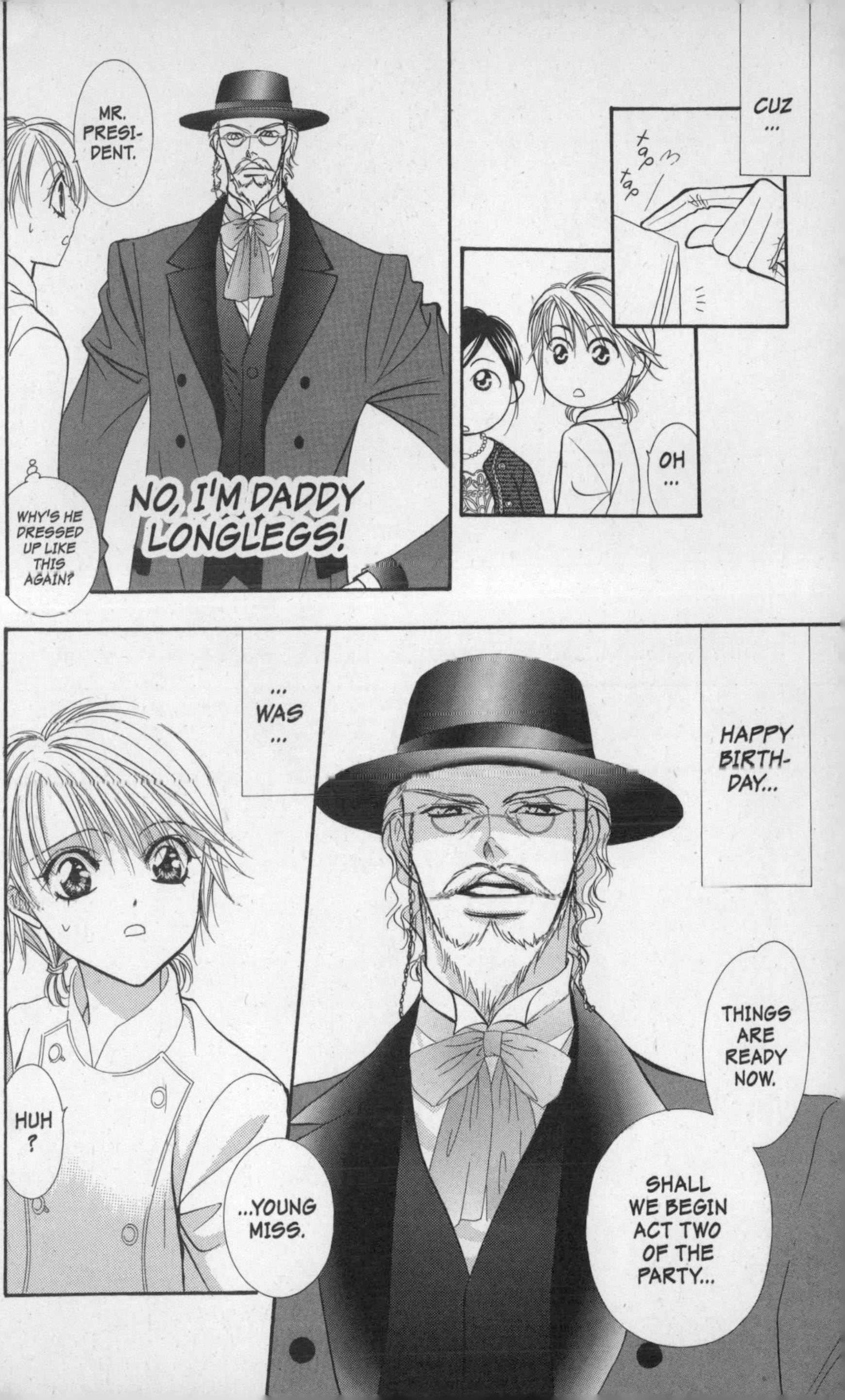
CUZ ...
tap tap
OH ...
MR. PRESIDENT.
NO, I'M DADDY LONGLEGS!
WHY'S HE DRESSED UP LIKE THIS AGAIN?
HAPPY BIRTHDAY...
... WAS ...
THINGS ARE READY NOW.
SHALL WE BEGIN ACT TWO OF THE PARTY...
...YOUNG MISS.
HUH ?

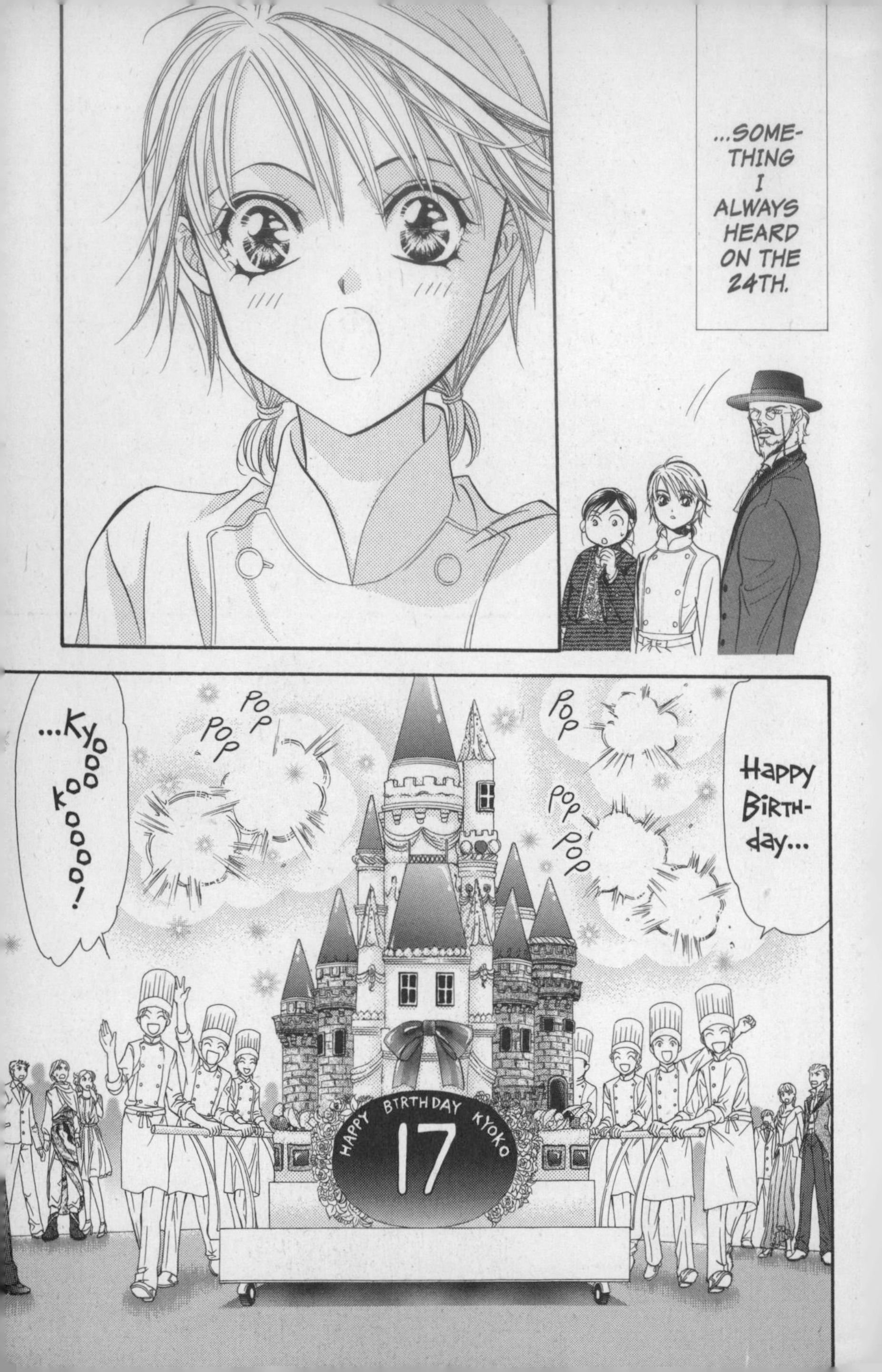
...SOME-THING I ALWAYS HEARD ON THE 24TH.
Happy Birth-day...
POP POP
POP POP
POP POP
...Kyoooko ooooo!
HAPPY BIRTHDAY KYOKO
17

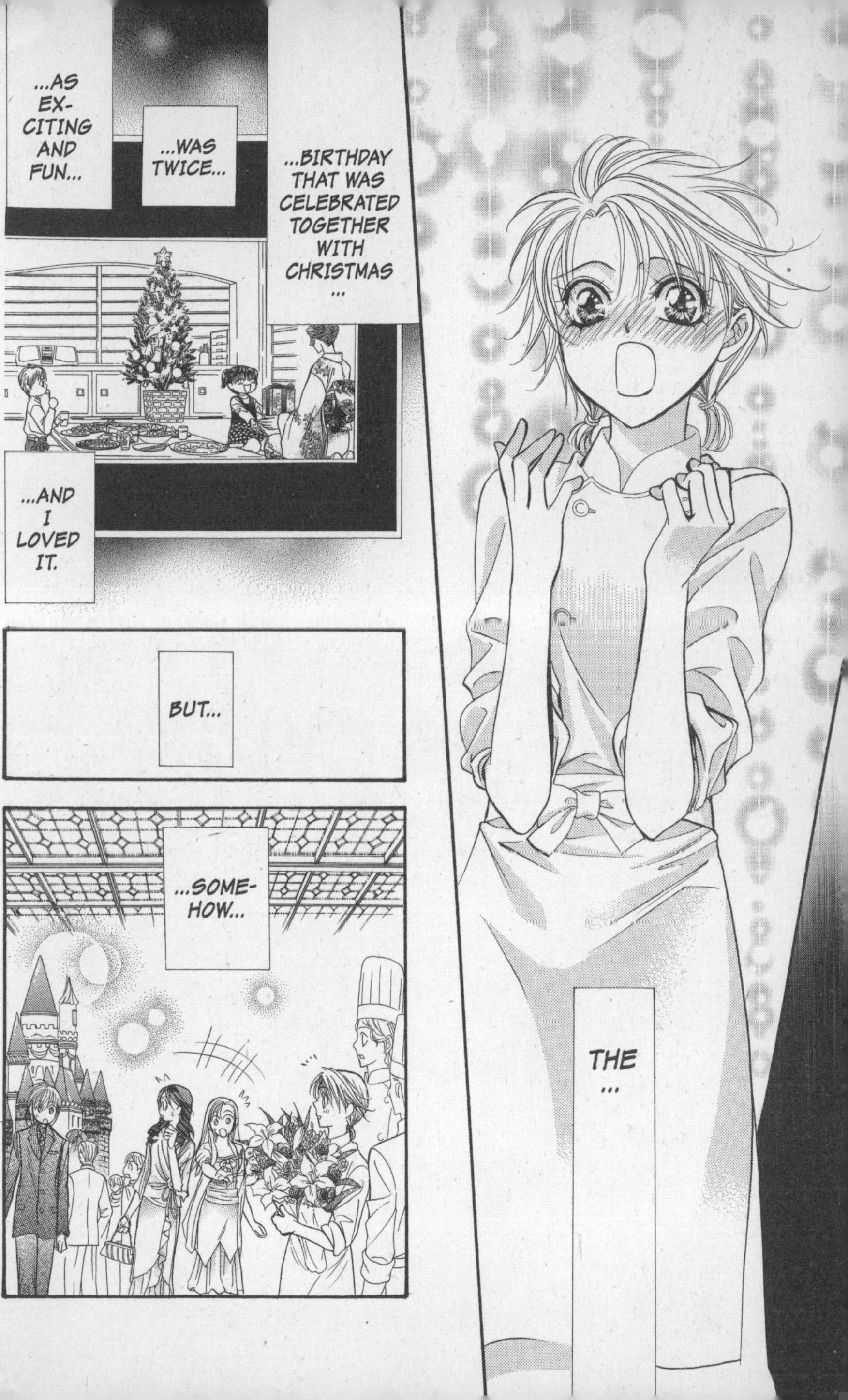
THE ...
...BIRTHDAY THAT WAS CELEBRATED TOGETHER WITH CHRISTMAS ...
...WAS TWICE...
...AS EX-CITING AND FUN...
...AND I LOVED IT.
BUT...
...SOME-HOW...

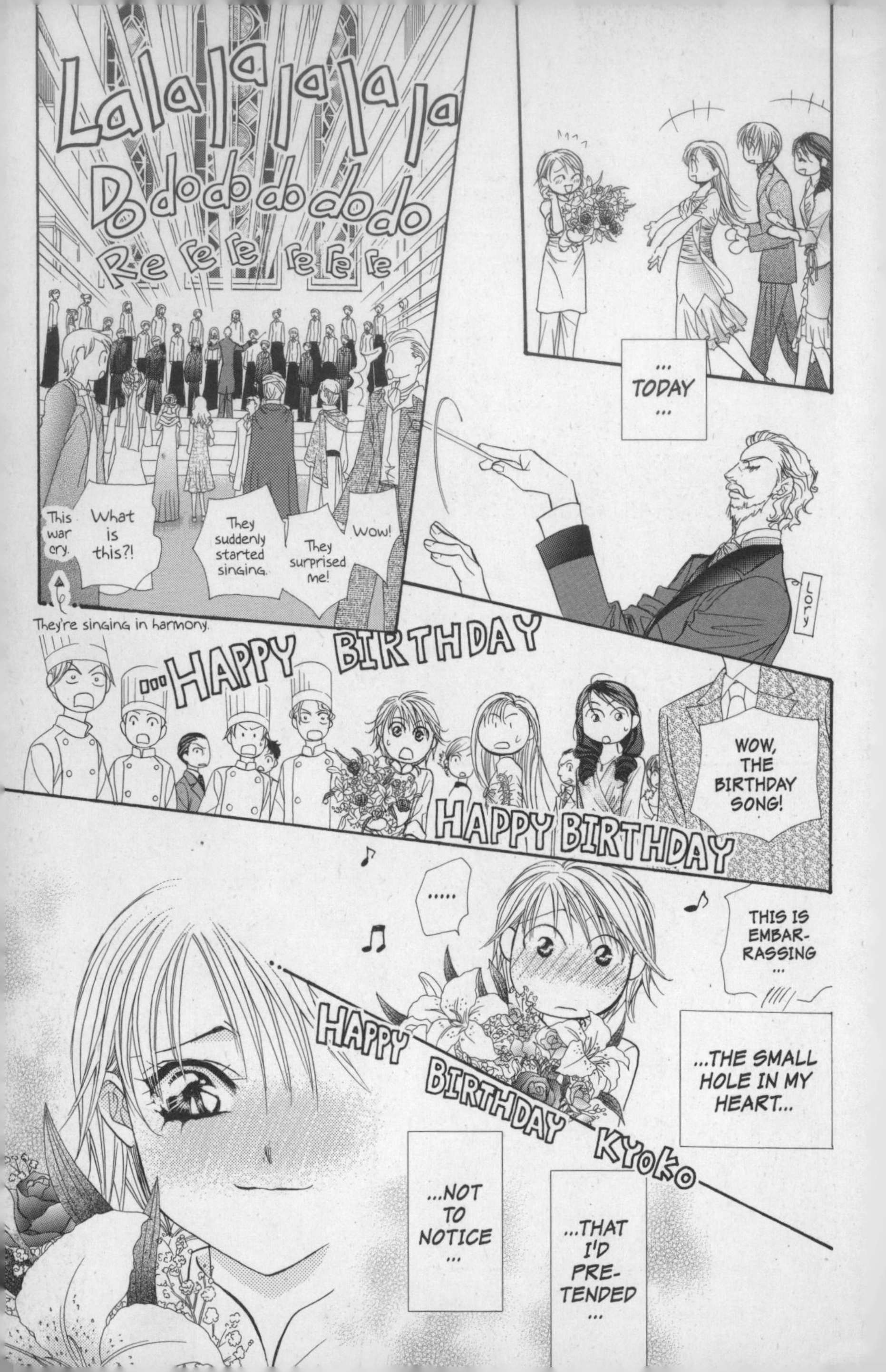
...TODAY...
Lory
Lalalalalala
Dodododododo
Rerererererere
Wow!
They surprised me!
They suddenly started singing.
What is this?!
This war cry.
They're singing in harmony.
...HAPPY BIRTHDAY
WOW, THE BIRTHDAY SONG!
HAPPY BIRTHDAY
THIS IS EMBARRASSING...
.....
HAPPY BIRTHDAY KYOKO
...THE SMALL HOLE IN MY HEART...
...THAT I'D PRETENDED...
...NOT TO NOTICE...

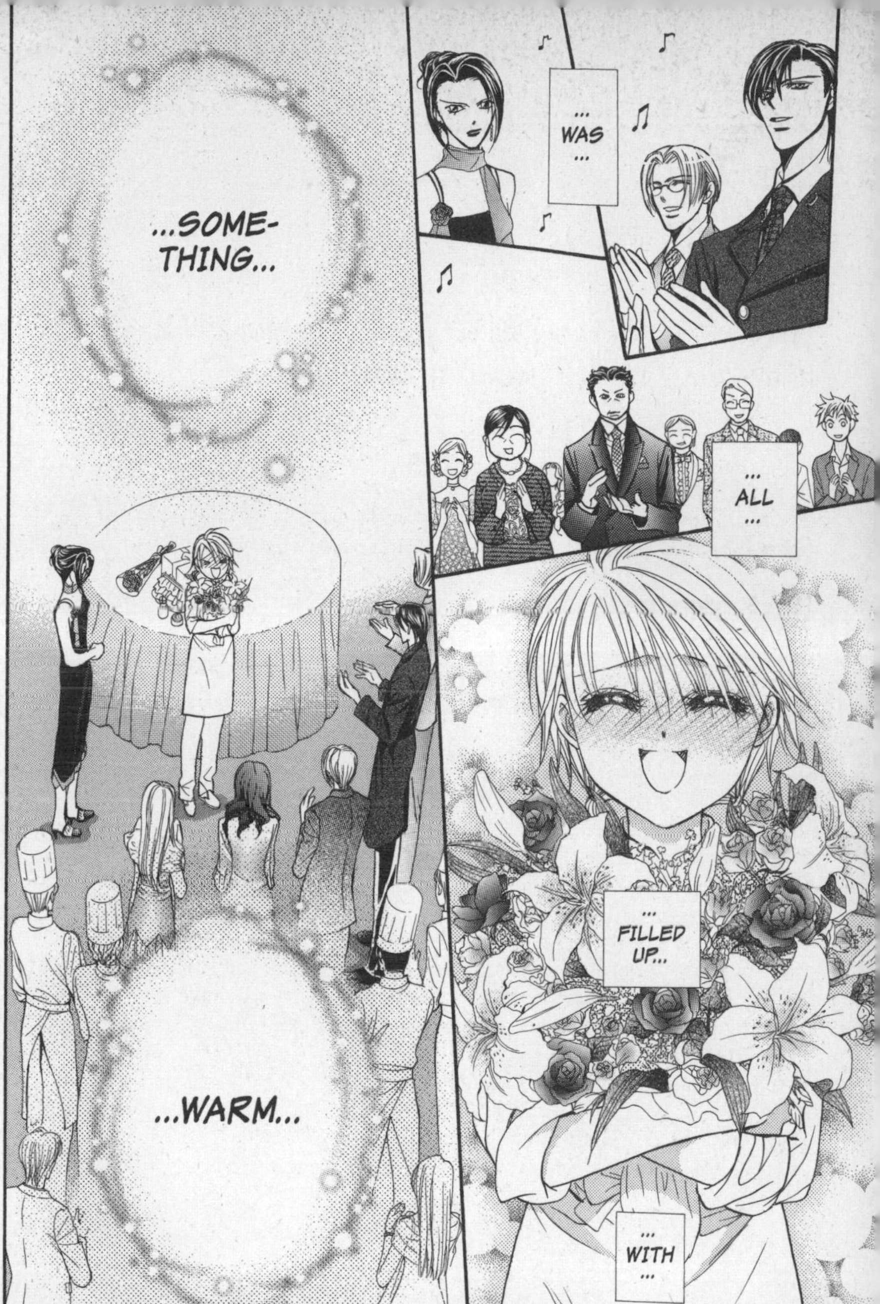
... WAS ...
... ALL ...
... FILLED UP...
... WITH ...
...SOME-THING...
...WARM...

End of Act 120

Skip-Beat! End Notes

Everyone knows how to be a fan, but sometimes cool things from other cultures need a little help crossing the language barrier.

Page 75, panel 8: Tora
This can mean "tiger" depending on the kanji used. In the Japanese, his nickname is spelled phonetically using katakana rather than kanji.

Page 92, panel 3: Yakuza
Moko is reacting to Maria's use of the phrase "good job." In the Japanese, the term she uses can also have the connotation of congratulating someone for finishing a prison sentence.

Page 92, panel 6: The idler
Kyoko is thinking of the character "Tora-san" from the movie series *Otoko wa Tsuraiyo*. In the series, Tora-san wanders all over Japan.

Page 92, panel 6: Tiger
Moko is thinking of the professional wrestler Tiger Mask.

Page 92, panel 7: Toraichi
Now Kyoko is thinking of a company that makes work uniforms for scaffolders. The kanji used for tora is the kanji that means "tiger."

Page 109, panel 3: Niagara
A type of big firework that looks like a waterfall.

Page 167, panel 1: Kyoko's thought balloon
This is a Hannya, a Noh mask with the face of a female demon.

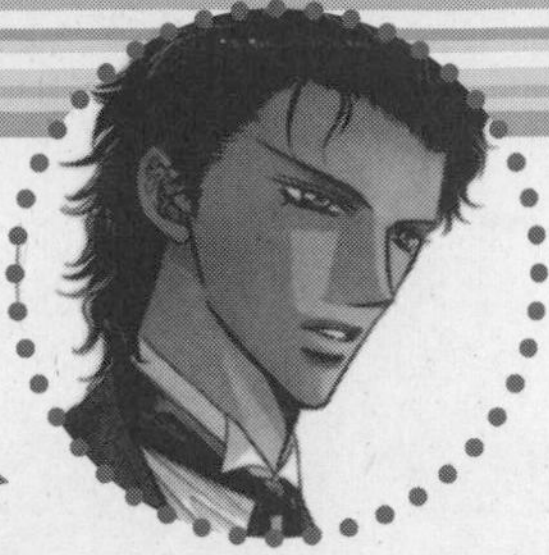

Yoshiki Nakamura is originally from Tokushima prefecture. She started drawing manga in elementary school, which eventually led to her 1993 debut of *Yume de Au yori Suteki* (Better than Seeing in a Dream) in *Hana to Yume* magazine. Her other works include the basketball series *Saint Love*, *MVP wa Yuzurenai* (Can't Give Up MVP), *Blue Wars* and *Tokyo Crazy Paradise*, a series about a female bodyguard in 2020 Tokyo.

SKIP·BEAT!
Vol. 20
Shojo Beat Edition

STORY AND ART BY YOSHIKI NAKAMURA

English Translation & Adaptation/Tomo Kimura
Touch-up Art & Lettering/Sabrina Heep
Design/Ronnie Casson
Editor/Pancha Diaz

VP, Production/Alvin Lu
VP, Sales & Product Marketing/Gonzalo Ferreyra
VP, Creative/Linda Espinosa
Publisher/Hyoe Narita

Skip-Beat! by Yoshiki Nakamura © Yoshiki Nakamura 2008.
All rights reserved. First published in Japan in 2008 by HAKUSENSHA, Inc., Tokyo.
English language translation rights arranged with HAKUSENSHA, Inc., Tokyo.

The stories, characters and incidents mentioned in this publication are entirely fictional.

No portion of this book may be reproduced or transmitted in any form or by any means
without written permission from the copyright holders.

Printed in Canada

Published by VIZ Media, LLC.
P.O. Box 77010
San Francisco, CA 94107

10 9 8 7 6 5 4 3 2 1
First printing, March 2010

www.viz.com

www.shojobeat.com

PARENTAL ADVISORY
SKIP-BEAT! is rated T for Teen and is
recommended for ages 13 and up. This
volume contains a grudge.
ratings.viz.com

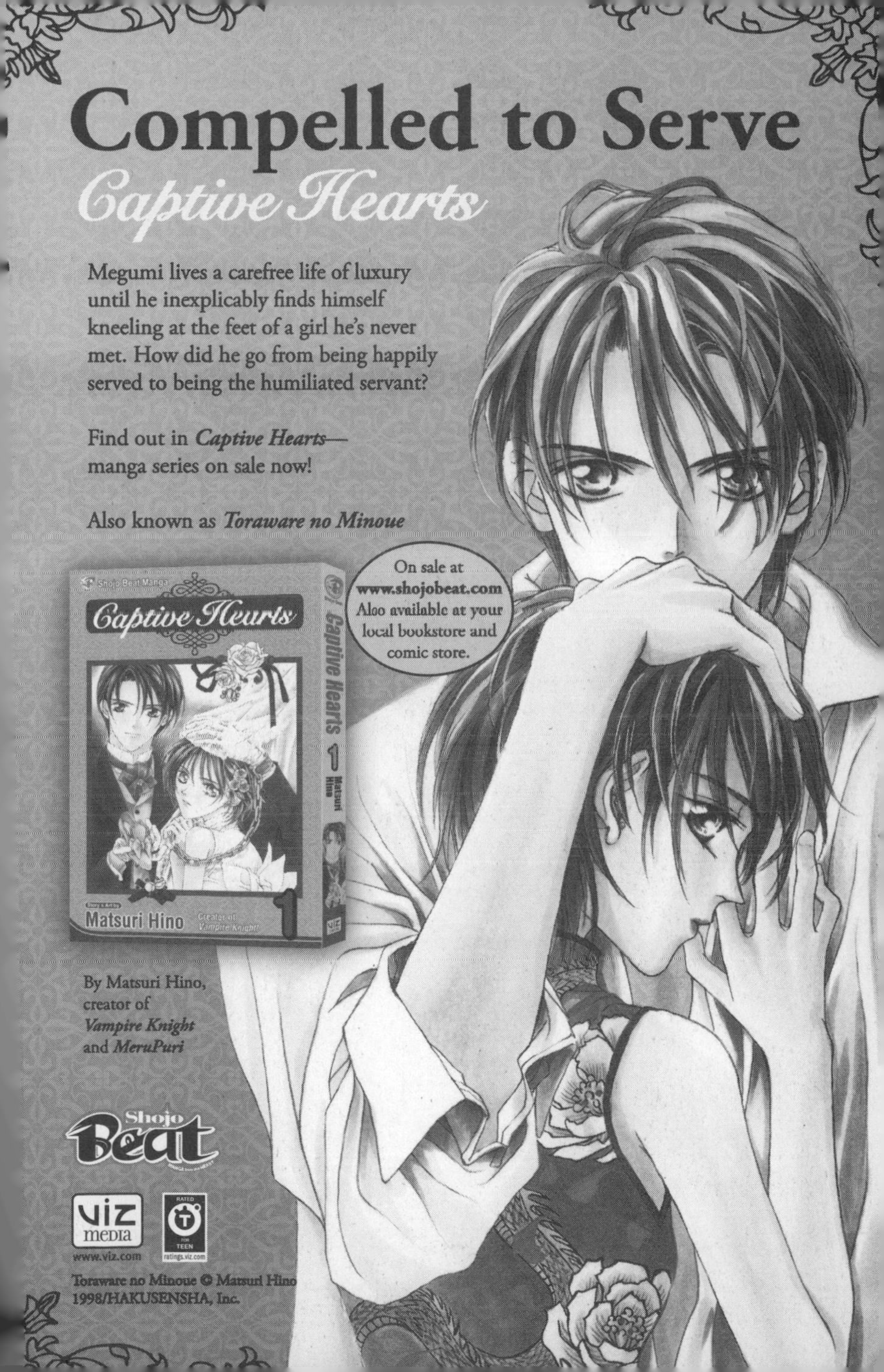
Compelled to Serve
Captive Hearts
Megumi lives a carefree life of luxury until he inexplicably finds himself kneeling at the feet of a girl he's never met. How did he go from being happily served to being the humiliated servant?
Find out in Captive Hearts—manga series on sale now!
Also known as Toraware no Minoue
On sale at www.shojobeat.com Also available at your local bookstore and comic store.
Shojo Beat Manga
Captive Hearts
Matsuri Hino
1
By Matsuri Hino, creator of Vampire Knight and MeruPuri
Shojo Beat
VIZ MEDIA
www.viz.com
RATED T FOR TEEN
ratings.viz.com
Toraware no Minoue © Matsuri Hino 1998/HAKUSENSHA, Inc.

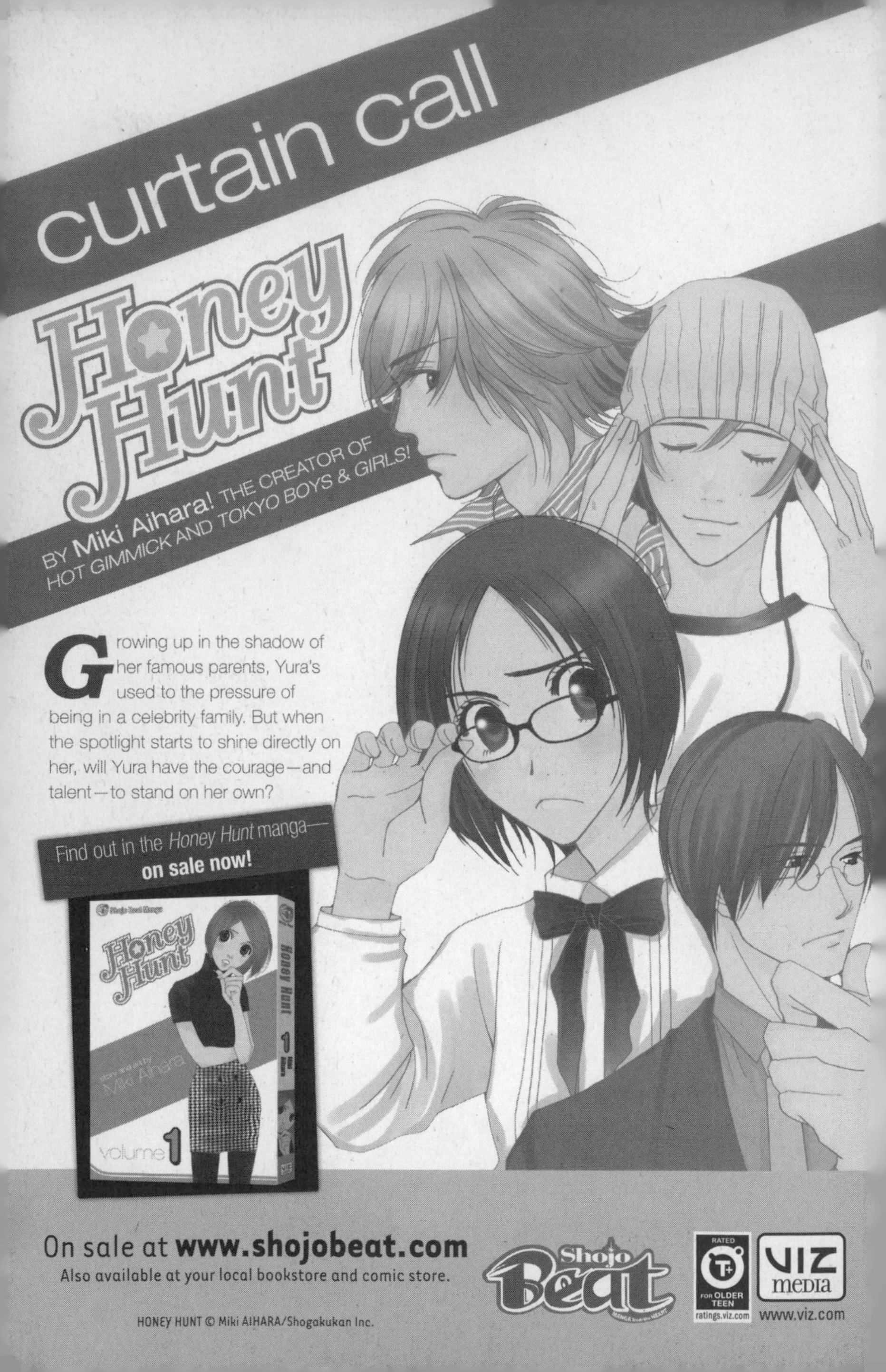
curtain call
Honey Hunt
BY Miki Aihara! THE CREATOR OF
HOT GIMMICK AND TOKYO BOYS & GIRLS!
Growing up in the shadow of her famous parents, Yura's used to the pressure of being in a celebrity family. But when the spotlight starts to shine directly on her, will Yura have the courage—and talent—to stand on her own?
Find out in the Honey Hunt manga—
on sale now!
Honey Hunt
story and art by Miki Aihara
volume 1
On sale at www.shojobeat.com
Also available at your local bookstore and comic store.
HONEY HUNT © Miki AIHARA/Shogakukan Inc.
Shojo Beat
RATED T+ FOR OLDER TEEN
ratings.viz.com
VIZ media
www.viz.com

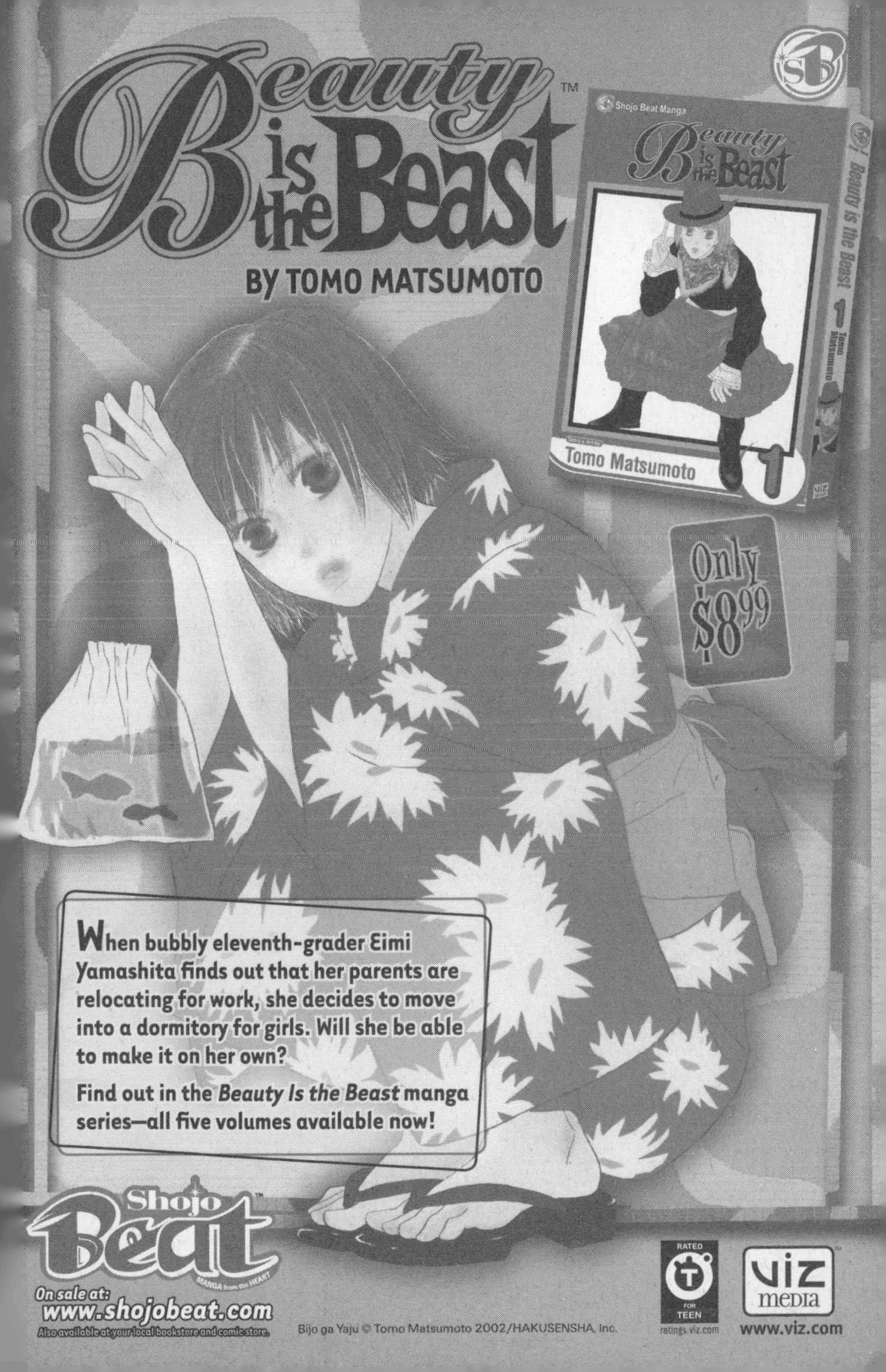
Beauty is the Beast™
BY TOMO MATSUMOTO
Shojo Beat Manga
Beauty is the Beast
Tomo Matsumoto
1
Only $8.99
When bubbly eleventh-grader Eimi Yamashita finds out that her parents are relocating for work, she decides to move into a dormitory for girls. Will she be able to make it on her own?
Find out in the Beauty Is the Beast manga series—all five volumes available now!
Shojo Beat™
MANGA from the HEART
On sale at:
www.shojobeat.com
Also available at your local bookstore and comic store.
Bijo ga Yaju © Tomo Matsumoto 2002/HAKUSENSHA, Inc.
RATED T FOR TEEN
ratings.viz.com
VIZ media
www.viz.com

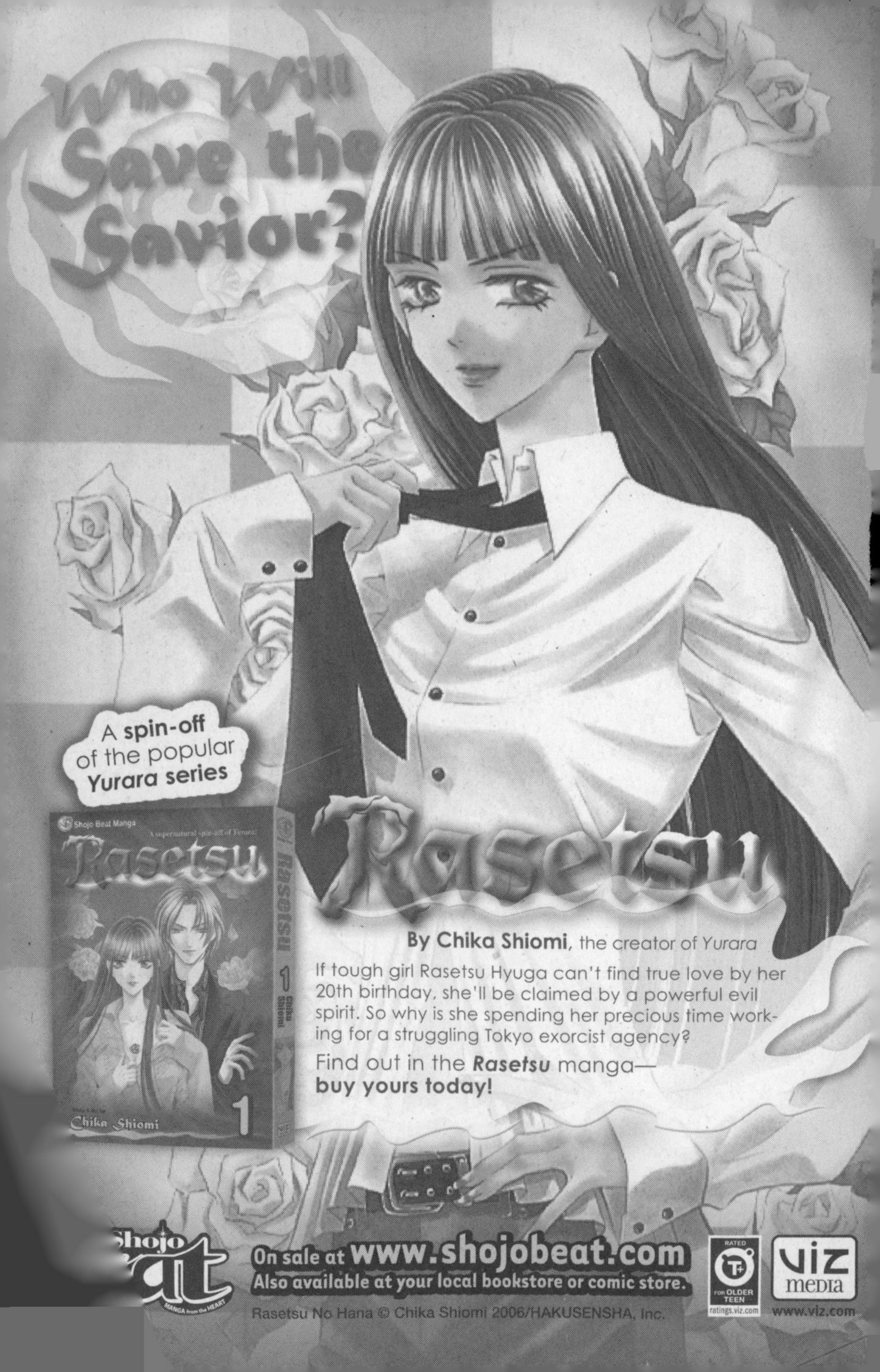

Who Will Save the Savior?
A spin-off of the popular Yurara series
Shojo Beat Manga
A supernatural spin-off of Yurara!
Rasetsu
1
Chika Shiomi
Rasetsu
By Chika Shiomi, the creator of Yurara
If tough girl Rasetsu Hyuga can't find true love by her 20th birthday, she'll be claimed by a powerful evil spirit. So why is she spending her precious time working for a struggling Tokyo exorcist agency?
Find out in the Rasetsu manga—buy yours today!
Shojo Beat MANGA from the HEART
On sale at www.shojobeat.com
Also available at your local bookstore or comic store.
Rasetsu No Hana © Chika Shiomi 2006/HAKUSENSHA, Inc.
RATED T+ FOR OLDER TEEN ratings.viz.com
VIZ media www.viz.com

Tell us what you think about Shojo Beat Manga!

Our survey is now available online. Go to:

shojobeat.com/mangasurvey

P9-DDM-516

CHASE BRANCH LIBRARY
17731 W. SEVEN MILE RD.
DETROIT, MI 48235

Help us make our product offerings better!

VIZ media

Shojo Beat

THE REAL DRAMA BEGINS IN...

FULL MOON WO SAGASHITE © 2001 by Arina Tanemura/SHU
Fushigi Yûgi: Genbu Kaiden © 2004 Yuu WATASE/Shogakukan
Ouran Koko Host Club © Bisco Hatori 2002/HAKUSENSHA, In